HODGES UNIVERSITY
P9-DZA-254

EXAMINING CRITICAL PERSPECTIVES ON HUMAN RIGHTS

Examining Critical Perspectives on Human Rights sets out a practical and theoretical overview of the future of human rights within the United Kingdom and beyond at this key juncture in the human rights project. A number of internationally renowned scholars respond to David Kennedy's contribution 'The International Human Rights Movement: Still Part of the Problem?' from a range of different perspectives. With its combination of the theory and practice of international and domestic human rights, this collection is of relevance to all scholars and practitioners with an interest in human rights.

ROB DICKINSON, ELENA KATSELLI, COLIN MURRAY and OLE W. PEDERSEN are lecturers at Newcastle Law School.

EXAMINING CRITICAL PERSPECTIVES ON HUMAN RIGHTS

Edited by

ROB DICKINSON, ELENA KATSELLI,
COLIN MURRAY and OLE W. PEDERSEN

CAMBRIDGE UNIVERSITY PRESS
Cambridge, New York, Melbourne, Madrid, Cape Town,
Singapore, São Paulo, Delhi, Tokyo, Mexico City

Cambridge University Press
The Edinburgh Building, Cambridge CB2 8RU, UK

Published in the United States of America by Cambridge University Press, New York

www.cambridge.org
Information on this title: www.cambridge.org/9781107006935

First published 2012

Printed in the United Kingdom at the University Press, Cambridge

A catalogue record for this publication is available from the British Library

Library of Congress Cataloging-in-Publication Data

Examining critical perspectives on human rights / [edited by]
Robert Dickinson... [et al.].
p. cm.
ISBN 978-1-107-00693-5 (Hardback)
1. Human rights. 2. Human rights–Great Britain. I. Dickinson, Robert, 1952–
K3240.E964 2012
341.4′8–dc23
2011029385

ISBN 978-1-107-00693-5 Hardback

CONTENTS

NOTES ON CONTRIBUTORS

PROFESSOR CHRISTINE BELL Christine Bell holds a Chair in Constitutional Law at the University of Edinburgh, was formerly Director of the Transitional Justice Institute at the University of Ulster and was a founder member of the Northern Ireland Human Rights Commission, established under the 1998 Belfast Agreement. Her research focuses on the role of human rights in transitional societies and her writings have been awarded the American Society of International Law's Francis Deake Prize, and include the influential *On the Law of Peace: Peace Agreements and the* Lex Pacificatoria (2008) awarded the Hart Socio-legal Book Prize.

PROFESSOR DAVID BONNER David Bonner has taught at the University of Leicester since 1974 and was appointed to a Chair in 2004. A renowned authority on civil liberties, human rights and counter-terrorism law, with publications covering conflicts from the Northern Ireland 'troubles' to the 'war on terror', his latest monograph, *Executive Measures, Terrorism and National Security* (2007) provides a detailed and well received contribution to the security debate.

DR ROB DICKINSON Robert Dickinson was appointed to a lectureship in Newcastle Law School in 2008 following the successful completion of his Ph.D. thesis, 'Self-Determination, Minority Rights and Oppression: A Chinese–Tibetan Perspective'. He is currently engaged in research focusing on self-determination and human rights arising out of this study.

PROFESSOR KEITH EWING Keith Ewing, Professor of Public Law at King's College London, is an academic working in the fields of public law and labour law. At the forefront of the bill of rights debate within the United Kingdom, his writings include his recent *Bonfire of the Liberties: New Labour, Human Rights and the Rule of Law* (2010), examining New Labour's assault on civil liberties.

PROFESSOR ERIC HEINZE Eric Heinze has been a member of the Queen Mary School of Law, University of London, since 1995, with his research focusing on human rights and legal theory. His research has centred on the theoretical underpinnings of the human rights project, including his trio of monographs *The Logic of Liberal Rights* (2003), *The Logic of Equality* (2003) and *The Logic of Constitutional Rights* (2005).

DR ELENA KATSELLI PROUKAKI Elena Katselli was appointed a lecturer in Newcastle Law School in 2005 and her research focuses (among other things) on international human rights law. Her writings include *The Problem of Enforcement in International Law: Countermeasures, the Non-Injured State and the Idea of International Community* (2009).

PROFESSOR DAVID KENNEDY David Kennedy returned to Harvard Law School in the autumn of 2009 to lead its new Institute for Global Law and Policy. He is acknowledged to be one of the leading figures in the Critical Legal Studies movement and is the author of *The Dark Sides of Virtue: Reassessing International Humanitarianism* (2004).

DR LIORA LAZARUS Liora Lazarus, Lecturer in Human Rights Law at the University of Oxford, is an established authority upon prisoners' rights, with works including *Contrasting Prisoners' Rights* (2004). Alongside her academic work, she has written public reports on aspects of human rights for the UK Ministry of Justice and the European Parliament. Her current research focuses on how the law shapes notions of security, and will culminate in the book *Juridifying Security.*

MR RICHARD MULLENDER Richard Mullender is a Reader in Law at Newcastle Law School. He has written a number of essays on human rights, including 'Hate Speech and Pornography in Canada: a Qualified Deontological Response to a Consequentialist Argument' (2007) 20 *Canadian Journal of Law and Jurisprudence* 241, 'Hegel, Human Rights, and Particularism' (2003) 30 *Journal of Law & Society* 554, and 'Tort Law, Human Rights, and Common Law Culture' (2003) 23 *Oxford Journal of Legal Studies* 301. He is also a contributor to *Religion and Human Rights* (2010) and to the forthcoming interdisciplinary *Handbook of Human Rights.*

MR COLIN MURRAY Colin Murray was appointed to a lectureship in Newcastle Law School in 2007. His current research is focused on the fields of national security law, legal history and public law with articles including 'In the Shadow of Lord Haw-Haw: Guantánamo Bay, Diplomatic Protection and Allegiance' [2011] *Public Law* 115.

DR OLE W. PEDERSEN Appointed to a lectureship in Newcastle Law School in 2008, Dr Pedersen's research focuses on issues of climate change and human rights. He has rapidly established a reputation as an authority on the relationship between human rights and environmental rights, with articles including 'European Environmental Human Rights and Environmental Rights: A Long Time Coming?' (2008) 21 *Georgetown International Environmental Law Review* 73.

PROFESSOR STEVEN WHEATLEY Steven Wheatley is Professor of International Law in the Law School at the University of Leeds. His research is focused on the relevance of democratic legitimacy for the exercise of political authority through law. A particular interest is the position of indigenous peoples and minorities, whose status as democratic minorities undermines arguments for any majority-rule based concept of democracy. Steven has published numerous articles in this area and is the author of *The Democratic Legitimacy of International Law, Studies In International Law* (2010) and *Democracy, Minorities and International Law* (Cambridge, 2005). He is a member of the Minority Rights Group (International) Expert Panel on Minorities Litigation and of the International Law Association International Research Committee on Indigenous Peoples.

ACKNOWLEDGEMENTS

This collection of papers is the outcome of a seminar series titled 'Human Rights in Retreat' which took place in November and December 2009 at Newcastle Law School and a symposium in January 2010 also hosted at Newcastle Law School titled 'Human Rights – Drop of Liberation or Fig Leaf of Legitimation?', both taking place during Colin Murray's tenure as Director of the Newcastle Human Rights Research Group. The symposium was generously supported by a grant from the *Modern Law Review* Seminar Fund, without which it is unlikely that the event would have been such a success. The willing engagement of the attendees and speakers at all of these events helped to make them very fruitful fora for the exchange of ideas. Each section of this collection has been edited by one of the team of editors, with Ole Pedersen assuming responsibility for the introduction, Colin Murray overseeing the 'Domestic Perspectives' section and Elena Katselli and Rob Dickinson handling the 'International Law Perspectives' and 'Theoretical Perspectives' sections respectively.

In addition, the editors wish to acknowledge the helpful assistance received from academic colleagues at Newcastle Law School in running the seminar series and the symposium. In particular the hard work and advice of Richard Mullender is gratefully acknowledged, as well as the assistance of Professors Ian Ward and Rhona Smith (Northumbria University) in taking the time to chair symposium panels. A special 'thank you' is reserved for Samantha Ryan, who in her time at Newcastle Law School played an important role in the Human Rights Research Group and provided much of the initial impetus behind this project. None of the above events would have run smoothly without the dedicated assistance of the administrative staff of Newcastle Law School, particularly Suzanne Johnson and Gemma Hayton who oversaw the project budget and arranged all room bookings.

Finally, this project has benefited from the dedicated guidance of Nienke van Schaverbeke. We would like to express our warm appreciation to her and to all the team from Cambridge University Press, in particular Richard Woodham, for supporting this project from its inception and despite any delays and setbacks that followed, and especially for undertaking the task of indexing the collection.

The Editors

PART I

Introduction

1

Examining critical perspectives on human rights: an introduction

OLE W. PEDERSEN & C.R.G. MURRAY

From political considerations to grand principles

As Costas Douzinas writes, it is possible to regard the Universal Declaration of Human Rights (UDHR) in 1948 as a turning point at which natural rights attained the dignity of law,[1] 'albeit of a somewhat soft kind'.[2] Over sixty years later, in the words of Francesca Klug, '[i]t is easy to forget that until the UDHR was adopted, virtually *any* criticism – let alone interference – by one government with the treatment of the citizens of another, was considered a breach of the principle of national sovereignty'.[3] But much as hindsight suggests that the general acceptance that '[s]tates now have duties to each other and to their subjects to observe human rights' amounted to an event by which traditional understandings of the relationship between the individual and the state had been 'turned upside down',[4] Douzinas's 'soft law' caveat remains essential.

Firstly, even as the idea of human rights was enshrined by Francis Fukuyama as part of the 'end of history' in the heady days for Western liberal democracies that followed the end of the Cold War,[5] there was a tension between the expansive vision of human rights advanced by the concept's proponents and the reality of the concept at work within the legal systems of liberal democracies. Conor Gearty allows that the concept needed to exude confidence to gain traction amongst policy makers:

Our thanks to Elena Katselli (Newcastle University) and Robert Dickinson (Newcastle University) for their advice and comments upon earlier drafts of this introduction. Any errors remain our own.

[1] GA Res. 217 A (III), UN Doc. A/810 (10 December 1948).

[2] C. Douzinas, *The End of Human Rights* (Oxford: Hart, 2000) p.9.

[3] F. Klug, 'The Universal Declaration of Human Rights: 60 years on' [2009] PL 205, 207.

[4] C. Palley, *The United Kingdom and Human Rights* (London: Sweet & Maxwell, 1991) p.37.

[5] F. Fukuyama, The End of History and the Last Man (New York: Free Press, 1992).

> The phrase 'human rights' is a strong one, epistemologically confident, ethically assured, carrying with it a promise to the hearer to cut through the noise of assertion and counter-assertion, of cultural practices and relativist perspectives, and thereby to deliver truth. To work its moral magic, human rights needs to exude this kind of certainty, this old-fashioned clarity.[6]

But, as David Kennedy came to recognise, in ascending to a role amongst the gamut of concerns feeding into governments' policy making, international human rights standards shed much of their transformative potential. From the outset, these standards were approached pragmatically by governments, which seek to gain the legitimacy of being 'rights respecting' whilst maintaining the maximum scope for their freedom of action. The employment of human rights as a 'status quo project of legitimation'[7] by the Government of the United States of America (USA) can be seen as early as the famous case of *Brown* v. *Board of Education*,[8] in which the US Supreme Court unanimously ruled that the segregation of public schools was unconstitutional. The US Government submitted an *amicus curiae* brief which argued that '[i]t is in the context of the present world struggle between freedom and tyranny that the problem of racial discrimination must be viewed'.[9] In other words, the existence of racial segregation within the southern states could be exploited by America's Cold War rivals in the battle for influence in the developing world. Human rights arguments were explicitly coupled to Cold War foreign policy objectives, creating a heady brew which 'could not fail to impress Cold War patriots sitting on the Court'.[10] Today *Brown* is regarded as one of the stepping stones by which the USA sought to extricate itself from its historical failures to secure the benefits of liberal democracy for citizens regardless of race. But, in light of the failure of the US Government to take action to enforce it for another decade, the decision's primary impact on the Eisenhower Administration was that it provided an opportunity to market the credentials of the US system of government to the world.

[6] C. Gearty, *Can Human Rights Survive?* (Cambridge University Press, 2006) p.19.

[7] See Chapter 2, p.33 below.

[8] *Brown* v. *Board of Education of Topeka* 347 US 483 (1954).

[9] P. Kurland & G. Casper, eds., *Landmark Briefs and Arguments of the Supreme Court of the United States* (Arlington, VA: University Publications, 1975) vol. 49, p.121.

[10] L. Powe, *The Warren Court and American Politics* (Cambridge, MA: Belknap Press, 2000) p.35.

Nor was the US State Department alone in co-opting human rights to the ideological battle of the Cold War. In May 1948, as tensions built towards the Berlin Blockade, Winston Churchill declared that:

> [t]he Movement for European Unity must be a positive force, deriving its strength from our sense of common spiritual values. It is a dynamic expression of democratic faith based upon moral conceptions and inspired by a sense of mission. In the centre of our movement stands the idea of a Charter of Human Rights, guarded by freedom and sustained by law.[11]

Despite Churchill's soaring rhetoric it was only in the 1970s that human rights began to gain traction within the policy-making circles of even Western governments. Churchill's 'Charter of Human Rights' for Europe had come into being in the form of the European Convention on Human Rights and Fundamental Freedoms (ECHR),[12] but the novel enforcement mechanism of the European Court of Human Rights had achieved little by the time the United Kingdom (UK) accepted the ability of individuals to petition the Court in January 1966, meaning that 'the Convention was a sleeping beauty (or slumbering beast, depending upon one's viewpoint)'.[13] Wiktor Osiatynski provides convincing reasons why the concept of human rights had largely lain fallow since 1948. Only in the 1970s had Western governments 'finally removed the human rights liabilities [by a process of decolonisation for many European countries and desegregation in the USA] that had made governments somewhat skeptical to the idea of human rights immediately after World War II'.[14] In his contribution to this collection David Kennedy remembers how the concept of human rights seized progressive thought:

> Jimmy Carter had made human rights a respectable vernacular for transposing what we remembered of sixties idealism to international affairs. I know my academic colleagues felt we were redeeming the better promise of Carter's diplomacy, turning the Cold War struggle from proxy wars to direct affirmation of democracy and citizens' rights.[15]

Taken in isolation, Kennedy's focus on 'citizens' rights' might be thought to betray some of his discomfort with the direction in which the human

[11] W. Churchill, *Europe Unite: Speeches 1947 and 1948* (London: Cassell, 1950) 310, p.312.
[12] 213 UNTS 222 (3 September 1953).
[13] A. Lester & K. Beattie, 'Human rights and the British constitution', in J. Jowell & D. Oliver (eds), *The Changing Constitution*, 6th edn (Oxford University Press, 2007) 59, pp.63–4.
[14] W. Osiatynski, 'Are human rights universal in an age of terrorism', in R. Wilson (ed.), *Human Rights in the 'War on Terror'* (Cambridge University Press, 2005) 295, pp.297–8.
[15] See Chapter 2, p.21 below.

rights movement was travelling, for the concept of human rights should in theory extend beyond an individual's allegiance to any particular state. However, in the context of his steadfast criticism of the failure of the human rights movement to close the 'protection gap' between international refugee law and national asylum law,[16] Kennedy's use of this phrase highlights his scepticism at the international human rights movement's capacity to secure its goals. This criticism notwithstanding, by the close of the twentieth century human rights appeared to be embedded as 'grand principles' underpinning liberal democracy. Gearty extolled their role as a bulwark against the excesses of capitalism at a time when socialism had failed to maintain its ideological challenge.[17] Human rights became, in Samuel Moyn's arresting description, 'the last utopia'.[18]

A lost Utopia: the crisis of human rights

A proliferation of academic commentary asserts that the international human rights system is in a state of crisis in the first decade of the twenty-first century. Even at the height of optimism surrounding the potential of human rights,[19] Costas Douzinas argued that they were 'veering away from their initial revolutionary and dissident purposes'[20] and feared 'that the extravagant boasts about the dawn of a new humanitarian age would be accompanied by untold suffering'.[21] In *Human Rights as Politics and Idolatry*, Michael Ignatieff identified both a spiritual and a cultural crisis facing human rights, as proponents struggle with both the 'intercultural validity of human rights norms' and 'the ultimate metaphysical grounding for these norms'.[22]

While a human rights revolution unfolded in the second half of the twentieth century, we now have grounds for thinking that success in advancing this agenda may be giving way to atrophy. In the first decade of the twenty-first century 'the hallmarks of the current era of human rights' became 'the controversial policies of torture, rendition, and of holding

[16] D. Kennedy, *The Dark Sides of Virtue: Reassessing International Humanitarianism*, (Princeton University Press, 2004) pp.208–9.

[17] Gearty, *Can Human Rights Survive?*, p.27.

[18] S. Moyn, *The Last Utopia: Human Rights in History* (Cambridge, MA: Belknap Press, 2010).

[19] See M. Ignatieff, *The Rights Revolution* (Toronto: House of Anansi Press, 2000).

[20] Douzinas, *The End of Human Rights*, p.380.

[21] C. Douzinas, *Human Rights and Empire: The Political Philosophy of Cosmopolitanism* (Oxford: Routledge-Cavendish, 2007), p.6.

[22] M. Ignatieff, 'Human Rights as Idolatry', in A. Gutmann (ed.), *Human Rights as Politics and Idolatry* (Princeton University Press, 2003) 53, p.77.

so-called enemy combatants without recourse to legal representation and without guarantee of just treatment'.[23] Indeed, judges and academics dispute whether terrorism has supplanted human rights as the defining concern of the present era of legal theory.[24] At the very least, the reasons to be sceptical of human rights discourse appear to have multiplied over the course of the last decade.[25] The USA's responses to the terrorist threat posed by al Qaeda, from the Guantánamo Bay detention facility to the Abu Ghraib prison in Iraq, have blighted its track record on human rights.[26] Even respected advocates of human rights, such as Alan Dershowitz, have questioned hitherto sacrosanct protections such as the prohibition of torture by debating how to 'manage' torture in the context of counter-terrorism.[27] Further difficulties lie ahead, given the growing geopolitical importance of China, a state which has exhibited a patchy commitment to human rights despite the 'compliance pull' of these norms.[28]

This collection makes no claims to constitute a comprehensive review of contemporary critiques of the human rights project. Instead, using David Kennedy's work as an anchor, the contributors seek to illuminate how aspects of his criticisms of human rights have played out in recent years, examining his work from theoretical, domestic and international perspectives. In doing so, this collection of essays is intended to shed new light on some of the challenges which have faced the concept of human rights in the last decade, and on the future direction of the international human rights movement.

Professor Kennedy's criticisms of the human rights movement

During recent years, in both the international and domestic spheres human rights lawyers and legal theorists have fixated upon whether the

23 A. Bullard, 'Introduction', in A. Bullard (ed.), *Human Rights in Crisis* (Aldershot: Ashgate, 2008) 1, p.3.

24 See M. Arden, 'Human rights in the age of terrorism' (2005) 121 LQR 604 and C. Warbrick, 'The European response to terrorism in an age of human rights' (2004) 15 *European Journal of International Law* 989.

25 See A. Tomkins, 'Introduction: on being sceptical about human rights' in T. Campbell, K. Ewing & A. Tomkins (eds.), *Sceptical Essays on Human Rights* (Oxford University Press, 2001) 1, pp.8–11.

26 See S. Mokhtari, *After Abu Ghraib: Exploring Human Rights in America and the Middle East* (Cambridge University Press, 2009) pp.63–66.

27 See A. Dershowitz, *Why Terrorism Works: Understanding the Threat, Responding to the Challenge* (New Haven, CN: Yale University Press, 2002) p.131.

28 T. Farer, *Confronting Global Terrorism and American Neo-Conservatism: The Framework of a Liberal Grand Strategy* (Oxford University Press, 2008) p.15.

concept of human rights provides a valid platform on which to assess human interactions with state bodies. This abstract debate as to the validity of the concept of human rights has often raged irrespective of 'real world' events which have seen millions of people continue to lose their lives in unlawful wars, persecuted on grounds of race or religion, or tortured by oppressive regimes which nonetheless claim to act on behalf of 'rights-respecting' states.

David Kennedy's study of the international humanitarian movement (a reference 'very generally to people who aspire to make the world more just')[29] openly challenges the assumption that human rights are a driver of benign social change. Rather, he claimed that after the Second World War the human rights movement became a distinctly Western project that ultimately serves to entrench the position of the politically and economically advantaged. Kennedy also urges proponents of human rights to subject the concept to robust analysis and not to treat it as a 'frail child' that might wilt under criticism.[30] Kennedy's opening foray regarding the international human rights movement was written on the cusp of events which have taken on the appearance of a turning point (the attacks of 11 September 2001 and their aftermath), not only for human rights as a concept, but also for the USA, the country most associated internationally with the human rights project.[31] Through this prescient discussion Kennedy (who further refined his thesis in his book, *The Dark Sides of Virtue: Reassessing International Humanitarianism*) cemented his reputation as 'one of the definitive critical voices in international law theory over the last two decades',[32] his scholarship challenging widely held assumptions regarding the nature of human rights and international humanitarianism. His work therefore provides the fulcrum upon which other contributors to this collection can develop their arguments.

In his contribution to this collection, revisiting and updating his analysis of the international human rights movement at the turn of the millennium, Kennedy reminds us that the idea of human rights is not an abstract theoretical construct, but has developed into a system of

[29] Kennedy, *The Dark Sides of Virtue*, p.236. [30] Ibid., p.267.

[31] D. Kennedy, 'The international human rights movement: part of the problem?' [2001] EHRLR 245.

[32] R. Dixon & D. Stephens, 'Book Review: *The Dark Sides of Virtue: Reassessing International Humanitarianism* by David Kennedy', [2004] *Melbourne Journal of International Law* 21 (available at www.austlii.edu.au/au/journals/MelbJIL/2004/21.html#Heading23), accessed 10 January 2011.

well-established norms supporting the activities of an international movement. When this movement makes claims regarding the universality of human rights Kennedy recognises that it is unsurprising that policy makers often choose to take human rights into consideration when formulating their foreign and domestic policies. A prominent example is the European Union's inclusion of human rights clauses in agreements concluded with third states. Kennedy moreover acknowledges that bodies within the human rights movement, most notably Human Rights Watch, have responded to these developments by evolving from 'watchdog' groups to bodies integrated within international human rights governance.

However, in light of the existence of the serious and widespread human rights abuses noted above, Kennedy identifies the conflicting temptations towards idolatry and pragmatism as threatening to undermine the successes of the human rights movement. He contends that idolatry of human rights standards has led human rights activists to overburden the concept with ever more ambitious social and economic rights, whilst preventing them from considering other solutions to these issues. The expression of vague values as legal norms opens them to selective interpretation and gives an advantage to litigious sections of society aware of how to manipulate the legal system to protect their interests. These criticisms are increasingly gaining traction within the human rights debate in the UK. In a much-quoted Policy Exchange report on the UK's place within the ECHR, Michael Pinto-Duschinsky warned that 'whenever vital political matters are decided in courts of law, the power of pressure groups will almost inevitably burgeon,'[33] skewing rights debates towards the interests of politically organised groups.

Pragmatism, according to Kennedy, also has its perils, as evidenced by the risks inherent in the application of human rights concepts when assessing whether causing the death of individuals during an armed conflict is necessary and proportionate. The law of war accepts that the use of armed force during a conflict is legitimate under specific circumstances, and that the loss of the life of an individual may be justifiable as collateral damage. Nonetheless, the inculcation of human rights values into military operations has enhanced the legitimacy of the actions of armed forces resulting, according to Kennedy, in a state

[33] M. Pinto-Duschinsky, *Bringing Rights Back Home: Making Human Rights compatible with Parliamentary Democracy in the UK* (Policy Exchange, February 2010), p.17.

of 'lawfare' which enables 'rights-respecting' states to rely more readily upon military responses to threats.

With these arguments providing the focal point, this collection analyses how, in the light of such chastening experiences, human rights can become a more responsive and more reliable mechanism for holding states to account, or whether, as Kennedy suggests, we need to look for new solutions to these problems. The collection will be divided into three sections, examining domestic, international and theoretical responses to the challenges laid down by Kennedy.

Domestic human rights perspectives

The first section of the collection will focus upon how domestic systems of rights protection, particularly in the UK and the USA, have withstood the crisis of human rights in the last decade. Since the enactment of the Human Rights Act (HRA) 1998, human rights hubris has gripped the legal systems of the UK. Comfortable assertions of the value of human rights in the face of evidence of serious abuses by the UK Government, in the form of compelling allegations of its complicity in torture overseas and use of information derived from such torture, provide the setting for Keith Ewing's paper. Ewing attacks the UK judiciary's supine response to such government activity, exposing the degree to which many judges have hidden behind impressive pronouncements of their abhorrence of torture, whilst delivering decisions which place minimal restrictions upon government. Moreover, he questions the usefulness of the HRA, concluding that, in the hands of domestic judges, the Act has played little role in strengthening protections for individuals against torture. Together, these arguments build into a powerful critique of a form of human rights 'idolatry'[34] which sees the courts do little more than 'pay lip-service'[35] to the importance of the principle that the UK's legal systems should be free from the taint of torture.

David Bonner's contribution picks up the baton from Ewing in analysing the performance of the judiciary on the related subject of non-*refoulement*. He sets out to analyse the efforts of the UK Government to circumvent Article 3 ECHR and case law before the European Court of Human Rights which restricts the deportation of foreign nationals to

[34] See Chapter 2 below.

[35] *A* v. *Secretary of State for the Home Department (No 2)* [2005] UKHL 71, para.80 (Lord Nicholls).

states where they are likely to face torture, or cruel or inhumane treatment. In the course of the legal battles over detention without trial, and subsequently control orders, the UK government developed an argument that these measures, and the infringements of human rights that they involved, could be justified on the basis that the government was subject to a positive obligation under Article 2 ECHR to protect the right to life. Ultimately, judges such as Lord Hope gave some credence to this argument, accepting that 'the first responsibility of government in a democratic society is owed to the public'.[36] Bonner's contribution illustrates the capacity of national governments to co-opt international human rights standards and language to serve their purposes, a powerful example of the 'risks, costs and unanticipated consequences of human rights activism' which Kennedy highlights.[37]

A more subtle crisis has also befallen the concept of human rights in the form of a division between those who see human rights as restricted to traditional civil and political rights and the advocates of wider socio-economic rights. Socio-economic rights advance human rights deep into the sphere of allocation of scarce resources, and to detractors mark the point at which human rights mount a challenge to democratic governance. Nonetheless, they also maintain the transformative value to human rights. As John Gray has noted, factors like exclusion of groups from participation in society, failure to maintain a stable economy or to provide adequate public services and security from crime, seem to lie at the root of a regime's legitimacy with individuals under its authority: '[r]egimes which meet these needs will be legitimate whether or not they are democratic, while regimes that do not will be weak and unstable however democratic they may be'.[38]

Examining Kennedy's assertions that the concept of human rights has been co-opted to the purposes of the state, particularly the idea that '[t]o be free ... is to have an appropriately organised state',[39] Liora Lazarus argues that political discourse around the conflict between security and rights since 9/11 has been complicated by the argument that the 'right to security' can be viewed as the meta-right (the right of rights). This argument, and the inherent ambiguity of the right to security, has the potential to lead to a 'securitisation' of human rights which threatens to erode the traditional foundations of human rights, and human rights themselves.

[36] *Secretary of State for the Home Department* v. *AF* [2009] UKHL 28, para.76.
[37] Kennedy, *The Dark Sides of Virtue*, p.1.
[38] J. Gray, *False Dawn, The Delusions of Global Capitalism* (London: Granta, 1998), p.18.
[39] Kennedy, *The Dark Sides of Virtue*, p.16.

Human rights norms are often couched in transformative language, with Claire Palley asserting that:

> [t]he dramatic language of 'human rights and fundamental freedoms', combined with talk of inalienability, immutability, imprescriptibility, universalism and absolutism, is emotive. The effect is the greater because human rights represent values in which people believe, for example, the worth of life, liberty, free speech, free trial, justice according to needs and absence of discrimination.[40]

Even within liberal democracies, however, the operationalised reality of human rights appears to be rather more prosaic. Such countries have endeavoured to constitutionalise their systems of government to a degree compatible with maintaining an important sphere of political debate. Some countries, like the USA and UK, have arrived at different accommodations of these concerns, producing atypical models of domestic rights protection. Colin Murray's chapter examines the consequence of these constitutional compromises which have emerged in both countries' responses to terrorism since the attacks of September 11. The constitutional rights protections in place within the USA serve not to prevent rights abuses but to channel responses to emergency situations against other, less well-protected, interests. Murray challenges the supposition that 'European human rights law would allow more infringements of liberty, in the name of national security and public order, than does the US Constitution',[41] contending that the ostensibly weaker rights protections in the UK carry the potential genuinely to constrain rather than simply redirecting the focus of counter-terrorism responses.

International human rights law perspectives

Kennedy's scepticism of the 'pragmatic' invocation of human rights norms in the context of the ongoing fight against terrorism provides the narrative basis for the second section of the collection, which relates to international human rights. The indefinite detention of individuals without charge or trial in Guantánamo Bay, the abuses amounting to torture in Abu Ghraib Prison in Iraq and the imposition of sanctions against individuals by the Security Council remain fresh in the memory

[40] C. Palley, *The United Kingdom and Human Rights* (London: Sweet & Maxwell, 1991), pp.75–6.

[41] S. Sottiaux, *Terrorism and the Limitation of Rights: The ECHR and the US Constitution* (Oxford: Hart, 2008) p.21.

of international human rights lawyers, tempting the human rights movement to engage pragmatically with the practices of these states and bodies to lessen abuses, even if the legitimacy of such actions is thereby enhanced.

The expanded role and competences of the Security Council in maintaining international peace and security have been particularly controversial. States have been presented with a conflict of norms and obligations when faced with the choice between observing international human rights obligations or meeting responsibilities which emanate from the United Nations Charter. This issue is analysed by Elena Katselli, who argues that the rule of law and respect for human rights are an integral part not only of the fight against terrorism but also of the regime for safeguarding international peace and security. Despite the sceptical view of some rule-of-law scholars that the rule of law is a virtue most notable on the international scene by its absence,[42] Katselli argues that stronger adherence to the rule of law in international legal settings can lend credibility to international law. This is partly based on her argument that the rule of law restricts state activities by requiring that states cannot act outside the confines of fundamental human rights when operating at the international level as a member of an international organisation. In a Fulleresque approach to the rule of law, which has arguably been developed further by the late Tom Bingham,[43] Katselli argues that the concept of human rights is central to any proper definition of the rule of law. Rather worryingly, though, her contribution highlights how one of the main threats to the international rule of law is found in the workings of the Security Council, which increasingly engages in activities usurping the rights of individuals with little recourse to individual review procedures for those affected. Again, Katselli puts forward a strong defence of the rights of individuals grounded in the rule of law. Importantly, she is aware of the siren song of 'idolatry' which Kennedy warns against.[44] Appropriately perhaps, Katselli argues that domestic and international courts have obligations to step in when the rule of law is overlooked by powerful international actors.

While David Kennedy claims that human rights are less compelling as a concept than they once were,[45] Steven Wheatley asserts a distinctive role for human rights law and that the concept of human rights

[42] See e.g. B. Tamanaha, *On the Rule of Law: History, Politics, Theory* (New York: Cambridge University Press, 2004), pp.127–36.

[43] See T. Bingham, 'The Rule of Law' (2007) 66 CLJ 67.

[44] See Chapter 2 below.

[45] See Chapter 2 below.

conditions the actions of states. He contends that the question which international lawyers must therefore address is one centred upon the legitimacy of these laws. In doing so, Wheatley examines in detail the role of the European Court of Human Rights and asks whether its teleological interpretation and emphasis on 'present day' conditions runs the risk of running counter to democratic and legitimate choices made at the state level. As suggested in Katselli's paper, it would seem that we are faced with a situation where competing norms conflict. Wheatley illustrates, through an examination of the Court's decision in *Sejdić and Finci*,[46] how the European Court of Human Rights grapples with the question whether blatant discrimination can be justified on consequentialist grounds by reference to the need to avoid civil war. Perhaps adopting a tone of pragmatism, Wheatley notes that it is 'difficult to conclude that a supranational court is better placed than the national constitutional court, which reached the opposite conclusion'.[47] Nevertheless, Wheatley argues that the situation in *Sejdić and Finci* is not one of conflict of norms. Instead it is one of deconstruction (by the Court) of the constitutional frame for democratic law-making found in Bosnia Herzegovina – a frame which the Court evidently does not approve of. When engaged in this activity, Wheatley argues that one way to understand the role of the European Court of Human Rights is to regard it as an 'other-regarding' institution which outlines conceptions of the democratic state moulded on the ECHR.

Striking a note of caution, though, he concludes that when international actors engage in activities in conditions of uncertainty, as in *Sejdić and Finci*, they cannot be certain that their activities are 'just' or 'right' in the absence of legitimate authority. Such legitimacy, in Wheatley's words, is absent from the ECHR as a result of the lack of political processes and deliberations through which legal actors can develop appropriate notions of political justice. Consequently, we can add his argument in favour of legitimacy to the dangers of idolatry and pragmatism, identified by Kennedy, as concerns which the human rights movement ought to take into account when embarking on human rights work.

Examining human rights in the context of struggles between different national groups, Rob Dickinson assesses Kennedy's contention that human rights have progressed from a utopian vision through a chastening

[46] *Sejdić and Finci* v. *Bosnia and Herzegovina*, Appl. nos. 27996/06 and 34836/06 (ECtHR, GC, 22 December 2009).

[47] See Chapter 8 below, p.163.

process. He argues that self-determination of peoples, an essential collective human right,[48] has been treated pragmatically by states rather than as being an indivisible interest, in a manner which calls into question the concept of universality of human rights. In his analysis, Dickinson argues that this pragmatism is vividly witnessed in the treatment afforded by the international community to Kosovo in its push for independence. Dickinson's assertion of self-determination (and by implication human rights) being subject to pragmatic influences is further highlighted by his argument that the recognition afforded Tibet stands in stark contrast to that of Kosovo. In Tibet, calls for secession are subjected to geopolitical considerations effectively blocking the application of any principle of self-determination as these were applied in Kosovo. As Dickinson appositely observes '[d]oes Kosovo . . . succeed in seceding because it can, rather than because it is entitled to do so on principle?'[49] Like Kennedy,[50] Dickinson notes that such pragmatism is not unreservedly positive. In Kosovo, for example, he points out that powerful elites today are not necessarily inclined to hold power for the benefit of the people.

Theoretical perspectives on human rights

The final section of the collection focuses upon theoretical responses to Kennedy's arguments. Whilst comprehensive coverage would prove difficult in a collection of this size, these responses probe Kennedy's key themes of idolatry, pragmatism and the co-option of the language of human rights by states in an attempt to legitimise their actions.

Eric Heinze neatly builds on Kennedy's arguments of idolatry in setting out to examine the role which the mass media play in shaping the public's perceptions of human rights violations.[51] Heinze argues that the mass media decisively shape global perceptions about human rights, despite failing to reflect the realities of global violations. The main reasons for this are to be found more in effect than in intent, arising more from entrenched journalistic conventions than from overweening editorial bias. Nevertheless, the human rights reporting by the mass media inevitably helps to spur notions of idolatry and of scepticism among both policy makers and the wider public. Heinze highlights how human rights discussions are often based, not on normative concerns,

[48] And one which, as Samuel Moyn recognises, has threatened at various times in the second half of the twentieth century to overshadow much of the remainder of the human rights project. See Moyn, *The Last Utopia*, pp.2–3.

[49] See Chapter 9 below, p.188. [50] See Chapter 2 below. [51] See Chapter 2 below.

but on what happens to receive most media attention. This is highlighted in the coverage afforded Israel's activities in the 'occupied territories' (a term which Heinze terms 'mediatised')[52] compared to the media coverage afforded the human rights abuses taking place in for example North Korea or the Democratic Republic of Congo. While it may be easy to dismiss such disparate media coverage as inconsequential, Heinze highlights how the coverage has significant effects on public perceptions of countries' human rights records. These problems, however, as Heinze observes, are not necessarily a problem for human rights *per se*. Nevertheless, the media coverage analysed by Heinze and its effect on the wider public represent a significant challenge for the international human rights movement.

Despite Moyn's pithy aphorism that, to date, human rights 'have done far more to transform the terrain of idealism than they have the world itself',[53] the influential role of the human rights movement in finally bringing peace and reconciliation to some parts of the world cannot be overlooked. This is emphasised by Christine Bell, who examines how the abuse of human rights, the structural inequality and the weak protection for the minority in Northern Ireland contributed to the escalation of the crisis and the outbreak of conflict. In the context of the 'Troubles', international mechanisms for the protection of human rights operated as mechanisms to exert pressure for reform and substantive improvement of the human rights situation. This reinforces the arguments that human rights and the rule of law have a determinative role to play in national and international conflicts and that politics cannot be disassociated from these fundamental principles. What is more, Bell's chapter highlights how human rights paradigms can play a significant role in local activist settings even where activists do not consider themselves part of an international human rights movement. In addition, Bell's contribution highlights that, while Kennedy's criticism of a legalistic human rights focus carries with it high costs,[54] some of the benefits (in particular in deeply divided societies) are easy to overlook. Likewise, Bell's on-the-ground experience is a fascinating example of how adherence to pragmatism (e.g. by trying to avoid politically fraught questions) in some instances served the human rights movement, and counters Kennedy's criticism of pragmatism.

Whilst Bell critiques Kennedy's accusations of idolatry from the practical but egalitarian perspective of a human rights activist, Richard Mullender examines Kennedy's argument that the concept of human

[52] See Chapter 10 below, p.201. [53] Moyn, *The Last Utopia*, p.9. [54] See Chapter 2 below.

rights is also under pressure from co-option of the language and technical detail of human rights, but not their underlying principles, by Western states and particularly by the military.[55] Mullender assesses the theoretical and historical roots of 'lawfare' (the process by which, Kennedy claims, states seek to enhance the legitimacy of military operations during conflicts by linking them to human rights standards) and the ability of governments in liberal democracies to assimilate the rhetoric of their opponents and thereby neutralise criticism of their own actions. Tracing a strong Anglo-American influence on the concept of 'lawfare' (while highlighting its universal agenda), Mullender argues that the concept presents the international human rights movement with a significant challenge. He warns that the proponents of 'lawfare' assume that it is possible to finely calibrate the use of military force in order to minimise its negative effects. While this focus on outcomes and consequences is in stark contrast to the deontological origins of the human rights movement, arguably the proponents of 'lawfare' are also prone to 'idolatry' as they suffer from what Mullender terms 'unjustified optimism' in assuming that they are in a position to make precise assessments of ends and means. He further argues that, in doing so, the proponents of 'lawfare' exhibit similarities with what Thomas Nagel considers ruthlessness in public life, insofar as they allow the overruling of deontological concerns by reference to consequentialist impulses. As a result, Mullender's contribution serves as a warning to the international human rights movement that they cannot have their cake and eat it.

An opportunity for reflection

As already noted, the aim of this collection is not to offer a comprehensive review of contemporary human rights critiques. More modestly, it is hoped that the contributions found in the collection will go some way towards shedding new light on past, present and future challenges facing the human rights movement. As observed by one of the greatest scholars of post-war European history, in the past the rights vocabulary has offered an opportunity to communicate across divides (be they political, geographical or cultural).[56] Whether this continues to be the case a decade on from the attacks of 11 September 2001 remains to be seen.

55 See Chapter 2 below.

56 T. Judt, *Postwar: A History of Europe since 1945* (London: William Heinemann, 2005) pp.564–66.

The intervening years of international adventuring by a cohort of states led by the USA and the UK has not simply undermined the international reputation of these states, but reignited debate as to whether human rights norms can adequately restrain powerful states on the international plane.[57] These events, coupled with the increasing introspection within legal systems regarding the 'trivialisation' of human rights norms,[58] create the opportunity for the reflections in this collection. It is hoped, therefore, that this collection will at least assist attempts to communicate across the existing and future divides which the human rights movement will need to span in the years to come.

57 See Farer, *Confronting Global Terrorism and American Neo-Conservatism*, pp.60–4.

58 See Lord Hoffmann, 'The Universality of Human Rights' (2009) 125 LQR 416, 430.

2

The international human rights regime: still part of the problem?

DAVID KENNEDY

Let me begin by expressing my gratitude to the editors of this volume, and to the University of Newcastle, for organizing the conversation from which these papers were developed. I was tremendously honored that colleagues would find my short essay on the human rights movement, first published a decade ago, still worthy of discussion.[1] I should start by emphasizing that more than sixty years after the adoption of the Universal Declaration of Human Rights there is much to celebrate. Human rights is no longer only an idea. Over the last half century, we have amassed an enormous library of legal norms and aspirational declarations. A complex institutional practice has grown up in the shadow of those pronouncements to promote, defend, interpret, elaborate, implement, enforce, and simply to honor them. There is no question the human rights movement has done a great deal of good, freeing individuals from great harm, and raising the standards by which governments are judged. It has cast light on catastrophic conditions in prisons around the world. Human rights advocacy became at once a professional practice and a movement.

It would be hard to date, but sometime not too long ago, human rights also became a practice of governance. Institutionally, it would be more accurate today to speak of international human rights as a 'regime' than as a movement or an idea. Governments have human rights departments, ombudsmen, special *rapporteurs*, and investigative divisions. If you are a diplomat, you can be assigned human rights as a specialty. If you are a law student, you can aspire to a career in the field of human rights. We have human rights networks, human rights courts,

[1] D. Kennedy, 'The international human rights movement: part of the problem?' *European Human Rights Law Review* 3 (2001) 245–67, reprinted in *Harvard Human Rights Journal* 14 (2002) 101–26.

non-governmental organizations, citizens' initiatives, government bureaus, international institutions, private foundations, military staffs, specialized journalists, authors, and media – all in one or another way 'doing' human rights. Diplomats denounce one another, citizens write letters and send checks, and a cadre of diverse professionals travels the world denouncing governments and promoting human rights.

Humanitarian voices are increasingly powerful on the international stage – often providing the terms through which global power is exercised, wars planned and fought. Human rights has elbowed economics aside in our development agencies, which now spend billions once allocated to dams and roadways on court reform, judicial training, and 'rule of law' injection. The UN High Commissioner for Refugees designs and manages asylum and immigration policies with governments around the world. And of course, human rights has also become an academic specialty – in law faculties, but also in departments of sociology, psychology, philosophy, political science, public health, and more. Some scholars go further, proclaiming ours the *age of human rights*. In this view, human rights has become more than an institutional regime – it is now a universal ideology, an international standard of legitimacy for sovereign power, a common vernacular of justice for a global civil society. Such an altered consciousness for the world's elites has long been among the movement's most fervent dreams. On this score, I am less sure, although it is certainly true that all manner of political maneuvers and strategies are now pursued in the rhetoric of human rights and the awareness of human rights violations now does seem to call forth – or delegitimate – political action.

There is no doubt that this is all a real achievement. At the same time, however, the discussions in Newcastle from which this volume has emerged took place at a moment of chastening for the human rights profession. Both beginners and seasoned veterans are far more savvy and pragmatic than any of us were when I started in the field almost thirty years ago. Painful lessons hard-learned have sown nagging doubts. There are so many unsavory things one simply cannot do anything about, so many unsavory things one finds *oneself* doing in the human rights business.

It is interesting how often we trace the origins of human rights to a *declaration* and locate the origins of the movement in a group of texts adopted after the Second World War. Human rights in the world is not a text. As a form of governance, a profession, a movement, a universal ideological practice, human rights was launched much later, in the late 1970s and early 1980s, just as the pendulum swung for a generation toward Thatcher, Reagan, and the politics of 'neo-liberalism.' I believe I taught a course on human rights at Harvard for the first time in 1982, and made my first human rights junket the next year, to visit prisons in Israel. The following year I was in Latin America, prisons again. By 1984, I was in Geneva working for the UN. In the heyday of human rights, it all seemed much simpler – we were turning text into deed, aspiration into institution. The language of human rights was everywhere, while the limits of what it could accomplish were only barely apparent.

Who were the first human rights professionals? Some had been liberals of the 1960s, taking their civil liberties commitments onto the global stage. Others, like myself, were children of the 1970s for whom Jimmy Carter had made human rights a respectable vernacular for transposing what we remembered of sixties idealism to international affairs. I know my academic colleagues felt we were redeeming the better promise of Carter's diplomacy, turning the Cold War struggle from proxy wars to direct affirmation of democracy and citizens' rights. Russian dissidents and their Western supporters were big players.

Over the next ten years, it seemed that democracy was on the rise and that we had ringside seats. I remember observing a trial in Prague on a grey and rainy October Tuesday in 1989, in a small dilapidated courthouse on the outskirts of town, only to return the following May, flowers in bloom, for a meeting of Harvard Law School's European alumni in a newly poshed-up hotel. I asked where to find the defendant whose trial I had sat through – a member of a John Lennon peace group – and was directed to 'the Castle.' It seems that, after the Velvet Revolution, he had gone to work in Václav Havel's office, where he was far too busy for an appointment. It was exciting stuff. After 1989, the human rights and humanitarian agendas benefited from an enormous burst of energy and self-confidence. On a recent visit, I was surprised to find that Human Rights Watch now takes up several floors in the Empire State Building, naming and shaming from a great height.

At the same time, since the early 1980s we have all learned a great deal about the dilemmas, dark sides, and disappointments of human rights as a tool for global governance. A surprising number of foot soldiers have left their jobs and written up their stories, stories of early faith confounded, lost amid the vagaries of politics and context and all the duplicities of good intentions brought to faraway places. Human rights today is at once more powerful and less innocent, urgent, compelling. It is hard to say why, or how this chastening has come about. Perhaps the movement bit off more than it could chew.

There were certainly many disappointments. So many interventions did not work out as we had planned. We learned that human rights can also legitimate a regime, even a regime we believe violates rights, if only by isolating the violation in a way which normalizes the rest of the regime's activities. As an absolute language of righteousness and moral aspiration came to be used strategically, human rights became less compelling, easy to interpret as nothing but strategy, cover for political objectives, particular interests clothing themselves in the language of the universal.

That human rights advocates and practitioners are no longer as naïve as we once were is itself worthy of celebration. Modern human rights professionals are often the first to know and to admit the limits of their language, their institutional practices, their governance routines. They know there are darker sides, they weigh and balance and think shrewdly and practically.

This, it seems to me, is the real promise of volumes like this one. Serious academic inquiry will also be critical inquiry, illuminating what has gone awry as well as what has been achieved. The human rights movement is up to it – indeed, it needs precisely this kind of serious interdisciplinary scrutiny.

Of course, the profession has also developed routine practices to disperse the nausea and still the confusion which go with human rights activism. They are careful to separate their public piety and their private cynicism, the pragmatism of the field and the earnestness of headquarters, the rhetoric of public relations and the reality of recruiting all those victims and gathering all that testimony, lest mixing the one with the other damage the endeavor or discourage the donors. We should bring these mechanisms into focus, for they permit knowledge of the dark side to remain as readily denied as admitted. In the field, it is denied in the name of the pragmatic, at headquarters in the name of ethical commitment.

I attribute the experience of chastening and disenchantment to increasing awareness of two related dangers of human rights work. First, the tendency of human rights idealism to veer toward idolatry, enchanting the tools and norms and practitioners of human rights, while remaining marginal to power, standing on the sidelines 'speaking truth.' For this, the traditional remedy is pragmatism. The activist practice of human rights should become more pragmatic.

Second, the pitfalls of pragmatism, of participation in governance, with all the tools of policy analysis, instrumental reason, and savvy evaluation of the costs and benefits of human rights initiatives that entails. For this, the traditional remedy is a return to ethics – and the dangers of idolatry.

There is no recipe or institutional roadmap to avoid these parallel difficulties, unfortunately. My worry is that, together, they chill the appetite for political decision, promoting the knowing routines of professional advocacy over the exercise of discretion and the experience of responsibility. What I do think we can hope for is a kind of professional, political, and moral vigilance, discipline, and renewal: a posture for the humanitarian professional which is neither ethically nor instrumentally self-confident, yet prepared to accept responsibility for the damage his or her initiatives will cause.

These twin difficulties – of idolatry and pragmatism – are not unique to human rights. They are common to many international humanist and humanitarian governance projects. Assessing – or celebrating – humanist governance requires that we focus on humanism as a political project: commitments that are widely shared and that have been transformed over the last thirty or forty years into concrete legal regimes and policy initiatives. In this light, we ought not to see humanism *against* power, talking to power, advising power, restraining power, but humanism *as* power; not humanism as the modest handmaiden of force, but humanism as the motive and method of force; humanism, moreover, as a professional *experience.* The experience of ruling – or perhaps, more modestly sometimes, of not ruling, of advising rulership – in the name of an appealing grab bag of ethical commitments.

Like any other attractive, professional self-image, the experience of ruling the world in the name of laudable commitments must be sustained. And yet tensions among humanist commitments – engage the world, but in the name of a cosmopolitan tolerance; reform the world, while renouncing the tools of power politics; rule the world, but live in an international community of modest humanist consensus – have gotten built into the legal and institutional tools we have constructed to give them expression. These tensions have left us ambivalent about rulership. And ambivalent rulership is often rulership denied. We sustain the experience of humanism by denying ourselves the experience of our own rulership. We prefer to think of ourselves off to one side, speaking truth to power – or hidden in the policy apparatus advising *other people* – the princes – to humanize *their* work. I suspect that the difficulties we encounter with humanist idealism and pragmatism arise from a reluctance to acknowledge the extent to which humanitarians have become rulers. Humanist rulers are chastened and disenchanted humanists.

They are unsettled at having become participants, rather than observers and critics, of global governance. To my mind, before they can become self-confident, empowered, and responsible partners in governance, humanitarians will need to learn to take responsibility for the costs as well as the benefits of their work.

Idealism and the problems of idolatry

The dangers of idolatrous rulership are well known. We are right to be worried when idealism takes over. Idealism becomes idolatry when it rules in the name of unambiguous virtue; when it overestimates the singularity of its vision and refuses to place the costs of its rulership centre-stage where they can be assessed and either refuted or taken into account. Human rights professionals know how this can happen – how they can get carried away by the human rights promise and lose sight of other virtues and other viewpoints.

It is nothing new to point out how *narrowly* the human rights tradition views human emancipation – focusing on what governments do to individuals, on participatory rather than economic or distributive issues, on legal, rather than social, religious, or other remedies. Problems which are hard to formulate as rights claims for individuals – collective problems, economic problems, problems of poverty or health – are easy to overlook. Emancipating people as *rights holders*, moreover, stresses their individual claims, their personal relationship with the state. This can encourage a politics of queue jumping among the disadvantaged, propagating attitudes of victimization and entitlement, while making cross-alliances and solutions which involve compromise and sharing more difficult.

As human rights activists, we know our profession can induce ethical deformations of various kinds. As we learn we can touch the barbaric and return unscathed, we discover there can be something voyeuristic in our gaze. We are often troubled when we acknowledge the suffering of others without abandoning our commitment to the system that produces it. We do worry that human rights so often legitimates and excuses government behaviour – setting standards below which mischief seems legitimate. We know it can be easy to sign a treaty – and then do what you want. But even compliance may do more harm than good – a well-implemented ban on the death penalty, for example, can easily leave the general conditions of incarceration unremarked, can make life-without-parole more legitimate, more difficult to challenge. The discourse of human rights speaks about torture and imprisonment and violence in a peculiar doubled way – and we worry when we come to think that way ourselves: on one hand, denunciation – somewhere a human right has been violated; but on the other, a balance – this right against that, these victims against those. We balance rights to free movement against rights of religious expression or speech. We balance security against freedom. And somehow the aura of the ethically absolute which accompanied our denunciation becomes affixed to whatever accommodative balance we strike, just as the right holders whose claims we balance come to seem equivalent, commutable, equally legitimate. Ripped from context, abstracted into rights to be balanced, the occupier and the occupied, the saviour and the sinner, can seem strangely similar.

I have repeatedly been surprised by the difficulty human rights lawyers have in acknowledging that there is law on the other side. When we invoke human rights against state power, we are pounding not only on the door of politics, but also on sovereign privilege and constitutional right. Yet we persist in thinking of inhumanity as a 'violation,' a barbarity, a lapse; as the exception, the extraconstitutional, the deviation; Guantánamo a black hole in the fabric of law – rather than one of the most intensely legalized spaces on the planet.

Human rights is all about focus – shining a light on this or that. With focus comes a common *tip of the iceberg* problem – focus on the real problems of refugees can make it more difficult to contest the closure of borders to economic migration. Indeed, the legal definition of 'refugee' has done as much to exclude people in grave need from protection as it has to legitimate UN engagement. After all, sexually humiliating, even torturing and killing prisoners is not the worst or most shocking thing the coalition has done in Iraq. Our horror at photos of 'human rights abuses' may also be a way of not thinking about other injuries, deaths, and mutilations the war has wrought.

By defining justice as a relationship to the state, rather than a condition in society, human rights can distract our attention from background norms and economic conditions which often do far more damage. Perhaps most disturbingly, the international human rights movement often acts as if it knows what justice means, always and for everyone – all you need to do is adopt, implement, interpret these rights. But justice is not like that. It must be built by people each time, struggled for, imagined in new ways. The most revered texts in the human rights canon are vague and open to interpretation. As a result, it is unlikely that any articulation of a global normative consensus will escape being perceived by those who disagree – and people will disagree – as partial, subjective, selective. These are the wages of speaking universally in a plural world.

Indeed, the crisis in confidence that crashed on the UN Human Rights Commission in recent years was not about only the appalling human rights record of governments that have served on the Commission. It also reflected the limits of turning the articulation and development of human rights over to *governments* in the first place. That governments would want to judge one another, to chastise their enemies and praise their friends, in a widely shared ethical vocabulary is not surprising. What is surprising is that the human rights community has been so enthusiastic about their taking up the task. The limits of a diplomatic ethics parallel the limits of any established church in a plural society: not good for the government, not good for the church.

We know we should worry that human rights (given its origins, its spokesmen, its preoccupations) has so often been a vocabulary of the center against the periphery, a vehicle for, rather than an antidote to empire. There are, moreover, real dangers to universal normative entrepreneurialism. Expressing the ethical conviction of the international community can suggest that there is, in fact, an 'international community' ready to stand behind one's pronouncements. It can lead people to intervene, multilaterally or otherwise, where there is no stamina, in fact, to follow through. It can suggest that those who disagree with this elite – and many do – are somehow outside the circuit of 'civilization.' Indeed, the ethical challenge for the next period will be to dissolve the hubris of a universal ethics, and to communicate modestly across ethical divisions, heightening our sense for the plural and heterogenous moral possibilities *within* the West, the rest, the center, the periphery.

These are all well-known worries. But they are terribly difficult to take into account – to weigh and balance against the real upsides of human rights work. It is easy for good-hearted people, humanitarians in the best senses, to get carried away with human rights. It can be all too easy to say 'let us at least begin' – let us light the first candle. Normally, of course, such an attitude in government would be completely irresponsible. Imagine a proposed road work – before the government builds the first mile, we expect them to have looked into the costs as well as the benefits. I have often spoken with human rights advocates who are proud of one or another of the movement's real achievements, but when you ask them 'what costs were associated with that success?' they rarely have a worked-out response – it is as if human rights improvements had no costs.

This kind of magical thinking should raise a red flag. We should be on guard when someone seeks to recruit us to a project that only has upsides. This is what it means for the exercise of power to fall victim to idolatry. The most significant challenges for the human rights movement in the years ahead will be to understand what it means to be a participant in governance, and not just a critic of it.

Pragmatism and the perils of humanist violence

To recount the pitfalls of idolatrous rulership is to call for the cool eyes and unsentimental calculations of a more pragmatic governance. There is something thrilling about learning to speak the practical language of policy if you think of yourself as a humanitarian – perhaps to leave the nostrums of human rights advocacy behind for a more nuanced engagement with the practical problems of rulership, with balancing harms, assessing benefits. Alongside enthusiasm for human rights as a rhetoric of global governance has grown a parallel, and equally promising rhetoric of practical wisdom about how one might bend the prince to humanist ends. The promise of this more practical humanism is nowhere better illustrated than in the modern laws of war and force, which (interestingly enough) have begun to merge with human rights as a vernacular for judging violence on the battlefield. Here also there has been enthusiasm and rapid development of norms and institutions and professional routines – and here also there has been a chastening.

We might say that the modern law of force represents a triumph for grasping the nettle of costs and benefits and infiltrating the background decision-making of those it would bend to humanitarian ends. Modern war is a legal institution. Once a bit player in military conflict, law now shapes the institutional, logistical, and physical landscape of war – and even more so for occupation. Law and human rights have infiltrated the military profession, and become – for parties on all sides of even the most asymmetric confrontations – a political and ethical vocabulary for marking legitimate power and justifiable death. Indeed, as law became an ever more important yardstick for legitimacy, legal categories became far too spongy to permit clear resolution of the most important questions – or became spongy enough to undergird the experience of self-confident outrage by parties on all sides of a conflict.

The triumph of humanist pragmatism opens opportunities and dangers. When things go well, law can provide a framework for talking across cultures about the justice and efficacy of wartime violence. At the same time, modern law is itself pragmatic – and surprisingly fluid. International law is no longer an affair of clear rules and sharp distinctions. Law today rarely speaks clearly, or with a single voice. As a result, the modern partnership of war and law often leaves all parties feeling their cause is just and no one feeling responsible for the deaths and suffering of war. Good legal arguments can make people lose their moral compass and sense of responsibility for the violence of war.

Just as we celebrate sixty years of human rights, we can be proud that modern war *is* a legal institution, not least because it has become a professional practice. Today's military is linked to the nation's commercial life, integrated with civilian and peacetime governmental institutions, and covered by the same national and international media. Officers discipline their force and organize their operations with rules. Operating across dozens of jurisdictions, today's military must also comply with innumerable local, national, and international rules regulating the use of territory, the mobilization of men, the financing of arms and logistics, and the deployment of force. If you want to screen banking data in Belgium, or hire operatives in Pakistan, or refuel your plane in Kazakhstan, you need to know the law of the place.

Law is perhaps most visibly part of military life when it privileges the killing and destruction of battle. If you kill *this way*, and not that, *here* and not there, *these people* and not those – what you do is privileged. If not, it is criminal. Moreover, if war remains, as Clausewitz taught us, the continuation of politics by other means, the politics continued by warfare today has itself been legalized. Political leaders act in the shadow of a knowledgeable, demanding, engaged, and institutionally entrenched national and global elite. Law has become the common vernacular of this dispersed elite, even as they argue about just what the law permits and forbids. This is what led opponents of the Iraq conflict – or Guantánamo – so often to frame their opposition in legal terms – what you are doing is *illegal*.

To grasp the dark sides of humanist pragmatism, we must understand two aspects of modern law: its antiformalism and its pluralism. Two hundred years ago, international law was rooted in ethics – to think about the law of war was to meditate on considerations of 'right' reason and natural justice. The call to professionalism – coinciding with the establishment of the ICRC – disengaged law from morality. One hundred years ago, law had become far more a matter of formal rules, delinked from morality and rooted in sovereign will. Law stood outside the institutions it regulated, offering a framework of sharp distinctions and formal boundaries. War and peace were legally distinct, separated by a formal 'declaration of war.' But ethical absolutes, let loose on matters of war and peace, can be dangerous – and seemed out of touch with an evolving practice of warfare. What was needed was something more practical – and antiformal.

We needed to translate our ethical worries into a workable wartime vernacular – not a series of idolatrous pronouncements. The International Committee of the Red Cross was again in the forefront, priding itself on its pragmatic relationship with military professionals. First, ICRC lawyers worked with the military to codify rules the military could live with – wanted to live with: no exploding bullets, respect for ambulances and medical personnel, and so forth. Of course, reliance on military acquiescence limited what could be achieved. Narrowly drawn rules permit a great deal – and legitimate what is permitted. Recognition of these costs encouraged a turn to principles and standards. Since at least 1945, a vocabulary of *principles* has grown up alongside tough-minded military bargains over weaponry. The detailed rules of The Hague or Geneva have morphed into standards – simple ideas which can be printed on a wallet-sized card and taught to soldiers in the field. 'The means of war are not unlimited, each use of force must be necessary and proportional' – these have become ethical baselines for a universal modern civilization. This move to principles has allowed the law in war to infiltrate the vocabulary of the military profession while blending smoothly with human rights.

As a framework for debate and judgment, this new law in war embraces the unavoidability of trade-offs, of balancing harms, of accepting costs to achieve benefit – an experience common to both military strategists and humanitarians. At the same time, the sharp distinction between war and peace, the need for a 'declaration,' even the legal status of 'neutrality' were abandoned. The UN Charter replaces the word 'war' with more nuanced – and vague – terms like 'intervention,' 'threats to the peace,' or the 'use of armed force,' which trigger one or another institutional response. In the process, the modern law of armed conflict became a confusing mix of principles and counter-principles, of firm rules and loose exceptions. Once-firm distinctions now melt into air when we press on them too firmly. Once 'war' itself becomes 'self-defense,' 'hostilities,' 'the use of force,' 'resort to arms,' 'police action,' 'peace enforcement,' 'peace making,' 'peacekeeping,' it becomes hard to keep it all straight.

Indeed, law now offers the rhetorical – and doctrinal – tools to make and unmake the distinction between war and peace, allowing the boundaries of war to be managed strategically. Take the difficult question – when does war end? The answer is not to be found in law or fact – but in strategy. *Declaring* the end of hostilities might be a matter of election theatre or military assessment. Just like announcing that there remains 'a long way to go,' or that the 'insurgency is in its final throes.' We should understand these statements as *arguments*: As messages – but also as weapons. Law – legal categorization – is a communication tool, and communicating the war is fighting the war. This is a war, this is an occupation, this is a police action, this is a security zone. These are insurgents, those are criminals, these are illegal combatants, and so on. All these are claims with audiences, made for a reason. Increasingly, defining the battlefield is not only a matter of deployed force – it is also a rhetorical and legal claim.

Law provides a vernacular for making such claims about a battlespace in which all these things are mixed up together. In the confusion, we want to insist on a bright line. For the military, after all, defining the battlefield defines the privilege to kill. But aid agencies also want the guys digging the wells to be seen as humanitarians, not post-conflict combatants – privileged not to be killed. Defining the not-battlefield opens a 'space' for humanitarian action.

When we use the law strategically, we change it. Moreover, strange as it may seem, there is now more than one law of armed conflict. Different nations – even in the same coalition – will have signed different treaties. The same standards look different if you anticipate battle against a technologically superior foe – or live in a Palestinian refugee camp in Gaza. Although we might disagree with one or the other interpretation, we must recognize that the legal materials are elastic enough to enable diverse interpretations. As a lawyer, advising the military about the law of war means making a prediction about how people with the power to influence our success will interpret the legitimacy of our plans.

It is easy to understand the virtues of a powerful legal vocabulary, shared by elites around the world, for judging the violence of warfare. It is exciting to see law and human rights become the mark of legitimacy as legitimacy has become the currency of power. It is more difficult to see the opportunities this opens for the military professional to harness law as a weapon, or to understand the dark sides of war by law. The American military have coined a word for this: 'Lawfare' – law as a weapon, law as a tactical ally, law as a strategic asset, an instrument of war. We might also think of human rights-fare: human rights as strategic asset and instrument of war.

This will take some getting used to. How should we feel when the military 'legally conditions the battlefield' by informing the public that they are *entitled* to kill civilians, or when our political leadership justifies warfare in the language of human rights? What is difficult for us to realize is that a war machine which used law more strategically might, in fact, be far more violent, more powerful, more ... well, legitimate. We need to remember what it means to say that compliance with international law 'legitimates.' It means, of course, that killing, maiming, humiliating, wounding people is legally privileged, authorized, permitted, and justified. And it is here that we can begin to see the darker side of humanitarian pragmatism.

The modern law of force has legitimated a great deal of warfare. Indeed, it is hard to think of a use of force that *could not* be legitimated in the language of the UN Charter. It is a rare statesman who launches a war simply to *be aggressive.* There is almost always something else to be said – the province is actually ours, our rights have been violated, our enemy is not, in fact, a state, we were invited to help, they were about to attack us, we are promoting the purposes and principles of the United Nations. Something. A parallel process has eroded the firewall between civilian and military targets – it is but a short step to what the military terms 'effects-based targeting.' And why *shouldn't* military operations be judged by their effects, rather than by their adherence to narrow rules that might well have all manner of perverse and unpredictable outcomes? The pragmatic assessment of wartime violence can be deeply disturbing.

Take civilian casualties. Of course, civilians *will* be killed in war. Limiting civilian death has become a pragmatic commitment – *no unnecessary damage, not one more civilian than necessary.* All we need to do is figure out just what is necessary. It is in this spirit that targets in the recent Iraq conflict were pored over by lawyers; and later, that those same lawyers, with a somewhat different strategy in view, pored over targets in Afghanistan, constantly revising the 'rules of engagement' to reflect the perceived strategic value of civilian life. We should not be surprised to hear that Human Rights Watch recently beefed up its ability to bring human rights to bear on the American practice of warfare – by hiring the man who had assessed the proportionality of American targeting for the Pentagon to do the same exercise for Human Rights Watch. Humanist pragmatism has become a partnership, within and without the government.

At the same time, the legitimacy of wartime violence is all mixed up with the legitimacy of the war itself. It is in this atmosphere that discipline has broken down in every asymmetric struggle, when neither clear rules nor broad standards of judgment seem adequate to moor one's ethical sense of responsibility and empowerment. Soldiers, civilians, media commentators, politicians, all begin to lose their ethical moorings. We can surely see that it will be hard for any Iraqi – or Lebanese – mother to feel it was necessary and proportional to kill her son. 'Why,' she might well demand to know, 'when America is so powerful and strong did you need to kill my husband?'

Here we can begin to see the dangers in turning the old distinction between combatants and civilians into a principle. The 'principle of distinction'. There is something oxymoronic here – it is either a distinction, or a principle. As the law in war became a matter of standards, balancing, and pragmatic calculation, the difficult, discretionary decisions were exported to the political realm. But when they get there, we find politicians seeking cover beneath the same legal formulations. Judgment, leadership, responsibility are in short supply.

There is no avoiding decisions about who to kill in warfare. The difficulty arises when humanitarian law transforms *decisions* about who to kill into *judgments;* when it encourages us to think death results, not from an exercise of human freedom, for which a moral being is responsible, but rather from the abstract operation of professional principles; or from a professional balance of competing human rights. Pretending that these decisions arise from the pragmatic assessment of competing principles can mean a loss of the experience of responsibility – command responsibility, ethical responsibility, political responsibility. Indeed, the greatest threat posed by the merger of law and war is loss of the human experience of moral jeopardy in the face of death, mutilation, and all the other horrors of warfare.

So, what can be done?

I certainly hope the humanitarian impulse will continue to mobilize people to become partners in rulership. My hope is for a more responsible, and more effective humanitarianism. We will need, however, to move beyond the twin dangers of an idolatry of rules and a pragmatism of principles. Ultimately, responsible rulership must be a practice of each humanitarian professional. We should encourage aspiring human rights activists to embrace the exercise of power and to develop an enhanced appetite for political conflict, and for the responsible exercise of human freedom – rather than the ethical self-confidence of idolatry or the evasions of instrumental reason.

We are up against some pretty daunting challenges on the global stage. Pandemics, global warming, financial instability, inequality – it is a long list. I worry that the human rights revolution may have been a delay and diversion: a status quo project of legitimation and an establishment career option for those who might otherwise have contributed to a new global politics. The global economic crisis is more than a challenge for technocrats and financial regulators. It presses upon us the limitations of a national politics in a global economy and a global society. The risks are not just those of unemployment or shrinking retirement savings. The risks are political and social – the impact of millions of individuals slipping away from their dreams. Speaking loosely, and to put it in the starkest terms, with economic globalization and the continued loss of public capacity, in twenty years large swaths of the world will have whatever social security system, whatever environmental regime, whatever labour law, whatever wage rate prevails in China. And there is the parallel challenge posed by economic failure in the developing world – by the revolution of rising frustrations among the hundreds of millions of individuals who can see in, but for whom there seems no route through the screen except by way of rebellion and spectacle.

Everywhere we confront an accelerating social and economic dualism. A rumbling fault line between two global architectures, between an insider and an outsider class, between leading and lagging sectors, both *within and between* national economies and political units. At the top and the bottom of the economy, we have deracinated ourselves, moving ever more often across ever greater distances. In relative terms, the middle classes are the ones who have become locked to their territory. Increasingly, the relative mobility of economics and the territorial rigidity of politics have rendered each other unstable as political and economic leadership have drifted apart. The result is a mismatch between a national politics on the one hand, and a global economy and society on the other.

These are the challenges facing humanists on the international stage in the coming decades. They are challenges about which human rights has very little to say – other than that state power must continue to be civilized and legitimate. What government – what NGO, what civil society – will be able to stem the revolutionary tide of resentment and desire unleashed along the fault lines of global politics today? Against this backdrop, I think we can begin to see the human rights moment for what it was – a status quo project for a stable time.

Perhaps a hundred years from now human rights professionals will still invoke norms, and shame governments, and publicize victims, and litigate injuries and indignities. But politics has moved on. Human rights is no longer the way forward – it focuses too longingly on the perfection of a politics already past its prime. Like constitutional orders before it, a new global governance regime will be imagined and built through collective hope, struggle, and disappointment. It took a long time to invent and civilize a national politics, to organize the world in nation states, and to subject them to one another's ethical judgment. Building a national politics across the planet had a strong emancipatory dimension – slaves, women, workers, peasants, colonial dominions obtained citizenship in relationship to the new institutional machinery of a national politics. We can see human rights as the apogee and epitaph for that politics. Building a new politics for a global society and a global economy will be every bit as difficult. Let us hope it does not take as long; and does not require as much violence in order to be born.

PART II

Domestic human rights perspectives

3

What is the point of human rights law?

K. D. EWING

Introduction

Binyam Mohamed is a British resident who was detained and tortured by the United States (USA) and others. His story is now well known, having been widely reported in the press, and since corroborated by a court in New York.[1]

In legal proceedings in the United Kingdom (UK), Mr Mohamed claimed that he had been unlawfully arrested in Pakistan in April 2002, and that he had then been detained without access to a lawyer or a court for almost four months. During that period, he was:

> interrogated by US officials, beaten, threatened with a gun, fed only every other day, suspended by his wrists, and given limited access to the lavatory, by the Pakistani authorities, and threatened by US officials with worse treatment elsewhere.[2]

Thereafter, Mr Mohamed 'was sent by way of so-called extraordinary rendition by the US authorities to Morocco, where he was interrogated further by US officials, and was beaten, subjected to sleep deprivation and cut on his private parts with a scalpel'.[3] In January 2004, he was then 'transferred' by the US authorities to Afghanistan, first to the 'Prison of Darkness' in Kabul, where he was again interrogated by US agents, and 'deprived of sleep, starved, and then beaten and hung up', and thence to Bagram in May 2004, where he said he was tortured and subjected to 'cruel, inhuman and degrading treatment'. In September 2004, Mr Mohamed was subsequently transferred to Guantánamo Bay, where he faced capital charges.[4]

As part of his defence to these charges, Mr Mohamed sought the disclosure of information held by the British government, which would

King's College, University of London.

[1] *Farhi Saeed Bin Mohammed (sic)* v. *Barack Obama* (Civil Action No 05–1347 (GK)).
[2] *R (Mohamed)* v. *Foreign Secretary* [2010] EWCA Civ 65, para.61 (Lord Neuberger MR).
[3] Ibid. [4] Ibid.

show that he had been tortured by the USA. Under general legal principles,[5] a court has the power to order a third party to disclose information which will be of assistance to a litigant (in this case Binyam Mohamed) against someone else (in this case the USA). That principle may be invoked where it can be shown that the third party (in this case the UK) had some role in the wrongdoing, and here there was evidence that a British intelligence official ('witness B') had questioned Mr Mohamed while he was in Pakistan. Once it was clear that this information could be disclosed, the British government issued a number of public interest immunity certificates objecting to its disclosure, on the ground that such disclosure would have an adverse impact on the willingness of the USA to share intelligence in the future. The case went to six hearings of the Administrative Court, before the Court of Appeal finally agreed that information about witness B's involvement should not be redacted from the public judgment, as the Foreign Office had argued. With strong echoes of another dispute between the courts and the government about the security and intelligence services,[6] the Court of Appeal was moved by the fact that the cat had been let out of the bag by the New York court, this having put into the public domain findings about Binyam Mohamed:

> being beaten with a leather strap, being subjected to a mock execution by shooting, being threatened with torture, being beaten, punched and kicked to the extent that he vomited and urinated, being tied to a wall, being left hanging, being left in darkness listening to other prisoners screaming, being cut on the chest and then on the penis and the testicles with a scalpel (about once a month for over a year), being subjected to a campaign of persistent very loud music, sleep interruption, drugs in his food, and sexually disturbing noises and sights, being chained and locked up in complete darkness, being 'hung up' by the wrists for two days, and being deprived of food and sleep. During this time he was interrogated by FBI and CIA agents, and 'his captors coached [him] on what to say during interrogations'.[7]

During the Administrative Court litigation, Mr Mohamed was released from US custody and returned to the UK. Along with a number of other victims, Mr Mohamed also brought proceedings in the English courts for damages on a number of grounds, relating to 'their respective

[5] *Norwich Pharmacal Co* v. *Customs and Excise Commissioners* [1974] AC 133.

[6] See the 'Spycatcher' case, *The Observer and The Guardian v United Kingdom* (1991) 14 EHRR 153.

[7] *Mohamed* v. *Foreign Secretary*, note 2 above, para.122.

detention and alleged mistreatment while detained', alleging 'false imprisonment, trespass to the person, conspiracy to injure, torture, breach of contract, negligence, misfeasance in public office, and breach of the Human Rights Act 1998'. On this occasion the government asked that the proceedings be held in secret on the ground that an open trial of the issue would be contrary to the public interest. But here too the government lost spectacularly in the Court of Appeal:

> [W]e should say firmly and unambiguously that it is not open to a court in England and Wales, in the absence of statutory power to do so or (arguably) agreement between the parties that the action should proceed on such a basis, to order a closed material procedure in relation to the trial of an ordinary civil claim for damages for tort or breach of statutory duty.[8]

The Court of Appeal took this view on the simple ground that the defendant's demands would 'undermine' one of the 'most fundamental principles' of the common law, and in any event would not be permissible under the Civil Procedure Rules.[9] Another defeat for the government; another vindication for the legal process; and another vindication for the common law. In neither of these cases did the Human Rights Act (HRA) 1998 play a significant part, on which more later.

Laws against torture

'There can be few issues on which international legal opinion is more clear than on the condemnation of torture.' So said Lord Bingham in *A* v. *Home Secretary (No 2)*.[10] But what constitutes torture to attract such unconditional condemnation? One starting point is the definition in the United Nations Convention against Torture (UNCAT), which defines torture as meaning:

> [A]ny act by which severe pain or suffering, whether physical or mental, is intentionally inflicted on a person for such purposes as obtaining from him or a third person information or a confession, punishing him for an act he or a third person has committed or is suspected of having committed, or intimidating or coercing him or a third person, or for any reason based on discrimination of any kind, when such pain or suffering is inflicted by or at the instigation of or with the consent or acquiescence of a public official or other person acting in an official

[8] *Al Rawi* v. *Security Service* [2010] EWCA Civ 482, para.11
[9] Ibid, para.12. [10] [2005] UKHL 71, para.33.

> capacity. It does not include pain or suffering arising only from, inherent in or incidental to lawful sanctions.[11]

It is important to emphasise that it is not the infliction of pain or suffering that constitutes torture. The key word in the foregoing definition is 'severe', a point reinforced by the European Court of Human Rights in *Ireland* v. *United Kingdom*,[12] where it emphasised that the use of the so-called 'five techniques' did not reach a sufficient level of gravity to constitute torture.[13]

An exhaustive account of the laws against torture is to be found in *A* v. *Home Office (No 2)* where Lord Bingham carefully traced the position under common law (which had 'set its face firmly against the use of torture') and statute.[14] According to Lord Bingham, the 'rejection of this practice was hailed as a distinguishing feature of the common law, the subject of proud claims by English jurists'.[15] This rejection was contrasted with 'the practice prevalent in the states of continental Europe who, seeking to discharge the strict standards of proof required by the Roman-canon models they had adopted, came routinely to rely on confessions procured by the infliction of torture'.[16] Despite this common law prohibition on relying on evidence produced by torture, it is clear from the historical record that torture was practised in England in the sixteenth and early-seventeenth centuries. But this, it is said, 'took place pursuant to warrants issued by the Council or the Crown, largely (but not exclusively) in relation to alleged offences against the state, in exercise of the Royal prerogative'.[17] It is important to emphasise, however, that neither the common law's total repugnance of torture, nor the abolition in 1640 of the Star

[11] United Nations Convention against Torture and Other Cruel, Inhuman or Degrading Treatment or Punishment (UNCAT), 1465 UNTS 85, Art. 1.

[12] (1978) 2 EHRR 25.

[13] The techniques in question were hooding, wall standing, noise, sleep deprivation, no food or water. *Plus ça change?*

[14] *A (No 2)*, note 10 above, para.11.

[15] Ibid, para.11. In rejecting the use of torture, Lord Bingham thought that 'the common law was moved by the cruelty of the practice as applied to those not convicted of crime, by the inherent unreliability of confessions or evidence so procured and by the belief that it degraded all those who lent themselves to the practice' (ibid). Compare Lord Brown, whose ethical starting point appeared to place great emphasis on the reputation of the legal system. In his view, one reason why torture evidence is excluded is because to do otherwise would 'bring British justice into disrepute' (para.165).

[16] Ibid, para.11.

[17] Ibid, para.12.

Chamber where torture evidence had been received, did enough to put an end to the practice, as we continue to be reminded.[18]

So mere condemnation is not enough. If the disapproval is to be meaningful, there is a duty on states to prevent torture from taking place, and to punish those who authorise or participate in such activity. This much is recognised by UNCAT which provides that '[e]ach State Party shall ensure that all acts of torture are offences under its criminal law',[19] and that '[e]ach State Party shall take effective legislative, administrative, judicial or other measures to prevent acts of torture in any territory under its jurisdiction'.[20] There are no exceptional circumstances 'whatsoever' ('whether a state of war or a threat or war, internal political instability or any other public emergency'),[21] and superior orders can never be invoked as a defence to an act of torture.[22] These provisions find a reluctant and inadequate home in British domestic law in the shape of the Criminal Justice Act 1988, section 134, which provides that 'a public official or person acting in an official capacity, whatever his nationality, commits the offence of torture if in the UK or elsewhere he intentionally inflicts severe pain or suffering on another in the performance or purported performance of his official duties'. UNCAT also provides that the criminal law should apply equally to attempts to commit torture, as well as to 'an act by any person which constitutes complicity or participation in torture'.[23]

The creation in the 1988 Act of a criminal offence in relation to torture is accompanied by provisions that ensure liability even though the perpetrator is acting at the instigation of another, and even where that other is acting in an official capacity.[24] But there is an important defence when someone claims to have been acting with lawful authority, justification or excuse,[25] reducing the chances of anyone being found guilty of torture and thereby facing a life sentence.[26] These provisions of the 1988 Act add to those of the Police and Criminal

[18] See *The Guardian*, 8 April 2011, referring to 'the most depraved torture, gruesome killings and mass hangings by Britain during Kenya's struggle for independence', in which 'about 160,000 black people were held in dire conditions in camps run by the British colonial authorities and tens of thousands were tortured to get them to renounce their oath to the Mau Mau rebellion against British rule in the 1950s'. According to the report, 'the Foreign Office doesn't deny there was torture and killings in the camps. How could it? Many of the abuses are documented in files discovered in its own archives. They includ[e] a telegram from the British governor of Kenya, Sir Evelyn Baring, documenting torture allegations against colonial district officers including "the burning alive of detainees".'

[19] Note 11 above, Art 4. [20] Art 2. [21] Art 2(2). [22] Art 2(3). [23] Art 4.

[24] Criminal Justice Act 1988, s.134(2). [25] Ibid, s.134(4). [26] Ibid, s.134(6).

Evidence Act 1984 (PACE), which contains a provision many might have hoped would not have been necessary in an Act passed by the Westminster Parliament. This requires confessions to be excluded in criminal proceedings where they were obtained by 'oppression', a word defined to mean 'torture, inhuman or degrading treatment, and the use or threat of violence (whether or not amounting to torture)'.[27] All this is now complemented by the HRA, which makes Article 3 of the ECHR enforceable in the British courts, thus prohibiting torture and inhuman or degrading treatment. An important gap has therefore been filled, in the sense that, as construed by the Strasbourg court, this should stop people being deported to regimes where they will be tortured.[28]

A cry for help

So much for the rhetoric and so much for the law. What about the courts? Here it might be thought that their first responsibility is to intervene to stop torture, by seeking to remove people from dangerous situations. The Court of Appeal was presented with an opportunity to do just this in the case of Feroz Abbasi, who was one of a number of British citizens detained at Guantánamo Bay on behalf of whom an approach was made to the British courts for diplomatic representations to be made to the US government, with a view to securing their release.[29] British judges were clearly very disturbed about what was going on at the US base on Cuba, with Lords Steyn and Hope speaking out in public condemnation of the treatment of detainees.[30] The Court of Appeal, which shared many of the concerns expressed extrajudicially by these law lords, was unable to approach the case other than on the basis that Mr Abbasi was arbitrarily detained in a 'legal black hole', in apparent contravention of fundamental principles recognised both by jurisdictions (the UK and the USA) and by

[27] Police and Criminal Evidence Act 1984 (PACE), s.76(8).

[28] *Chahal* v. *United Kingdom* (1997) 23 EHRR 413.

[29] *R (Abbasi)* v. *Foreign Secretary* [2002] EWCA Civ 1598. See also *R (Al Rawi)* v. *Foreign Secretary* [2006] EWCA Civ 1279. For a fascinating account of these cases, see C. R. G. Murray, 'In the shadow of Lord Haw Haw: Guantánamo Bay, diplomatic protection and allegiance' [2011] PL 115.

[30] As reported in *The Independent*, 29 January 2004, Lord Hope said: 'We must not allow the smiling charming faces of our American allies to divert us from seeking to discover what is being done by their interrogators. How can we expect to eliminate torture elsewhere if there is no way of knowing whether or not it has been practised at Guantanamo Bay?' For the even more outspoken remarks of Lord Steyn, see *BBC News*, 26 November 2003.

international law.[31] At the time of the legal proceedings it was unclear whether Mr Abbasi had been subjected to torture below the high threshold set by the European Court of Human Rights. Nonetheless, a report by the University of California contains allegations that, along with other detainees, Mr Abbasi had been exposed to loud music during interrogation and that he was kept in solitary confinement for more than a year.[32] Otherwise, it is very clear that Guantánamo was a place where:

> [c]aptives . . . were chained hand and foot in a fetal position to the floor for 18 hours or more, urinating and defecating on themselves, an FBI report has revealed. . . . Besides being shackled to the floor, detainees were subjected to extremes of temperature. One witness said he saw a barefoot detainee shaking with cold because the air conditioning had brought the temperature close to freezing. On another occasion, the air conditioning was off in an unventilated room, making the temperature over 38°C (100°F) and a detainee lay almost unconscious on the floor with a pile of hair next to him. He had apparently been pulling out his hair throughout the night.[33]

The question for the Court of Appeal was whether it could intervene in an area which was governed by the prerogative power of the Crown in the field of international relations. This would have been a no-go area in the past, with the courts refusing to scrutinise the exercise or non-exercise of the prerogative.[34] That position changed a little in the GCHQ case,[35] so that there is no automatic assumption that prerogative powers are not justiciable. In *Abbasi*, however, the Court rejected the argument that it has a duty to protect British citizens who are being abused by the governments of another state. The most it was prepared to accept was the existence of a right to intervene to protect such citizens, though it is a right which is highly discretionary, exercisable only in the event of

[31] *Abbasi*, note 29 above, para.64.

[32] See http://humanrights.ucdavis.edu/projects/the-guantanamo-testimonials-project/testimonies/prisoner-testimonies/report-on-torture-cruel-inhuman-and-degrading-treatment-of-prisoners-at-guantanamo-bay-cuba-abbasi. For allegations of torture made by Moazzam Begg, one of Mr Abbasi's fellow detainees, see *BBC News*, 1 October 2004.

[33] *The Guardian*, 3 January 2007. The accounts of mistreatment were contained in FBI documents released as part of a lawsuit involving the American Civil Liberties Union. See also Steyn, note 30 above. A former Guantánamo guard has since told the BBC that 'what he saw amounted to "torture" and that some of his fellow guards were so violent as to be "psychotic"' (*BBC News*, 9 January 2009).

[34] See A. W. Bradley and K. D. Ewing, *Constitutional and Administrative Law* (15th edn, 2011), ch.12.

[35] *Council of Civil Service Unions* v. *Minister for Civil Service* [1985] AC 374.

irrationality or the frustration of a legitimate expectation. Yet although 'the expectations are limited', it was nevertheless accepted that:

> [i]t is highly likely that any decision of the Foreign and Commonwealth Office, as to whether to make representations on a diplomatic level, will be intimately connected with decisions relating to this country's foreign policy, but an obligation to consider the position of a particular British citizen and consider the extent to which some action might be taken on his behalf, would seem unlikely itself to impinge on any forbidden area.[36]

But having established – albeit reluctantly and to a limited extent – that it had the power to intervene, the Court of Appeal was unwilling to use its power in this case, saying that:

> [e]vidence of action taken by the United Kingdom Government in relation to Mr Abbasi and the other British detainees in Guantánamo Bay has been provided in a witness statement by Mr Fry, a Deputy Under-Secretary of State for Foreign and Commonwealth Affairs. He speaks of close contact between the United Kingdom Government and the United States Government about the situation of the detainees and their treatment and of the consistent endeavour of the government to secure their welfare and ensure their proper treatment. To that end, we are told, the circumstances of the British detainees have been the subject of regular representations by the British Embassy in Washington to the United States Government. They have also been the subject of direct discussions between the Foreign Secretary and the United States Secretary of State as well as 'numerous communications at official level'.[37]

According to the Court of Appeal, Mr Abbasi could not 'reasonably expect more than this',[38] taking the view also that '[o]n no view would it be appropriate to order the Secretary of State to make any specific representations to the United States, even in the face of what appears to be a clear breach of a fundamental human right, as it is obvious that this would have an impact on the conduct of foreign policy, and an impact on such policy at a particularly delicate time'.[39]

This seems an extraordinarily timid response, which fails to meet the gravity of the situation or reflect the repulsion of torture expressed subsequently in *A (No 2)*. It also renders completely hollow the Court of Appeal's condemnation of the 'legal black hole' and the 'clear breach of international law, particularly in the context of human rights'.[40] This rhetoric is revealed as no more than hot air, it being enough that the government had considered Mr Abbasi's request for assistance, and that

[36] *Abbasi*, note 29 above, para.106. [37] Ibid, para.4. [38] Ibid, para.107. [39] Ibid.
[40] Ibid, para.57.

discussions had taken place at various levels between the UK and US governments. There was no need to go further, not even for the British to express the view that the treatment of Mr Abbasi might violate international law. Even this perfunctory performance is diminished by an apparent failure to go beyond the witness statement produced by the Foreign Office, indicating the Court's reluctance to examine the nature of the representations that were being made to the Americans. This is all the more unfortunate in light of the valuable insights produced (albeit long after the event) by Chris Mullen in his acclaimed diaries. The following are a few entries from Mullin's time as junior minister at the Foreign and Commonwealth Office:

> 7 July 2003
>
> The line is that we are making the strongest representations, but are we? Certainly Jack [Straw] is sending a tough letter to Colin Powell, but the trouble is we are up against Rumsfeld and the Pentagon and strong messages to the State Department won't make the blindest difference. If we are to get anywhere, The Man [i.e. Tony Blair] will have to tackle George Bush and there is no evidence so far that he has done so.
>
> 5 January 2004
>
> Liz Symons expressed concern about the lack of progress with the Americans re Guantánamo. She said, 'it will go badly wrong soon'.
>
> 11 May 2004
>
> 'We have to put some clear blue water between us and the Americans, even if it means embarrassing Himself', remarked Liz Symons at this morning's meeting. 'Guantánamo is the way to do it', said Mike O'Brien. 'I have written to Colin Powell', said Jack, adding that he had taken care to agree the text of his letter with Powell in advance.[41]

'Paying lip-service' to principle

On 9 December 2005, the Tory-leaning *Daily Telegraph* published an article by its legal correspondent under the heading 'Torture law victory for terror suspects'. The article was a report of the decision in the *A (No 2)* case considered above, in which the fine rhetoric of the House of Lords addressed whether the Special Immigration Appeals Commission could consider evidence obtained by torture in deciding whether

[41] C. Mullin, *A View from the Foothills* (London: Profile Books, 2009), pp.420, 438 and 468 respectively.

someone should be detained indefinitely on suspicion of being an international terrorist.[42] This might be said to be the second responsibility of the courts. If they are unprepared to take steps to secure the release of citizens who are exposed to a regime of personal terror over a long period (as measured in years rather than hours, days or months), they at least have an opportunity to discourage the use of torture by ensuring that any evidence obtained in this way cannot be relied upon. Although this would not necessarily stop the practice, it would go a long way to making it counter-productive to the gaoler, depending of course on the extent to which the use of evidence procured by torture was forbidden. It might be thought from the *Daily Telegraph's* headline that the courts had risen to the occasion. This is not the case.

It is true that the House of Lords held unanimously that confession 'evidence' obtained by torture is inadmissible. To that extent the *Daily Telegraph* was correct: Lord Brown said that 'SIAC [the Special Immigration Appeals Commission] could never properly uphold a section 23 detention order where the sole or decisive evidence supporting it is a statement established to have been coerced by the use of torture'.[43] But this was the easy part, with the House of Lords dividing 4:3 on the more difficult question of the burden of proof. It is one thing to say that evidence obtained by torture cannot be admitted, but this begs the question what has to be shown and by whom, in order to establish that torture has been used in the first place. As we have seen, legislation makes the use of evidence obtained by torture inadmissible in criminal proceedings, although the legislation applies only to confessions, and not also to evidence that might be yielded by the confession.[44] The courts are required to exclude confession evidence where representations are made that it may have been obtained by torture, 'except in so far as the prosecution proves to the court beyond reasonable doubt that the confession (notwithstanding that it may be true) was not [so] obtained'.[45] That is a high standard for the prosecution to meet.

It is unclear why this could not have been used as a template in *A (No 2)*. True, the detention under the 2001 Act did not involve the conviction and imprisonment of the individual in question. But in some respects the consequences of relying on evidence of this kind would be

42 Anti-terrorism, Crime and Security Act 2001, ss.21–3.
43 *A (No 2)*, note 10 above, at para.165.
44 But, incongruously, PACE, s.78 gives the courts a discretion to exclude such evidence in the interests of 'fairness', which does not necessarily include a breach of human rights.
45 Ibid, s.76(2).

even greater than in a criminal prosecution. Under the 2001 Act, the individual in question could be interned indefinitely without having committed an offence and without having been convicted of an offence, following a secret 'trial' in which the respondent had not been permitted to see the evidence against him or her and during which he or she had not been entitled to choose legal representation. Nevertheless, a majority of the House of Lords adopted a position much diluted from that found in PACE, and also much diluted from that accepted by the minority. The majority position is best represented by the following passage from the speech by Lord Brown, who said:

> [T]he burden of proof. I agree with Lord Hope of Craighead (at para 121 of his opinion) that SIAC should ask itself whether it is 'established, by means of such diligent inquiries into the sources that it is practicable to carry out and on a balance of probabilities, that the information relied on by the Secretary of State was obtained under torture'. Only if this is established is the statement inadmissible. If, having regard to the evidence of a particular state's general practices and its own inquiries, SIAC were to conclude that there is no more than a possibility that the statement was obtained by torture, then in my judgment this would not have been established and the statement would be admissible.[46]

The difference between the majority and the minority on this question of the burden is not simply a difference on a technical question about a procedural point of law. Rather, it is a difference on a technical point which has profound practical implications, as pointed out in the powerful dissents of Lords Bingham and Nicholls in particular (Lord Hoffmann also dissented). The minority would have set the bar at a much more realistic level, taking the view that if 'SIAC is unable to conclude that there is not a real risk that the evidence has been obtained by torture, it should refuse to admit the evidence'.[47] The reason for this was given by great cogency by Lord Bingham who in an Atkinesque criticism of the majority said that:

> [m]y noble and learned friend Lord Hope proposes, in paragraph 121 of his opinion, the following test: is it *established*, by means of such diligent enquiries into the sources that it is practicable to carry out and on a balance of probabilities, that the information relied on by the Secretary of State *was* obtained under torture? This is a test which, in the real world, can never be satisfied. The foreign torturer does not boast of his trade. The security services, as the Secretary of State has made clear, do not wish to imperil their relations with regimes where torture is practised. The

[46] *A (No 2)*, note 10 above, para.172.

[47] Ibid, para.56. (Lord Bingham).

> special advocates have no means or resources to investigate. The detainee is in the dark. It is inconsistent with the most rudimentary notions of fairness to blindfold a man and then impose a standard which only the sighted could hope to meet. The result will be that, despite the universal abhorrence expressed for torture and its fruits, evidence procured by torture will be laid before SIAC because its source will not have been 'established'.[48]

All of which is to say that, despite the *Daily Telegraph's* headline, confession evidence obtained by torture will still be admissible, following a decision that hardly justifies the extraordinary claim by Keir Starmer (now the Director of Public Prosecutions), that *A (No 2)* was a 'great victory for those engaged in the campaign to end torture', and still less his even more extravagant claim that *A (No 2)* is 'a landmark judgment, in fact, the leading judgment in the world [on torture]'.[49] In failing to read the small print, everyone seems to have overlooked Lord Bingham's conclusion in which he expressed 'regret that the House should lend its authority to a test which will undermine the practical efficacy of the Torture Convention and deny detainees the standard of fairness to which they are entitled under Article 5(4) or 6(1) of the European Convention'.[50] They appear also to have overlooked the trenchant criticisms of Lord Nicholls (with whom Lord Bingham expressly agreed) that the approach of the majority would 'place on the detainee a burden of proof which, for reasons beyond his control, he can seldom discharge'. Not only would this 'largely nullify the principle, vigorously supported on all sides, that courts will not admit evidence procured by torture', but it 'would be to pay lip-service to the principle', which in the words of Lord Nicholls 'is not good enough'.[51]

A cry of pain

Rangzieb Ahmed is one of a number of men whose torture is described by Ian Cobain in his brilliant *Guardian* exposé of the practice.[52] According to Cobain, Greater Manchester police and MI5 'drew up questions and handed them to the Pakistani security services. By the time Ahmed was deported back to Britain, he had three fingernails missing from his left hand'.[53] He was subsequently charged with a number of terrorism-related offences, the gist of the case against him

[48] Ibid, para.59. [49] *Daily Telegraph*, 9 December 2005.
[50] *A (No 2)*, note 10 above, para.62. [51] Ibid, para.80.
[52] *The Guardian*, 8 July 2009. [53] Ibid.

being that he was heavily involved in general terrorist planning and the coordination of agents and sympathisers in the UK.[54] His application to have the proceedings against him discontinued on the ground of abuse of process was based on a number of considerations, Mr Ahmed asserting that:

> after arrest on 20 August 2006 he been (i) held incommunicado, without charge, without access to lawyers or contact with any person outside the prison until December when he was taken to court and allowed to speak although unrepresented, (ii) kept, at least initially, handcuffed and shackled in a cell without daylight or furniture, (iii) deprived of sleep and fed poorly, (iv) beaten with sticks, a piece of tyre on a handle and electric wire and further that (v) on each of days 7, 9 and 11 his captors had removed one fingernail from his left hand by use of pliers. On one occasion only during his year of captivity, he said that he had been seen and questioned by British officers; that, he said, was on day 12.[55]

The application to have the proceedings discontinued was dismissed principally because the evidence against Mr Ahmed was unrelated to his detention in Pakistan, though doubt was also expressed about whether his treatment amounted to torture. Nevertheless, in an important judgment the Court of Appeal did consider a number of questions relating to torture and the use of evidence obtained by torture. One of these related to a second caveat entered in *A (No 2)* (which was considered at some length by the court in *Ahmed*). In *A (No 2)* the House of Lords held, not only that confessions obtained by torture may be admitted (unless the individual could prove that torture had indeed taken place), but also that it is not unlawful for ministers and others to rely on material obtained by torture, despite the fact that the material is not admissible in legal proceedings. Even Lord Bingham acknowledged that 'the Secretary of State does not act unlawfully if he certifies, arrests, searches and detains on the strength of . . . foreign torture evidence'.[56] For his part, Lord Nichols accepted that, in using torture evidence in this way, the government is 'open to the charge that it is condoning torture'. So what? 'So, in a sense, it is. The government is obtaining information obtained by torture.' This is justified on the ground that 'the government cannot be expected to close its eyes to this information at the price of endangering the lives of its own citizens'.[57]

[54] *Ahmed* v. *R* [2011] EWCA Crim 184, para.1 (Hughes LJ). [55] Ibid, para.14.
[56] *A (No 2)*, note 10 above, at para.47. [57] Ibid, para.69.

Perhaps predictably, Lord Brown appeared to go further still, articulating explicitly a duty which also finds expression in the *Ahmed* case where Hughes LJ adopted the following passage from his speech:

> Generally speaking it is accepted that the executive may make use of all information it acquires: both coerced statements and whatever fruits they are found to bear. Not merely, indeed, is the executive entitled to make use of this information; to my mind it is bound to do so. It has a prime responsibility to safeguard the security of the state and would be failing in its duty if it ignores whatever it may learn or fails to follow it up. Of course it must do nothing to promote torture. It must not enlist torturers to its aid (rendition being perhaps the most extreme example of this). But nor need it sever relations even with those states whose interrogation practices are of most concern. So far as the courts are concerned, however, the position is different. Generally speaking the court will shut its face against the admission in evidence of any coerced statement (that of a third party is, of course, in any event inadmissible as hearsay); it will, however, admit in evidence the fruit of the poisoned tree.[58]

This passage was seized upon with alacrity by Hughes LJ, concerned that 'public authorities are likely to be faced with conflicting duties' and that 'the duty to preserve the safety of those within a State's borders means that some measure of co-operation, and information-sharing with regimes whose standards may sometimes fall below what is internationally acceptable, is a practical necessity if the duty is to be done'.[59]

But are there no limits on the power of the state to use evidence obtained by torture? An attempt was made in *Ahmed* to distinguish the House of Lords decision in *A (No 2)* on the ground that it does not apply to information supplied by a regime where there is a 'suggestion of complicity by the UK authorities in any torture which might be in question'.[60] The Court of Appeal found nothing in *A (No 2)* to support such a conclusion and in any event was unable to agree on whether information sharing constitutes complicity. Support for this view that it does was to be found in the work of the UN Special Rapporteur on Human Rights and the Countering of Terrorism who reported that:

> [s]tates must not aid or assist in the commission of acts of torture or recognize such practices as lawful, including by relying on intelligence information obtained through torture. States must introduce safeguards preventing intelligence agencies from making use of such intelligence.[61]

[58] Ibid, para.161. [59] *Ahmed*, note 54 above, para.36. [60] Ibid, para.37.
[61] As quoted ibid., at para.45.

That position was reinforced by a passage from Lord Neuberger's judgment in the Court of Appeal in *A (No 2)* where he said that 'even by adopting the fruits of torture, a democratic State is weakening its case against terrorists, by adopting their methods, thereby losing the moral high ground an open democratic society enjoys'.[62] But all this was much too wide for the Court of Appeal in *Ahmed*, which thought that it goes well beyond the ordinary principles of the common law for 'secondary liability' where someone aids or assists another in the commission of a crime, and also beyond 'the standards of international law', as represented by the 'general principles of law recognized by civilized nations'.[63]

This is a rather bleak outcome. The only concession made by the Court of Appeal over what might count as complicity (or in its words 'secondary participation in torture') was that 'extraordinary rendition for the purposes of outsourcing torture would of course amount to secondary participation in torture on ordinary common law principles'.[64] But if everything below such rendition is to be permitted this amounts to a very high ceiling. It should be noted, however, that much of the discussion was incidental, simply because of the Court's affirmation of the first instance finding that no torture had occurred in this case. According to the Court of Appeal:

> The judge expressly rejected the suggestion of outsourcing torture by British authorities; there was, he found, simply no evidence that they had assisted or encouraged the Pakistani detainers to detain him unlawfully or to ill-treat him in any way, whether amounting to torture or not. Further, he found that no part of any product of questioning in Pakistan (by anyone) was relied on in the trial before the judge, nor had the prosecution case against Rangzieb or Habib been informed by any material emanating from such questioning. At the request of the appellants we have reviewed his findings of fact. We are quite satisfied that there are no grounds for impugning them. We have also looked, at the request of the appellants, at some additional material on the basis of which it is contended that questions asked of Rangzieb when in Pakistan informed actions in relation to other suspects. Whether that is so or not, it does not affect the judge's conclusions that there was simply no connection between Rangzieb's questioning in Pakistan and this trial.[65]

But for all the controversy about what happened to Mr Ahmed, the importance of the case lies in (i) what it says to the security and intelligence services in the future, and (ii) the immunity from complicity

[62] [2004] EWCA Civ 1123. [63] *Ahmed*, note 54 above, para.48.
[64] Ibid, para.45. [65] Ibid, para.20.

which it extends to the international trade in intelligence created by torture. The unequivocal line of the court is that the equivocal line of the government has its full blessing.

A licence to torture

Deaf to cries for help. Deaf to cries of pain. Deaf now to cries of complicity? Complicity is a key provision of UNCAT, the complicity provisions having attracted a great deal of publicity in recent years since Western powers are alleged to have outsourced by various devices the task of torturing prisoners to what are politely referred to as 'regimes whose standards may sometimes fall below what is internationally acceptable'.[66] The relevant provisions of UNCAT are to be found in Article 4, which states that:

> [e]ach State Party shall ensure that all acts of torture are offences under its criminal law. The same shall apply to an attempt to commit torture and to an act by any person which constitutes complicity or participation in torture.

As pointed out by the UK Parliament's Joint Committee on Human Rights (JCHR) 'the UK is therefore under a positive obligation under UNCAT, both to make it a criminal offence in UK law for any person to commit an act which constitutes complicity or participation in torture, and to investigate credible allegations of complicity or participation in torture, including by detaining any person present in the UK who is alleged to have committed any such act'.[67] There is, however, no reference to complicity in the Criminal Justice Act 1988, and no definition in UNCAT.

One of the most extended discussions of the meaning of complicity in torture is to be found in the JCHR report on *Allegations of UK Complicity in Torture*,[68] published on 4 August 2009. There the Committee was faced with allegations of British complicity in torture, some of which had been reported in a chilling account by Ian Cobain.[69] The alleged complicity is said to have taken a number of different forms, including (but not necessarily confined to):

- 'requests by UK agents to foreign intelligence services, known for their systematic use of torture, to detain and question a terrorism suspect;

[66] Ibid, para.36. [67] HL 152/HC 230 (2008–9), para.22.
[68] Ibid. [69] *The Guardian*, 8 July 2009. Also HL 152/HC 230, above, paras.6–16.

- 'the provision of information by UK agents to such foreign intelligence services enabling them to apprehend a terrorism suspect or facilitate the suspect's extraordinary rendition;
- 'the provision of questions by UK agents to such foreign intelligence services to be put to a detainee who has been, is being or is likely to be tortured;
- 'the sending of UK interrogators to question detainee(s) who are, or should have been, known to have been tortured by those detaining and interrogating them;
- 'the presence of UK intelligence personnel at interviews with detainees being held in a place where it is known, or should be known, that they are being tortured;
- 'the lack of any apparent action taken by the UK personnel to establish whether torture was occurring and to prevent it from continuing; and/or
- 'the systematic receipt by UK agents of information known or thought likely to have been obtained from detainees subjected to torture, without apparent comment on, concern about or action to establish its provenance.'[70]

In responding to the uncertainty caused by the lack of a definition of complicity, the Committee concluded that its meaning depends on the context, and on whether the accused is a person or a state. Thus:

> In our view, it is necessary to distinguish between complicity for the purposes of individual criminal responsibility and complicity for the purposes of State responsibility. We consider that a narrower meaning is likely to be adopted in the context of individual criminal responsibility, but principles of State responsibility more readily recognise positive obligations on States (as opposed to individuals) to take action to prevent torture from occurring or continuing. Complicity may therefore be given a wider meaning for the purposes of deciding whether the State is responsible for particular acts which have the effect of allowing torture to occur or continue.
>
> We therefore conclude that complicity has different meanings depending on whether the context is individual criminal responsibility or State responsibility:
>
> for the purposes of individual criminal responsibility for complicity in torture, 'complicity' requires proof of three elements: (1) knowledge that torture is taking place, (2) a direct contribution by way of assistance that (3) has a substantial effect on the perpetration of the crime;

[70] HL 152/HC 230, para.17.

> for the purposes of State responsibility for complicity in torture, however, 'complicity' means simply one State giving assistance to another State in the commission of torture, or acquiescing in such torture, in the knowledge, including constructive knowledge, of the circumstances of the torture which is or has been taking place.[71]

Applying these principles to the liability of states, two questions arise. The first is to determine in what circumstances complicity may be said to occur for the purpose of state responsibility. Here the Committee suggested the list of circumstances quoted above, dwelling on the particular difficulty of circumstances involving the systematic receipt of information known or thought likely to have been obtained from detainees subjected to torture. It accepted that the mere receipt and use of information would not necessarily constitute complicity, on the ground that 'passive receipt of information is . . . not obviously a form of "assistance" or facilitation, because it seems likely that the torture will continue to take place anyway whether the information is received or not by the other State'.[72] That said, however, the JCHR appeared to take a much more robust approach than the Court of Appeal in *Ahmed*, being clear that the passive receipt of information could constitute complicity in certain circumstances:

> This would not apply, however, to circumstances where the receipt of such information (that it is reasonable to suspect is produced as a result of torture) is so regular that it becomes an expectation, or where it is part of a reciprocal arrangement (regardless of whether the arrangement is formal or explicit), or where the information is received over a long period with no apparent concern being raised about its provenance.[73]

The second question arising from the foregoing definition of complicity is one of enforcement. In cases of individual complicity, the position is relatively straightforward in principle in the sense that this could lead to a prosecution, however unlikely that might be in practice. But how do we deal with the question of complicity as a state responsibility? As the JCHR pointed out, there is the possibility of liability under international law:

> [C]omplicity in torture would be a direct breach of the UK's international human rights obligations, under UNCAT, under customary international law, and according to the general principles of State Responsibility for internationally wrongful acts.[74]

[71] Ibid., paras.34–5. [72] Ibid, para.38. [73] Ibid. [74] Ibid, para.27.

But that is not likely to cause any sleepless nights in government departments or in the dark corners of the security and intelligence community. The only way by which states can be held true to their commitments is by the domestic courts taking a robust view about the fruits of torture, and refusing in the process to allow prosecutors or others to allow any evidence to be admitted where there is a suspicion that it carries a taint of torture. Otherwise, complicity becomes a dead letter, and our attempts to prohibit torture merely become a licence to use it. All of which leads back to *A (No 2)* and *Ahmed*, and to uncomfortable conclusions about the complicity in torture of those who (i) fail to protect those in vulnerable locations, or (ii) diminish laws that are designed to protect the victims of what everyone appears unequivocally to accept is 'wrong'.[75] It is a matter of great regret that the exceptional report on complicity by the JCHR was not given more weight by the Court of Appeal, and a matter of further regret that the JCHR should be sniffily dismissed by that court as a body which does not purport to be 'empowered to make authoritative declarations of the law'.[76]

Rendition and torture

These uncomfortable conclusions are very heavily underlined when we turn to the question of rendition. Here we are concerned not with 'extraordinary rendition' (one of only a few judicial red lines), but with the lawful removal of an individual from one state (the UK in this case), and his or her return to another. It is true – of course – that a suspected international terrorist cannot lawfully be rendered to a country where he or she is likely to be tortured or to suffer inhuman or degrading treatment or punishment. The European Court of Human Rights has put paid to that, and it is because of that court's decisions that the British government instituted the indefinite detention without trial of people whose presence was unwelcome but whose removal would be unlawful.[77] The government has managed to get round this problem by negotiating memoranda of understanding (MOU) with the dodgy regimes in question, in which diplomatic assurances of various degrees of credibility are given that the returning individual will not be mistreated.[78] But even if these assurances are genuinely effective in the sense that the rendered individual is not then tortured, that is only half of the problem resolved.

[75] Ibid, para.40. [76] *Ahmed*, note 54 above, para.47.
[77] See especially *Chahal*, note 28 above. [78] For full details, see Chapter 4 below.

There is also the possibility that the rendered individual will be put on trial in the course of which evidence obtained by torturing someone else may be used against him or her. When will the removal of the individual be stopped in such circumstances? This was one of the question raised in the case of Abu Qatada (referred to in the case as Mr Othman), in which SIAC not only rejected his complaint that he would be ill-treated if rendered to Jordan (on the strength of an MOU), but also his complaint that he would be deprived of his right to a fair trial under Article 6 of the ECHR.[79] In the latter instance this was because it was likely that he would be retried for a number of terrorist offences for which he had been tried and found guilty in his absence. Although these concerns were dismissed by SIAC, they were upheld by the Court of Appeal,[80] which ruled that the former had 'erred by applying an insufficiently demanding test to determine the issue of whether Article 6 rights would be breached'.[81] According to the Court of Appeal – in what is at times a damning judgment – SIAC 'treated the possible use of evidence obtained by torture *pari passu* with complaints about the independence of the court'; the Commission failed 'to recognise the high degree of assurance that is required in relation to proceedings in a foreign state before a person may lawfully be deported to face trial that may involve evidence obtained by torture';[82] and it was led to 'undervalue the importance of the risk that the impugned evidence would in fact be used at the retrials'.[83]

But although Abu Qatada succeeded in the Court of Appeal, the House of Lords reinstated SIAC's decision. In another quite remarkable judgment in which Lord Hope was 'astonished at the amount of care, time and trouble that has been devoted to the question whether it will be safe for the aliens to be returned to their own countries',[84] Lord Phillips rejected the view that 'a high degree of assurance [would be required] that evidence obtained by torture would not be used in the proceedings in Jordan before it would be lawful to deport Mr Othman to face those proceedings'.[85] The need to 'stand firm' against torture 'does not require this state, the United Kingdom, to retain in this country to the detriment of national security a terrorist suspect unless it has a high degree of assurance that evidence obtained by torture will not be adduced against him in Jordan'.[86] What was relevant was 'the degree of

[79] *RB and OO* v. *Home Secretary* [2009] UKHL 10.

[80] *Othman* v. *Secretary of State for the Home Department* [2008] EWCA Civ 290.

[81] Ibid, para.[46]. [82] Ibid, para.[49]. [83] Ibid, para.[53].

[84] *RB and OO*, note 79 above, para.[209]. [85] Ibid, para.[153]. [86] Ibid.

risk that Mr Othman will suffer a flagrant denial of justice if he is deported',[87] Lord Phillips having observed in an earlier passage that

> [i]f an alien is to avoid deportation because he faces unfair legal process in the receiving state he must show that there are substantial grounds for believing that there is a real risk not merely that he will suffer a flagrant breach of his Article 6 rights, but that the consequence will be a serious violation of a substantive right or rights.[88]

It has been said that this decision reflects the 'old cancer in Britain that we prefer to forget', namely the 'casual racism that allows our society to treat these men's human rights as different from our own'. Whether or not we agree with this assessment, what seems less contentious is the associated claim that the decision underlines an attitude that 'the issue of torture in the countries where these people are being deported is not the business of the court'.[89] As such it raises fresh questions about the complicity of the state in torture, though the rendering of an individual to a state where torture is practised was not an issue considered by the JCHR in the landmark report referred to above, and was thus not an example of conduct that fell within its definition of state complicity. Nevertheless, such conduct would fall squarely within the general definition of state complicity expressed by the Committee, that is to say:

> [O]ne State giving assistance to another State in the commission of torture, or acquiescing in such torture, in the knowledge, including constructive knowledge, of the circumstances of the torture which is or has been taking place.

There can be no question that the courts knew of concerns about torture in Jordan. True, they are not giving assistance to Jordan to commit such torture. But by sending someone back to be tried on evidence that may have been obtained by torture, the judges have left themselves exposed to the charge that they are acquiescing in torture, and exposed to the charge that their decision falls within the definition of complicity offered by the JCHR. If we are serious about torture, it should make no difference that the evidence against a man is a confession obtained by torturing him, or one obtained by torturing his wife, and if we are serious about torture we should not be rendering people to countries where evidence obtained by torture from any source is likely to be used. In the words of Lord

[87] Ibid. [88] Ibid, para.[138]. [89] *The Guardian*, 18 February 2010.

Nicholls in *A (No 2)*, merely 'pay[ing] lip-service to the principle' that torture evidence is not to be used 'is not good enough'.[90]

Conclusion

All in all, a sorry tale of judicial neglect and legal failure, if not worse. Here we have the courts (i) refusing to assist those in conditions where torture (or something as close to torture as is possible) appears to have been practised, (ii) allowing evidence to be admitted where it has been obtained as a result of torture, (iii) permitting agents of the state to use torture evidence supplied by a country where torture takes place, and (iv) authorising the rendition of individuals to a country where evidence obtained by torture may be used against them. So what is left? No rendering of an individual to a country where he or she may be the direct rather than the vicarious victim of torture? And no extraordinary rendition for the purposes of outsourcing torture?[91] Is that really where the English courts are prepared to draw the line? If so, one may be forgiven for asking an even more uncomfortable question, about precisely the very point of human rights law. What is the point of human rights law if it is unable to deal with something as fundamental as torture? And what is the point of human rights law when senior judges in a country such as the UK are willing in practice to allow evidence obtained by torture to be used by the public authorities, and in some cases to be admitted in legal proceedings?[92] At the very least, such an apparently abysmal response from the courts raises hard questions for the human rights brigade, with the HRA 1998 having been singularly absent from much of this evolving jurisprudence, and generally unresponsive when it was called upon.

Notwithstanding the formal 'rebalancing' of the constitution in favour of liberty, the judges at the highest level continue to reveal themselves as much too preoccupied with the interests of the executive. This is perhaps

[90] *A (No 2)*, note 10 above, para.80.

[91] *Ahmed*, note 54 above: '[e]xtraordinary rendition for the purposes of outsourcing torture would of course amount to secondary participation in torture on ordinary common law principles' (para.45).

[92] Just to help the debate along, it is not an answer (*pace* Lord Brown) to say that torture material should be used because it is available. It is available because those who indulge themselves in the practice know that it will be used and that they will not be punished. Nor is it an answer (*pace* Hughes LJ) to say that the rules on evidence do not exist to discipline the executive, the police or the intelligence services. Perhaps on the issue of torture it is time that they did.

most clearly indicated in the speech of Lord Brown in *A (No 2)*, where he was able to offer the following reassurances to the security and intelligence services:

> To what extent, it is perhaps worth asking, does such a ruling impede the executive in its vitally important task of safeguarding the country so far as possible against terrorism? To my mind to a very limited extent indeed. In the first place it is noteworthy that the ruling will merely substitute an exclusionary rule of evidence for the Secretary of State's own publicly stated policy not in any event to rely on evidence which he knows or believes to have been obtained by torture abroad. Secondly, the intelligence case against the suspect would, we are told, ordinarily consist of material from a large number of sources – a 'mosaic' or 'jigsaw' of information as it has been called; it is most unlikely that the sole or decisive evidence will be a coerced statement.[93]
>
> . . .
>
> It follows from all this that your Lordships' decision on these appeals should not be seen as a significant setback to the Secretary of State's necessary efforts to combat terrorism. Rather it confirms the right of the executive to act on whatever information it may receive from around the world, while at the same time preserving the integrity of the judicial process and vindicating the good name of British justice.[94]

This is not the only time that Lord Brown has provided the decisive swing vote in a terrorism case.[95] His role is particularly significant for the fact that while he was sitting in judgment over government actions he was also acting as the Intelligence Services Commissioner, a role which he occupied with distinction from 2000 to 2006. This is a role that involves working closely with the intelligence services and the making of secret reports to the Prime Minister. That a person performing such a role should (a) occupy high judicial office, and (b) sit in a case involving the powers of the services he supervises, hardly needs comment.[96]

Is this not the final futility of the Human Rights Act?[97] No doubt the human rights brigade will blether that the bold decision of the Court of Appeal in *Al Rawi* allowed a number of victims of torture to recover compensation for the injuries suffered,[98] following the government's

[93] *A (No 2)*, note 10 above, at para.166. [94] Ibid, para.171.
[95] See Secretary of State for the Home Department v. JJ [2007] UKHL 45.
[96] See further, K. D. Ewing, *Bonfire of the Liberties* (Oxford University Press, 2010), chapters 3 and 7.
[97] See further, K. D. Ewing, 'The Futility of the Human Rights Act' [2004] PL 829; and K. D. Ewing and J-C. Tham, 'The Continuing Futility of the Human Rights Act' [2008] PL 668.
[98] *Al Rawi*, note 8 above, confirmed by the Supreme Court: [2011] UKSC 34.

speedy offer to settle rather than face the humiliation of proceedings in the full glow of publicity.[99] But to that there are three responses. The first is that the nature of the conduct which the government was so desperate to hide by making generous settlements on the individuals in question must have been quite something, given the reluctance of the courts in this country to take the question of torture as seriously as their condemnation of it would seem to require. In other words, we can only speculate that British officials were involved in conduct of the most questionable kind. The second is that it would have been much better if the courts had been prepared to be as vigorous in their defence of the victim as in that of their own self-importance and the procedures they administer. In other words, better if they were to intervene to protect the individual from torture in the first place, than to facilitate his or her compensation after the event, as an intended or unintended consequence of a decision on a collateral matter, albeit one of great importance (that is to say, open justice).[100] But finally, the third is that even in this moment of 'triumph', the HRA remained all but invisible, denied even a bit part either in the *Mohamed* case with which this chapter started,[101] or the *Al Rawi* case in which Binyam Mohamed was a party. In other words, these cases were decided under common law principles without the need for the HRA, at a time when senior judges jealously expressed concern about the vitality of the common law as it operates in the shadow of the ECHR.[102]

In light of the foregoing, it is about time human rights lawyers – the supercilious, the self-important and the gullible – were heard to explain what is going on, and why they deceived so many into thinking that the HRA would make a difference to human rights practice (as opposed to human rights law practice, with which some human rights lawyers appear arrogantly to conflate human rights practice). At a time when human rights appear to have gone AWOL, perhaps they will explain also why the British courts do so little to prevent the use of the torturer's scalpel.

[99] On which, see *BBC News*, 16 November 2010 for a good account.

[100] *Al Rawi*, note 8 above. [101] *Mohamed* v. *Foreign Secretary*, note 2 above.

[102] See *The Guardian*, 7 April 2010, where the Lord Chief Justice is reported as having said in a public lecture that 'it would be a sad day if the home of the common law lost its standing as a common law authority', and that 'perhaps we should reflect on the way in which I detect that our Australian colleagues (and those from other common law countries) seem to be claiming bragging rights as the custodians of the common law'. There is much of this in *Al Rawi*, note 8 above, decided on 4 May 2010, in which the HRA is mentioned once.

4

If you cannot change the rules of the game, adapt to them: United Kingdom responses to the restrictions set by Article 3 ECHR on 'national security' deportations

DAVID BONNER

Introduction

This chapter chronicles the United Kingdom's (UK) attempts to deal with an interpretation of Article 3 ECHR by the European Court of Human Rights (the Court), a controversial part of the Court's settled jurisprudence, recently unanimously reaffirmed by its Grand Chamber to the chagrin of the UK Government which has argued against the interpretation's legitimacy since its inception and has since sought to reverse or modify it. The principle predates *Chahal* v. *UK* (the UK's *bête noire*),[1] but finds its apotheosis in its extension there to the highly sensitive context of national security deportation:

> State A (the 'host' State, a party to the ECHR) will breach Article 3 if it expels or extradites someone from its jurisdiction to State B (the 'destination' State) where there are substantial grounds for believing that there is a real risk that the person will be subjected in State B to torture, inhuman or degrading treatment or punishment.

There are no exceptions. Article 3 is absolute and is non-derogable in times of war or other public emergency threatening the life of the nation.[2] Neither the conduct of the putative deportee(s) nor the danger they present to the security of the state is relevant. Assurances of no maltreatment from the 'destination' state are relevant but not in themselves determinative.

That interpretation is one which the government regards as unjustifiably limiting its right to deport non-nationals (aliens) where this would be

[1] (1997) 23 EHRR 413. [2] Art. 15(2) ECHR.

conducive to the public good on grounds of national security, relations with another state or international organisation or for other reasons of a political nature ('national security' deportation).[3]

The chronicle responds to Professor Kennedy's chapter firstly by illustrating the pragmatic policy and national security arguments which the UK has raised as a result of international human rights decisions;[4] and secondly, by illustrating the way in which it deployed the political imperative and the positive obligation set by Article 2 ECHR to take action to protect life, as if that were one that trumps every other obligation, when clearly the positive action taken must be regarded by the polity as necessary and proportionate and conform to the human rights obligations in the Convention and other instruments.[5] To achieve this, the chapter first considers the legal and factual background to, and the decision in, *Chahal*. It then examines the initial governmental and legislative response to the ruling. It next considers the first post-9/11 response to curtailed ability to deport: Anti-Terrorism, Crime and Security Act (ATCSA) detention without trial of foreign-national terrorist suspects, the contrasting response the Opposition proposed and the subsequent response in terms of control orders under the Prevention of Terrorism Act 2005 (PTA).

After 7/7,[6] Prime Minister Blair proclaimed that the 'rules of the game' were changing;[7] that the UK would act in response to what it perceived as the deleterious effects of *Chahal*: first to try to effect change through litigation; second to effect legislative change at national and/or international level; and third to comply with *Chahal* by deporting only where suitable assurances had been obtained from the 'destination' state. The next element of the chronicle considers two attempts to effect change by seeking to persuade the Court to modify *Chahal* by intervening in 'security' deportation cases against other states (the litigation

[3] See Immigration Act 1971, s.3(5). Basing the 'conducive to the public good' decision on national security etc takes the case out of the ordinary immigration appellate processes and instead appeal lies to the Special Immigration Appeals Commission (SIAC), rather than, as prior to 1998, to non-binding review by three advisers: see D. Bonner, *Executive Measures, Terrorism and National Security: Have the rules of the game changed?* (Aldershot: Ashgate, 2007), pp.127–34.

[4] See Chapter 2 above. [5] Ibid.

[6] The shorthand term for the bomb attacks by four 'home-grown' Islamist terrorists on London's transport network on 7 July 2005: see further Intelligence and Security Committee, *Report into the London Terrorist Attacks on 7 July 2005* (2006) Cm 6785.

[7] *The Guardian*, 5 August 2005, available at www.guardian.co.uk/uk/2005/aug/05/july7.uksecurity5 (accessed 13 January 2010).

option). The chapter then surveys the legislative option: amending the Human Rights Act 1998 (HRA) or the ECHR itself. Next, it examines arguably the most fruitful response: comply with the rule by putting in place a memorandum of understanding (MOU) with the would-be 'destination' state, contending that the nature and effectiveness of the agreement is such as to reduce or obviate the risk that the deportee would be ill-treated contrary to Article 3 ECHR if returned there. The relationship of such assurances to the *Chahal* principle is again before the Court in an application against the UK by Abu Qatada (Othman). The chapter then notes that there is no evidence of UK governmental consideration of a non-compliance option, which, sadly, appears to be part of Italy's approach to interim measures ordering suspension of removal pending final resolution of the proceedings by the Court. Access to executive records in the next fifteen years may cast light on whether such an approach was ever seriously considered by the Labour Government. Finally, the chapter offers a number of general conclusions from the chronicle.

The *Chahal* principle

Article 3 ECHR states simply:

> No one shall be subjected to torture or to inhuman or degrading treatment or punishment.

In *Chahal*, the Court reminded everyone that, under well-established international law, the sovereign right of states to control the entry, residence and expulsion of aliens was, however, subject to ECHR and other treaty obligations and that there was no explicit right of political asylum in the ECHR.[8] *Chahal* was not the first case in which was considered the matter of whether state A (the 'host' state) could have responsibility under Article 3 ECHR for returning an individual within its jurisdiction (and thus entitled to ECHR protection through Article 1 ECHR) to state B (the 'destination' state) where there was a risk that in state B the individual would suffer torture, inhuman or degrading treatment or punishment.[9] It was, however, the first case on national security deportation. The principle to which *Chahal* gives dramatic effect and which has become such a fundamental element in the Court's settled

[8] *Chahal*, note 1 above, para.73. [9] Ibid., para.74.

jurisprudence originates from the jurisprudence of the European Commission on Human Rights and the Court in the extradition context and that of removal of failed asylum seekers.[10]

In *Soering* v. *UK*,[11] despite the UK's argument that this constituted an intolerably strained interpretation, in order to make practical and effective the safeguard afforded by Article 3 (one of the fundamental values of European democratic societies), the Court implied an absolute non-*refoulement* principle into Article 3. It did so despite the fact that such a principle was only explicitly to be found in a specialised treaty, the UN Convention Against Torture (UNCAT), and there only in respect of torture. The Court subsequently held the principle applicable beyond extradition to decisions to remove, or removal of, failed asylum seekers, but in neither case did it find a breach on the facts.[12]

Chahal saw the extension and application by the majority of the Court of the *Soering* principle to national security deportation. In 1990 the Home Secretary decided that it would be conducive to the public good, for reasons of national security and other reasons of a political nature (the international fight against terrorism), to attempt to deport Chahal to his national state, India, because he was believed to be involved in financing, equipping with arms, planning and directing terrorism connected with the creation of a separate Sikh state, and to detain him pending deportation. Chahal denied all the allegations against him. He founded his case for political asylum and the protection of the *Soering* principle on his having been tortured on a visit to India in 1984 and fear of a repeat if he were to be deported there. His parents, relatives and contacts of his had been tortured by the Indian authorities in 1989. He supported his claim by reference to consistent evidence of the murder and torture of Sikh militants by Indian authorities, particularly the Punjabi police. His application for judicial review of the second refusal of asylum and the decision to proceed with deportation was rejected by the High Court and on appeal by the Court of Appeal. Leave to take the case to the House of Lords was refused. The Court of Appeal endorsed a 'balancing exercise'. It held that in combination the Refugee Convention 1951 and the Immigration Rules giving effect to its provisions required the Home Secretary to weigh the threat deportation posed to Chahal's life or freedom against the danger to national security if he were allowed

10 *Kirkwood* v. *UK* (1984) 6 EHRR CD373, 379.

11 *Soering* v. *UK* (1989) 11 EHRR 439.

12 *Cruz Varaz* v. *Sweden* (1991) 14 EHRR 1; *Vilvarajah* v. *UK* (1992) 14 EHRR 238.

to stay. The Court could only interfere with the balance struck by the Home Secretary if Chahal could show the decision to be irrational, something nigh impossible given that neither he nor the Court knew the evidential basis for the decision.[13]

Part of the government's case before the Court was that there was no evidential basis for holding that Chahal faced any risk of maltreatment if returned to India. In support of this it relied on assurances from the Indian government and a much improved security situation in the Punjab. It was prepared to return him to any part of India. Before the Commission, the government also contested the legitimacy of the *Soering* principle, reiterating the arguments it had unsuccessfully deployed in that case. It contended, in the alternative, that a national security case was different to those in which the principle had been developed. Just as the principle had been implied from Article 3 so there was an implied limitation to it comparable to exceptions in the Refugee Convention 1951, entitling a 'host' state to expel a national security threat even where a real risk of ill-treatment existed. In such cases, either Article 3 guarantees were not absolute or the degree of threat to the national security of the host state was a factor to weigh in the balance when applying the *Soering* test: the greater the risk of ill-treatment, the less weight should be accorded to the threat to national security, and vice versa. It was at the very least open to serious doubt whether the alleged risk of ill-treatment to Chahal would materialise. Consequently, the serious threat he posed to the security of the UK justified his deportation.

The Commission gave these arguments short shrift. The Court's jurisprudence was clear; the guarantees afforded by Article 3 were absolute in character, admitting of no exception. The national interests of the state could not be invoked to override the interests of the individual where substantial grounds had been shown for believing that he would be subjected to ill-treatment if expelled. Before the Court, the furthest the Commission delegate would go was to suggest that, in a case where there were serious doubts as to the likelihood of a person being subjected to treatment or punishment contrary to Article 3, this might enable the benefit of that doubt to be given to the deporting state the national interests of which were threatened.[14]

The Court split both on the terms of the rule to be applied and on the application to Chahal of the formulation endorsed by the majority of the

[13] *R. v. Secretary of State for the Home Department, ex parte Chahal* [1994] Imm AR 107.
[14] *Chahal*, note 1 above, para.78.

Court. The majority were adamant that the national security context made no difference. Nor did the immense difficulties faced by states in modern times of protecting their communities from terrorist violence. The prohibition was equally absolute in expulsion cases:

> [T]he activities of the individual in question, however undesirable or dangerous, cannot be a material consideration. *The protection afforded by Art. 3 is thus wider than that provided by Articles 32 and 33 of the United Nations 1951 Convention on the Status of Refugees.*[15]

The Court made clear that its remarks on 'balance' in *Soering* went only to the matter of interpreting the descriptors of maltreatment in Article 3, *and not to the matter of state responsibility under its expulsion aspect.* Given that the situation in the 'destination' state may fluctuate, a key consideration was to identify the point in time at which the risk was to be assessed. Where expulsion had already been effected the focus would be on what was known, or should have been known, by the expelling state at the time of the expulsion.[16] Where expulsion had yet to be effected, the risk was to be assessed as at the time of consideration of the matter by the Court.[17] The focus should be on the present, but the historical position was relevant to the extent that it could illuminate the current position and its likely evolution.

In assessing the risk, the Court was not confined to material produced by the parties, any interveners or the fact-finding elements of the Commission's investigations, hearings and report. The absolute nature of Article 3, a fundamental value of the democratic societies of which the Council of Europe was formed, demanded a rigorous approach by the Court looking also at material obtained of its own motion. Given that the material time was the date of consideration by the Court, circumstances since the delivery of the Commission's report had to be considered.[18] The Court examined all the material before it by looking at the evidence relating to general conditions in the Punjab and (since the

15 Ibid., para.80 (emphasis added). On this aspect and for comparisons with other international instruments, see C. Harvey, 'Expulsion, national security and the European Convention' (1997) EL Rev 626; H Lambert, 'Protection against *refoulement* from Europe: human rights law comes to the rescue' (1999) 48 ICLQ 515; R. Bruin and K. Wouters, 'Terrorism and the non-derogability of non-*refoulement*' (2003) 15 *International Journal of Refugee Law* 5.

16 *Cruz Varas*, note 12 above, para.76; *Vilvarajah*, note 12 above, para.107. The Court may also look at events after the expulsion since this might help confirm or refute the government's appreciation of the situation or the applicant's fears.

17 *Chahal*, note 1 above, para.86.

18 Ibid., paras.95–7.

government was willing to return Chahal to anywhere in India) in India as a whole, and at factors particular to Chahal: material from Amnesty International as intervener in the case; a 1994 report by the Indian National Human Rights Commission (an autonomous statutory body established by the Indian legislature in 1994)[19] which 'substantiated the impression of a police force completely beyond the control of lawful authority'; the US State Department's 1995 and 1996 reports on India; relevant material on the risk from a UK Immigration Appeal Tribunal decision; material from the UN Rapporteur on torture as endemic in the Indian police and a lack of accountability for police actions; and information from the monitoring of the changing situation by the UK High Commission in India. It also noted Chahal's high profile as a Sikh militant, the decision to deport having effectively branded him very publicly as a terrorist. There was also the matter of assurances from the Indian government that Chahal would not be maltreated.

All this persuaded the majority that there were significant problems of human rights abuses in the Punjab; that the security forces operated against Sikh militants both within and outside the Punjab; that there was evidence of their involvement in extrajudicial killings; 'that, until mid-1994 at least, elements in the Punjab police were accustomed to act without regard to the human rights of suspected Sikh militants and were fully capable of pursuing their targets into areas of India far away from Punjab';[20] and that, while there was evidence of improvements in the human rights situation in India, in democracy in the Punjab, in the legal accountability of its police force to the courts there, and an abatement of violence since its height in 1984, there remained evidence of sporadic 'disappearances' of leading Sikh figures and continued assassinations of Sikh militants. Most significantly, no concrete evidence had been produced of any recent fundamental reform or reorganisation of the Punjab police.[21] Given this, the Court was not persuaded that the assurances of good faith from the Indian government could provide Chahal with an adequate guarantee of safety, the risk to him being heightened by his high profile.[22] All this, but particularly the evidence of the involvement of the Punjab police in killings and abductions outside that state and the ongoing allegations of serious human rights violations by members of the Indian security forces elsewhere, led the Court to find

[19] Under the Protection of Human Rights Act 1993. See further www.nhrc.nic.in.
[20] *Chahal*, note 1 above, para.100. [21] Ibid., paras.102–3. [22] Ibid., para.105.

a real risk that Chahal would have been subjected to treatment contrary to Article 3 if he were to be returned to India.

The approach of the dissentients was rather different: Article 3 is absolute as regards ill-treatment by a High Contracting Party within its own jurisdiction, but the indirect effect (extraterritorial application) was subject to a 'fair balance' exception in national security cases. In short, they accepted the government's second argument.[23] In any event, whether applying that approach or the Court's test, the dissentients considered that neither was met on the evidence. The tests involved a matter of evaluation of the risk. Chahal's high profile and the assurances of the Indian government made it less likely that, if returned, he would be subjected to maltreatment.[24]

Initial executive and legislative responses

In public at least, the initial government response to *Chahal* was, in retrospect, rather muted. There was no histrionic overreaction as with the 'Death on the Rock' case.[25] Little appeared by way of comment in the press. It was accepted that effect would have to be given to the judgment. Chahal and others in a like situation were very quickly released from detention and the threat of deportation lifted.[26]

It was further accepted that the processes for reviewing national security deportations would have to change in light of the Court's other findings that the neither the adviser system nor judicial review satisfied the requirements of Article 5(4) that detention be reviewable by a court, and neither did they provide the effective remedy required by Article 13 ECHR. In late May 1997 the new Labour Government brought forward the Special Immigration Appeals Commission Bill to provide a right of appeal to an expert body for those adversely affected by national security immigration decisions. The Commission (SIAC) would be able to review all of the material seen by the Home Secretary and its decision would be binding. The Bill would have been brought forward whichever party had won the general election in early May 1997 and was unopposed. Conservative spokespeople raised the need to balance the rights of deportees with the general interest of the community, and concerns were expressed that Labour plans to incorporate the Convention would

[23] Ibid., p.481, para.1. [24] Ibid., p.483, paras.8–9.
[25] *McCann* v. *UK* (1996) 21 EHRR 97. [26] *The Times*, 16 November 1996, 2.

impede deportation.[27] Labour and Liberal Democrat spokespeople made clear that national security deportation would have to operate within the parameters of the absolute nature of the non-*refoulement* principle.[28]

Within the executive branch, both under Conservative and Labour governments, however, it would appear that the *Chahal* principle gave much more cause for concern than the public debates so far examined would suggest. It is reported that David Cameron, at the time of the decision a Home Office adviser, was very much affected by it. Material disclosed in a 2004 case on the failed deportation of four militants to Egypt (considered later) reveals graphically Prime Minister Blair's frustration. A number of concerns along similar lines were raised during the debates on the Human Rights Bill. But a major difference of approach between government and opposition became manifest when considering the appropriate response to 9/11, since the impediment set by *Chahal* would no longer apply only to a small number of cases.

9/11: ATCSA detention without trial and PTA control orders

How to respond to the dangers exemplified by 9/11 and to those threats which could not be dealt with by the criminal process, produced divergent responses from government and opposition. *Chahal* had also held that detention for deportation (enabled by Article 5(1)(f) ECHR) was only permissible so long as deportation was a realistic prospect, so that the type of detention pending deportation deployed against foreign nationals in the UK during the first Gulf War was not now available.[29] Both government and opposition saw the post-9/11 problem in immigration terms – the threat posed by foreign nationals in the country. Government, 'caught between a rock and a hard place' because of *Chahal*,[30] unable to derogate from Article 3, derogated from Article 5 under Article 15 ECHR, enabling indefinite detention of terrorist suspects believed to be a threat under immigration powers that would

[27] J. Clappison, MP, HC Debs., vol.299, cols.1058–9, 30 October 1997; Baroness Blatch, HL Debs., vol.580, cols.737–8, 5 June 1997; Baroness Anelay of St Johns, HL Debs., vol.580, col.749, 5 June 1997.

[28] Lord Williams of Mostyn, HL Debs., vol.580 cols.753–4, 5 June 1997; Lord Lester of Herne Hill, HL Debs., vol.580, col.739, 5 June 1997.

[29] D. Bonner and R. Cholewinski, 'The response of the United Kingdom's legal and constitutional orders to the 1991 Gulf War and the post-9/11 "war" on terrorism', in A. Baldaccini and E. Guild (eds.), *Terrorism and the Foreigner: A Decade of Tension around the Rule of Law in Europe* (Leiden: Nijhoff, 2007) 123, pp.125–32.

[30] 'Editorial' [2002] Crim LR 159, 160.

otherwise have been time-limited by *Chahal*.[31] In short, the government claimed that this approach would be consistent with its legal obligations under the Convention.[32] Conservative spokespeople colourfully categorized this as sacrificing Magna Carta and habeas corpus for the ECHR, or as having mumps but taking a treatment for measles.[33] The problem lay with the *Soering/Chahal* jurisprudence. The opposition 'solution' was to use Articles 57 and 58 ECHR to withdraw from the Convention and immediately rejoin making a reservation with respect to Article 3, which would in some way disapply *Chahal*.[34] That approach was legally questionable (arguably reservations cannot be valid if inconsistent with the fundamental object and purpose of a treaty)[35] and, in a European context, a mode of proceeding which our European partners would be unlikely to accept.[36]

In December 2004, the House of Lords in *A and others* held ATCSA detention to be incompatible with Convention rights as a disproportionate and discriminatory response to a public emergency in the face of the terrorist threat from al Qaeda, and the derogation order to be invalid since the measures taken went beyond what was required by the exigencies of an Article 15 ECHR 'public emergency'. ATCSA detention was abolished in March 2005 when control orders under the PTA came into effect. These can be made in respect of any terrorist suspects. The scheme was very much shaped by the obligations in the ECHR in that non-derogating control orders – the only ones ever deployed – cannot impose restrictions so extensive as to amount to a 'deprivation of liberty' contrary to Article 5 ECHR. The line between mere 'restrictions' on liberty and a 'deprivation' of it is imprecise and uncertain, and has generated significant litigation, but currently seems to permit curfews lasting up to sixteen hours.[37] Twenty-four-hour house arrest could have been enabled through a derogating control order, but this would require

[31] ATCSA 2001, Part 4.

[32] It was giving effect to its legal duty under Art. 3 while trying, within the bounds set by the ECHR, to deal with threats to the lives of the public which could not be managed by the criminal process: see C Warbrick, 'Diplomatic assurances and the removal of terrorist suspects from the UK' (2006) *Archbold News* 6.

[33] D. Cameron, MP, HC Debs., vol.375 cols.144–5, 19 November 2001.

[34] J. Paice, MP, HC Debs., vol.375, col.133; O. Letwin, MP, HC Debs., vol.375, cols.49–50, 19 November 2001.

[35] N. Grief and M. Addo, 'Some practical issues affecting the notion of absolute right in Article 3 ECHR' [1998] EL Rev 17 at 24.

[36] Report from the Joint Select Committee on Human Rights (JCHR), *A Bill of Rights for the UK?*, HC (2007–8) 150–II, Ev 106, 107 (Centre for Public Law, University of Cambridge).

[37] C. Walker, 'The threat of terrorism and the fate of control orders' [2010] PL 4, 5.

derogation under Article 15 ECHR and both Houses to approve an Article 15 derogation order, and the decision on the issuing and terms of any derogating control order would be one for the High Court.

During the passage of the Control Order Bill, the opposition focused on the option of maintaining for a short time ATCSA detention without trial, despite the declaration of incompatibility, in order to further explore alternatives that might be better (such as deployment of surveillance powers), be capable of generating evidence which could be used in court, and improve the chances of criminal conviction in terrorist cases (through use of intercept evidence and introducing an 'acts preparatory' offence into the armoury of terrorist criminal offences).[38] It did not propose changing the *Chahal* rule to enable deportation. The Liberal Democrats made some criticism of the government's long-term objective of more deportations with assurances:

> [W]e would like much stronger reassurances on human rights issues. It is not satisfactory for Ministers to be exchanging memorandums on these issues. The orders must be binding and tested, and we must have some reassurance that, before we proceed with any deportations, proper human rights principles are in place.[39]

Since non-derogating control orders could provide only partial protection in security terms, the government continued to seek other ways of changing the *Chahal* principle. Efforts intensified after the 7 July 2005 bombing attacks on London's transport network ('7/7'). Those options pursued – the 'litigation option', the 'legislative' option and the compliance/MOU option – must now be examined in turn.

The litigation option

The UK government was keen to find another opportunity to persuade the Court that its approach in *Chahal* had been in error. It intervened in two cases on national security deportation brought against other states. The first lodged in 2005 was *Ramzy* v. *Netherlands*. Proceedings in *Ramzy* stalled, but the UK found another vehicle, intervening in *Saadi* v. *Italy*.[40] The interventions were criticised by human rights NGOs and

[38] D. Davis, MP, HC Debs., vol.431, cols.354–6, 367, 404; D. Hogg, MP, HC Debs., vol.431, cols.402–5, 23 February 2005.

[39] M. Oaten, MP, HC Debs, vol.431, col.370, 23 February 2005.

[40] *Saadi* v. *Italy* (2009) 49 EHRR 30.

by the JCHR as aiming to weaken the prohibition against torture and as damaging the UK's standing on human rights.[41]

Saadi v. *Italy* concerned the proposed deportation to Tunisia on security grounds of this Tunisian national, said by intelligence sources to have spent time in an al Qaeda training camp in Iran and to be part of an Islamist cell involved in a large-scale enterprise involving the production of false identity papers and their distribution to its members. Saadi was convicted of forgery by an Italian court but maintained that the offence was not linked to terrorism.

The Italian government, also supporting the arguments made by the UK, argued that the risk of being exposed to maltreatment contrary to Article 3 had to be corroborated by 'appropriate evidence'. None had been presented. There was a more positive picture of Tunisia. The country was a signatory to numerous international human rights instruments which constitutionally took precedence over statute law. It permitted the International Committee of the Red Cross to visit its prisons and places of detention. It had an association agreement with the EU and bilateral agreements with Italy on emigration and terrorism, which 'presupposed a common basis of respect for fundamental rights'.[42] All this established that it could not be presumed that Tunisia would default on its international agreements.[43] Italy had sought diplomatic assurances from Tunisia, in response to which Tunisia had given 'an undertaking to apply in the present case the relevant Tunisian law . . . , which provided for severe punishment of acts of torture or ill-treatment and extensive visiting rights for a prisoner's lawyer and family'.[44]

As intervener, the UK stressed both the changed nature and the increased danger of the terrorist threat after 9/11 and the significant problems the *Chahal* ruling posed to states trying to counter that threat and thus to protect the lives of their citizens. The threat from al Qaeda and other groups willing to kill and maim members of the public was real, its level had significantly increased in recent years, showed no signs of diminishing and was of 'a particularly serious kind'. The UK government cited the highly organised nature of the groups and networks posing the threat, the phenomenon of suicide bombers and operatives willing to die for the cause, and the threat to use 'atrocities of the most serious and appalling kind' involving chemical, nuclear, radiological or biological material. Article 5(1)(f) ECHR, legitimising detention

[41] Warbrick, 'Diplomatic assurances', pp.7–8.

[42] *Saadi*, note 40 above, paras.111–12. [43] Ibid., para.112. [44] Ibid., para.116.

pending deportation, recognised that deportation or expulsion was a 'classic method' by which states 'have sought to protect themselves against foreign nationals on their territory who are judged to be a threat to national security'. *Chahal* severely limited its practicality. While 'diplomatic assurances' might in some cases enable deportation consistently with *Chahal*, that turned on the uncertainties of whether such assurances provided 'adequate and effective protection', something on which reasonable decision makers could disagree in any particular case. Where someone was identified as a terrorist suspect, no state, other than the one of which the person was a national (with which he was likely in practice to be at odds and thus at risk of maltreatment if returned there), was likely to take the individual. Thus, the potential impediment to removal was likely to arise in a significant number of cases. Nor were the alternatives to deportation always effective. Recourse to criminal prosecution could not provide adequate protection. Evidence indicating that someone posed a serious threat to national security through involvement in terrorism might not suffice to satisfy the criminal standard of proof. There might be problems with the admissibility of some evidence, because of the 'equality of arms' facet of criminal proceedings. Some probative material might not be able to be put before the court because of the need to protect the identity of an informant or undercover agent or a desire not to reveal the nature of a method of surveillance. The criminal law and process are not well suited to *preventing* terrorist acts. The individual suspect might be careful not to commit any offences before the deadly attack or any he did commit might be of a minor nature where sentencing had to reflect the severity of the offence itself and not be based on the principle of preventing other terrorist acts. Measures such as indefinite detention without trial could provide that protection, but had been declared incompatible with Convention rights. Lesser measures such as surveillance or control orders provided only partial protection. The government questioned the appropriateness of *Chahal*; while there could be, in a particular case, a very high risk to the security of the state, a real risk of maltreatment in the 'destination' state only just attaining the level of severity for treatment to be 'degrading' would nonetheless preclude deportation of a dangerous terrorist.

The UK submitted that the *Chahal* approach should be clarified and adapted to meet the threat currently posed by international terrorism after 9/11. First, it restated the 'fair balance' argument advanced in *Chahal* and accepted there by the dissentients. The Court should weigh against the possibility and nature of anticipated maltreatment the threat posed to the 'host' state's national security by the person whose putative removal is at issue. This modification was warranted because it better recognised the relative nature of the issues and the rights in play, enabling the rights of the deportee and those of the public properly to be weighed and respected. In contrast, the 'absolute' approach left out of account rights of the public, including the right to life, and meant that a risk of mild degrading treatment precluded deportation that might save lives. Moreover, the absolute approach was inconsistent with the nature of the obligation placed on the state. The obligation is implied from Article 3 and is positive rather than negative. Given that, the Court should recognise, as it does elsewhere in the Convention in respect of implied positive obligations, that the content of the obligation must take account of other facets of the general interest and, where other ECHR rights are involved, the necessity for an appropriate balancing exercise, much as it had seemed to do in *Soering* with respect to the scope and application of 'inhuman and degrading treatment'. The 'absolute' approach was out of step with general international law on refugees and the terms and structure of the Refugee Convention with its exceptions enabling *refoulement* of a national security threat,[45] or those who had committed acts contrary to the purposes and the principles of the United Nations, including a variety of acts connected with terrorism.[46] The government contended that it was by no means clear that UNCAT supports an absolute obligation and that interpretations by its Committee Against Torture were not binding. And it only applies to torture, whereas *Soering/Chahal* had also taken the unjustified further leap of applying the 'absolute' approach to the lesser forms of maltreatment in Article 3. The approach of the dissentients in *Chahal* was preferable. The 'absolute' approach reflected no universally recognised moral imperative, as was plain from the provisions of the Refugee Convention. The government contended that there were states which did not follow the absolute approach, citing here the Supreme Court in Canada,[47] as well as the legal position in the United States, which had entered an express understanding with respect to a higher standard of proof when ratifying UNCAT. The government acknowledged that a considered judgment would be required in every case, weighing all the relevant circumstances. National security could not always be the trump card enabling removal; even in such cases, the appropriate balance of risks would mean that

[45] Art. 33(2). [46] Art. 1F(c). [47] *Suresh* v. *Canada* [2002] 1 SCR 3.

deportation was not inevitable in security cases. Its argument was a narrower one; that national security considerations were relevant.

The government's second submission concerned the appropriate standard of proof. It noted here the concession made in *Chahal* by the Commission's delegate that where there were serious doubts as to the likelihood of a person being subjected to treatment or punishment contrary to Article 3, this might enable the benefit of that doubt to be given to the deporting state whose national interests were threatened. The government submitted, however, that it would be more appropriate clearly to set the applicant in national security cases a significantly higher standard of proof ('more likely than not') of maltreatment contrary to Article 3 if removal was to be precluded. This was compatible with the wording of Article 3 UNCAT, which had been based on the case law of the Court itself.

The result of the litigation option was the firmer establishment of the absolute approach as the settled jurisprudence of the Court. The Grand Chamber unanimously endorsed the 'absolute' approach and it has been further maintained in a variety of case contexts since *Saadi*.[48] Under the approach of the UK courts to section 2 of the HRA, the rule must be applied by the courts, even where they might think it wrong.[49] The Court was fully conscious of the immense difficulties facing states in modern times of protecting their communities from terrorist violence. But while it could not underestimate the scale of the danger of modern terrorism and its threat to the community, that could not call into question the absolute nature of Article 3. It considered the balancing argument 'misconceived':

> The concepts of 'risk' and 'dangerousness' in this context do not lend themselves to a balancing test because they are notions that can only be assessed independently of each other. Either the evidence adduced before the Court reveals that there is a substantial risk if the person is sent back or it does not. The prospect that he may pose a serious threat to the community if not returned does not reduce in any way the degree of risk of ill treatment that the person may be subject to on return. For that reason it would be incorrect to require a higher standard of proof, as submitted by the intervener, where the person is considered to represent a serious danger to the community, since assessment of the level of risk is independent of such a test.[50]

[48] Human Rights Watch, *Not the Way Forward: the UK's Dangerous Reliance on Diplomatic Assurance* (October 2008) *Toumi* v. *Italy* (App. 25716/09), 5 April 2011.

[49] I. Leigh and R. Masterman, *Making Rights Real: the Human Rights Act in its First Decade*, (Oxford: Hart, 2008), ch.3.

[50] *Saadi*, note 40 above, paras.138–9.

This was so even if, as the two governments asserted, the terrorist threat had increased since *Chahal.* Nor was the Court prepared to modify the standard of proof. One detects some frustration at the actions of the two governments: first, when the Court observes that similar arguments to those advanced in the present case had already been rejected in *Chahal*;[51] and second, when, as regards the standards set by the test, it reminded everyone that:

> it applies rigorous criteria and exercises close scrutiny when assessing the existence of a real risk of ill-treatment As a result, since adopting the *Chahal* judgment it has only rarely reached such a conclusion.[52]

This, however, was one such case. The Court held unanimously that substantial grounds had been shown for believing that there was a real risk that the applicant would be subjected to maltreatment contrary to Article 3 if returned to Tunisia. There had been problems with visits of the International Red Cross, and Human Rights Watch (an NGO) had been refused access. The statement by Tunisia in response to the Italian request for diplomatic assurances about Saadi's treatment if returned did not go so far as to provide such assurances. But even if they had been forthcoming, the Court would have had to consider whether in their practical application they afforded:

> a sufficient guarantee that the applicant would be protected against the risk of treatment prohibited by the Convention. *The weight to be given to assurances from the receiving State depends, in each case, on the circumstances prevailing at the material time.*[53]

The legislative option

In his 'rules of the game are changing' press conference, Prime Minister Blair stated very clearly that

> [s]hould legal obstacles arise, we will legislate further, including, if necessary, amending the Human Rights Act, in respect of the interpretation of the ECHR. In any event we will consult on legislating specifically for a non-suspensive appeal process in respect of deportations.[54]

Similar threats/promises of legislation to amend the HRA so that UK courts could not apply the *Chahal* ruling directly but would have to

[51] Ibid., para.141. [52] Ibid., para.142 (emphasis added). [53] Ibid., para.148.
[54] Press conference, quoted in *The Guardian*, note 7 above.

accord greater weight to national security, were made by the Lord Chancellor and Home Secretary Charles Clarke.[55] At different times Clarke also made contrary statements that such amendments would not happen.[56] There was clearly division and confusion within the Cabinet on the matter. Prime Ministerial frustration with *Chahal* can be seen in his interventions during 1999 in specific cases in connection with return to Egypt which came to light in 2004.[57] These included a scribbled 'get them back' and 'why do we need all these things?' on one item of interdepartmental correspondence about assurances, 'this isn't good enough. I don't believe we shld *(sic)* be doing this. Speak to me' on another letter, and a willingness to accept very basic assurances which in the end were never forthcoming from Egypt.[58] It was clear that his priority throughout was the return of the individuals to Egypt, and that his 'gung ho' approach was out of line with the more legally driven nature of the Home Office and Foreign Office responses.[59] Another Home Secretary, Dr John Reid, variously described *Chahal* as 'imbalanced',[60] a 'gross misjudgement',[61] and 'outrageously disproportionate' and 'outrageous'.[62]

No such legislation to amend the HRA was brought forward under the Blair or Brown governments. A suspensive right of appeal (exercisable only after departure from the country) now applies with respect to national security deportation but, significantly, challenges with respect to the ECHR are an exception to that: they are heard by way of an 'in-country' appeal.[63] Labour remains committed to a UK Bill of Rights that will be 'HRA/ECHR plus', thus embodying the *Chahal* principle as binding on UK courts; the 'no amendment' faction seems to have prevailed.

The Conservatives have long been keen to change the *Chahal* ruling. On 24 August 2005, David Cameron, then Shadow Education Secretary, delivered a speech to the Foreign Policy Centre think tank on the challenges of global terror. On 'Homeland Security', he stated that:

> under the European Convention on Human Rights (ECHR) and in particular through important cases such as *Chahal*, it has become close

[55] A. Lester and K. Beattie, 'Risking torture' [2005] EHRLR 565, 565.

[56] Report from the JCHR, *Counter-Terrorism Policy and Human Rights: Terrorism Bill and Related Matters*, HC (2005–6) 561–I (oral evidence, 24 October 2005, q4).

[57] *Youssef* v. *Home Office* [2004] EWHC 1884 (QB). [58] Ibid., paras.15, 29, 38.

[59] Ibid., para.18. [60] HC Debs., vol.448, col.743, 25 July 2006. [61] Ibid.

[62] HC Debs., vol.460, col.1433, 24 May 2007.

[63] Nationality, Immigration and Asylum Act 2002, s.97A, inserted by Immigration, Asylum and Nationality Act 2006, s.7.

> to impossible to deport foreign nationals that may pose a threat to the UK. Being able to balance the danger they may pose to the UK if they stay with the danger to them if they are returned to their country of origin, is no longer possible. That is wrong. . . . If the government succeeds in its attempts to achieve memorandums of understanding with countries to which these people would be returned, so much the better. If not, we must . . . amend the Human Rights Act, or, if necessary, leave – perhaps temporarily – the ECHR.[64]

By July 2006, he had eschewed the option of leaving the ECHR and instead saw the solution in abolishing the HRA and replacing it with a 'British' Bill of Rights. This 'enduring solution' would nonetheless mean:

> there may still be a need to deal at times with the European Court's interpretation of the Convention – as in the *Chahal* case. And so one of the challenges for our panel of jurists and legal experts will be to determine how the nature of our participation in the ECHR can be aligned with the principles and legal effect of our modern British Bill of Rights.[65]

David Pannick QC thought this 'ill informed about basic principles of law . . . incoherent as an expression of policy aims, and inevitably doomed to failure as a response to the *Chahal* judgment'.[66] There is also a certain irony in that, to try to limit potential activism by UK judges, during the passage of the Human Rights Bill the Conservatives unsuccessfully tried to make Strasbourg jurisprudence binding on them.[67] The Liberal/Conservative Coalition Government, clearly divided on the matter, is to subject the matter to review.[68]

Amending the HRA in the way envisaged is pointless in terms of achieving the end they sought, and appears mere populist political posturing. Short of withdrawal from the ECHR (an option now ruled out by the major political parties), *Chahal* would govern any application made to Strasbourg and bind the UK to give effect to any adverse judgment of the Court. Exactly the same preclusive rule is embodied in the UN International Covenant on Civil and Political Rights and

[64] As reported in *The Guardian*, 24 August 2005, available at www.guardian.co.uk/politics/2005/aug/24/conservatives.faithschools (accessed 13 January 2010).

[65] D. Cameron MP, 'Balancing freedom and security', Centre for Policy Studies, 26 June 2006. Available at www.guardian.co.uk/politics/2006/jun/26/conservatives.constitution. (accessed 14 January 2010).

[66] 'Crisis, what crisis? It's just political posturing: Britain does not need a modern Bill of Rights, it needs a properly trained Civil Service', *The Times*, 11 July 2006.

[67] Leigh and Masterman, *Making Rights Real*, pp.59, 89–90.

[68] See C. R. G. Murray at www.humanrights.ie/index.php/2010/05/19/did-the-uk-general-election-save-the-human-rights-act/ (accessed 14 September 2010).

jurisprudence under it.[69] The same prohibition, albeit confined to torture, is found in Article 3 UNCAT. The prohibition against torture is now a peremptory norm of international law and (it has been argued) so is the prohibition on *refoulement* to torture.[70] While possible, through denunciation under Article 58, withdrawal from the ECHR would be 'far from straightforward'.[71] Denunciation in order to re-ratify subject to a reservation narrowing Article 3 as applied in *Chahal* is both legally questionable and politically highly unlikely: 'considerable political difficulty – both domestically and internationally – would presumably attend a decision by the UK government that it was unwilling to guarantee to those within its jurisdiction a set of human rights currently binding upon 47 European states'.[72] Membership of the EU presupposes adherence to the ECHR. Withdrawal from the EU – again legally possible – is not on the political agenda of any major political party. Moreover, as Professor Klug has noted, there are major foreign policy implications of the 'British' Bill of Rights proposal: 'the message to the rest of the world – that a domestic bill of rights can be used to opt out of a commitment to fundamental human rights – could be quite catastrophic. Any dictatorship would have carte blanche to do likewise'.[73] It could arguably breach Article 17 ECHR prohibiting acts aimed at limiting the ECHR protected rights and freedoms to an extent greater than the Convention permits.[74]

There is some evidence of attempts to persuade our European partners to seek to change the *Chahal* principle. An EU Commission working paper indicated some support for persuading the Court to modify its stance,[75] but the UK found few partners willing to intervene with it in *Ramzy* and none are recorded as interveners in *Saadi*. Whether the option of an amending Protocol narrowing the principle was considered or pursued is unclear. This might legally be possible, but no Protocol to date has yet sought to narrow a Court ruling; all have added extra rights or modified structures and procedures of the ECHR's enforcement machinery. The response in the Committee of Ministers Declaration on Countering Terrorism, cited in *Saadi* as a basis for maintaining the absolute rule on non-*refoulement*, and the limited number of interveners in *Ramzy*, indicate that pursuit of any such option would not have borne fruit.

[69] Art. 7; *Ng* v. *Canada* (1994) 15 HRLJ 149.

[70] Report from the JCHR, *The UN Convention Against Torture*, HC (2005–6) 701–I and II, Ev 150, paras.3–4 (Immigration Law Practitioners Association).

[71] JCHR, *A Bill of Rights for the UK?* [72] Ibid.

[73] Ibid., Ev 146 (F. Klug). [74] Ibid.

[75] Bruin and Wouters, 'Terrorism and the non-derogability of non-*refoulement*', pp.8–11.

The compliance option (deportation with assurances)

In his 'rules of the game are changing' press conference, Prime Minister Blair stated that:

> we believe we can get the necessary assurances from the countries to which we will return the deportees, against their being subject to torture or ill-treatment contrary to Article 3. We have concluded a Memorandum of Understanding with Jordan . . .[76]

In its 2006 counter-terrorism strategy document,[77] the government reported that it had concluded further MOUs with Lebanon and Libya. Bodies to monitor the agreements had been appointed in Jordan and Libya and an agreement in principle had been reached with such a body in Lebanon. Negotiations were ongoing with a number of other countries in the Middle East and North Africa. Less codified arrangements are in place to deal with deportations to Algeria,[78] a particular difference being the failure to specify independent monitoring.

The JCHR, in two reports, and a raft of NGOs giving evidence to it, were sceptical in the light of experience of the value of 'no ill-treatment agreements' or diplomatic assurances in specific cases from states with a bad record on torture.[79] Similar scepticism has been expressed by the Council of Europe High Commissioner on Human Rights and the UN Special Rapporteur on Torture.[80] The UK courts have been very much aware of these concerns through both the arguments of counsel for the putative deportees and NGOs intervening in a number of the cases coming before the courts.[81]

MOUs and the less formal arrangements with Algeria have been taken into account by SIAC and the appellate courts when applying the *Soering/Chahal/Saadi* test,[82] with mixed outcomes. It is clear that whether the *Chahal* test is met in any particular case is situation-, time-, regime- and individual-specific. It is not a matter within the exclusive province of the executive.[83] The matter is one of weighing

76 Press conference, quoted in *The Guardian*, note 7 above.

77 *Countering International Terrorism: The United Kingdom's Strategy*, Cm 6888 (2006), para.74.

78 *RB (Algeria)* v. *SSHD*, *OO (Jordan)* v. *SSHD* [2009] UKHL 10.

79 JCHR, *UNCAT*, note 70 above, HC 701–I, paras.110–31; HC 701–II: 105–10 (Amnesty International), 110–38 (British Irish Rights Watch), 145–50 (Human Rights Watch), 153–9 (Liberty and Justice).

80 Ibid., HC 701–I, para.131.

81 *AS (Libya)* v. *SSHD* [2008] EWCA Civ 289 (Liberty).

82 See Appendix to this chapter, extracted from material on http://www.siac.tribunals.gov.uk/outcomes2007onwards.htm.

83 *SSHD* v. *Rehman* [2003] 1 AC 153, Lord Hoffmann, paras.54, 57; *AS*, note 81 above, paras.47–50.

the credibility of any MOU or other diplomatic exchanges and of other specific assurances in respect of the particular individual in order to assess, in the light of information about the 'destination' state, the level of risk should that individual be returned. The acceptance of assurances depends on the facts of each case, rather than any rule of law or thumb. In application the test, involving close scrutiny of the circumstances of each case, is one of fact to be decided by the expert tribunal (SIAC), equivalent to the High Court since 2001.[84] An appellate court can overturn it only on a point of law: so, if SIAC has stated the test correctly and applied the appropriate level of scrutiny, its decision is impugnable by the higher court only on grounds of irrationality.[85] Moreover, the appellate courts are conscious of the need not lightly to interfere with a decision of SIAC as an expert tribunal which hears all the evidence, both 'open' and 'closed'.[86] The House of Lords noted the high level at which these MOUs and other agreements had been concluded.[87]

Assurances do not have to eliminate all risk of torture or inhuman and degrading treatment faced by the individual before the goverment can rely on them.[88] Applying *Saadi*, in a case on Libya the Court of Appeal held that the test is one of 'real risk' – 'more than a mere possibility but something less than a balance of probabilities or more likely than not'.[89] The test is not whether the risk is 'real or immediate'.[90] The test is, however, stringent.[91] In cases involving Algeria and Jordan, the House of Lords stated that 'the terms on which assurances were given, the opportunities for monitoring and the extent to which the risk would be reduced required careful evaluation, especially where the assurances were given by a country where inhuman treatment by state agents was endemic'.[92] The question is whether, 'after consideration of all the

[84] See, on SIAC's status, ATCSA 2001, s.35. *OO*, note 78 above, paras.52, 114–15, 117–18, 124–5, 126, 185, 187, 236, 238, 241; *AS*, note 81 above, paras.41, 52, 69, 81–3. The approach reflects wider judicial opinion as indicated in a *Guardian* report of interviews on condition of anonymity with 37 appeal court judges. See C. Dyer, 'Judges ready to defy ministers over terror deportations', *The Guardian*, 12 September 2005, available at www.guardian.co.uk/uk/2005/sep/12/terrorism.uksecurity (accessed 13 January 2010).

[85] *AS*, note 81 above, paras.81–3.

[86] *RB/OO*, note 78 above, paras.118 (Lord Phillips of Worth Matravers); 235 (Lord Hope); *AS*, note 81 above, paras.15–19.

[87] *RB/OO*, note 78 above, paras.106 (Lord Phillips); 192 (Lord Hoffmann); 235 (Lord Hope).

[88] Ibid., paras.114 (Lord Phillips); 242 (Lord Hope).

[89] *AS*, note 81 above, para.60. [90] Ibid., para.64. [91] Ibid., paras.65–7.

[92] *RB/OO*, note 78 above, paras.114 (Lord Phillips); 241 (Lord Hope); *AS*, note 81 above, paras.81–2.

relevant circumstances of which assurances form part, there are no substantial grounds for believing that a deportee will be at real risk of inhuman treatment'.[93] If there are no such grounds, there can then be no basis for holding that deportation will contravene Article 3. There is no legal requirement for external monitoring in each and every case; while it is important that 'fulfilment of the assurances can be verified, external monitoring is only one possible form of verification'.[94] SIAC can take account, for example, of the sensitivities of sovereign states, which (like Algeria) might baulk at a specific requirement for external monitoring. It was entitled to hold that, in the Algerian cases, there were other ways – the sort of state and NGO reports on which SIAC and the Court have relied in the cases under study – in which non-compliance could be made known. Moreover, it was entitled to look at the political incentives in the relationship between 'host' and 'destination' states and the likelihood of those incentives ensuring compliance.[95]

In nine cases (PP, YB, BB, U, W, Z, B, Y and G) over a three-year period, SIAC determined (in carefully constructed judgments, some running to hundreds of paragraphs) that the *Chahal* principle did not operate to preclude their deportation to an Algeria much changed since 2001 and, indeed, in the last four years. SIAC has considered material from the FCO, the United States State Department, from NGOs (including Amnesty), oral testimony from FCO representatives and from an academic expert on North Africa. In particular it focused on the moves towards reconciliation in Algeria, attempts to draw a line under the past by a President democratically elected and a government thought less subject to control by the military. Important here were the terms and applicability to the individuals of an effective 'amnesty' in respect of relevant offences in a Charter and Ordonnance and also the release of many terrorist prisoners. Also of weight were the circumstances of others who had earlier returned to Algeria. That there was no formal MOU was immaterial, given the nature of the diplomatic exchanges and correspondence between the two governments. Nor, given the low level of risk to the individuals, was the lack of explicit formal monitoring structures a problem, given the mutual interests of the two governments in making the return process work, given ongoing scrutiny by NGOs both within and outside Algeria, and given that Algeria seemed committed to signing

[93] *RB/OO*, note 78 above, para.114 (Lord Phillips); *AS*, note 81 above, paras.74–5.
[94] *RB/OO*, note 78 above, para.193 (Lord Hoffmann).
[95] Ibid., paras. 126 (Lord Phillips); 192–3 (Lord Hoffmann); 236 (Lord Hope).

the Optional Protocol to UNCAT.[96] A similar approach was taken in *Abu Qatada* against the backdrop of the MOU with Jordan.[97] That country might torture other Islamist extremists but was unlikely, because of the diplomatic cooperation and the attention focused on the case, to maltreat Abu Qatada. The decision was controversial but was upheld both by the Court of Appeal and the House of Lords.[98] It resonates with the approach by the dissentients in *Chahal* to application of the test set by the majority in that case. Removal to Ethiopia has also been allowed.

In contrast, reinforcing that all depends on the circumstances of the particular case, the Court of Appeal upheld SIAC's refusal to sanction the national security deportation of AS and DD to Libya.[99] Given the mercurial nature of Colonel Qaddafi and his regime and its pragmatic approach to foreign relations, there was a risk that it might not keep its word.[100] The monitoring agency in the agreement bore his name, was headed by one of his sons, and was thus not independent of the regime.[101] In May 2010, SIAC refused to return to Pakistan two appellants it regarded as national security threats, holding that it could take no account of confidential assurances of no maltreatment given only in closed session.[102]

JUSTICE, however, characterised their Lordships' decisions to sanction two Algerians and one Jordanian's deportation on national security grounds as:

> a step backwards in the international fight against torture. A promise not to torture from a regime that tortures its own people is worth nothing. It is shameful that the government negotiated these deals in the first place, and saddening that the courts have refused to stop them. At a time when the Obama administration is cleaning house and renouncing torture, today's ruling shows the UK still clinging to paper promises from torturers.[103]

The matter of Abu Qatada's national security deportation to Jordan is now before the Strasbourg Court, giving it the opportunity to give further guidance on the place in the test of assurances by way of MOUs. The case also raises questions of the 'extraterritorial application' and

[96] SC/36/2005 (Y: 24 August 2006); SC/39/2005 (BB: 5 December 2006); SC/02/2005 (G: 8 February 2007).
[97] SC/15/2005, Judgment 26 February 2007.
[98] *OO*, note 78 above; [2008] EWCA Civ 290.
[99] *AS*, note 81 above.
[100] Ibid., paras.69–78.
[101] Ibid., para.79.
[102] SC/77/09 (Abid Naseer, 18/5/10); SC/80/09 (Ahmad Faraz Khan).
[103] JUSTICE, Press Release, 18 February 2009.

'application in a "foreign" case' of the fair trial guarantees in Article 6, and of the guarantee in such a case of liberty and security under Article 5. Pending resolution of the application, the Court has indicated non-removal as an interim measure of protection.[104]

The non-compliance option

There is no public evidence of the government considering an approach of simply ignoring the decisions of the Court of Human Rights on Article 3 or, in an Article 3 case, of it being prepared to ignore suspension of removal as an interim measure of protection under rule 39 of Strasbourg's Rules of Court. It is now established that such measures are considered binding so that, in an extradition or expulsion case, a failure to abide by them will breach Article 34 as an interference with exercise of the right of individual petition.[105] Italy has been criticised by the Council of Europe's Human Rights Commissioner in respect of cases in which it has ignored suspensive interim measures and returned individuals to Tunisia.[106] In this context, a recent decision finding the UK in breach is troubling.[107] The UK transferred prisoners in its custody in Iraq to the Iraqi authorities for trial on a capital crime in apparent disregard of interim measures indicated by the Court, a transfer held to violate Articles 3, 4 and 13. But this seems less a case of a switch to a policy of plain lawlessness than one of confusion over the proper priority of conflicting legal rules in the mess that is Iraq. The decision became final on 4 October 2010.

Conclusions

The expulsion cases under Article 3 graphically illustrate the ECHR as a living instrument, capable of being interpreted and applied in ways never conceived of by its framers. They reveal the absolute nature of Article 3 prohibitions: applicable whatever the circumstances, whatever an individual has done, even in the sensitive field of national security. The bold and teleological interpretation accords with the principle of the practical effectiveness of the ECHR and with international obligations on torture. The interpretative approach accords with the Vienna Convention of the

[104] European Court of Human Rights, press release 131, 19 February 2009.

[105] D. Harris, M. O'Boyle, E. Bates and C. Buckley, *Law of the European Convention on Human Rights* (Oxford University Press, 2nd edn, 2009), pp.842–6.

[106] 'Annual Activity Report 2009', Comm(DH)(2010) 8.

[107] *Al-Saadoon and Mufdhi* v. *UK* (2010) 51 EHRR 9.

Law of Treaties.[108] The principle is in line with a key counter-terrorism principle that in responding the state must act lawfully and retain the moral high ground.[109]

This chronicle confirms the view expressed by the Council of Europe's Human Rights Commissioner that the UK has a tendency to 'consider human rights as excessively restricting the effective administration of justice and the protection of the public interest'.[110] But it does not show the UK as cavalier with human rights when responding to terrorism.[111] Arguably it shows a rule-oriented entity seeking to find a solution to a difficult governmental problem in a way that conforms with, rather than flouts, its ECHR obligations. The UK took the wrong step with ATCSA detention, but a time-restricted control order regime applying due process, as demanded by their Lordships in *AF*, could have continued to constitute a workable response if sparingly used.[112]

The chronicle gives cause for concern about the commitment of leading politicians to the HRA. The Conservatives have always opposed it and intended to replace it with a 'British' Bill of Rights, but under the Lib/Con Coalition the matter is subject to review. The ambivalence of members of the Labour Cabinet to one of their flagship constitutional reforms is more troubling. A range of views competed for consideration within that Cabinet, giving an impression of 'shifting sands', even with the same spokesperson. Fortunately, Labour came round to backing the HRA with a UK Bill of Rights envisaged as 'HRA/ECHR plus'. It is more encouraging to note that there seems no real evidence of desire in the major political parties to follow the 'non-compliance' route taken by Italy. Even the picture of Prime Minister Blair's attempts to secure the deportation of four militants to Egypt has its positive side. The Home Office and Foreign Office, each more 'rule-oriented', won out in the battle with No. 10.

The UK case law confirms that it is possible to deport foreign national terrorist suspects from the UK. The *Chahal* 'rule' is revealed as highly case-sensitive in terms of the character of the destination state and its regime, the identity and prominence of the individual to be deported, and the dynamics of the political relationship between 'host' and 'destination' states, at a particular time. This is shown by the contrasting outcomes in

[108] H. Battjes, 'In search of a fair balance: the absolute character of the prohibition of *refoulement* under Article 3 reassessed' (2009) 22 *Leiden Journal of International Law* 583.

[109] D. Feldman, 'Deprivation of liberty in anti-terrorism law' (2008) 67 CLJ 4.

[110] 'Report on his visit to the United Kingdom', 4–12 November 2004, Comm(DH)(2005) 6, para.3.

[111] Warbrick, 'Diplomatic assurances'.

[112] Walker, 'The threat of terrorism', pp.16–17.

respect of deportation to Algeria/Jordan, on the one hand, and to Libya or Pakistan on the other. Had the events of the 'Arab Spring' not intervened it might have been possible that, over time, the 'rehabilitation' of the Qaddafi regime could have developed in such a way as to remove the SIAC concerns currently precluding removal to Libya. Instead, Qaddafi's reaction to popular protest against his rule bears out the wisdom in SIAC's approach. The picture in Pakistan may also change.

Commentators await with interest the Court's decision in Abu Qatada's case, the more so since it recently held that a deportation by France to Algeria would contravene Article 3. It will probably take a 'case by case' approach to assurances, rather than absolutely set its face against them, but this will not necessarily produce the same outcomes as in UK courts. If so, the UK government will simply have to adapt once again, rethink its approach to control orders, but preferably be more imaginative – within the bounds set by the ECHR – about possible reforms of the criminal law and criminal procedure, including the use of intercept evidence and reconceptualising 'fair trial' rights.

Appendix

Table of SIAC national security deportation cases dealing with Article 3

Date determined	SIAC Ref	Name	Result of appeal	Country
11/7/11	SC/98/2010	JJ	Dismissed	Ethiopia
10/9/10	SC/61/2007	XX	Dismissed	Ethiopia
18/5/10	SC/77/09	Abid Naseer	Allowed	Pakistan
18/5/10	SC/80/09	Ahmad Faraz Khan	Allowed	Pakistan
23/11/07	SC/54/2006	PP	Dismissed	Algeria
02/11/07	SC/32,36,39/2005	Y, BB, U	Dismissed	Algeria
02/11/07	SC/59/2006	VV	Dismissed	Jordan
14/05/07	SC/32/2005	U	Dismissed	Algeria
14/05/07	SC/34/2005	W	Dismissed	Algeria
14/05/07	SC/37/2005	Z	Dismissed	Algeria
27/04/07	SC/42/2005 & SC/50/2005	DD, AS	Allowed	Libya
26/02/07	SC/15/2005	Abu Q	Dismissed	Jordan
08/02/07	SC/02/2005	G	Dismissed	Algeria
5/12/06	SC/39/2005	BB	Dismissed	Algeria
24/08/06	SC/36/2005	Y	Dismissed	Algeria

5

The right to security – securing rights or securitising rights?

LIORA LAZARUS

Introduction

There are an increasing number of ways to think about security and the attainment of security. Some of us believe that security comes from the ground up,[1] some of us believe it is achieved by a civilized state,[2] some of us think security is access to resources, water or health,[3] others talk of environmental security or a 'right to security from climate change'.[4] We also talk about human security, personal or individual security, national security and global security. There is plenty to say about what security is and how it can achieved: Zedner is quite right to frame security as a 'promiscuous concept'.[5] What we know at the very least is that the level

This paper is the culmination of two lectures and two seminars, which I delivered in Newcastle, New York, Cape Town and Oxford respectively. I am, consequently, indebted to a number of people in the development of this piece. Thanks in particular to Colin Murray, Ian Loader, Clifford Shearing, Carol Sanger and Lucia Zedner for their important contributions in these discussions. I am especially indebted to Jeremy Waldron who acted as respondent to the lecture in New York, and for various associated discussions. Henry Shue was also very generous in allowing me to discuss my thoughts and in offering reflections on my previous piece 'Mapping the right to security' in B. Goold and L. Lazarus (eds.), *Security and Human Rights* (Oxford: Hart, 2007). Finally, special thanks to my research assistants, Christopher Boulle and Natasha Simonsen. Natasha not only assisted in the research for this piece, but offered me important comments and insights during the writing process.

1 L. Johnston and C. Shearing, *Governing Security: Explorations in Policing and Justice* (London: Routledge, 2003).

2 I. Loader and N. Walker, *Civilizing Security* (Cambridge University Press, 2007).

3 S. Fredman, 'The positive right to security' in B. Goold and L. Lazarus (eds.), *Security and Human Rights* (Oxford: Hart, 2007), 307; E. Burleson, 'Water is security', 31 *Environs Environmental Law & Policy Journal* (2008) 197.

4 A. Sinden, 'An emerging human right to security from climate change: the case against gas flaring in Nigeria', Temple University Beasley School of Law Legal Studies Research Paper Series, Research Paper No. 2008–77.

5 L. Zedner, *Security* (London: Routledge, 2009), p.9.

of controversy about what security is, whether it is something that is self-defining or in effect relates to something else,[6] brings with it all sorts of difficulties when it comes to defining the notion of a *right* to security.

There is, as readers of this volume will be aware, plenty of controversy about the nature of human rights, the basis of their universality or normative legitimacy, their political implications, and which rights are more important than others (particularly when we engage in the difficult enterprise of 'balancing' rights).[7] Some of us think rights derive from our understanding of essential human nature,[8] others argue that they arise from a particular liberal commitment to state limitation and political community.[9] Some people reject rights altogether, argue rights divide us and undermine our communities and would prefer to talk about responsibilities.[10] Still, many others think that rights liberate us and bring us justice.[11] The controversy surrounding the rights project, and the conditions in which those who define or even adjudicate upon rights are placed, brings a further level of difficulty in determining the contours of the right to security.

Why is it so important to define the right to security? Calls for tighter definition of legal concepts are usually founded on familiar rule-of-law arguments that clarity and consistency are important in law.[12] Normally, we think of laws as coercive and hence as requiring justification because they impose and infringe upon our autonomy. Why then should we require clarification, or even delimitation, of a right that directly protects our autonomy, at least to the extent that it protects us from invasions on

[6] R. Powell 'The relational concept of security' (2006), available at http://papers.ssrn.com/sol3/papers.cfm?abstract_id=959266 (accessed 2 August 2011); M. Valverde, 'Governing security, governing through security', in R. Daniels, P. Macklem and K. Roach, *The Security of Freedom: Essays on Canada's Anti-Terrorism Bill* (Toronto University Press, 2001) 83, p.85.

[7] A. Ashworth, 'Security, terrorism and the value of human rights', in Goold and Lazarus, *Security and Human Rights*, 203, p.208.

[8] J. Griffin, *On Human Rights* (Oxford University Press, 2008); J. Gardner, 'Simply in virtue of being human: the whos and whys of human rights' (2008) 2:2 *Journal of Ethics & Social Philosophy* 1; T. Endicott, 'What human rights are there – if any – and why?' (2010) 23 *Studies in Christian Ethics* 172.

[9] J. Rawls, *Political Liberalism* (New York: Columbia University Press, 2005); J. Raz, 'Human rights without foundations', Oxford Legal Studies Research Paper No. 14/2007; J. Raz, 'Human rights in the emerging world order', (2010) *Transnational Legal Theory* 31.

[10] A. Etzioni, *The Spirit of Community: Rights, Responsibilities and the Communitarian Agenda* (New York: Crown Publishers, 1993).

[11] See, eg, S. Caney, *Justice Beyond Borders: A Global Political Theory* (New York: Oxford University Press, 2005), p.93.

[12] L Fuller, *The Morality of Law* (New Haven, CN: Yale University Press, 1964).

our sense of personal security? Moreover, if security is indeed 'the right of rights' why should we clarify it at all? This chapter argues that the project of clarification is important because identifying the contours of the right to security results in a delimitation of the state's correlative duty to coerce.

It is because the right to security is frequently taken to imply (both legally and rhetorically) a correlative duty on the state or third parties to coerce others, that it is distinctive from many other rights. While other rights might give rise to such duties, there are few rights so centrally directed at the establishment of coercive duties than the right to security. The term coercive here does not refer to any state limitations on liberty (such as taxation for example), but rather the type of coercion which we typically associate with the state's law enforcement or military apparatus. To that extent, the right to dignity, for example, does not possess a similar coercive sting. Although it might be possible to express criminal laws and police powers as protectors of our dignity, it is less frequently the case that we hear politicians or lawyers calling on the right to dignity when seeking to strengthen law enforcement. In contrast, assertions of the right to security can imply, and increasingly have been politically exploited to mean, increasing police powers, powers of surveillance, powers of pre-trial detention and pre-emptive measures aimed at risk prevention. Also, the right to security is frequently used to legitimate invasions or incursions into countries seen to be a threat to security.

So the right to security is inherently ambiguous. It encapsulates on one hand a commitment to rights, which we commonly associate with absence from coercion, but on the other hand a commitment to coercion in the name of individual and collective security. This ambiguity has been exploited in complex ways, and has particular implications. The political implications of the extension of the right to security, and the direction in which political rhetoric is taking the right, raise the stakes required in clarifying and delimiting the right even further. This chapter will thus seek to present reasons for limiting the right to security to the narrowest possible set of claims and correlative duties on the state, and even to think of a 'right to insecurity'. It will be divided into four further parts: the next will explore the varied legal meanings attributed to the right to security; the third will examine rhetorical expressions of the right to security; the fourth will explore attempts to cast security as a meta-right and the problems involved with this; and the fifth will examine the risks inherent in the symbiotic process of 'securitising rights' and 'righting security'.

Defining the right to security

What then is the right to security? Is it even a right? And if it is a right, what is it a right to?

First, a clarification. There are a number of ways in which the right to security is rhetorically expressed which are not reflected in law. Politicians and government officials frequently refer to the 'right' of a particular state to 'security', but it isn't entirely clear to what they are referring in law.[13] There are rights in international and domestic law which are so closely aligned with the right to security that distinguishing them is difficult. On the international plane, the UN Charter preserves the right of states in certain circumstances to use force in individual and collective self-defence, but this strictly circumscribed right does not alter the Security Council's broad mandate to take action to preserve or restore 'international peace and security'.[14] On the domestic level, the US Constitution (for example) protects 'the right of the people to keep and bear Arms' as 'being necessary to the security of a free State'.[15]

None of these examples are really what I am referring to when I talk about the right to security. This is not to say that self-defence isn't closely aligned with, and a means of, attaining security, or even a justification for the pursuit of security. But the right to security is broader than the right to self-defence. The narrower concept of self-defence refers to action taken in response to some kind of serious threat, though the extent to which that threat must be imminent is now a matter of extensive debate.[16] However,

[13] For example, al-Abbass Abdul Rahman Khalifa, Sudanese army spokesman, said that the army 'was not powerless to deal with such aggressions' and 'we will stay awake guarding our rights of security, peace and stability', reported by Panafrican News Agency *Daily Newswire*, 'Sudan, Chad still trading charges over rebel attacks in Darfur', 30 November 2005.

[14] UN Charter, Art. 51:

> Nothing in the present Charter shall impair the inherent right of individual or collective self-defence if an armed attack occurs against a Member of the United Nations, until the Security Council has taken measures necessary to maintain international peace and security. Measures taken by Members in the exercise of this right of self-defence shall be immediately reported to the Security Council and shall not in any way affect the authority and responsibility of the Security Council under the present Charter to take at any time such action as it deems necessary in order to maintain or restore international peace and security.

[15] Second Amendment of the United States Constitution.

[16] See, eg, A. Dershowitz, *Preemption: A Knife That Cuts Both Ways*, (New York: WW Norton, 2006); cf. H. Shue and D. Rodin (eds.) *Preemption: Military Action and Moral Justification* (Oxford University Press, 2007). For an excellent analysis see S. Wallerstein,

as will become clear throughout this piece, the right to security is now expressly associated with a range of goods and values which encompass much more than responding to actual and imminent threats. So, to be clear, what we are examining here is the right to security, as expressed in these terms in law. We will then examine the term the 'right to security' as expressed in these terms in political rhetoric in the next part of this chapter.

The clearest example of an express right to security is the right to *personal* security laid down in various national constitutions and human rights treaties. What follows is a brief comparative survey of these existing legal expressions, and interpretations, of this right.[17] What do these tell us about the coherence of the right to security? Do they give it clear meaning or substance? At the very least, this exercise can demonstrate law's present ambiguity as to the possible meanings of the right, and the concerns that arise from this. If there is little agreement between legal systems as to what the right to personal security might entail, how can politicians be blamed for their expansive claims for the right in other ways?

Express legal provisions on the right to personal security

The right to personal security is enshrined as a constitutional right in a number of jurisdictions. In the European Convention on Human Rights (ECHR), Canada, South Africa and Hungary the right to personal security is inextricably linked with conceptions of freedom and liberty. For example, Article 5 of the ECHR states that 'everyone has the right to liberty and security of person'. Section 7 of the Canadian Charter of Rights and Freedoms provides that 'everyone has the right to life, liberty, and security of the person, and the right not to be deprived thereof except in accordance with the principles of fundamental justice'. Article 55(1) of the Constitution of Hungary declares that 'everyone has the right to freedom and personal security; no one shall be deprived of his freedom except on the grounds and in accordance with the procedures specified by law'. Finally, Article 12 of the South African Constitution provides that 'everyone has the right to freedom and security of the person.'

'The state's duty of self-defence: justifying the expansion of criminal law' in Goold and Lazarus, *Security and Human Rights*, 277, pp.283–5.

[17] See more in-depth analysis of the law in L. Lazarus, 'Mapping the right to security' in Goold and Lazarus, *Security and Human Rights*, 325, pp.332–43. See also R. Powell, 'The right to security of person in European Court of Human Rights jurisprudence' (2007) 6 EHRLR 649.

In both South Africa and Ireland, the right to security is framed to explicitly include protection from threats to security which arise from non-state sources. The right protected by Article 12 of the South African Constitution includes a number of further specific rights such as the right not to be arbitrarily detained, to be free from violence whether from public or private sources, freedom from torture and cruel, inhuman or degrading treatment or punishment, and the right to bodily and psychological integrity. Similarly, the Northern Ireland Human Rights Commission's now-stalled efforts to draft a Bill of Rights had sought to include a 'the right to be protected from violence', including threats of violence from private sources.[18] The draft bill articulates this right in two ways. In the Preamble, it is expressed as a self-standing principle: 'everyone has the right to live free from violence, fear, oppression and intimidation, with differences to be resolved through exclusively democratic means without the use of threat or force'. The right to be protected against violence is also explicitly grounded in the 'right to dignity and physical integrity' under section 6 of the draft bill.

Legal interpretations of the express right to personal security

A short survey of case law from a range of jurisdictions shows a variety of judicial interpretations of the right to personal security. Some courts take a very broad conception of the right to security. For example, the Canadian Supreme Court held in *Rodriguez* that:

> there is no question that personal autonomy, at least with respect to the right to make choices concerning one's own body, control over one's physical and psychological integrity, and basic human dignity are encompassed within security of the person, at least to the extent of freedom from criminal prohibitions which interfere with these.[19]

Other courts, like the European Court of Human Rights, take a very narrow view of the right to security of person. Reflecting the wording of Article 5 ECHR, which omits any further mention of security after the first sentence, the court often elides security with liberty under Article 5.[20]

[18] Northern Ireland Human Rights Commission, 'Progressing a Bill of Rights for Northern Ireland: an update', April 2004.

[19] *Rodriquez* v. *British Columbia (Attorney General)* [1993] 3 SCR 519.

[20] Powell, 'The relational concept of security'.

In *Adler and Biuvas* v. *Federal Republic of Germany*, the Court noted that the terms 'liberty' and 'security' should be read as a whole,[21] while in *Bozano* v. *France*, it stipulated that Article 5 deals with arbitrary deprivation of liberty rather than protecting against threats to a person's safety by other private individuals.[22] The concept of security has received passing mention in a small number of cases,[23] but the consensus remains 'that the case law has not ascribed any separate meaning to 'security of person' in Article 5'.[24] Comparing the Canadian and the European approaches we can see that the right to security may mean everything – including the right to personal autonomy, control over physical and psychological integrity, and human dignity – or nothing at all.

The approach of the South African Constitutional Court has been exacting, though pragmatic. The right to security has been developed to protect against domestic violence in *Baloyi*,[25] and to protect against the risk of rape in *Carmichele*.[26] In *Metrorail* the Court found a constitutional duty to protect rail commuters from violent assault.[27] Given the security environment in South Africa, the correlative obligation resulting from the right to security has centred on reasonableness, proximity and resource constraints. Nevertheless, the principle of constitutional accountability was held to require 'decision-makers to disclose their reasons for their conduct'.[28]

The South African Constitutional Court has restricted protective duties mainly to freedom from violence and construed the state's duty towards individual citizens with due regard to resource constraints and proximity issues (analogous to private law considerations such as

[21] Appls 5573/72, Yearbook XX (1977) p.102 (146).

[22] *Bozano* v. *France* (1986) 9 EHRR 297. See also *X* v. *Ireland* (1973) 16 YB 388, EComm HR.

[23] *Orhan* v. *Turkey* [2002] ECHR 25656/94, para.368; *Kurt* v. *Turkey* (1999) 27 EHRR 373, 378, para.6(b); *Cyprus* v. *Turkey* (2001) 11 BHRC 45, paras.223–7; *Khudoyorov* v. *Russia* [2005] ECHR 6847/02, para.142.

[24] R. Clayton and H. Tomlinson, *The Law of Human Rights* (Oxford University Press, 2009) p.628.

[25] *State* v. *Baloyi (Minister of Justice Intervening)* 2000 (1) BCLR 86 (CC). Article 12(1)(c) of the South African Constitution 'obliges the State directly to protect the right of everyone to be free from private or domestic violence'.

[26] *Carmichele* v. *Minister of Safety and Security and Another* 2001 (4) BCLR 938 (CC). The state is under a duty to fulfil this right, and deviation is only warranted in the public interest.

[27] *Rail Commuters Action Group and Others* v. *Transnet Ltd t/a Metrorail and Others* 2005 (4) BCLR 301 (CC).

[28] Ibid.

tort/delict). As it happens, the European Court of Human Rights,[29] the Indian Supreme Court,[30] and the German Federal Constitutional Court,[31] have implied similar obligations from the right to life, the right to freedom from torture and the right to private life. As I have argued elsewhere,[32] the development of these implied rights raises the question whether an express right to security is needed at all.

A slightly different manifestation of personal security has arisen on the international stage in the form of a non-justiciable right to 'human security', most recently in Article 143 of the United Nations General Assembly 2005 World Summit Outcome Document. The language of Article 143 is striking in its breadth:

> We stress the right of people to live in freedom and dignity, free from poverty and despair. We recognize that all individuals, in particular vulnerable people, are entitled to freedom from fear and freedom from want, with an equal opportunity to enjoy all their rights and fully develop their human potential. To this end, we commit ourselves to discussing and defining the notion of human security in the General Assembly.

The UN conception of human security now encompasses rights which many of us consider to be long-established, fundamental and free-standing. So, under Article 143, human security expressly encompasses a right to 'dignity', 'equality' in the broadest sense of having an 'equal opportunity to enjoy all their rights and fully develop their human potential', and 'liberty' in the broadest positive sense of being 'free from fear and want' and 'poverty and despair'. This breadth, and the matter of

29 *Osman* v. *UK* (1998) 29 EHRR 245 states that 'Article 2 (ECHR) may also imply in certain well-defined circumstances a positive obligation on the authorities to take preventive operational measures to protect an individual whose life is at risk from the criminal acts of another individual'. The case law on rape is particularly interesting here with protective obligations arising from Arts. 3 and 8 ECHR against invasions of 'sexual autonomy' and 'security'. See *MC* v. *Bulgaria* (2005) 40 EHRR 20 and L. Lazarus, 'The human rights framework relating to the handling, investigation and prosecution of rape complaints', Annex A to the *Stern Report on The Handling of Rape Complaints* (Government Equalities Office and Home Office, March 2010), available at www.equalities.gov.uk/download_links/s/stern_review.aspx.

30 *National Human Rights Commission* v. *State of Arunachal Pradesh and another* AIR 1996 SC 1234; *Manjit Singh Sawhney* v. *Union of India* 2005 Indlaw DEL 379; K. Cooper-Stephenson, 'The emergence of constitutional torts worldwide', presented at the Conference on Comparative Constitutionalism on 12 December 2005, University of Kwazulu, Natal, South Africa.

31 BVerfGE 46, 160/164; 56, 54/80ff; 79, 174/202; 85, 191/212.

32 Lazarus, 'Mapping the right to security', p.341.

whether the right to security should be viewed as the right upon which equality, dignity and liberty rest, is an issue we will return to below.

To sum up the domestic and international law position: if we take a sweeping view of the Canadian, European and South African approaches to the right to personal security, and the United Nations approach to human security, we can see that the right to security can protect dignity, equality, liberty, physical and psychological autonomy, freedom from fear and freedom from want. The range of goods and interests this right promises to protect is extensive,[33] and we are left with a sneaking suspicion that the right to security can be deployed to protect most things that we want in life.[34]

Rhetorical expressions of the right to security

If the law has left us unclear about the contours of the right to security, politics has shed even less light. What we do know is that politicians deploy the right to security with enthusiasm, and the right is becoming an increasingly important rhetorical tool in security politics globally.

A global search on Lexis for references to the phrase 'the right to security' over the past twelve years in the English-speaking press yielded over 400 deployments of that phrase. Almost half of those dated from the last two years, which may suggest an increasing trend. The number of politicians, public figures, newspaper editors and journalists that use this language, not to mention the range of jurisdictions and issues to which the right is connected, is significant.

It will come as little surprise to readers that the phrase 'the right to security' is used most frequently with respect to the Middle East (ninety-nine results). As George W. Bush declared:

> I can understand the deep anger and anguish of the Israeli people. You've lived too long with fear and funerals, having to avoid markets and public transportation, and forced to put armed guards in kindergarten classrooms. The Palestinian Authority has rejected your offered hand and trafficked with terrorists. You have a right to a normal life. You have *a right to security*. And I deeply believe that you need a reformed, responsible Palestinian partner to achieve that security.[35]

[33] Powell also arrives at this conclusion. See R. Powell, 'Security and the right to security of person', doctoral thesis, University of Oxford Faculty of Law, 2008.

[34] See, eg, Fredman, 'The Positive Right to Security'.

[35] George Bush, 'Remarks on the Middle East', speech from the Rose Garden of the White House, 24 June 2002. Full text available at http://www-cgi.cnn.com/2002/ALLPOLITICS/06/24/bush.mideast.speech/index.html (accessed 14 September 2010) (emphasis added).

George Bush has been joined by Barack Obama, Nicolas Sarkozy, Vladimir Putin, Franco Fini, David Milliband and Colin Powell (amongst others) who have all asserted the collective right to security of the Israeli people, although they vary as to the extent to which this right is to be balanced against the 'right to security' of Palestinians and their 'right to an independent State'. This language is all well and good, but it's also worth noting that other states, such as North Korea, also invoke their own 'right to security' in the context of nuclear or other military threats.[36]

It will come as no surprise to readers that the right to security is frequently deployed in the discussion on the 'war on terror'. The right has been deployed to justify tightening anti-terrorism measures both within and outside the USA or even to justify military invasion of or responses in Afghanistan,[37] Kosovo,[38] Pakistan[39] and, in Colombia's case, Ecuador.[40] There are many examples, but two will demonstrate this point well enough. When introducing the EU counter-terrorism strategy, Franco Frattini stated 'our political goal remains to strike the right balance between the fundamental right to security of citizens, which is first, right to life, and the other fundamental rights of individuals, including privacy and procedural rights'.[41] Similarly,

36 See *The Associated Press*, 'Non-aligned meeting backs calls for Iraq to disarm; Malaysia warns attack on Iraq would be considered a "war against Muslims"', 23 February 2003: 'On Sunday, Pyongyang insisted on additional guarantees for its right to security and self defense, Asian delegates said on condition of anonymity. Pyongyang has never admitted having nuclear weapons but cites its right to develop nuclear weapons for self defense.'

37 E. Cochrane, 'Troops deserve our support', *Carstairs Courier* (Alberta), 6 November 2007.

38 *The Vancouver Sun*, 'Yeltsin's final fling: The Russian leader, often portrayed in the West as a boorish drunk, had substance that belied his unvarnished style', 27 January 2001: 'The Kosovo conflict demonstrated the worst political tendencies and double standards of modern Europe. It was claimed, for example, that human rights were more important than the rights of a single state. But when you violate the rights of a state, you automatically and egregiously violate the rights of its citizens, including their rights to security.'

39 *The Press Trust of India*, 'Pak should give firm assurance against abetting terrorism', 30 December 2001: 'Stating that terrorism had crossed the *lakshman rekha* (the limit of patience) with the December 13 attack on Indian Parliament, Advani said, "no sovereign nation which is conscious of its right to security can sit silent. It has to think as to what steps need to be taken to check this menace".' (Quoting India's Federal Home Minister L. Advani in a programme on national broadcaster, Doordarshan).

40 *BBC Worldwide Monitoring*, 'Colombia defends its incursion into Ecuador' 23 March 2008: Communiqué issued by the Presidency of the Republic in Bogota on 22 March. 'The Colombian Government hereby expresses:

1. Its full observance of the decisions adopted by the OAS.
2. Reminds the world that the camp of alias "Raul Reyes" was a site of terrorists who acted against the *right to security* of the Colombian people.' (Emphasis added.)

41 European Commissioner responsible for Justice, Freedom and Security 'EU counter-terrorism strategy' European Parliament, 5 September 2007, Speech/07/505.

discussing UK counter-terrorism policy in 2006, John Reid, former Home Secretary, stated: 'as we face the threat of mass murder we have to accept that the rights of the individual that we enjoy must and will be balanced with the collective right of security and the protection of life and limb that our citizens demand'.[42]

Politicians are not alone in deploying this language. Citizens too articulate the right to security in relation to the 'war on terror'. As Emily Cochrane wrote in the *Carstairs Courier* in Alberta:

> The Canadian Charter of Rights and Freedoms, ... declares the right of security of person. When members of the Taliban terrorist organization crashed those planes in a calculated attack against America on 9/11, killing 2,973 people, those that supported those actions and those who would offer them refuge, forfeited their rights of security as they had caused the loss of life of so many others. The US people have a right to security – to live without fear, and the only way to achieve that end was to neutralize the threat from the source.[43]

These references tell us two important things: firstly, that the right to security is deployed to strengthen political rhetoric in the context of international military disputes and the war on terror in a subtle and important way. This process of legitimisation (or perhaps sanitisation) by reference to rights discourse is what we might term 'righting' security. The framing of the right to security allows politicians to present their coercive actions as the necessary correlative of a right. In other words, pursuing security is not merely a political choice in pursuance of a public good, it is the fulfilment of a duty imposed upon the state by each individual's basic right to security.

Crucially, too, framing such state actions as having been taken in pursuit of our basic right is central to the rhetoric of 'rebalancing' between security and human rights. This language of rebalancing commonly poses the rights to security of the majority against the rights of minorities which might be infringed. The intrinsic 'othering' in this rebalancing rhetoric is well exemplified by the former Attorney-General Lord Goldsmith, who argued that it is difficult to strike a 'simple utilitarian calculation of balancing the right to security of the many against the legal rights of the few'.[44] Nevertheless, politicians do disagree as to the weight the right to security carries, and hence where to strike

[42] J. Reid, 'Rights, security must be balanced', *Associated Press Online* 16 August 2006.

[43] Cochrane, 'Troops deserve our support'.

[44] Full text of speech reported by *BBC News* 'Lord Goldsmith's speech in Full' 25 June 2004, available at http://news.bbc.co.uk/2/hi/uk_news/politics/3839153.stm (accessed 14 September 2010).

the balance between security and competing defensive rights. While John Reid believes that 'the right to security, to the protection of life and liberty, is and should be the basic right on which all others are based',[45] Sir Menzies Campbell notes that while 'the public has a right to security' it 'also has a right to security against the power of the state'.[46] Such a framing of security as a defensive right against state intervention is less commonly deployed in political rhetoric, however, than the positive dimension of the right that results in state coercive duties.

These varying ideas on the right to security, and its weight in the balance between security and liberty, play directly into how governments strengthen policing powers and evaluate military activity in the face of a security threat. There is very little clarity or guidance on how to balance the right to security where it is invoked to legitimate state force either in the international or the domestic context. This is problematic, because the scope of the right to security, its weight in relation to other rights, its permissible limitations, and the correlative duties that it imposes on the state, are all prior questions that need answering before we can determine how any 'balance' might be achieved.

Is security a basic right?

In this environment a key question is whether security is a basic right; or a specific right derived from broader grounding rights or principles; or a meta-right, in other words a right which grounds other rights. The claim to the right to security being a basic right is one many politicians are inclined to make. As noted above, John Reid described the right to security as 'the basic right on which all others are based'.[47] Similarly, Franco Frattini, European Commissioner responsible for Justice, Freedom and Security, considers the right to be 'a precondition for all other freedoms'.[48]

[45] Full text of speech reported by *BBC News* 'Reid urges human rights shake-up' 12 May 2007, available at http://news.bbc.co.uk/2/hi/uk_news/politics/6648849.stm (accessed 14 September 2010).

[46] Speech made in the House of Commons debates into extending the limits of pre-charge detention, 25 July 2007, HC Deb., vol. 463, col. 851. Ironically, this framing of security as a defensive right against state action was part of the rationale behind the Second Amendment of the US Constitution which allowed for an armed citizenry to defend against abuses by undemocratic government (L. Emery, 'The Constitutional right to keep and bear arms' 28(5) *Harvard Law Review* (1915) 473, 476).

[47] Reid, HC Deb, note 46 above.

[48] Speech, 14 July 2005, reported by M. Rice-Oxley in *Christian Science Monitor*, 'How far will Europe go to stop terror', available at www.csmonitor.com/2005/0715/p01s02-woeu.html/ (accessed 14 September 2010).

Again, politicians and judges are not alone. Henry Shue also argues that security constitutes a basic right because without it enjoyment of all other rights would be impossible.[49] Shue's account of the right to security is essentially instrumentalist: security is a precondition to the enjoyment of all other rights. But Shue also argues that the instrumental nature of a right to security does not destroy the claim to recognise security as a basic right. In one sense it seems obvious that we can't enjoy other rights if our lives are constantly at risk. Locke is clear that liberty is integrally linked to personal security. In his Second Treatise, he casts as a slave someone who cannot exert power over his own life.[50] But does Shue's instrumental argument regarding the relationship between personal security and the enjoyment of rights support the much broader proposition that the right to security is the right of rights: the meta-right upon which all other rights rest?

There are a number of arguments why the right to security cannot, and must not, displace the non-instrumental values of liberty, dignity and equality, as the grounding foundation of human rights.[51] In order to understand the first difficulty of conceiving of security as a meta-right, we have to read this claim against the background of the global security environment since 9/11 in which security is constantly pitted against rights. Framing security as a meta-right gives it a subtle and different weight in the balancing process to what it would have if it is considered to be only a collective goal (or for that matter a specific right). Jeremy Waldron explains this well:

> Many people think we would be safer if we were to abandon some of our rights or at least cut back on some of our more aggressive claims about the extent and importance of our civil liberties. Or maybe the trade-off should go in the other direction. Many people think we should be a little braver and risk a bit more in the way of security to uphold our precious rights. After all, security is not the be-all and the end-all; our rights are what really matter. But this alternative line will not work if it turns out that our security is valuable, not just for its own sake, but for the sake of our rights. What if the enjoyment of our rights is possible only when we

[49] H. Shue, *Basic Rights: Subsistence, Affluence, and US Foreign Policy* (2nd edn.) (Princeton University Press, 1996).

[50] John Locke, *Second Treatise of Government* (1690) ch. 4, paras.22–4. This has been linked by Norris to Agamben's discussion of 'bare life' (A. Norris, 'The exemplary exception: philosophical and political decisions in Giorgio Agamben's *Homo Sacer*', in A. Norris (ed.) *Politics, Metaphysics and Death* (Durham,, NC: Duke University Press, 2005) 262, p.273).

[51] Lazarus, 'Mapping the right to security'.

> are already secure against various forms of violent attack? If rights are worth nothing without security, then the brave alternative that I alluded to is misconceived.[52]

But of course the danger of making a claim doesn't necessarily make it implausible. How plausible is it that security is a meta-right?

Let us first ask what a right to security (as a basic right or meta-right in Shue's language) entails. For Shue the answer is simple: it is a right not to be subjected to murder, torture, mayhem, rape or assault, i.e. to physical security.[53] But this sounds very close to a specific right. If this is to be a claim to a meta-right, as a foundational platform giving rise to other more specific rights, surely the claim must be broader than this.

From an objective perspective, the right to security entails the establishment of the factual conditions which give rise to the achievement of someone's actual security – namely the absence from threats or risks of threats – which results in her being able to enjoy other rights. From a subjective perspective, we may require a *feeling* of security which entails the absence of anxiety or apprehension. Clearly, subjective security does not establish a sound basis, on its own, upon which to frame a right to security. There would have to be some rational objective test to evaluate the absence of risk – which should correlate with a reasonable person's perception of the existence of that risk. In both these subjective and objective states, the relationship to risk is crucial. But the important point here is that, even if we can establish some objective framework for evaluating the existence of the risk, we only really give the right substance if it bears a relationship to the enjoyment of other rights. Shue argues that security is a basic right because its fulfilment provides the factual preconditions to the enjoyment of other rights. The right to security is therefore *a right to secure rights.*

So, let's try to formulate this argument for a basic right to security again: the right to security is a right giving rise to a correlative duty on the state to establish the factual conditions in which objective risks of imminent and future threats that give rise to reasonable subjective feelings of apprehension or insecurity, are minimised to such a degree that the enjoyment of all other rights is possible.

When looked at in this way, the basic right to security is a description of the factual preconditions relating to the absence of risks, which

[52] J. Waldron, 'Security as a basic right (after 9/11)' in *Torture, Terror and Trade-Offs: Philosophy for the White House* (Oxford University Press, 2010) p.166.

[53] Shue, *Basic Rights*, pp.69–71.

enables the enjoyment of other rights. There are a number of problems with this proposition. They are: first, the problem of vagueness and indeterminability; second, the problem of duplication; third, the weakness of the precondition argument; fourth, the confusion of preconditions with foundations; and fifth, the risk of securitisation.

The first objection – vagueness – is the typical lawyer's objection. The right is simply too broad and too vague. You cannot pin it down sufficiently to frame the rights that flow from it as a result, or even the correlative duties that might allow for such rights to be fulfilled. We might argue that such a problem exists for other grounding rights, such as dignity for example. But the breadth of the right to security is particularly problematic because of the right's close relationship with inscrutable perceptions of future risk. This particularly undermines jurisprudential constraints on the potential range of associated rights claims. We have created a right that is all about the avoidance of risks that might undermine the enjoyment of other rights. But how foreseeable do these risks have to be? And how much risk can we live with in order to exercise our rights?

The second objection is duplication. It is not clear that the right to security adds anything to the other rights that are meant to be secured. And, conversely, we could also say that the constituents of the right to security are provided by the fulfilment of other rights. It seems, then, that the meta-right to security is nothing more than a hologram: a right you can put your hand through. At the very least, it is not a thing (or a right) in itself.

Third, security is not necessarily always a precondition to the exercise of all rights. Waldron argues convincingly that it may be possible to exercise certain rights even in conditions of insecurity, that is, because 'security is not an all-or-nothing matter, but a matter of more or less'.[54] Security may be provided in a patchy way, but rights may be exercised in any event and there are many countries in the world today where this is the case. I could vote in the morning and get mugged in the afternoon. Moreover, there is the danger that Waldron also warns us about, that we may become so fixated on the fulfilment of the necessary preconditions in order to exercise rights that we might end up not fulfilling our rights at all. We might have perfect security but very little liberty. As Waldron warns us, security is a 'voracious ideal'.[55]

[54] Waldron, 'Security as a Basic Right', p.177. [55] Ibid.

Fourth, as I have also argued elsewhere,[56] there is a difference between foundational rights and preconditional rights. The confusion between them is a confusion of *value-based* claims with *factual* claims. Take the right to life, for example. Clearly, being alive is a necessary precondition to the enjoyment of other rights. Yet we do not view this as a foundational *value*, but rather as a factual state. In value terms, life would have very little meaning beyond bare existence unless we were able to live our lives as freely as possible (liberty) so as to enable our personal development as individuals (dignity), with the same opportunities as others (equality).[57] What is different, you might say, about security? Why are the values of liberty, equality and dignity foundational, if security is not? Surely, living life 'securely' is a precondition to the enjoyment of life? The question, however, is whether this is enough to make security a foundational value.

To say that a right is foundational is to argue that it grounds (or provides a value-based platform for) other, more specific, rights in *value-based* terms.[58] Let us take the right to a fair trial for example. Because we accept that the liberty of individuals is a fundamental right, we establish specific rights (such as the right to an independent and impartial tribunal, or the right to silence in a police station) that protect the innocent from being convicted for crimes they have not committed. Judges, when they reason about rights, often resort to arguments about the value of liberty, in asserting specific rights to fair-trial protections. Another example might be dignity-based rights. Jurisdictions which seek to protect the basic right to dignity normally accept that they should protect against torture and inhuman treatment.

What would a fundamental right to security add to this? Many legal provisions refer to 'liberty and security' of person. But it is very unclear what the word 'security' adds, as the European Court of Human Rights jurisprudence reflects. The right to liberty is both the absence of coercion, and the capacity to utilise our freedom. The right to security, as a basic right in the formulation above, either means the same thing, or it means that this right to liberty will be secured. Liberty is the foundational right here; security only adds the factual guarantee that liberty will be secured. It cannot be said to add anything in and of itself.

[56] Lazarus, 'Mapping the right to security'.

[57] See also G. Agamben, *Homo Sacer: Sovereign Power and Bare Life* (Palo Alto, CA: Stanford University Press, 1998).

[58] This value-based approach is often the one adopted in constitutional systems that apply foundational principles and rights (such as those of South Africa or Germany) in their interpretation of rights.

The other way to think about this is to imagine what a right to security would mean in a society without dignity, equality or liberty. What rights would it give rise to? Does it have any grounding value? Here we confront the difficulty that security means very little in and of itself. As Powell argues, 'security is a *relational* rather than a *substantive* concept. It provides a framework for integrating other concepts but it has no "content" of its own.'[59] Security in itself cannot be understood without answering the questions: security of what? Security of whom? In other words, it is almost impossible to understand security without some 'referent': a right to security of 'person' or of 'goods', for example.

We might argue that, at the very least, the right to security could mean the absence of threats to life. But it would have very little meaning beyond the bare fact of survival, unless we understood and accepted as a society that liberty, dignity and equality were fundamental values to be secured. And in any event, it could just as easily be argued that, if we only had one right, it would be the right to life, and the right to security would be a superfluous one if it only meant the right to secure life.

All of these are strong objections. But I argue that the most serious risk in calling the right to security a meta-right is the risk that we will slip from a sense that the right to security merely exists to affirm other rights, to a belief which actively 'securitises' those rights. In the process we may also end up 'righting' security.

Securitising rights

Securitisation, simply put, is an act of speech which results in security becoming the lens through which more and more social issues, problems and categories are viewed.[60] Loader and Walker argue persuasively that securitisation occurs when security is 'elevated to an unhealthily hegemonic category and comes to mean the unreflexive, parochial and anxious cleaving to a security-driven conception of a risk-free society'.[61]

Why does the meta-right to security potentially risk securitising rights? I argued above that there is a strong difference between seeing rights as preconditional and seeing them as foundational. But with respect to the right to security, political and popular rhetoric show few signs of appreciating the subtle distinction between the two. And here is the real danger: if we think security is the 'foundation' of rights

59 Powell, 'Security and the Right to Security of Person'.

60 Zedner, *Security*, pp.23–5.

61 Loader and Walker, *Civilizing Security*, p.168.

(confusing *fact* and *value*), we risk securitising rights. The double trump of rights (normatively) and security (politically) means that claims to a right to security are potent when used in political rhetoric, legitimating coercive action. In this environment, the narrative shifts in subtle ways to favour the protective role of the state. As Lord Hope argues 'the first responsibility of government in a democratic society is owed to the public. It is to protect and safeguard the lives of its citizens'.[62]

How does this securitisation occur? Let's return for a moment to John Reid's statement noted earlier: 'the right to security, to the protection of life and liberty, is and should be the basic right on which all others are based'. Here the former Home Secretary argues that the rights to life and liberty are essentially subsumed in the notion of security. In other words, life and liberty have become securitised values. But isn't the right to liberty essential to the pursuit of human development? We need to be free to make our own choices in order to become the people we are. So liberty might mean something entirely different to security; it might, in fact, mean that we have to embrace risk. But if we look at this through the lens of security, as the foundational right for life and liberty, we don't associate liberty necessarily with human flourishing which may necessitate risk – we associate it with the absence of foreseeable risk. Hence, the order matters – at least for liberals. Security does not come first.[63]

If we think of security as the root of liberty, we risk reducing liberty to a single dimension. Or at least, we might forget that the two may mean very different things. Perhaps liberals need to think less about security. Perhaps the most liberal response is in fact to stand for a right to *insecurity*. To argue for such a right would be to argue for a right to unknowns, surprise and risk taking necessary to a process of self-creation. It would be to argue in effect for a right to freedom, as 'the point is, with freedom comes risk and insecurity; it is a necessary concomitant of the liberal society'.[64] For those who think that arguing for a right to insecurity is frivolous at times like this, we ought at the very least to argue for restraint in the deployment of the right to security. If there is to be such a thing as a right to security, it must be a specific right which captures the difference between the right to

[62] *Secretary of State for the Home Department* v. *F* ([2009] 3 WLR 74, para.76.

[63] As opposed to the argument of A. Etzioni in *Security First: For a Muscular, Moral Foreign Policy* (New Haven, CN: Yale University Press, 2007).

[64] L. Lazarus, 'Inspecting the tail of the dog' in M. McCarthy (ed.), *Incarceration and Human Rights* (Manchester University Press, 2010).

security and the right to be secure (incorporating as it would a right to a range of valuable human goods).[65]

So it is important that human rights advocates are more sceptical of the right to security, and resist securitising rights. The temptation is considerable because rights appear to be losing out in the political battle with security. Rights seem no longer to be politically animating claims in and of themselves. Hence, when faced with the ostensible opposition between security and human rights since 9/11, rights advocates often seek to protect rights by arguing that there is no conflict because security is a basic right.[66] Equally, those seeking to advance socio-economic rights have begun to advance them using the human security agenda.[67]

But the difficulty here is that this language of the right to security also serves those less interested in rights. As the third section of this chapter clearly demonstrates, the right to security is frequently deployed to legitimise and justify coercive force and military activity. It is clear, from that analysis, that those seeking to advance the security agenda are very well served by the right to security. It is much easier to sanitise security measures by referring to them as the correlative of a right, as the pursuance of a duty, than it is simply to describe them as a political decision in the face of a supposed threat. As I have explained, this process of legitimating security through rights talk, is the process of 'righting' security.

We see then a complex interaction in the deployment of the language of the right to security. On one hand, the right to security is deployed by rights activists to legitimate rights through security; on the other hand, political actors deploy the right to legitimate security. The normative appeal of rights and the political appeal of security mean claims to a right to security are potently used by politicians and rights activists alike to legitimate both security and rights.

Conclusion

How then do we avoid this vicious circle: securitising rights and righting security? Simply put, we must begin with a sceptical analysis of broad claims to the content of the right to security. If a right to security is to

[65] Fredman, 'The positive right to security'.

[66] See, e.g., W. Schulz: 'Amnesty International is not criticizing the war on terror in and of itself by any means. We condemned unequivocally the 9/11 events. That is a horrific human rights violation. The right to security is a basic human right.' *Safer or Scared? Impact of the War on Terror* – CNN, 28 May 2003.

[67] See, e.g., Fredman, 'The positive right to security'.

exist at all, it ought to be a specific right which can cover something distinctive that other self-standing fundamental rights do not capture. Thus, we should argue that a duty correlative of a right to security can mean only the development of structures and institutions capable of responding to and minimising 'critical and pervasive threats' to human safety, namely absence from harm in the most central, physical sense of harm to person. Importantly, the right to security must be grounded in dignity, equality and liberty, and not the other way round.

If we fail to keep the right to security securely in its place, there is a real danger that the right to security might not result just in the erosion of rights which protect liberty. This chapter has argued that there is a more sinister danger in securitising rights, namely that the rhetoric of the 'right to security' as a meta-right could displace a hard-won, carefully reasoned, yet fragile, consensus around the foundation of fundamental rights. In parallel, this rhetoric, when deployed by certain political actors, also has the potential to 'right' security. In other words, to sanitise coercive measures which might otherwise be less palatable. Courts, legal practitioners, scholars are in a unique position to safeguard the integrity of human rights. It is imperative that we keep the scope of the right to security distinct and its content specific. By limiting the scope of the right to security, not only can we tame extensive claims to security, we can secure rights.

6

Of fortresses and caltrops: national security and competing models of rights protection

C. R. G. MURRAY

Introduction

The preamble of the Universal Declaration of Human Rights (UDHR) famously asserts the significance of the 'recognition of the inherent dignity and of the equal and inalienable rights of all members of the human family' as 'the foundation of freedom, justice and peace in the world'.[1] If a country is to be regarded as 'rights-respecting', therefore, the state must endeavour to secure these interests in its dealings with all individuals subject to its jurisdiction. As David Kennedy argues, however, human rights standards are often approached pragmatically by governments, which seek to accrue legitimacy from their recognition as being 'rights-respecting' whilst, at the same time, seeking to maintain the maximum scope for freedom of action.[2] Moreover, in spite of the claims made within the UDHR, states still attach profoundly different values to certain rights and maintain widely varying mechanisms for securing them.

Focusing specifically upon the United States of America and the United Kingdom, this chapter examines whether the operation of human rights norms within domestic legal systems constitutes evidence of what Costas Douzinas describes as 'the – incomplete – legalisation of politics which made positive law the terrain of both power and its critique'.[3] The key word in this statement is 'incomplete'. The tension inherent in Douzinas's observation is that the potential to legalise (or

My thanks to Tom Frost (Newcastle University), Aoife O'Donoghue (Durham University) and Ole Pedersen (Newcastle University) for their advice and comments upon earlier drafts of this article. Any errors remain my own.

[1] GA Res. 217 A (III), UN Doc. A/810 (10 December 1948).

[2] See Chapter 2 above.

[3] C. Douzinas, *The End of Human Rights* (Oxford: Hart, 2000) p.20.

constitutionalise)[4] systems of government is not limitless and all states must engineer a zone for political decision-making and democratic discussion which is neither settled nor conducted in the courtroom. This chapter first addresses how the USA and the UK adopted what, by the late twentieth century, were atypical domestic approaches to civil and political rights. Despite these atypical rights-protection structures, the two countries' signature and ratification of the International Covenant on Civil and Political Rights was intended to convey their governments' belief that their domestic arrangements sufficed to protect such interests.[5] This belief requires an examination of whether these rights-protection approaches have adequately secured civil and political rights, especially where such rights have been affected by legislation and policy decisions made in response to the attacks of 11 September 2001. In both countries, these attacks precipitated major security responses. In both, the aftermath of the attacks saw the executive branch display a 'security bias'[6] stemming from the political dangers of underaction in response to terrorism.[7] But, it will be argued, the form of domestic rights-protection arrangements plays a role in shaping executive responses to terrorism, potentially channelling such measures against certain groups or interests which are less firmly protected under a country's domestic law.

Human rights in the United States and the United Kingdom: an uneasy constitutional fit

The USA and the UK, despite their shared history, have approached the question of the constitutionalisation of their systems of governance, and particularly the place of rights within this process, very differently.

4 See A. Peters, 'Compensatory constitutionalism: the function and potential of fundamental international norms and structures' (2006) 19 *Leiden Journal of International Law* 579, 582.

5 999 UNTS 171 (13 March 1976). Neither state has made the ICCPR as a whole enforceable under its domestic law. See, however, in the context of the UK's incorporation of Article 14(6) ICCPR, *R.* v *Secretary of State for the Home Department, ex parte Mullen* [2004] UKHL 18, at [35]–[36] (Lord Steyn).

6 F. de Londras and F. Davis, 'Controlling the executive in times of terrorism: competing perspectives on effective oversight mechanisms' (2010) 30 OJLS 19, 21. See also P. Thomas, 'September 11th and good governance' (2002) 53 *Northern Ireland Legal Quarterly* 366.

7 See D. Bigo and E. Guild, 'The worst-case scenario and the man on the Clapham omnibus' in B. Goold and L. Lazarus, *Security and Human Rights* (Oxford: Hart, 2007) 99. For a succinct defence of the need for the executive to maintain the capacity to react, and even overreact, see A. Vermeule, 'Self-defeating proposals: Ackerman on emergency powers' (2006) 75 *Fordham Law Review* 631.

Sir Igor Judge, delivering a sweeping paean to the two countries' shared constitutional heritage at the 2010 Bench & Bar Conference in Colorado, attempted to diagnose the source of this divergence: '[I]n our [UK] arrangements the potential for tyranny was gradually removed by insisting on the parliamentary legislative process, and victory in battle.... For you a sovereign Parliament was the problem. It could therefore not be the solution.'[8] So it was, according to the Lord Chief Justice, that the seventeenth-century victories of Parliament's armies came to establish parliamentary sovereignty in the UK whilst the rebellion by the colonies which went on to form the USA, fomented in response to Parliament's passing of the Duties in American Colonies Act 1765, produced a form of government limited by the US Constitution (including the Bill of Rights).

The USA provides a useful focal point in assessing the operation of human rights within domestic legal systems because, as Claire Palley recognises, it was in the early days of the independence of what were previously Great Britain's American colonies that 'human rights ideals were first given effect in institutional form'.[9] Nonetheless, this venerable constitutional system is difficult to reconcile with consequent developments in the concept of human rights. Francesca Klug contrasts the Enlightenment preoccupations of the 'first-wave' US Bill of Rights with the UDHR and the European Convention on Human Rights and Fundamental Freedoms (ECHR),[10] which she casts as 'second-wave' human rights documents:

> In essence the transition from the first to the second wave of rights is represented by a shift from a preoccupation with the rights and liberties of individual citizens within particular nation states to a preoccupation with creating a better world for everyone. Both waves were aimed at protecting individuals from tyranny but the vision of how to achieve that goal had shifted. In the earlier era the main target was to set people free; in the later period it was to create a sense of moral purpose for all humankind.[11]

[8] I. Judge, '"No taxation without representation': a British perspective upon constitutional arrangements' (28 August 2010), pp.9–10, available at www.judiciary.gov.uk/media/speeches/2010/lcj-speech-no-representation-without-taxation (accessed 2 August 2011).

[9] C. Palley, *The United Kingdom and Human Rights* (London: Sweet & Maxwell, 1991) p.1.

[10] 213 UNTS 222 (3 September 1953).

[11] F. Klug, 'The Human Rights Act – a "third way" or a "third wave" Bill of Rights' (2001) EHRLR 361, 364. See also S. Moyn, *The Last Utopia: Human Rights in History* (London: Belknap, 2010) p.12.

Later human rights documents provide for a more extensive range of human rights than were originally enumerated under the US Constitution, although many of the rights contained within treaties such as the ECHR were also subject to nuanced formulations which accounted for countervailing community interests which could be invoked by states to enable them to restrict rights.

If the rights provided for under the US Constitution do not map perfectly to modern conceptions of civil and political rights, the centrality of parliamentary sovereignty to the UK's constitution made its legal system even less hospitable ground for the concept of human rights. The Wilson government's decision to allow applicants to petition the European Court of Human Rights from 1966 onwards provided a neat ruse, maintaining the UK's credentials as a rights-respecting democracy whilst keeping the ECHR at arm's length from the domestic legal system. But as the volume of cases brought against the UK before the ECHR's judicial organs began to increase, and as figures including Lord Scarman and Lord Hailsham began to advocate a Bill of Rights in the 1970s,[12] the writing appeared to be on the wall for the 'political' constitution. In the face of this onslaught J. A. G. Griffith mounted his famous defence of a constitutional system which did not repose ultimate authority in the courts:

> For centuries political philosophers have sought that society in which government is by laws and not by men. It is an unattainable ideal. Written constitutions do not achieve it. Nor do Bills of Rights or any other devices. They merely pass political decisions out of the hands of politicians and into the hands of judges and other persons.[13]

Griffith's howl of defiance was profoundly out of step with the apparent trajectory of constitutional developments in the UK.[14] In its 1979 manifesto (at Lord Hailsham's instigation), even the Conservative Party committed itself to all-party discussions on a Bill of Rights. These plans, however, were shelved soon after Margaret Thatcher entered office.[15] At the same time as the Thatcher government was moving to ensure its freedom of action, scholars from the left of the political spectrum also

[12] Sir Leslie Scarman, *English Law – The New Dimension* (London: Stevens & Sons, 1974). Q. Hogg, *The Dilemma of Democracy: Diagnosis and Prescription* (London: Collins, 1978).

[13] J. A. G. Griffith, 'The political constitution' (1979) 42 MLR 1, 16.

[14] See T. Poole, 'Tilting at windmills? Truth and illusion in "The political constitution"' (2007) 70 MLR 250, 260.

[15] See F. Klug, 'A bill of rights: do we need one or do we already have one?' [2007] PL 701, 703–4.

asserted the inappropriateness of a traditional Bill of Rights within the UK's constitution. Picking up the mantle from Griffith, figures such as Keith Ewing and Conor Gearty argued that permitting the judiciary to review legislation on the basis of human rights norms would serve to strengthen the hand of the UK's historically conservative judiciary against the will of the people as expressed through their representatives.[16] When Tony Blair's newly elected Labour Government came to transpose human rights norms into the domestic legal systems of the UK through the Human Rights Act 1998 (HRA), these voices carried considerable weight. Whilst the Act gave the courts the duty to interpret statutory provisions to conform to a range of provisions from the ECHR where it was possible to do so, and where this was not possible to make a declaration identifying the breach, it did not extend to the courts the ability to strike down legislation which breached human rights. Lord Steyn considered that this model of rights protection was specifically designed to protect Parliament's sovereignty:

> It is crystal clear that the carefully and subtly drafted Human Rights Act 1998 preserves the principle of parliamentary sovereignty. In a case of incompatibility, which cannot be avoided by interpretation under section 3(1), the courts may not disapply the legislation. The court may merely issue a declaration of incompatibility which then gives rise to a power to take remedial action.[17]

The UK and the USA therefore offer examples of states which bought into the late twentieth century's human rights project only partially. When, in the aftermath of 9/11, this project was thrown into crisis, these states offered crucial proving grounds on which to test the resilience of the concept. As Conor Gearty felt obliged to recognise, '[i]f we ask the question . . . "Can Human Rights Survive?", then we must admit that an optimistic answer is least obvious in this field of national security, which these days invariably means counter-terrorism'.[18] Critics of the response of these states were quick to highlight the weakness of their rights-protection regimes. This chapter assesses these critical perspectives. Against the backdrop of the national security discourse prevalent in both countries during the last decade, this study examines the role of human rights norms (with a specific focus, in this context, upon civil

[16] See K. Ewing and C. Gearty, *Democracy or a Bill of Rights* (London: Society of Labour Lawyers, 1991).

[17] *R* v. *Director of Public Prosecutions, ex parte Kebilene* [2000] 2 AC 326, Lord Steyn, p.367.

[18] C. Gearty, *Can Human Rights Survive?* (Cambridge University Press, 2006) p.102.

and political rights), not as trumps, but as factors in the policy mix, conditioning and channelling a state's responses to terrorism.[19]

United States experience: the 'fortress' model of rights protection

In the febrile atmosphere engendered by the 9/11 attacks on New York and Washington DC, legislators, law enforcement agencies and the military were all involved in a multifaceted US response. Within little over a month, Congress enacted the USA PATRIOT Act.[20] In signing the Act into law, President George W. Bush focused upon its implications for sharing intelligence between law enforcement and security agencies within the USA.[21] This was because, whilst the PATRIOT Act 'grants vastly expanded investigatory and surveillance powers to the federal government',[22] it made relatively limited amendments to the substantive criminal law. Notwithstanding these new powers, the US government was able to conduct large-scale deportations of foreign nationals from the United States under existing immigration laws.[23] Beyond these domestic responses, as suspected terrorists were apprehended by the USA and its allies in the course of the invasion of Afghanistan, and thereafter across the globe, the Bush administration sought to formalise the detention and interrogation of these individuals. Under the authority of a Presidential Order,[24] many were transferred to the secure compound at Camp Delta, part of the US Naval Base at Guantánamo Bay, Cuba.

For critics of the Bush administration's actions, the decision to employ military force (rather than focus on domestic responses using the criminal justice system) is often portrayed as having been taken to

[19] For a thorough evaluation of the contrasting approaches to limitation of rights under both the US Constitution and the ECHR than is possible in this article, see S. Sottiaux, *Terrorism and the Limitation of Rights: The ECHR and the US Constitution* (Oxford: Hart, 2008), pp.35–65.

[20] Uniting and Strengthening America by Providing Appropriate Tools Required to Intercept and Obstruct Terrorism Act 2001, Pub. L. No. 107–56, 115 Stat. 272.

[21] See B. Goold, 'Privacy, identity and security' in Goold and Lazarus, *Security and Human Rights*, 45, p.47.

[22] R. Brooks, 'War everywhere: rights, national security law, and the law of armed conflict in the age of terror' (2004) 153 *University of Pennsylvania Law Review* 675, 696.

[23] See D. Cole, 'The priority of morality: the emergency constitution's blind spot' (2003–4) 113 *Yale Law Journal* 1753, 1778 and L. Volpp, 'The citizen and the terrorist' (2001–2002) 49 *UCLA Law Review* 1575, 1577.

[24] Military Order of November 13, 2001: Detention, Treatment and Trial of Certain Non-Citizens in the War Against Terrorism, 3 CFR 918 (2002).

display US military strength, to maximise Presidential approval ratings and to access Presidential war powers.[25] A combination of these factors steered the US response away from tackling the threat using the criminal law, which was cast by the administration as containing too many procedural safeguards to provide an adequate response to an emergency of this magnitude.[26] This attitude explained Congress's relatively minor extensions to the criminal offences tackling the provision of material support for terrorist organisations,[27] originally enacted in the aftermath of the Oklahoma City bombing.[28] For some writers, including Conor Gearty, the Bush administration's readiness to dismiss the criminal justice process out of hand indicates a wilful misreading of the criminal law's flexibility and evidences its eagerness to go to war.[29] Nonetheless, it remains at least arguable that the model of rights protection under the US Constitution played its part in channelling the Bush administration away from proposing adjustments to the criminal justice system of the type employed in the UK to combat terrorism,[30] and influenced its largely military response.

In the USA a dominant 'cultural norm' favours almost absolute freedom of expression.[31] A network of constitutional jurisprudence forms what Lee Bollinger and Geoffrey Stone describe as a 'fortress' around the right to freedom of speech under the First Amendment to the US Constitution. The key strongpoint amongst these defences is *Brandenburg* v. *Ohio*.[32] This decision saw the US Supreme Court abandon the restricted vision of freedom of speech espoused in

[25] See T. Farer, *Confronting Global Terrorism and American Neo-Conservatism: The Framework of a Liberal Grand Strategy* (Oxford University Press, 2008) pp.85–6.

[26] See B. Ackerman, *Before the Next Attack: Preserving Civil Liberties in an Age of Terrorism* (New Haven, CN: Yale University Press, 2006), pp.39–57.

[27] Most importantly 18 USC §2339B, which makes it an offence to provide 'material support or resources ... [to] designated foreign terrorist organizations'. For a thorough evaluation of the introduction of these measures and the addition of groups to which they applied after 9/11, see R. Chesney, 'The sleeper scenario: terrorism-support laws and the demands of prevention' [2005] 42 *Harvard Journal on Legislation* 1, pp.18–21.

[28] Antiterrorism and Effective Death Penalty Act of 1996, Pub. L. No. 104–132, 110 Stat. 1214.

[29] C. Gearty, 'The superpatriotic fervour of the moment' (2008) OJLS 183, 189.

[30] See E. Parker, 'Implementation of the UK Terrorism Act 2006 – the relationship between counterterrorism law, free speech, and the Muslim community in the United Kingdom versus the United States' (2007) 21 *Emory International Law Review* 711, pp.734–5.

[31] L. Donohue, 'Terrorist speech and the future of free expression' (2005) 27 *Cardozo Law Review* 233, 237.

[32] *Brandenburg* v. *Ohio*, 395 US 444 (1969). Bollinger and Stone describe *Brandenburg* v. *Ohio* as an effort by the US Supreme Court to 'create a fortress of constitutional

Dennis v. *United States* at the zenith of the McCarthyite 'Red Scare'.[33] In that decision, the Supreme Court had ruled that freedom of speech varied according to circumstances, creating a flexible test to assess 'whether the gravity of the "evil," discounted by its improbability, justifies such invasion of free speech as is necessary to avoid the danger'.[34] The activities of senior members of the Communist Party in the USA, advocating the eventual overthrow of the US government, were considered by the Court to be so pervasive, notwithstanding the small chance that such an uprising would begin, as to render their conspiracy convictions constitutional. Almost two decades later in *Brandenburg* (and with the 'Red Scare' a receding memory), the Court resiled from this position, asserting that only speech which is 'directed to inciting or producing imminent lawless action and is likely to incite or produce such action' is capable of being criminalised under the US Constitution.[35] Essentially the Court had accepted a categorical approach to the right of freedom of speech, admitting only the narrowest exceptions to this right.[36]

Laura Donohue's assertion that 'few justices would want to be remembered for the modern-day equivalent of *Dennis* v. *United States*',[37] goes some way towards explaining the US government's reluctance to assault 'fortress' *Brandenburg*, even after the attacks of 9/11. Despite the encouragement of writers influential within the Bush administration that such 'constitutional understandings ... are liable to change rapidly during emergencies',[38] the executive refused to shoulder the political risk inherent in an effort to radically change such understandings. Any attempt to persuade the courts to retreat from *Brandenburg* would have been uncertain of success and would have acted as a lightning rod for opposition, as is evident in the US Supreme Court's approach to some of the PATRIOT Act's limited extensions to the substantive criminal law. When, in *Holder* v. *Humanitarian Law Project*,[39] the Court considered

protection around valued speech and debate': L. Bollinger and G. Stone, *Eternally Vigilant: Free Speech in the Modern Era* (University of Chicago Press, 2002) p.25.

33 *Dennis* v. *United States* 341 US 494 (1951). 34 Ibid., 510.

35 *Brandenburg*, note 32 above, 447.

36 See M. Tushnet, 'Defending *Korematsu*?: Reflections on civil liberties in wartime' (2003) *Wisconsin Law Review* 273, 281–2.

37 Donohue, 'Terrorist speech and free expression', p.237.

38 E. Posner and A. Vermeule, *Terror in the Balance: Security, Liberty and the Courts* (New York: Oxford University Press, 2007), p.9. Donohue herself concluded, on a similar basis, that '[r]elying on *Brandenburg* as a guarantee that speech necessary to the liberal, democratic discourse is protected, however, may be somewhat naïve': Donohue, ibid, p.248.

39 *Holder* v. *Humanitarian Law Project* 561 US ____ (2010).

the offence of providing material support for terrorism, six of the justices upheld the constitutionality of the current provisions. But even the justices making up the majority emphasised that these restrictions only applied to actions taken at the behest of listed terrorist groups,[40] and impinged on exercises of pure speech only in exceptional circumstances:

> Under the material-support statute, plaintiffs may say anything they wish on any topic. They may speak and write freely about the PKK and LTTE, the governments of Turkey and Sri Lanka, human rights, and international law. They may advocate before the United Nations. . . . Rather, Congress has prohibited 'material support,' which most often does not take the form of speech at all. And when it does, the statute is carefully drawn to cover only a narrow category of speech to, under the direction of, or in coordination with foreign groups that the speaker knows to be terrorist organizations.[41]

With regard to resident US citizens, the US government felt obliged to adopt a 'business as usual' approach to terrorism when it came to the substantive criminal law (if not, as we have seen, to executive surveillance powers).[42] In contrast, when David Cole writes of the government's willingness to adopt 'administrative measures to avoid the safeguards associated with the criminal process',[43] he is referring to efforts to deal with resident foreign nationals suspected of terrorism under an immigration system which provided far fewer safeguards than the criminal law.[44] The following statement by then US Attorney-General John Ashcroft illustrates not simply this approach but the assumption, underpinning it, that foreign nationals within the USA presented an especially grave terrorist threat:

> [L]et the terrorists among us be warned. If you overstay your visas even by one day, we will arrest you. If you violate a local law, we will . . . work to make sure that you are put in jail and . . . kept in custody as long as possible. We will use every available statute. We will seek every

[40] In this case the Kurdistan Workers' Party (PKK) and the Liberation Tigers of Tamil Eelam (LTTE).

[41] *Holder*, note 39 above, pp.20–21.

[42] F. Ní Aoláin and O. Gross, *Law in Times of Crisis: Emergency Powers in Theory and Practice* (Cambridge University Press, 2006) p.252.

[43] D. Cole, 'The new McCarthyism: repeating history in the war on terrorism' (2003) 38 *Harvard Civil Rights-Civil Liberties Law Review* 1, 28.

[44] See N. Hussain, 'Beyond norm and exception: Guantánamo' (2007) *Critical Inquiry* 734, 743.

> prosecutorial advantage. We will use all our weapons within the law and under the Constitution to protect life and enhance security for America.[45]

The model of rights protection operative within the USA in effect persuaded the Bush administration of the advantages of adopting a two-tier response to terrorism which differentiated between citizens and foreign nationals. Ashcroft spoke at a time when the USA was engaged in the summary detention and deportation of thousands of Asian and Middle Eastern immigrants,[46] and two months before members of his own Office of Legal Counsel circulated internal memos regarding the possibility that the detention of individuals at Guantánamo Bay would not be subject to the jurisdiction of the Federal courts.[47] The aim of these memos was to skirt the Constitutional protections relating to habeas corpus. Like freedom of speech this writ, which enables individuals to challenge deprivations of liberty which do not follow from criminal convictions, is protected by a fortress of jurisprudence.

Although the US Constitution allows for the suspension of habeas corpus in wartime,[48] once again the Bush administration sought to avoid engaging this right directly, given the restrictions imposed on such suspensions by the Supreme Court's post-Civil War decision in *Milligan*.[49] At the time these efforts to restrict habeas corpus to the borders of the United States resulted in the characterisation of Guantánamo Bay as a 'legal black hole'.[50] This 'magisterial rebuke'[51] resonates in a way which belies the dense 'normative and institutional' framework which does indeed apply to Guantánamo Bay.[52] The Bush administration did not attempt to oust

45 D. Eggen, 'Tough anti-terror campaign pledged Ashcroft tells mayors he will use new law to fullest extent' *The Washington Post* (26 October 2001) p.A01.

46 These deportations were primarily carried out under s.236, Immigration and Nationality Act, 8 USC §1226. See D. Weissbrodt, *The Human Rights of Non-Citizens* (Oxford University Press, 2008) p.4.

47 See J. Margulies, *Guantánamo and the Abuse of Presidential Power* (New York: Simon & Schuster, 2006) pp.44–59.

48 Art. One, s.9, cl.2 US Constitution: 'The privilege of the writ of habeas corpus shall not be suspended, unless when in cases of rebellion or invasion the public safety may require it'.

49 *Ex parte Milligan*, 71 US 2 (1866). See Ní Aoláin and Gross, *Law in Times of Crisis*, pp.89–98.

50 J. Steyn, 'Guantánamo Bay: the legal black hole' (2004) 53 ICLQ 1. The description was first employed by Mr Nicholas Blake QC in *R (Abbasi)* v. *Secretary of State for Foreign and Commonwealth Affairs* [2002] EWCA Civ 1598, para.22.

51 C. Warbrick, 'The European response to terrorism in an age of human rights' (2004) 15 EJIL 989, 996.

52 F. Johns, 'Guantánamo Bay and the annihilation of the exception' (2005) 16 EJIL 613, 618. See also Hussain, 'Beyond norm and exception', pp.740–41.

all law from Guantánamo, only the domestic and international rights protections which it sought to avoid applying to the detainees. The legal framework which the US government erected around the Guantánamo detainees therefore constituted the most ambitious of its efforts to exploit the weaknesses in the US model of rights protection. It was part of a political conjuror's trick, by which the government attempted to persuade the American public that it was capable of pursuing its 'War on Terror' whilst simultaneously deflecting opposition with claims that no constitutional rights were even engaged by its actions, much less infringed.

The example of measures undertaken during the Second World War which infringed civil liberties loomed large in accounts which sought to justify the security measures adopted in response to 9/11. In these accounts, the long-term detention without trial of hundreds of foreign nationals in Guantánamo marked a quantitative improvement upon the detention of thousands of Japanese Americans for the duration of hostilities. Even Mark Tushnet has admitted that this comparison with the powers adopted during the Second World War 'diminishes contemporary threats to civil liberties'.[53] Some writers have gone further, identifying in these comparisons a trend towards ever-closer limitation of state power in response to perceived threats, a limitation resulting from 'America's distinctive history' and the central place of civil liberties within its legal culture.[54] In this vein William Rehnquist, writing when Chief Justice of the US Supreme Court (but before 9/11), concluded his study of habeas corpus with the assertion that 'there is every reason to think that the historic trend against the least justified of the curtailments of civil liberty in wartime will continue in the future'.[55] Such assertions appear to be underpinned by Whiggish historiography, conditioned to regard US constitutional arrangements as existing in a 'transcendent' state of continuous and progressive improvement towards some utopian ideal.

Oren Gross offers an alternative view of these events; national crises have historically been, and will continue to be, used as a pretext to

[53] Tushnet, 'Defending *Korematsu*?', p.274.

[54] J. Goldsmith and C. Sunstein, 'Military tribunals and legal culture: what a difference sixty years makes' (2002) 19 *Constitutional Commentary* 261, 262. Goldsmith and Sunstein conclude, at 289, that 'with respect to actions of the Executive branch that might endanger civil liberties, the Nation is now far less trusting of government, and far more solicitous of the accused, than it was sixty years ago'.

[55] W. Rehnquist, *All the Laws but One: Civil Liberties in Wartime* (New York: Vintage, 2000) p.224.

extend the executive's powers, resulting in 'the concomitant contraction of individual freedoms and liberties'.[56] If the above analysis of the US government's response to 9/11 bears out this conclusion, it also requires that the conclusion be slightly refined; in the course of any efforts to enhance its powers, the executive will first attempt what David Cole describes as the 'course of least resistance'.[57] The implications of the responses to 9/11 for civil liberties differ in scale and emphasis from the measures adopted during the Second World War because the course of least resistance has changed. Just as few judges today would like to be remembered for retreating from *Brandenburg*, the Bush administration considered that there would be as little enthusiasm from the bench for reaffirming decisions such as *Korematsu* v. *United States*,[58] which upheld the constitutionality of the internment of Japanese Americans during the Second World War. Moreover, by seeking to circumvent, rather than assault, constitutional protections, the Bush administration at the very least bought itself time in which to detain and interrogate individuals at Camp Delta on its own terms, until the legal process caught up.[59] Only by a series of decisions over several years, running from *Rasul* v. *Bush*,[60] via *Hamdan* v. *Rumsfeld*,[61] to *Boumediene* v. *Bush*,[62] did the US Supreme Court assert the jurisdiction of the Federal courts over Guantánamo Bay and ultimately recognise that the prisoners held there enjoyed a constitutional right to habeas corpus. At some indeterminate point hereafter, the course of least resistance will once again ordain a different response to a future crisis in an effort to circumvent these authorities.

Alongside the standard explanations of the US government's response to 9/11, more attention needs to be given to the channelling effect of the model of rights protection under the US Constitution. The US government's ability to adapt the criminal law to counter the threat of terrorism (by creating new offences or special procedural rules) remains severely curtailed by the fortress model of rights protection. Given the imperative of being seen by the public to respond quickly and effectively to the

[56] O. Gross, 'Chaos and rules: should responses to violent crises always be constitutional?' (2003) 112 *Yale Law Journal* 1011, 1029.

[57] Cole, 'The new McCarthyism', p.15.

[58] *Korematsu* v. *United States*, 323 US 214 (1944).

[59] See, by way of comparison, the thoughts of Francis Biddle, US Attorney-General during the Second World War, on the advantages enjoyed by the executive by exploiting delays in the judicial process and the reluctance of the courts to impose injunctions on the executive in wartime: F. Biddle, *In Brief Authority* (New York: Doubleday, 1962), p.219.

[60] *Rasul* v. *Bush*, 542 US 466 (2004).

[61] *Hamdan* v. *Rumsfeld* 548 US 557 (2006).

[62] *Boumediene* v. *Bush*, 553 US 723 (2008).

attacks, it is therefore unsurprising that the Bush administration rapidly dismissed the idea of overhauling the criminal justice system (and the assault on cases like *Brandenburg* which this would entail). In comparison, the establishment of Camp Delta, the deportation of foreign nationals under immigration laws and flexing America's military muscle overseas must have all seemed like more accessible means of responding to the threat of terrorism.

United Kingdom experience: the 'caltrop' model of rights protection

In contrast to the USA, the UK was not slow to adapt the criminal law to the needs of counter-terrorism. Even before the 9/11 attacks, the UK maintained some of the most stringent criminal-law responses to terrorism in Europe.[63] In assessing these provisions, writers like Colin Warbrick have accepted the necessity, 'in some cases', of altering the ordinary operation of the criminal justice system to enable responses to terrorism.[64] Indeed, the security framework provided by the Terrorism Act 2000 was developed in light of the acceptance by the European Court of Human Rights that, in 'interpreting and applying the relevant provisions of the Convention, due account will be taken of the special nature of terrorist crime, the threat it poses to democratic society and the exigencies of dealing with it'.[65] In essence, the hallmark of the UK's criminal justice system is its adaptability:

> What does exist is a framework of criminal law which is informed by principle certainly and controlled to some degree . . . by a range of more or less embedded rights but which is nevertheless always on the move, the substance of the crimes themselves and the procedural framework for their detection and punishment being in a perpetual state of flux.[66]

Under the HRA 1998 the 'more or less embedded rights' to which Gearty refers are more often limited or qualified rights than absolute ones, and function as factors which must be properly considered in policy making, with the courts overseeing the adequacy of such consideration.[67] Under section 4 of the HRA 1998 not even absolute rights, such as the prohibition of torture under Article 3 ECHR, can be described as

63 C. Walker, 'Terrorism and criminal justice: past, present and future' (2004) Crim LR 311, 317.
64 Warbrick, 'European response to terrorism', p.990.
65 *Murray* v. *UK* (1994) 19 EHRR 193, para.47.
66 Gearty, 'Superpatriotic fervour', p.189.
67 See R. Dworkin, *Taking Rights Seriously* (London: Duckworth, 1977) pp.184–205.

'fortress' rights since, faced with clear legislation that breaches these prohibitions, the courts can at most issue a declaration of incompatibility that does not undermine the legal validity of the legislation. In contrast to the near-impregnable protections surrounding freedom of speech under the US Constitution, the right to freedom of expression provided under Article 10 ECHR functions like the policy-making equivalent of a caltrop. Used on battlefields from antiquity onwards, caltrops are spiked metal devices strewn in the path of an expected enemy advance to slow their progress by risking injury to the feet of soldiers or horses.[68] This may look like a pale shadow of the protection afforded to freedom of speech in the USA, but the qualified right to freedom of expression (and other qualified rights such as the right to private and family life and to freedom of assembly)[69] operating under the HRA is a comprehensive tool, used by courts in the UK to shape policy-making decisions rather than channel government policy against less well-protected interests. Thus, although legislative measures can be introduced banning organisations involved in political violence[70] or criminalising expressions which directly or indirectly encourage others to commit acts of terrorism,[71] if such measures operate in a manner which the courts believe to be incompatible with the ECHR, a declaration to this effect will at the least provide a government's opponents strong political arguments in favour of their repeal or amendment.

Nonetheless, despite the adaptability of the UK criminal law, the enactment of the Anti-Terrorism Crime and Security Act in October 2001 showed that the US government was not alone in rushing to circumvent the operation of criminal law in favour of executive responses to terrorism. Part 4 of this Act provided a system of detention without trial (in HM Prison Belmarsh) for foreign-national terrorist suspects who are present in the UK,[72] but cannot be deported to their home countries owing to the risk of their being subject to inhuman and degrading treatment there,[73] and cannot be charged with terrorism offences due to a lack of admissible evidence.[74] These detentions could

[68] See C. Gilliver 'Hedgehogs, caltrops and palisade stakes' (1993) 4 *Journal of Roman Military Equipment Studies* 49.

[69] Private and family life: Art. 8 ECHR; assembly, Art. 11 ECHR.

[70] Terrorism Act 2000, s.3.

[71] Terrorism Act 2006, s.1.

[72] Anti-Terrorism, Crime and Security Act (ATCSA) 2001, ss.21–32.

[73] Art. 3 ECHR. See *Chahal* v. *UK* (1997) 23 EHRR 413 and *Saadi* v. *Italy* (2009) 49 EHRR 30.

[74] This often means that the evidence against the individuals is made up of intercepted communications, which, to protect the secrecy of the UK's capacity to intercept

only be challenged, at first instance, before the Special Immigration Appeals Commission, a body which could sit in closed session and exclude the defendant from hearings.[75] Looking back over the operation of these provisions in January 2005, the then Home Secretary Charles Clarke explained that '[t]he Government believed that the part 4 powers were justified, because the threat appeared to come predominantly, albeit not exclusively, from foreign nationals, [and] because foreign nationals do not have the same right to be here as British nationals . . . .'[76]

The executive's desire to subject foreign nationals to a unique counter-terrorism regime was understandable given that the 9/11 hijackers were foreign nationals resident in the USA, but a few months after Clarke's statement the supposed predominance of the threat posed by foreign nationals would be shown to be a tragic misjudgement, when the 7/7 attacks highlighted the seriousness of the 'home-grown' terrorist threat.[77] Charles Clarke's second reason for focusing security policy on foreign nationals, however, suggests that these measures can be characterised as a learned response by an executive conditioned to attempt the course of least resistance in responding to emergencies. With the HRA not yet well established within the UK's constitutional arrangements, foreign nationals must have seemed like the ideal focus of security policy, especially to long-serving members of the security services and the civil service. Not only could these advisers point to the judiciary's long-standing acceptance that, where the rights of a foreign national conflict with the needs of national security, then 'the alien must suffer, if suffering there is to be',[78] but moreover the interests of foreign nationals are less well-protected in a political system in which they are disenfranchised.[79]

On this occasion, however, the UK government suddenly found that the path of least resistance was blocked. As Trevor Allan asserts, 'a provision for the detention of suspected terrorists, which extends only to aliens or foreigners even though some British nationals admittedly present a similar threat, suggests a type of irrational discrimination

communications, remain inadmissible in court. See J. Chilcot *et al.*, *Privy Council Review of intercept as evidence: Report to the Prime Minister and the Home Secretary* (4 February 2008) Cm 7324.

75 ATCSA 2001, s.25.

76 Charles Clarke, MP, HC Deb. vol. 430, col. 306, 26 January 2005.

77 See C. Walker, 'The treatment of foreign terror suspects' (2007) 70 MLR 427, 428.

78 *R* v. *Home Secretary, ex parte Hosenball* [1977] 1 WLR 766, Lane LJ, p.784.

79 See D. Cole, 'Enemy aliens' (2001–2) 54 *Stanford Law Review* 953, 955.

inconsistent with the fundamental principle of legal equality'.[80] And so a specially convened nine-judge panel of the House of Lords found in the *Belmarsh Detainees* case.[81] One judge, Lord Hoffmann, went even further than the majority in asserting that the UK faced no emergency threatening the life of the nation sufficient to justify detention without trial, on the basis that '[t]errorist violence, serious as it is, does not threaten our institutions of government or our existence as a civil community'.[82]

As important as this decision was, Keith Ewing reminds readers, no individuals were released as an immediate result of their detention being found discriminatory and disproportionate, since the House could only issue a declaration of incompatibility. When they were eventually released in mid-2005 they were immediately subject to the newly minted control orders regime.[83] Much of the government's justification for introducing control orders, under the Prevention of Terrorism Act 2005, was to deal with those same individuals who, following *Belmarsh Detainees*, could no longer be detained without trial, but who 'continue to pose a threat to national security'.[84] Control orders imposed restrictions which varied according to the threat supposedly posed by the individual in question, potentially relocating controlees to unfamiliar cities, restricting and monitoring their access to telecommunications, their movements and their visitors.[85] By tailoring a control order to each controlee and by applying control orders to both nationals and foreign nationals, the government had addressed the specific criticisms made in *Belmarsh Detainees*. Nonetheless, control orders rested on a very similar system of closed evidence justifying detention without trial,[86] raising concerns about whether the new orders breached the right to fair trial and,[87] with the government not having issued a derogation with regard to the right to liberty,[88] many of the control orders were challenged on the basis that their restrictions were so severe that this right was infringed.

[80] T. Allan, 'Deference, defiance, and doctrine: defining the limits of judicial review' (2010) 60 *University of Toronto Law Journal* 41, 44.

[81] *A* v. *Secretary of State for the Home Department* [2004] UKHL 56.

[82] Ibid., para.96.

[83] K. Ewing, *Bonfire of the Liberties: New Labour, Human Rights and the Rule of Law* (Oxford University Press, 2010), p.238.

[84] Charles Clarke, MP, HC Deb. vol. 430, col. 307, 26 January 2005.

[85] Prevention of Terrorism Act 2005, s.2.

[86] Civil Procedure (Amendment No. 2) Rules 2005 SI 2005/656.

[87] Art. 6 ECHR. [88] Art. 5 ECHR.

Having obliged the government to compromise on this key plank of its security policy, however, the courts became less sure how to address the many claims made against control orders.[89] Labour ministers complained that the new measures were 'far from being the best option' in terms of ensuring security by comparison to detention without trial,[90] an assertion leant credibility by the number of controlees who were able to abscond despite the restrictions placed upon them.[91] This stance put pressure on the courts not to dilute such compromised arrangements still further. In the *JJ* case a number of controlees challenged the eighteen-hour control orders to which they were subject, on the basis that such severe restraints amounted to a deprivation of liberty.[92] Lord Bingham and the majority of the court accepted that such orders did infringe the right to liberty, finding that an 'analogy with detention in an open prison was apt, save that the controlled persons did not enjoy the association with others and the access to entertainment facilities which a prisoner in an open prison would expect to enjoy'.[93] The right to liberty served in this instance as a caltrop screen (albeit, as we will see, a weak one), employed by the Court to reduce the maximum length of curfew imposed each day rather than providing a basis on which to invalidate this aspect of the control orders regime. Lest the Court's findings be thought to impose too much of a restriction upon government policy, Lord Brown clarified that, whilst eighteen-hour curfews constituted unacceptable infringements to the right to liberty and would be quashed, lesser restrictions would be acceptable.[94] Even this compromise was too much for Lord Hoffmann, who dissented from the decision, arguing that if the courts were to preserve the distinction between the right to liberty and lesser interests such as freedom of movement, it was essential not to give an overexpansive interpretation to the concept of deprivation of liberty.[95]

This hesitant decision was compounded by the refusal of the House of Lords in *MB*,[96] decided on the same day as *JJ*, to declare the control

[89] See, asserting that in the context of these cases 'marginal gains are better than no gains at all and some measure of rights protection is better than flagrant violation across the board', A. Kavanagh, 'Judging the judges under the Human Rights Act: deference, disillusionment and the "war on terror"' [2009] PL 287, 304.

[90] John Reid, MP, HC Deb. vol. 460 col. 1428, 24 May 2007.

[91] See D. Campbell 'The threat of terror and the plausibility of positivism' [2009] PL 501, 511.

[92] *Secretary of State for the Home Department* v. *JJ* [2007] UKHL 45.

[93] Ibid., para.24. [94] Ibid., para.105. [95] Ibid., paras.45–7.

[96] *Secretary of State for the Home Department* v. *MB* [2007] UKHL 46.

orders regime as a whole incompatible with the right to a fair trial on the basis of the lack of information provided to detainees regarding the case against them. Whilst the majority of the House of Lords satisfied themselves with a slight reinterpretation of the rules for disclosure of evidence under the Prevention of Terrorism Act,[97] Lord Hoffmann again sought to shield the control orders regime from challenge, emphasising that the preventative nature of these orders set them apart from criminal proceedings in terms of the standards applicable under the right to fair trial.[98]

Together, according to Ewing, these decisions 'are more important for what they appeared to permit rather than what they purported to prohibit'.[99] They were not, however, allowed to stand as the final word on the matter. When the Belmarsh detainees took their fight for compensation to Strasbourg, the European Court of Human Rights found that the extensive reliance on closed evidence undermined the UK government's claims that detention without trial had been compatible with Article 6 ECHR:

> While this question must be decided on a case-by-case basis, the Court observes generally that, where the evidence was to a large extent disclosed and the open material played the predominant role in the determination, it could not be said that the applicant was denied an opportunity effectively to challenge the reasonableness of the Secretary of State's belief and suspicions about him.[100]

This decision rendered untenable the position adopted by the House of Lords in *MB*, which had essentially permitted similar closed proceedings in control orders cases. It also meant that, if many of the control orders were to remain in place and undiluted, the government would have to disclose more information to the detainees regarding the basis for the suspicions against them and thereby potentially disclose sources of intelligence. The House of Lords, for all their efforts to maintain the viability of the control orders regime, had to come into line with Strasbourg in the *AF* case.[101] In his decision in *AF*, however, Lord Hoffmann made no secret of the fact that he would extend the material available to controlees only 'with very considerable regret, because

[97] Ibid., Baroness Hale, para.73. [98] Ibid., para.49. See also Lord Bingham, para.24.

[99] Ewing, *Bonfire of the Liberties*, p.247. See also E. Bates, 'Anti-Terrorism Control Orders: liberty and security still in the balance' (2009) 29 LS 99, 125.

[100] *A* v. *UK* (2009) 49 EHRR 29, para.220.

[101] *Secretary of State for the Home Department* v. *AF* [2009] UKHL 28.

I think that the decision of the [European Court] was wrong and that it may well destroy the system of control orders which is a significant part of this country's defences against terrorism'.[102]

Lord Hoffmann cuts an enigmatic figure in these cases, from railing against detention without trial in *Belmarsh Detainees* to buttressing the control orders regime in *JJ*, *MB* and *AF*. His speeches, nonetheless, should be considered in the context of the transitional state of the UK's domestic legal systems. As Thomas Poole notes, Lord Hoffmann's decision in *Belmarsh Detainees* deliberately eschews reference to the ECHR,[103] proceeding instead on the basis that detention without trial 'calls into question the very existence of an ancient liberty of which this country has until now been very proud: freedom from arbitrary arrest and detention'.[104] Writing in the immediate aftermath of the decision, Poole postulated that this conscious attempt to recruit the ancient protections of habeas corpus to the cause of challenging detention without trial could be regarded as 'as an attempt to circumvent the widespread sentiment against judges using "foreign" law [i.e. the ECHR] to tamper with the policy choices of the British government'.[105] With the benefit of Lord Hoffmann's control order speeches, however, a less sophisticated rationale for this decision appears to be increasingly plausible. These speeches displayed his reluctance to accept the extent to which the right to liberty granted by the ECHR (and the right to a fair hearing which supports it) outstrip historic, domestic protections of similar interests.[106] They therefore reflect the degree to which judicial acceptance of ECHR principles within domestic law remained, unsurprisingly, incomplete in the first decade following the passing of the HRA.

The experience of detention without trial and control orders reaffirms the dangers of sidelining the criminal law as a state's primary response to those engaged in political violence. In late 2001 the government sought

[102] Ibid., para.70.

[103] T. Poole, 'Harnessing the power of the past? Lord Hoffmann and the *Belmarsh Detainees* case' (2005) 32 *Journal of Law & Society* 534, 537–8.

[104] *A* v. *SSHD*, note 81 above, para.86.

[105] Poole, 'Harnessing the power of the past?', pp.554–5.

[106] This conclusion is buttressed by Lord Hoffmann's extrajudicial assertion that '[s]ince 9/11 there have been enough real and serious invasions of traditional English freedoms to make it tragic that the very concept of human rights is being trivialized by silly interpretations of grand ideas'. M. Pinto-Duschinsky, *Bringing Rights Back Home: Making human rights compatible with parliamentary democracy in the UK* (Policy Exchange, February 2010), p.7.

to enact robust counter-terrorism legislation in order to reassure the public of its grip on the security situation, but failed to appreciate the implications of the human rights regime it had brought into domestic law. This combination of factors persuaded ministers to focus their counter-terrorism proposals against foreign nationals, a supposedly soft target. They were ultimately deflected from this course in *Belmarsh Detainees* by a senior judiciary largely committed to the model of rights protection provided by the HRA, but thereafter divided as to the limits of the rights to liberty and fair trial. Probably, many of the Law Lords were also uncertain whether they should exercise their mandate with restraint to prevent a now rights-sceptical executive from revisiting and restricting the HRA. The whole saga suggests that the UK's constitution is still in transit into the human rights era and that, as Claire Palley forewarned, '[u]nless public, officials and lawyers are imbued with human rights ideology, lip-service to, rather than respect in practice for, human rights will frequently be the outcome'.[107]

Conclusion

This chapter has focused upon two states which have long asserted their commitment to the human rights project whilst maintaining domestic legal systems set apart from the model of rights protection most commonly found amongst liberal democracies. Such diversity should not be surprising. All systems of government are unique in their capacity for legalisation. As Griffith asserted, 'law is not and cannot be a substitute for politics ... [t]o require a supreme court to make certain kinds of political decisions does not make those decisions any less political'.[108] But the 'caltrop' model of rights protection, exemplified here by the UK's adoption of the ECHR into domestic law, carries the potential to spread human rights standards widely through a legal system, unlike the 'fortress' model established under the US Constitution, which focuses the finite capacity for legalisation on a limited number of virtually absolute rights.

The caltrop model of rights protection in place in the UK allows courts to assert human rights standards in the face of executive action and to bring attention and political weight to attempts to repeal or amend legislation which permits an abuse of human rights, but does

[107] Palley, *The United Kingdom and Human Rights*, p.3.
[108] Griffith, 'The political constitution', p.16.

not place the power to strike down in the hands of the courts. Often the rights protected are themselves flexible standards which may be subject to qualification, limitation or balancing exercises alongside other rights. Nonetheless, the above analysis supports Stefan Sottiaux's conclusion that 'flexible styles of limitation [of rights], combined with non-deferential judicial review, provide fertile ground for generating well balanced trade-offs between liberty and security in the context of terrorism'.[109] Sottiaux's identification of the need for 'non-deferential judicial review' is emphasised by the courts' response to cases involving national security concerns heard in the UK since 9/11. Whilst the ministers who championed the HRA aspired to create 'a culture of rights and responsibilities in the UK',[110] this culture had little time to take root before it was buffeted by the efforts of the same ministers to respond to 9/11. As a result, the judiciary has struggled to reconcile its new role under the HRA with historic jurisprudence providing for deference to the executive in response to security threats.[111] In particular, having declared in *Belmarsh Detainees* that detention without trial is incompatible with the ECHR, the senior judiciary were thereafter reluctant to test the boundaries of their authority by challenging the control orders regime established in its stead. These circumstances highlight the usefulness of the continued role adopted by the European Court of Human Rights, as a backstop, 'detached and further removed from the immediate turmoil',[112] in safeguarding against abuses of human rights which slip past the domestic courts.

In contrast, cultural veneration of rights protection is not lacking in the USA, where Clinton Rossiter was moved to celebrate the American people for their 'healthy distrust of emergency departures from the normal ways of government'.[113] If human rights protection in the UK regime suffers from *transitional* difficulties, for much of the first decade of the twenty-first century this culture of respect for rights in the USA struggled to keep pace with efforts of government to circumvent constitutional restrictions on its freedom of action. The *systemic* weakness exposed in this chapter as inherent in the US Constitution's model of

[109] Sottiaux, *Terrorism and the Limitation of Rights*, p.406.
[110] Jack Straw, MP, 'Building a human rights culture', Address to the Civil Service College, 19 December 1999.
[111] See Allan, 'Deference, defiance, and doctrine', p.52.
[112] O. Gross and F. Ní Aoláin, 'From discretion to scrutiny: revisiting the application of the margin of appreciation doctrine in the context of Article 15 of the European Convention on Human Rights' (2001) 23 *Human Rights Quarterly* 625, 639.
[113] C. Rossiter, *Constitutional Dictatorship* (Princeton University Press, 1948), p.210.

rights protection is that it serves to funnel executive action against less well-protected interests. This ensures that, unless the nature of a threat is such as to imbue future US administrations facing emergency situations with sufficient political capital to assault fortress rights, they will continue to seek a course of action which outflanks constitutional rights protections.

PART III

International human rights law perspectives

7

The rule of law and the role of human rights in contemporary international law

ELENA KATSELLI

Introduction

To talk about the rule of law and human rights when clearly the system of law, both national and international, still fails to provide effective protection to millions of individuals around the world is a particularly difficult task.[1]

Yet again, this may suggest that human rights are independent of law and the rule of law and therefore that the individual is not entitled to human rights if the legal system within which they exist does not incorporate human rights principles. This would make human rights protection subjective and thereby individuals in different parts of the world would, and in reality do, enjoy different standards of protection, if any at all.

Nevertheless, if there is a lesson to be learned from the Second World War it is that using the law as justification for a state's policies is incredibly dangerous. It was by operation of law that Hitler pursued the genocidal persecution of Jews before and during the war. It was also on the law that the racist regime in South Africa based its apartheid policies against the black majority. Whilst, surely, both systems used the law as a shield for atrocities, it can hardly be argued that these practices were in compliance with the rule of law.[2]

The author is grateful to her co-editors for their useful comments and advice, to her colleagues at Newcastle Law School for their feedback and questions, and particularly to Dr Ole Pedersen. The author remains solely responsible for any mistakes.

1 Some of the issues considered in this chapter were presented by the author in her invited Aisha Ibrahim Duhulow 2nd Annual Memorial Lecture organised by Newcastle Amnesty Group on 27 October 2010. The lecture signified two years from the stoning to death of 13-year-old Somali girl Aisha Ibrahim Duhulow by the authorities in control in a failed state.

2 S. Chesterman, 'An international rule of law?', 56 *American Journal of Comparative Law* (2008) 331, p.337. On apartheid laws see W. B. Harvey, 'The rule of law in historical perspective', 59 *Michigan Law Review* (1960–61) 487, p.495.

One therefore needs to be particularly cautious when the law is invoked as justification for the oppression of the individual. Law has frequently been used without 'the deepest interests of humanity' in mind, contrary to what Professor Orentlicher believed.[3]

This reservation does not apply just to national law. It applies perhaps even more compellingly in relation to international law since this still is very much the product of a non-democratic and highly political process which reflects predominantly the interests of powerful states. In this regard, in some instances, reliance on international law such as state sovereignty and consent becomes a dangerous tool for violating fundamental rights. Whilst in these situations apparent compliance might be in accordance with the letter of international rules, it may not necessarily be in accordance with the rule of law.

For the purposes of this chapter, the law and the rule of law are treated as two different concepts. Whilst the two may overlap, with international laws in most circumstances promoting the rule of law, this is not always the case.

This chapter examines whether one can speak of an international rule of law in an international legal order which is so inherently diverse, pluralistic, primitive and anarchic. It considers this question together with the role, if any, that human rights play in the international rule of law. Significantly, the chapter considers the relevance of the rule of law and human rights when international peace and security are under threat, particularly within the context of mandatory United Nations (UN) Security Council action. As human rights principles gain ground, the Security Council emerges as a powerful player and at the same time as a threat to human rights.

It is argued that the rule of law is a significant legal concept that restricts the powers of states in their relations with other states and the individual. It is also a concept continuously evolving and developing, making respect for it a necessity for the peaceful coexistence and cooperation of states and for the protection of human rights. The rule of law is significantly undermined when human rights are disregarded. At the same time, international rules that do not comply with the rule of law threaten the credibility of the international legal order. In this context, traditional concepts such as absolute state sovereignty have given way to fundamental community interests that coincide with the rule of law. The

[3] L. Henkin, G. L. Neuman, D. F. Orentlicher, D. W. Leebron, *Human Rights* (New York: Foundation Press, 1999) p.v.

Security Council must ensure conformity of its actions with these significant developments. The division between legal and political disputes must be extinguished with the rule of law and human rights prevailing in international affairs. It is in this context that the conflict between obligations arising from Security Council resolutions and obligations regarding human rights must be decided, as explored in the final section of this chapter.

Law and rule of law

The sole fact that a certain conduct is authorised by law does not necessarily make it right, contrary to Hobbes' understanding that justice is what is enacted in law. This is because the law does not always coincide with principles of justice.[4] The Nazi and racist regimes in Germany and South Africa respectively clearly illustrate this. In a more contemporary context the adoption of the PATRIOT Act after the 2001 terrorist attacks in the United States raises doubts regarding the compliance of the Act with justice or the rule of law.[5] The power under section 106 of the Act to 'use all necessary and appropriate force' against those that the President determines were involved in the attacks is but one such example.[6] This was employed in practices of extraordinary rendition. Individuals suspected, as opposed to being convicted, of terrorism were kidnapped and flown to other states, not to stand trial but rather to be interrogated (the means of interrogation did not matter).

Similar legal concerns arose from Part 4 of the 2001 Anti-terrorism, Crime and Security Act (ATCSA) adopted in the United Kingdom. This Act introduced discriminatory practices of indefinite detention and deprivation of liberty without charge or trial, applied to non-nationals who could not be deported.[7] Following the ruling of the House of Lords in the *Belmarsh* case, it was held that the Act was in violation of the European Convention on Human Rights (ECHR).[8]

4 See Harvey, 'The rule of law in historical perspective', pp.487 and 489.

5 Uniting and Strengthening America by Providing Appropriate Tools Required to Intercept and Obstruct Terrorism Act 2001, Pub. L. No. 107–56, 115 Stat. 272. For criticism of the Act see D. Cole, *Enemy Aliens* (New York: The New York Press, 2003) p.58.

6 PATRIOT Act, ibid.

7 Anti-terrorism, Crime and Security Act 2001, Chapter 24, Part 4, available at www.legislation.gov.uk/ukpga/2001/24/enacted (accessed 21 February 2011). For analysis see E. Katselli and S. Shah, 'September 11 and the UK response', ICLQ 52 (2003) pp.245–55.

8 *A (FC) and others (FC)* v. *Secretary of State for the Home Department*, [2004] UKHL 56. For analysis see T. Bingham, *The Rule of Law* (Harmondsworth, Middx.: Penguin, 2010) pp.137–58.

Accordingly, states frequently use the law (rule *by* law) as a pretext for imposing arbitrary and discriminatory restrictions on human rights contrary to the rule *of* law.[9]

Nevertheless, the serious terrorist and other contemporary threats against international peace and security must not stand in the way of the observation of the rule of law, as this both protects public interests and protects from state abuse.[10] For this reason, as will be discussed further below, it cannot be seen in disassociation from the protection of human rights. This was confirmed by the European Court of Human Rights (ECtHR), according to which the Convention 'draws its inspiration' from the rule of law.[11] Hence, a state that infringes human rights cannot be regarded as acting within the rule of law.[12]

The concept of the rule of law has been used in different contexts to refer to law or to legality, as a broader idea of justice, or even as a political idea.[13] In a more recent context, the rule of law is understood as a system of rules that aims to protect against abuse of those who exercise power; a system of rules that relies on courts for its application and that extends equally to everyone without discrimination.[14] As Lord Steyn noted, the rule of law sets out 'minimum standards of fairness' which must be reflected in the law and the acts of Parliament.[15] Whilst recognising that 'belief in the rule of law does not import unqualified admiration of the law, or the legal profession, or the courts, or the judges', one would much prefer to live in a society which adheres to the rule of law than in one that does not.[16]

In a contemporary context the individual faces threats not only from states but also from other international actors such as the Security Council. In this regard, the rule of law should be understood as a set

9 J. Raz, 'The rule of law and its virtue' in J. Raz, *The Authority of Law: Essays on Law and Morality* (Oxford University Press, 1979) 211, p.221. The distinction between rule by law and rule of law is owed to Li Shuguang in B. Z. Tamanaha, *On the Rule of Law: History, Politics, Theory* (Cambridge University Press, 2004) 3.

10 Bingham, *The Rule of Law*, pp.158–9; Harvey, 'The rule of law in historical perspective', p.491.

11 *Engel* v. *The Netherlands*, No. I (1976), I EHRR 647, p.672 para.69.

12 Bingham, *The Rule of Law*, p.496.

13 Chesterman, 'An international rule of law?', p.332. Also, on the different conceptions of the rule of law, see Bingham, ibid., p.5.

14 See for instance, E. P. Thompson, *Whigs and Hunters: The Origin of the Black Act* (Harmondsworth, Middx.: Penguin, 1977) p.266 quoted in Bingham, *The Rule of Law*, p.331.

15 *R* v. *Secretary of State for the Home Department, ex parte Pierson* [1998] AC 539, p.591.

16 Bingham, *The Rule of Law*, p.9.

of rules which aim to protect the individual or the state from abusive exercise of power irrespective of where this power comes from. Nevertheless, in an inherently divergent and decentralised international legal community does it make sense to speak of an international rule of law?

An international rule of law?

In the international context, the rule of law has the same compelling significance as at a national level,[17] albeit of a different nature due to the significant differences between the two legal systems in terms of structure, purposes and functions.[18] Many states today, whether powerful or weak, democratic or authoritarian, human rights-abiding or notorious human rights violators, condone the rule of law.[19] Whilst the rule of law is increasingly endorsed in many legal systems, its meaning however may still have not achieved universal consensus due to the varied political agendas of states.[20] Even those states that often invoke the rule of law have a different understanding of what this concept actually encapsulates. For some states the rule of law protects freedom, whilst others view it as the foundation of order within society.[21] This is particularly so in the context of international law. It is therefore a difficult, almost an impossible task to agree a common definition of the international rule of law in the form of 'one size fits all'. Instead, one can identify some of its features on the basis of legal developments that occurred particularly in the period following the Second World War.

This principle lies at the heart of the UN system,[22] the primary objectives of which are the maintenance of international peace and security, the settlement of international disputes by peaceful means, 'in conformity with the principles of justice and international law' and on the basis of respect for equal rights and the self-determination of peoples. The UN also aims to promote international cooperation and respect for human rights and fundamental freedoms without discrimination.[23] Hence, at the 2005 UN World Summit participating states affirmed adherence to 'the purposes and principles of the Charter and

[17] Ibid., p.110. [18] Tamanaha, *On the Rule of Law*, p.129. [19] Ibid., pp.1–2.

[20] R. Peerenboom, 'Human rights and rule of law: what's the relationship?', 36 *Georgetown Journal of International Law* (2004–5) 809, pp.825–6.

[21] Tamanaha, *On the Rule of Law*, pp.2–3.

[22] Report of the United Nations Secretary-General on the Rule of Law and Transitional Justice in Conflict and Post-Conflict Societies, S/2004/616, 23 August 2004, para.6.

[23] Art. 1, Charter of the United Nations, 892 UNTS 119.

international law and to an international order based on the rule of law and international law, which is essential for peaceful coexistence and cooperation among States'.[24] The former UN Secretary-General perceived the rule of law among other things as a system that adheres to international human rights as a safeguard against arbitrariness.[25]

Even in the presence of deep ideological and political division among states, the international rule of law is based on a significant body of rules which are followed by most states most of the time.[26] The international rule of law aims to restrict state power and incorporates some rules which are of superior status (peremptory norms) and provide equal protection to all (obligations owed to the international community of states).[27] States are therefore obliged to conduct their functions in conformity with the rule of law. The distinction between rule by law and rule of law is also becoming relevant at the international level. Accordingly, states cannot rely on international rules such as state sovereignty and consent to justify action that disregards fundamental community and universal principles. Moreover, the protection of the rule of law at a domestic level would be severely compromised if the rule of law was not respected at an international level. In this regard, a state which is bound by national laws to respect fundamental human rights and the rule of law cannot step outside these confines when acting at the international level as a member of an international organisation.

[24] Resolution adopted by the General Assembly, 2005 World Summit Outcome, A/RES/60/1, 24 October 2005, para.134.

[25] Report of the United Nations Secretary-General, note 22. Nevertheless, one wonders whether the UN have always acted in such a manner that 'politically charged issues, such as . . . abuse of power, denial of the right to property or citizenship and territorial disputes between States' have indeed been addressed 'in a legitimate and fair manner'. One cannot but make reference to the former Secretary-General Kofi Annan's Plan for the Settlement of the Cyprus Problem of April 2004, which did not take into account that the problem is one of foreign occupation in violation of both the *jus ad bellum* and the *jus in bello*. The plan, among other goals, aimed to legitimise the division of the Cypriot population on grounds of race (see in particular the restrictions on settlement), and by closing the door to the ECtHR failed to protect property rights effectively. For analysis see C. Palley, *An International Relations Debacle: The UN Secretary-General's Mission of Good Offices in Cyprus, 1999–2004* (Oxford: Hart, 2005). Also see 'A principled basis for a just and lasting Cyprus settlement in the light of international and European law', International Expert Panel convened by the Committee for a European Solution in Cyprus, paras.20–22. The Panel consisted of Professors Auer, Bossuyt, Burns, De Zayas, Silvio-Marcus, Kasimatis, Oberndoerfer Dieter and Shaw, and its report is available at http://alfreddezayas.com/Law_history/Cyprusproposal.shtml.

[26] Tamanaha, *On the Rule of Law*, p.128.

[27] Peerenboom, 'Human rights and rule of law', p.827.

The international rule of law therefore stands firmly against unilateral and arbitrary action by states either against other states or against the individual.[28] It is accordingly the answer to 'arbitrary power in international relations', it substitutes for the settlement of disputes by the use of force and is used to protect community interests, including fundamental rights.[29] In an international community where nuclear weapons have become a reality, the rule of law becomes even more important as a substitute for such forceful means.[30] It aims to ensure the peaceful coexistence of its subjects for their common good.[31]

Nevertheless, one may question whether the international rule of law actually exists. The unlawful bombing of Kosovo in 1999 and the invasion of Iraq in 2003 are illustrations of this.[32] Moreover, even the laws of war raise legitimate questions of whether they comply with the rule of law since any manner in which war is carried out results in devastation.[33] Such laws are 'vague and easily manipulated to serve political ends. They may even legitimate the use of force by providing superpowers the legal fig leaf needed to cover their acts of naked aggression.'[34]

To an even greater extent, the lack of centralised enforcement mechanisms and also of compulsory jurisdiction before the International Court of Justice and other international courts and tribunals undermines the rule of law at the international level. This was identified by Brierly as a significant weakness since the strength of a legal system lies in the mechanisms it sets out for its enforcement.[35] Whilst the international legal system has developed alternative enforcement mechanisms,[36] there is no doubt that its consent-based nature still leaves it exposed to ineffectiveness, selectivity and dysfunction.[37] This undoubtedly

[28] Ibid., p.814.

[29] W. Bishop, 'The international rule of law', 59 *Michigan Law Review* (1960–61) 553. Also Chesterman, 'An international rule of law?', p.359.

[30] Bishop, ibid., p.571.

[31] Bingham, *The Rule of Law*, pp.110 and 112. On the objective of law generally see Harvey, 'The rule of law in historical perspective', p.488.

[32] Peerenboom, 'Human rights and rule of law', p.869.

[33] Ibid., p.877. [34] Ibid., pp.877 and 899.

[35] J. L. Brierly, *The Law of Nations*, 4th edn (Oxford University Press, 1949) at 73 quoted in Bishop, 'The international rule of law', pp.562–3. Also see Chesterman, 'An international rule of law?', p.357.

[36] Such as counter-measures in response to violations of community interests. For analysis see E. Katselli-Proukaki, *The Problem of Enforcement in International Law: Countermeasures, the Non-Injured State and the Idea of International Community* (London: Routledge, 2010).

[37] Tamanaha, *On the Rule of Law*, pp.130–31.

undermines the international rule of law and constitutes a stumbling block to the fulfilment of community interests such as the peaceful coexistence of states and the universal respect for human rights and freedoms in a meaningful way. Similarly, states are normally bound by different rules which may be applied by different national and international courts leading to different legal outcomes.[38] This polymorphy threatens the integrity of the international rule of law. At the same time, the dominance of powerful actors make international law less well-represented. In addition, collective action is greatly preferred to unilateral state action and very much more needed,[39] although political realities make this difficult to achieve in many circumstances.

Nevertheless, even recalcitrant states obey most international rules, and when they do not, they never openly admit this. Moreover, the period after the Second World War signifies the changing nature of the international legal system.[40] International human rights law emerged as an expression of the international rule of law for the purpose of protecting the individual regardless of any other conditions such as nationality, religion or status. Even if its values are not universally recognised they are at least widely accepted, as is evident from the numerous human rights treaties, now an integral part of the international legal order.[41] Although pragmatism illustrates that human rights are not effectively implemented or adhered to worldwide, no human rights progress could be achieved outside the rule of law.[42]

That the rule of law is closely linked to respect for human rights as a constraint on the state and society is well established today.[43] The Universal Declaration of Human Rights envisaged in its preamble that 'it is essential, if man is not to be compelled to have recourse, as a last resort, to rebellion against tyranny and oppression, that human rights

38 Ibid., p.132.

39 P. C. Jessup, *A Modern Law of Nations* (London: Macmillan, 1948) at 2 in Bishop, 'The international rule of law', p.565.

40 Tamanaha, *On the Rule of Law*, p.131.

41 Bingham, *The Rule of Law*, pp.116–17. On the universal character of human rights also see O. Yasuaki, 'A transcivilizational perspective on international law. Questioning prevalent cognitive frameworks in the emerging multi-polar and multi-civilizational world of the twenty-first century', *Recueil des Cours* (2009) 77, 344; Henkin *et al.*, *Human Rights*, p.3. For a thorough account of reservations felt about incorporating human rights within the Australian legal order and a response to sceptics, see S. Ratnapala, 'Bills of rights in functioning parliamentary democracies: kantian, consequentialist and institutionalist scepticisms', 34 *Melbourne University Law Review* (2010) 591.

42 Peerenboom, 'Human rights and rule of law', p.812.

43 See Harvey, 'The rule of law in historical perspective', p.497.

should be protected by the rule of law'.[44] This principle is also entailed in the preamble of the ECHR as commonly shared by all member states of the Council of Europe.[45] Extensive reference to the rule of law is also incorporated in the Treaty on the European Union. Significantly, in delimiting the Union's actions in the international sphere Article 21(1) also provides that:

> [t]he Union's action on the international scene shall be guided by the principles which have inspired its own creation, development and enlargement, and which it seeks to advance in the wider world: democracy, the rule of law, the universality and indivisibility of human rights and fundamental freedoms, respect for human dignity, the principles of equality and solidarity, and respect for the principles of the United Nations Charter and international law.[46]

Although the 1966 International Covenant on Civil and Political Rights does not expressly make reference to the rule of law, the concept is inherent in the Covenant.[47] Whilst Article 4 permits the adoption of measures in response to a public emergency under stringent conditions, it also provides that such measures must not be in breach of states' 'other obligations under international law' and must not 'involve discrimination solely on the ground of race, colour, sex, language, religion or social origin'. Accordingly, restrictions are not unqualified. This ensures the protection of the individual against arbitrary or excessive state power in violation of the rule of law, an interpretation confirmed by the Human Rights Committee which emphasises that '[s]afeguards related to derogation, as embodied in Article 4 of the Covenant, are based on the principles of legality and the rule of law inherent in the Covenant as a whole'.[48]

The Westphalian model, under which states enjoyed absolute sovereignty and dominion often at the expense of the individual, has gradually given way to recognition of the individual's own legal personality within the international legal system. The international rule of law is thus linked closely with the protection of human rights and with the idea

[44] The Universal Declaration of Human Rights, adopted by General Assembly Resolution 217–A (III), 10 December 1948.

[45] Convention for the Protection of Human Rights and Fundamental Freedoms, ETS No. 5 (Protocol 11, ETS No. 155) Rome, 4 November 1950.

[46] Consolidated version of the Treaty on European Union, *Official Journal of the European Union* C83/13, 30 March 2010.

[47] International Covenant on Civil and Political Rights, 999 UNTS 171.

[48] General Comment No. 29, States of Emergency (Article 4), Human Rights Committee, CCPR/C/21/Rev.1/Add.11, 31 August 2001.

of restraining force among states.[49] A relevant question to consider is whether the rule of law is associated with democracy. Indeed, one can see that the reconciliation of justice with non-democratic regimes that violate human rights and freedoms is difficult to achieve.[50] Yet again, as argued above, the rule of law is not necessarily linked with what the majority of the population wants, as expressed through democratic procedures. In this context, human rights entail an element of democracy: the right of the people to take part in government. However, only to the extent permitted by the rule of law can democracy, in other words the right of the majority, circumvent human rights.[51]

The significance of human rights as a concept that is part and parcel of the rule of law is considered next.

Human rights and international rule of law

Few can actually doubt that the Second World War was a period of great significance: for the devastation that it caused to millions of people, but also for the hope that the postwar era brought. Truly, the years that followed the cessation of hostilities signified a new momentum in the international legal order and brought about ground-breaking developments in relation to the rights of the individual at an international level. Gradually emerging in a traditionally state-dominated legal order as an actor and not merely as an object, the individual begins to be regarded as the holder of international rights and obligations.[52] The principles of absolute state sovereignty, consent and non-interference are challenged by principles of fundamental, universal and inalienable human rights, *jus cogens* norms and obligations owed to the international community as a whole.[53] These developments have been motivated, although not

[49] UN Secretary-General, Report on the Rule of Law and Transitional Justice, para.6. Also see analysis in Bishop, 'The international rule of law', pp.554–5.

[50] See analysis in Peerenboom, 'Human rights and rule of law', pp.863–4.

[51] Henkin *et al., Human Rights.* Also see Ratnapala, 'Bills of rights in functioning parliamentary democracies', p.596.

[52] Sir Hersch Lauterpacht, *International Law and Human Rights* (London: Stevens & Sons, 1950), p.61 in H. J. Steiner, P. Alston and R. Goodman, *International Human Rights in Context (Law, Politics, Morals)*, 3rd edn. (Oxford University Press, 2008) p.144.

[53] A. A. C. Trindade, *International Law for Humankind: Towards a New* Jus Gentium (Leiden: Martinus Nijhoff, 2010), p.282. Also see R. B. Bilder, 'An overview of international human rights law' in H. Hannum, *Guide to International Human Rights Practice*, 4th edn. (Ardsley, NY: Transnational Publishers, 2004), p.3.

incontestably,[54] by a strong belief that promoting respect for human rights and strengthening the system of protection of the individual are for the common good. Respect for human dignity and the prohibition of conduct that violates fundamental community interests constitute a part of general international law and are no longer made conditional on the existence or ratification of a treaty.[55]

The wealth of treaty and customary human rights rules, the establishment of the two ad hoc international criminal tribunals for the former Yugoslavia and Rwanda, and the creation of the first permanent International Criminal Court demonstrate that human rights create *legal* rights.[56] Increasingly, violations and massive atrocities are not tolerated.[57] Moreover, the House of Lords' judgment in *Pinochet* signified a new era in which a state official cannot hide behind immunities for serious violations of international law such as torture. Even more significantly, it no longer matters where the atrocity took place.[58] The principle of universal jurisdiction enables the prosecution of individuals responsible for atrocities regardless of where they occurred or the nationality of the victim. As pointed out, violations in one part of the world are now felt everywhere.[59]

Furthermore, in 2005 the UN General Assembly referred to the duty of states to protect not just their own populations but also non-nationals from genocide, war crimes, ethnic cleansing and crimes against humanity.[60] According to Judge Buergenthal, this responsibility to protect will 'become an important tool in fighting these international crimes'.[61]

Hence, human rights have exercised a significant influence on national and international theory and practice, they have infiltrated foreign affairs and they have promoted the idea of global justice. The policy of former US President Jimmy Carter to see human rights guiding foreign affairs and influencing foreign policies has contributed to a different approach

54 M. Koskenniemi, 'International law in Europe: between tradition and renewal', 16 *EJIL* (2005) 1, 113, p.116.

55 Trindade, *International Law for Humankind*, pp.276–7.

56 Henkin *et al., Human Rights*, pp.3–4.

57 See C. Tomuschat, *Human Rights: Between Idealism and Realism*, 2nd edn. (Oxford University Press, 2008) 95. Tomuschat quotes Walzer, according to whom there exists a 'minimal and universal moral code'.

58 *R* v. *Bow Street Magistrates ex parte Pinochet* (1999) 2 WLR 827.

59 Kant quoted in D. O'Byrne, *Human Rights: An Introduction* (London: Pearson, 2003) p.35.

60 General Assembly Resolution, note 24 above, para.134.

61 T. Buergenthal, 'The contemporary significance of international human rights law', 22 *Leiden Journal of International Law* (2009) 217, p.221.

in relation to serious violations by other states.[62] This policy was of course far from perfect. Foreign affairs were still influenced by geostrategic, economic, political and other interests as demonstrated by the support for dictatorial and racist regimes in the Americas and South Africa. Nonetheless, such ideas might be seen behind the countermeasures imposed against the genocidal regime of Amin in Uganda in the 1970s and against South Africa in the 1980s, which both have something important to say about the protection of fundamental community interests. Closer to home, the European Union (EU) often imposes human rights clauses before agreeing to provide economic and other assistance to third states that do not respect human rights.[63]

States increasingly realise that their disregard for human rights has economic and political costs.[64] Human rights are not just a political idea or a movement, but rather law which extends beyond the 'naming and shaming' of the recalcitrant states.[65] Respect for them reaffirms the rule of law. Increasing awareness that the conduct of a certain state is illegitimate has the potential 'to have an effect on the behaviour of some governments and possibly also on their grip on power'.[66] This is far from just disillusion or idolatry as the 2011 revolts in Tunisia, Egypt and Libya demonstrate. Taking into consideration the political realities, as Judge Buergenthal himself recognises, not every case will be a success story. However, the dynamics of human rights cannot be reversed and one can only hope for stronger and more effective protection in the future. In this context it is often argued that the concept of human rights constitutes 'one of the most important values of the twenty-first century world'.[67]

Nevertheless, human rights ideas should not be taken for granted. Often regarded as a Trojan horse advanced for the purpose of a new form of imperialism and oppression of the people, human rights ideas have not yet brought about consensus among states and commentators. There are still those who argue that cultural, economic, political and social differences dictate a different understanding of 'human rights', one that will respect the diversity of the various actors in international law.[68] This echoes Weil's warning that 'injecting' community ideas into the

[62] President Carter's Inaugural Address, 20 January 1977, *New York Times*, 21 January 1977.
[63] See Katselli Proukaki, *The Problem of Enforcement*.
[64] Buergenthal, 'Contemporary significance', p.219.
[65] Ibid., p.221. Also see Chapter 2 above.
[66] Buergenthal, 'Contemporary significance', p.223.
[67] Yasuaki, 'A transcivilizational perspective', p.342. [68] Ibid., p.344.

theory and practice of international law endangers its neutrality and its primary purpose: to achieve consensus in a pluralistic and inherently diverse community of states.[69]

Hence, hanging between idolatry and pragmatism as Professor Kennedy rightly points out in this volume,[70] the concept of human rights is in danger of falling into disrepute. On one hand, there may be those who would argue that international law, despite the advances of the last six decades, has not done much to provide effective and credible protection to all (disassociated from double standards, hypocrisy and dysfunction). On the other hand, others would argue that international law can only do as much as its primary subjects, namely states, want it to achieve. In this sense, international law is closely linked with state consent and its fate is entirely reliant upon, and submissive to such consent.

Professor Kennedy is right when he says that awareness of the limitations of the human rights language is fundamental. This is because adopting an absolute language of morality, righteousness and universality gives rise to concerns at how genuine are the motives of those invoking them, and makes the debate on human rights counterproductive. It also disregards pragmatism which is nothing but the recognition that states are still guided by different interests. Hence, states are only too willing to comply with international rules that do not interfere with such interests.[71] As human rights law gains ground states are less keen to support its further development. For as long as human rights were perceived as the answer to Communism and as the transposition of 'liberal' ideals into developing countries, they had the full support and backing of the developed.[72] Today however, developed states are concerned that what they have long passionately preached is turning against them. In the light of international terrorism and other serious threats to international peace and security, human rights create a legal obstacle in the reformulated policies of these states: torture (whether through water-boarding or not), presence of state agents during questionable interrogation methods abroad, extraordinary rendition, detention without charge or trial, freezing of economic assets, the inclusion of individuals in lists of terrorists and thereby removing them from any concept of due process, discriminatory practices against non-nationals and increased executive powers of control orders.

69 P. Weil, 'Towards normative relativity', 77 *American Journal of International Law* (1983) 3, 413, p.420.

70 See Chapter 2 above.

71 Buergenthal, 'Contemporary significance', p.218.

72 Peerenboom, 'Human rights and rule of law', p.824.

The *Realpolitik* could not be more evident here: preaching that other states must respect the rule of law, whilst placing themselves outside any such context.

Ironically, at times states rely on international law such as state sovereignty and equality to justify action that in effect undermines the rule of law, such as human rights violations.

It is therefore shown that the end of the Second World War and the creation of the UN often did not meet the aspirations towards an international rule of law that would bring about friendly relations among states and fruition of fundamental rights. The genocide in Rwanda in 1994 and the war that traumatised the Balkans in the 1990s are but two examples of this: the list is long and disappointing.[73] Despite the significant steps taken for the protection of human rights, atrocities and massive violations continue to occur. Still, and as Judge Buergenthal points out, 'it would be naïve not to expect such setbacks, but it would be equally wrong to assume that no progress has been made'.[74] As pointed out by US President Obama, the recent revolt in Libya 'represents the aspirations of people who are seeking a better life' through respect for their 'universal' and 'not negotiable' human rights.[75]

For this reason, the need to respect the international rule of law in state affairs, through among other things respect for human rights, is particularly compelling, as explained in the next section. Notably however, '[i]f there is to be an enduring international rule of law, it must be seen to reflect the interests of the entire international community'.[76]

The political–legal divide and the rule of law

In the light of the pragmatism which permeates inter-state relations, there is often a call to accept the political reality, the *Realpolitik*,[77] at the expense of the rule of law and human rights. The distinction between the political and the legal is frequently resorted to by states, and even by the UN when settling international disputes. The plan proposed by the former UN Secretary-General Kofi Annan for the settlement of the Cyprus problem in 2004 is an illustration of an attempt to impose the political reality on the rule of law.[78] This was even in breach of the UN's

[73] Buergenthal, 'Contemporary significance', p.218. [74] Ibid., p.218.

[75] Obama's speech on Libya, *The New York Times*, 23 February 2011.

[76] Tamanaha, *On the Rule of Law*, p.136. [77] Ibid., p.128.

[78] Palley, *An International Relations Debacle*. Also see F. Hoffmeister, *Legal Aspects of the Cyprus Problem: Annan Plan and EU Accession* (Leiden: Martinus Nijhoff, 2006).

basic aim to settle international disputes 'in conformity with the principles of justice and international law'.

For Professor Lauterpacht, the distinction between legal and political disputes was but yet another attempt 'to give legal expression to the State's claim to be independent of law'.[79] In any case, states often invoke vital national interests in an attempt to justify their action. Nevertheless, all disputes between states are subject to the rule of law regardless of whether the dispute in question involves fundamental state interests.[80] The legal–political divide is often reflected in domestic laws which prevent the consideration of issues that fall within foreign policy,[81] and also in the non-justiciability of the acts and decisions of the UN Security Council. As Professor Koskenniemi observes, there exists 'a more pragmatic concern about who should have the say about foreign policy – and thus occupy the place political theory has been accustomed to calling "sovereignty"'.[82] This is further reflected in the composition of international courts such as the International Court of Justice which requires national or ad hoc judges. Whilst the judges in each instance must act independently of their national state, this might not always be the case.[83]

Nevertheless, the international legal order is a dynamic, constantly evolving system of rules which adjusts to the needs of the international community.[84] This is evident from the fact that international rules such as those protecting human rights have developed in deviation from positivist rules for the purpose of protecting the individual.[85] The necessity of looking at the evolutionary element of international law is hindered by political realism and legal positivism, however, to the extent that they insist that 'current needs and aspirations of humankind' must take into account the state-centric character of the international legal order.[86] In this sense, state interests dominate the law regardless of justice.[87] Yet,

> [n]o positivist could anticipate, in the mid-forties, the emergence and consolidation of the International Law of Human Rights. No realist could foresee, in the mid-fifties, the advent of the phenomenon of

[79] Sir Hersch Lauterpacht, *The Function of Law in the International Community* (Oxford: Clarendon Press, 1933) p.6.

[80] M. Koskenniemi, 'The function of law in the international community: 75 years after', *British Yearbook of International Law* (2008) 353, pp.358 and 360–61.

[81] See for instance the ruling of the Court of Appeal in *R (Abbasi)* v. *Foreign Secretary* [2002] EWCA Civ 1598.

[82] Koskenniemi, 'The function of law in the international community', p.365.

[83] Tamanaha, *On the Rule of Law*, p.134.

[84] Trindade, *International Law for Humankind*, pp.32 and 36.

[85] Ibid., pp.36–7. [86] Ibid., p.47. [87] Ibid.

> decolonisation. The emancipation of the human person *vis-à-vis* his own State and the emancipation of peoples in International Law took place much to the amazement of legal positivists and political 'realists'. No realist could forecast the fall of the Berlin wall, in the late eighties. Neither legal positivists, nor political 'realists', can understand – and have difficulties to accept – the profound transformations of contemporary International Law in pursuance of the imperatives of justice.[88]

International law, as it emerged from the ruins of the Second World War, could not dissociate itself from principles of 'ethics' and 'justice'.[89] The concept of 'moral relativism' is in this regard criticised.[90] There is an imperative need for 'an international legal order capable of regulating effectively the relations between all its subjects, and of fulfilling the needs and aspirations of the international community as a whole, among which [are] the realisation of justice'.[91]

However, in recent years the international legal community has witnessed a new predator. The Security Council's growing interference with fundamental rights using its Chapter VII powers has raised legitimate questions about the boundaries of its powers. Most significantly, it has provoked criticism that it has become a politicised body which appears to be acting outside the rule of law. These concerns are addressed in the next section by reference to how these questions have been addressed before regional and national courts.

The rule of law, human rights and international peace and security

The preceding analysis established that the international rule of law requires respect for human rights. Nevertheless, new challenges have emerged in recent years which threaten the integrity of the international legal order and the rule of law. Since the end of the Cold War in the early 1990s, the Security Council has adopted a more active role in the exercise of its primary responsibility to maintain international peace and security. This has undoubtedly brought about many positive results, such as the establishment of the two ad hoc international criminal tribunals for the prosecution of serious atrocities. Nevertheless, it has also resulted in

[88] Ibid., pp.47–8. [89] Ibid., p.49.

[90] Sir Hersch Lauterpacht, 'On realism, especially in international relations' in *International Law Being the Collected Papers of Hersch Lauterpacht*, vol. 2, part 1 (Cambridge University Press, 1975) pp.53 and 57–62. Quoted in Trindade, ibid., p.49.

[91] Trindade, ibid., p.50.

more controversial action which has led to the violation of human rights. Legitimate questions arise in this respect as to whether the rule of law extends to Security Council actions or not.[92]

The Security Council, in responding to international terrorism or other threats to peace and security, has authorised significant restrictions on, among other things, the financial assets of individuals and their rights to run for election, to effective judicial review, and to liberty.

The fact that the Security Council is an undemocratic political body the acts of which cannot be subject to judicial review is still a thorn in the side for critics. In truth, the rule of law becomes devoid of meaning if the law is applied in a selective way and permits no review of certain actions. However, this has not prevented individuals from seeking judicial protection. The cases discussed below highlight some of the legal difficulties whilst courts have not always taken a consistent stance on significant issues, such as those relating to conflicting international obligations of compelling significance (e.g. human rights and the rule of law) on one hand, and obligations emanating from Security Council resolutions on the other. The dilemma therefore is, as Lord Brown recognised, that to act 'contrary to fundamental principles of human rights' is however 'the inevitable consequence' of implementing such resolutions.[93]

In *al Jedda*, the appellant challenged his indefinite detention by British troops in Iraq as a breach of his rights to liberty and a fair trial. This detention relied on Security Council Resolution 1511. Whilst the House of Lords accepted that the detention was attributed to the UK directly and not to the UN,[94] controversially it held that in such cases the obligation to detain prevailed over the obligation to protect the appellant's fundamental rights emanating from the ECHR.[95] In other words, the House qualified the enjoyment of human rights and the application of the ECHR in the light of overriding obligations under Article 103 of the UN Charter. The ruling raises serious concerns regarding the power of the Security Council to compromise rights recognised not only in numerous treaties but also in customary law. It is a clear illustration of the dominance of a political body, in reflection of political reality, over the rule of law. Nevertheless, the

92 Chesterman, 'An international rule of law?', p.349.

93 *Her Majesty's Treasury* v. *Ahmed and others*, [2010] UKSC 2, para.203.

94 Deviating from the findings of the ECtHR in *Behrami* v. *France*, Application No. 71412/01, and *Saramati* v. *France, Germany and Norway*, Application No. 78166/01, Judgment of 2 May 2007, (2007) 45 EHRR SE10, para.144.

95 *R (on the application of al-Jedda)* v. *Secretary of State for Defence*, Judgment of 12 December 2007, [2007] UKHL 58, para.35.

drafters of the ECHR never intended to qualify the rights under the Convention in the light of UN obligations. As recognised by Baroness Hale in *al Jedda*, the drafters of the ECHR had not 'become disillusioned with the United Nations as a reliable source of human rights protection'. Significantly however, in its landmark judgment on the same case, the ECtHR held that it was not the Security Council's expressed intention to authorise the detention of individuals in violation of international human rights law. The Court did not accept that in this instance there existed a conflict between the relevant Security Council resolutions and human rights obligations. Nor did it accept that the Council had authorised through the resolution under consideration the indefinite detention of individuals without charge or trial. Instead, emphasising the Security Council's responsibility to act in compliance with the principles of the United Nations, including respect for human rights, the ECtHR concluded that the detention of the applicant lacked legal basis.[96] Similar issues were raised before the European Court of Justice (ECJ) in *Kadi* and *al Barakaat.*

In these cases the applicants challenged the lawfulness of a Council regulation, based on Security Council resolutions, which authorised the freezing of their financial assets without enabling them to judicially challenge the decision against them. The ECJ held that the contested regulation was indeed in breach of the appellants' fundamental rights as incorporated in EU law representing 'a higher rule of law in the Community legal order'.[97] Significantly however, in determining whether Community legislation which gives effect to Security Council resolutions but violates human rights is lawful the Court stressed:

> [T]he Community is based on the rule of law, inasmuch as neither its Member States nor its institutions can avoid review of the conformity of their acts with the basic constitutional charter, the EC Treaty, which established a complete system of legal remedies and procedures designed to enable the Court of Justice to review the legality of acts of the institutions . . .[98]

As further pointed out, EU member states cannot rely on other international agreements as a justification for compromising the constitutional principles of the Community, including their obligation to protect fundamental rights.[99]

[96] Ibid., para.125. See also *al Jedda* v. *United Kingdom*, Application no. 27021/08, 7 July 2011, paras.102, 105 and 107.

[97] C–402/05 P, *Kadi* v. *Council of the European Union and Commission of the European Communities* and C–415/05 P, *al Barakaat International Foundation*, Joined cases, Judgment of the European Court of Justice, 3 September 2008, ECR 2008 I–06351, paras.285–8.

[98] Ibid., paras.281–2.

[99] Ibid., para.285.

By taking such a strong constitutional line the ECJ aimed to protect the integrity of the European legal order which it has been tasked by the EU treaties with protecting. Nevertheless, the question is not one relating to the dominance of the European legal order over general international law. Rather, it is a question of upholding general international law, in which fundamental rights and freedoms and the rule of law constitute an integral part. The EU itself is legally bound by such principles regardless of whether the EU treaties expressly provide for their respect. This argument is supported by Ziegler who takes a sceptical view of the ECJ's conclusion since according to her it contributes to the fragmentation of international law. What the ECJ should have done is to interpret Security Council resolutions in the light of international human rights standards, as the ECtHR did in *al Jedda*.[100] As she points out, '[a]fter all, the standards and values enforced by the ECJ are also those pursued by the international legal order'.[101] Indeed, fundamental rights are 'part and parcel of a common identity of the international community'.[102]

Yet the ruling in *Kadi* demonstrates the significant role of institutions in upholding the rule of law and fundamental rights and in restraining arbitrary action on grounds of international peace and security. It further upholds previous case law according to which Community legislation must comply with these fundamental principles and Community courts must extend judicial review to all legislation that might impinge on the principles on which it is founded.[103]

Another significant judgment was given by the UK Supreme Court in its first ever case. The Supreme Court was called to determine the lawfulness of the restrictions on the appellants' financial assets applied under the Terrorism (United Nations Measures) Order 2006 and the Al Qaida and Taliban Order 2006.[104] Both Orders were adopted by the Treasury under section 1 of the United Nations Act 1946 in order to give

[100] K. S. Ziegler, 'Strengthening the rule of law, but fragmenting international law: the *Kadi* decision of the ECJ from the perspective of human rights', 9 *Human Rights Law Review* (2009) 2, 288, pp.297–8.

[101] Ibid., pp.304–5.

[102] A. Bianchi, 'Security Council's anti-terror resolutions and their implementation by member states: an overview', *Journal of International Criminal Justice* (2006) 1073.

[103] C. Tomuschat, 'Case T–306/01, *Ahmed Ali Yusuf and Al Barakaat International Foundation* v. *Council and Commission*, 21 September 2005, Court of First Instance; Case T–315/01, *Yassin Abdullah Kadi* v. *Council and Commission*, 21 September 2005, Court of First Instance', 43 CMLR (2006) 541. See also Art. 6, para.2 TEU.

[104] See *Ahmed and others*, note 93 above.

effect to Security Council Resolutions 1267 and 1373 against those listed as terrorists by the Sanctions Committee.

Lord Hope, recognising the 'paralysing' effects of the imposed measures on the enjoyment of private and family life which made the individual a 'prisoner of the State',[105] stressed that the executive was not free from increased scrutiny. This was particularly so whenever fundamental rights were at stake. This duty persisted even under the 1946 Act which authorised the executive to take 'necessary or expedient' measures for the implementation of Security Council decisions. Notably,

> If the rule of law is to mean anything, decisions as to what is necessary or expedient in this context cannot be left to the uncontrolled judgment of the executive ... The undoubted fact that section 1 of the 1946 Act was designed to enable the United Kingdom to fulfil its obligations under the Charter to implement Security Council resolutions does not diminish this essential principle.[106]

As noted, granting the executive unlimited power in implementing such resolutions, which it had taken part in formulating, 'conflicts with the basic rules that lie at the heart of our democracy'.[107]

The Supreme Court concluded that both orders lacked Parliament's authorisation in imposing 'draconian' restrictions on the individual on reasonable suspicion of involvement in terrorist activities which were 'so great, so overwhelming and so timeless'.[108] According to Lord Hope, the listing and delisting procedures did not comply with principles of natural justice or basic procedural guarantees.[109]

If individuals are unable to judicially challenge their inclusion in the terrorist list this amounts to a violation of a significant principle of the rule of law.[110] Such severe interference had not been foreseen by the legislator when adopting the 1946 Act. Accordingly, the principle of legality requires the presumption that the intention of Parliament was not to provide such extensive power to the executive.[111]

[105] Ibid., paras.38 and 60. [106] Ibid., para.45. [107] Ibid.

[108] Ibid., para.76. According to Lord Hoffmann, 'Parliamentary sovereignty means that Parliament can, if it chooses, legislate contrary to fundamental principles of human rights. The Human Rights Act will not detract from this power. The constraints upon its exercise by Parliament are ultimately political, not legal. But the principle of legality means that Parliament must squarely confront what it is doing and accept the political cost': *R* v. *Secretary of State for the Home Department, ex parte Simms* [2000] 2 AC 115, 131. Whilst the state is entitled to restrict fundamental human rights in order to protect the rights of others and in the public interest, its power to do so is not unlimited.

[109] *Ahmed and others*, note 93 above, para.80. [110] Ibid., para.146.

[111] Ibid., para.154.

The ruling was welcomed as upholding human rights 'over executive decisions founded on international law, including those originating from the United Nations Security Council. International law cannot be a round-about means of bypassing citizens' most basic fundamental rights.' Significantly, it was stressed that Security Council-authorised sanctions should respect minimum standards of fundamental rights.[112]

Whilst this ruling is indeed significant, the Supreme Court was reluctant to deviate from the findings in *al Jedda* that Security Council resolutions prevail over human rights. Moreover, the issues dealt with by the Court were restricted to the limits of executive power and the relationship between the executive and Parliament. The Court also expressly stated that fundamental rights could lawfully be restricted if this is approved by Parliament. This suggests that conduct that undermines fundamental principles could be lawful if authorised by the Security Council and given effect domestically by legislation.

This highlights again the necessity to delimit the Security Council's powers. The Security Council is not itself above the rule of law. It is bound by the legal rules that brought it into existence, and in particular the UN Charter.[113] It is therefore clear that, since respect for human rights constitutes one of the primary objectives of the Charter, the Security Council does not possess carte blanche to disregard such obligations when exercising its mandatory powers.[114] Like the EU and any other international organisation, the Security Council is a body that has been created by and, as a result, is subject to the rules and principles of general international law.[115] This includes respect for human rights which is, according to Brownlie, a 'legal necessity'.[116]

In this regard, international peace and security cannot be used by a political body in a manner contrary to fundamental principles on which the international rule of law is founded. Such was the position of the ECJ

[112] 'Anti-terrorist blacklists: Dick Marty welcomes British court ruling', 28 January 2010, Rapporteur of Parliamentary Assembly, Council of Europe.

[113] *Reparations for Injuries Case* ICJ Reports (1949) 180.

[114] For analysis see E. Katselli, 'Holding the Security Council accountable for human rights violations', 1 *Human Rights and International Legal Discourse* (2007) 2, pp.301–33.

[115] B. Fassbender, 'The United Nations Charter as constitution of the international community', 36 *Columbia Journal of Transnational Law* (1998) 529, p.594; J. L. Brierly, 'The Covenant and the Charter', 23 *British Yearbook of International Law* (1946) 83.

[116] I. Brownlie, 'The decisions of political organs of the United Nations and the rule of law' in R. Macdonald, *Essays in Honour of Wang Tieya* (Leiden: Martinus Nijhoff, 1994), p.102; Report of the Special Rapporteur, Mr Martin Scheinin, on the promotion and protection of human rights and fundamental freedoms while countering terrorism, 28 December 2005, E/CN.4/2006/98, para.60.

in *Kadi* and *al Barakaat*, in which the court rejected the view that Security Council decisions prevail to the detriment of fundamental Community principles and fundamental rights.[117]

Conclusion

The rule of law is a significant concept inherent in the idea of justice and legality and gains prominence in many different legal systems, both domestic and international, as a restriction of state abuse. Blind adherence to rules and the law in disregard of these principles is no longer acceptable. This is particularly so in an international legal order in which state rights have given way, to a certain extent, to fundamental community interests. The continuing attempts of states to confine international law to principles of state sovereignty, consent and non-interference no longer fit with the ground-breaking developments that took place in the aftermath of the Second World War. Furthermore, no pragmatism and no political realism were sufficient to stop the wind of change which placed significant emphasis on the rights of the individual and on state restraint.

Whilst the establishment of a truly effective international rule of law is painstaking due to the weaknesses of the international legal system, it has been illustrated that the legal changes that occurred in the last six decades provide hope for the future.

In this context, the Security Council is itself in desperate need of adjusting to these significant legal developments. It must therefore ensure that in carrying out its responsibility for international peace and security it does not act outside the ambit of the rule of law. The UN Charter and general international law dictate that the Security Council, a political and undemocratic body, does not have unlimited powers. The Security Council cannot therefore act at will, at the expense of fundamental rights, without legal consequences. National and international courts have a paramount obligation to protect the individual against abuse and to uphold fundamental rights, justice and the rule of law, even when considering Security Council-authorised action. This is particularly so given that the Security Council is not itself subject to judicial review.

The analysis in this chapter has therefore demonstrated that the international rule of law, in which human rights hold a prominent place, infiltrates the political sphere in an irreversible manner with which states and international bodies such as the Security Council are required to conform.

[117] *Kadi*, note 97 above, Opinion of Advocate-General Maduro, 16 January 2008, para.34.

8

The construction of the constitutional essentials of democratic politics by the European Court of Human Rights following *Sejdić and Finci*

STEVEN WHEATLEY

Introduction

In his contribution to this collection, David Kennedy observes that the concept of human rights is no longer just an idea: both in debates and formal institutional settings, 'human rights' are relied upon to denounce the conduct of states and promote global justice. Human rights activists, professionals and lawyers should accept the responsibilities of rulership and re-imagine the idea of human freedom in more expansive terms – freedom from hunger, disease and war etc – to remake world society by establishing a new system of rulership with a greater potential for the emancipation of human persons.[1] The analysis is compelling in highlighting the ways in which the idea of 'human rights' constrains the ways in which we understand justice in world society, and the limits of that understanding. What is self-consciously absent is any requirement to legitimate the rulership of a new humanitarian elite by reference to standards of normative political or democratic legitimacy. This chapter accepts the possibilities of rulership (or 'governance') through formal institutions and the discourse of human rights, which constructs identities, claims, relationships and democratic politics, but rejects any argument that the concept of authority, i.e. the right to determine the normative situation of others, can be disengaged from the idea of democratic legitimacy, at least in relation to democratic societies.[2]

[1] See Chapter 2 above. Elsewhere, Professor Kennedy observes 'the exuberance of humanitarians who see a constitutional moment of the first order . . . in the emergence of human rights . . . as a global vocabulary of legitimacy': David Kennedy, *The Dark Sides of Virtue: Reassessing International Humanitarianism* (Princeton, NJ: Princeton University Press, 2004), p.336.

[2] See, generally, Steven Wheatley, *Democratic Legitimacy of International Law* (Oxford: Hart, 2010).

The chapter first outlines the regime established under the European Convention on Human Rights (ECHR) and the dynamic and teleological approach of the European Court of Human Rights (ECtHR) to the interpretation of the Convention. It then evaluates the judgment of the Grand Chamber in *Sejdić and Finci v Bosnia and Herzegovina*, from which there is no possibility of appeal, which subjected the imposed constitutional settlement in Bosnia and Herzegovina (BiH) to supranational judicial review. The chapter then proceeds to consider the relationship between the autonomous legal order constituted by the ECHR and the autonomous legal orders of states parties, and the complexities that emerge from the establishment of competing conceptions of political justice. Drawing on the work of John Rawls, the chapter considers the possibility of developing a political conception of justice through judicial reasoning by a supranational constitutional court (the ECtHR), and the limits of those possibilities. The analysis suggests the development of an 'other-regarding' conception of justice by the ECtHR, limited to the constitutional essentials of political law-making in states parties and the scope and content of the fundamental Convention rights in the ECHR. The chapter concludes by emphasising the requirement to establish political legitimacy for 'human rights', and the need for democratic engagement – not rulership – by humanitarians (and others who claim to know better) in order to exercise legitimate governance in conditions of complexity and reasonable disagreement.

International human rights law

Reference to 'human rights' suggests a universal moral code applicable to all persons in world society. Consider, for example, the foundational statement in Article 1 of the Universal Declaration on Human Rights (UDHR): 'All human beings are born free and equal in dignity and rights.'[3] The Universal Declaration does not, however, prescribe the scope and content of human rights for all persons, in all places; it establishes a political conception of rights, containing a limited number of absolute prohibitions,[4] and 'rights' that may be subject to such limitations as required for securing the rights and freedoms of others

[3] Art. 1, GA Res. 217(III)A, adopted 10 December 1948, 'Universal Declaration of Human Rights'.

[4] The UDHR prohibits slavery (ibid., Art. 4), torture and cruel, inhuman or degrading treatment or punishment (Art. 5); equal protection under the law (Art. 7) is likewise absolute.

and for 'meeting the just requirements of morality, public order and the general welfare in a democratic society'.[5] The scope and content of human rights norms must be worked out through democratic procedures in each sovereign political community, a point emphasised in Article 21, which provides that the will of the people is the basis for the authority of government, expressed in periodic and genuine elections.[6]

Since the adoption of the UDHR, a *corpus* of international human rights law has emerged in both 'hard' international treaties and 'softer' instruments. The ECHR, introduced to give effect to the rights recognised in the Universal Declaration and to preserve the rule of law and principles of democracy,[7] is a hard international law treaty establishing a legal regime for the protection of civil and political rights at the regional level. Responsibility for the interpretation of its provisions is accorded to the ECtHR.[8] The ability of the Court to develop the ECHR regime is not unlimited; the ECtHR is not an international common law court – its interpretative function is constrained by the constitutive text: the ECHR and its protocols.[9] The indeterminate nature of the treaty provisions and the Court's dynamic and teleological approach to interpretation have, though, allowed the ECtHR to develop the scope and content of the provisions of the ECHR beyond the literal text. The Court has not felt constrained by the *Lotus* principle or established international law rules for the interpretation of treaties.[10] The ECtHR does not regard the ECHR as an international treaty of the 'classic kind', involving 'mere reciprocal engagements between contracting States'.[11] In the interpretation of the Convention, 'regard must be had to its special character as a treaty for the collective enforcement of human rights and fundamental

[5] Ibid., Art. 29(2). [6] Ibid., Art. 21(3).

[7] Convention for the Protection of Human Rights and Fundamental Freedoms, CETS 005, Rome, 4 November 1950 (as amended) (hereafter, European Convention on Human Rights), preamble.

[8] Ibid., Art. 32(1): 'The jurisdiction of the Court shall extend to all matters concerning the interpretation and application of the Convention'.

[9] *Johnston and others* v. *Ireland*, Ser. A112, App. No. 9697/82, para.53: 'the Court cannot, by means of an evolutive interpretation, derive from these instruments a right which was not included therein at the outset. This is particularly so here, where the omission was deliberate.' Cf. *Öcalan* v. *Turkey*, App. No. 46221/99, judgment 12 May 2005 [GC], paras.163–5.

[10] Cf. Art. 31(1), Vienna Convention on the Law of Treaties (VCLT), 1155 UNTS 331. See *Golder* v. *United Kingdom*, Ser. A18, App. No. 4451/70, Separate Opinion of Judge Sir Gerald Fitzmaurice, para.37.

[11] *Ireland* v. *United Kingdom*, Ser. A25, App. No. 5310/71, para.239.

freedoms'. Its object and purpose, as an instrument for the protection of individual human rights, requires that the provisions of the ECHR be interpreted 'so as to make its safeguards practical and effective'. In addition, the interpretation of Convention rights must be consistent with its general spirit, as 'an instrument designed to maintain and promote the ideals and values of a democratic society'.[12] Further, the ECHR is a 'living instrument which must be interpreted in the light of present-day conditions[;] [its provisions] cannot be interpreted solely in accordance with the intentions of their authors as expressed more than forty years ago'. This approach 'is not confined to the substantive provisions of the Convention, but also applies to those provisions ... which govern the operation of the Convention's enforcement machinery'.[13]

The provisions of the ECHR are given an autonomous meaning within the context of the Convention, i.e. it is for the ECtHR to determine the meaning of terms in the ECHR and not the sovereign will of the states parties – individually or collectively.[14] The approach of the ECtHR to the interpretation of the Convention is guided principally by the requirement to establish the ordinary meaning of words in their context, in the light of the object and purpose of the ECHR as an instrument for the protection of human rights and in a manner that promotes internal consistency between the various provisions. The ECtHR will also have reference to any relevant rules and principles of international law applicable in relations between the states parties and the 'living' nature of the instrument, which must be interpreted in the light of present-day conditions, taking into account evolving norms of national and international law.[15] The meaning of indeterminate provisions may also be clarified through the identification of a 'European consensus' on the interpretation of a term in the Convention.[16]

In relation to the structure of the ECHR, certain Convention rights cannot be subject to an interference in any circumstances (consider, for example, the absolute prohibition on torture (Article 3) – which is not framed as a right); others may be subject to an interference in defined and limited circumstances (right to life (Article 2)). These rights are

[12] *Soering* v. *United Kingdom*, Ser. A161, (1989) 11 EHRR 439, para.87.

[13] *Loizidou* v. *Turkey* (Preliminary Objections), Ser. A310 [GC], App. No. 15318/89, Reports 1996–VI, para.71.

[14] *Engel and others* v. *The Netherlands*, Ser. A22 (1976) I EHRR 647, para.81.

[15] *Demir and Baykara* v. *Turkey*, App. No. 34503/97, [GC] judgment 12 November 2008, paras.65–8.

[16] *Vo* v. *France*, App. No. 53924/00, [GC] judgment 8 July 2004, Reports of Judgments and Decisions 2004–VIII, para.82. Cf. Dissenting Opinion of Judge Ress, para.8.

enjoyed equally by all persons under the jurisdiction of the ECHR, with the ECtHR developing an autonomous understanding of the scope and content of the rights, which are not subject to the democratic wills of the peoples of states parties. In contrast, the rights that structure the exercise of private autonomy (rights to private and family life, religion, expression and association (Articles 8–11)) may be subject to an interference for defined and limited reasons 'where necessary in a democratic society'. The scope and content of these rights emerge through domestic democratic procedures with the ECtHR accepting that states parties enjoy a certain 'margin of appreciation' in balancing the rights of the individual against the general interest, depending on a number of factors.[17] One part of the justification for the recognition of a margin of appreciation lies in the fact that the national authorities enjoy 'direct democratic legitimation'.[18]

Sejdić and Finci

The European Court of Human Rights exercises a governance function where it elaborates the scope and content of the obligations in the ECHR, constraining the political choices available to the democratic governments in states parties; introduces tests, such as proportionality, for 'balancing' the rights of the individual against the general interest; and establishes the necessary conditions for the conduct of democratic politics and required procedures for decision making in domestic societies (the democracy 'norm' and the procedural aspect of Convention rights). Whilst democracy is a condition of membership of the Council of Europe and a normative requirement of the ECHR, the establishment of a supranational judicial body with compulsory jurisdiction creates an international counter-majoritarian difficulty where the ECtHR limits the legitimate political choices available to the peoples of the democratic states party to the ECHR.

Sejdić and Finci v Bosnia and Herzegovina raises further – arguably more fundamental – questions around the governance role of the ECtHR.[19] The application did not request the review of political law

[17] *S. and Marper* v. *United Kingdom*, Apps. No. 30562/04 and 30566/04, [GC] judgment 4 December 2008, para.102.

[18] *Hatton and others* v. *United Kingdom*, Reports of Judgments and Decisions 2003–VIII [GC], para.97.

[19] *Sejdić and Finci* v. *Bosnia and Herzegovina*, Apps. no. 27996/06 and 34836/06, [GC] judgment 22 December 2009.

norms established by the democratic institutions of a state party, but supranational judicial review of the compatibility of the BiH Constitution with the provisions of the ECHR and its protocols, as interpreted by the ECtHR. The Constitution of Bosnia and Herzegovina was imposed by the international community as one part of the settlement that ended the violent ethnic conflict in the country (1992–5).[20] A majority of the people of the territory constituted a sovereign and independent state through an act of democratic will-formation (the external aspect of self-determination),[21] but the international community established the political system of government – the opposite of (internal) *self*-determination. Following the consociational model proposed for deeply divided societies,[22] the constitutional architecture introduced as one part of the Dayton Peace Accords established a complex model of power sharing between the 'constituent peoples' of BiH (Bosniacs/Bosniaks, Croats and Serbs), but excluded persons belonging to other groups and those refusing to designate themselves as belonging to a constituent people from full rights of political participation, and specifically from election to the House of Peoples (the second chamber of the state parliament) and the Presidency (the collective head of state).[23]

In *Sejdić and Finci*, the applicants, respectively members of the Roma and Jewish communities, argued that the BiH constitution violates certain provisions of the ECHR and its protocols: *inter alia*, Article 3,

[20] Annex 4, 'Constitution', The General Framework Agreement for Peace in Bosnia-Herzegovina, 35 ILM (1996) 89.

[21] The State of Bosnia and Herzegovina emerged following the forced dissolution of the Socialist Federal Republic of Yugoslavia in accordance with the guidelines established by the Conference on Yugoslavia Arbitration Commission. See Opinions on Questions Arising from the Dissolution of Yugoslavia, 31 ILM 1488 (1992). The Commission did not initially recommend the recognition of Bosnia and Herzegovina since no referendum on independence had been held. Subsequently, a referendum was held in which an overwhelming majority voted in favour of independence, although the Serb minority boycotted the vote. Bosnia and Herzegovina was recognised as a sovereign and independent state and admitted to the United Nations on 22 May 1992.

[22] See, for example, Arend Lijphart, 'Self-determination *versus* pre-determination of ethic minorities in power-sharing systems', in Will Kymlicka (ed.), *The Rights of Minority Cultures* (Oxford University Press, 1995) 275, p.278.

[23] The Constitution provides for an upper House of Peoples containing fifteen Delegates, 'two-thirds from the Federation (including five Croats and five Bosniacs) and one-third from the Republika Srpska (five Serbs)': Art. IV (Parliamentary Assembly), Annex 4, BiH Constitution, note 20 above. A three-member Presidency comprises 'one Bosniac and one Croat, each directly elected from the territory of the Federation and one Serb directly elected from the territory of the Republika Srpska': Art. V (Presidency), ibid.

Protocol to the ECHR (hereafter P1–3)[24] and Article 14, ECHR (non-discrimination in the enjoyment of Convention rights).[25] Whilst framed in terms of obligations, i.e. 'to hold free elections to ensure the free expression of the opinion of the people in the choice of the legislature', the ECtHR has interpreted P1–3 as including the rights to vote and to stand in elections.[26] In relation to the establishment of criteria for standing for elective office (the 'passive' aspect of the right), the ECtHR accepts that states parties enjoy a 'broad latitude to establish constitutional rules' and the criteria will vary in accordance with the 'historical and political factors specific to each State'. In an expression that is much repeated, although without explication, the Court has concluded that 'features that would be unacceptable in the context of one system may be justified in the context of another'.[27] Relevant historical and political factors include the transition to full democracy in states parties in Central and Eastern Europe. The issue in the instant case was the extent to which the avoidance of civil war was capable of justifying a constitutional system that expressly discriminated on grounds of ethnicity or race.[28]

In its judgment, the Grand Chamber observed that the Constitution of Bosnia and Herzegovina, as one part of a peace treaty, 'was drafted and adopted without the application of procedures which could have provided democratic legitimacy'.[29] According to the narrative developed by the Court, the impugned provisions were not included in the basic outline of the Dayton Peace Accords but introduced at a later stage, 'because of strong demands to this effect from some of the parties to the conflict'.[30] The Court further concluded the following: 'Fully aware that

[24] Art. 3, Protocol to the Convention for the Protection of Human Rights and Fundamental Freedoms (1952) CETS No. 9: 'The High Contracting Parties undertake to hold free elections at reasonable intervals by secret ballot, under conditions which will ensure the free expression of the opinion of the people in the choice of the legislature.'

[25] Art. 14, ECHR, note 7 above: 'The enjoyment of the rights and freedoms set forth in this Convention shall be secured without discrimination on any ground such as . . . race . . . [or] association with a national minority'.

[26] *Hirst* v. *United Kingdom* (No. 2), Reports of Judgments and Decisions 2005–IX [GC], para.58. On the limitations of the rights, see *Yumak and Sadak* v. *Turkey*, App. No. 10226/03, [GC] judgment 8 July 2008, para.109.

[27] *Podkolzina* v. *Latvia*, Reports of Judgments and Decisions 2002–II, para.33.

[28] Cf. the Good Friday Agreement (Northern Ireland), which avoids direct reference to ethno-cultural identity: *Agreement Reached in the Multi-Party Negotiations*, Belfast, 10 April 1998, 37 ILM (1998) 751, 'Strand One: Democratic Institutions in Northern Ireland'.

[29] *Sejdić and Finci*, note 19 above, para.6.

[30] Ibid., para.13.

[the constitutional] arrangements were most probably conflicting with human rights, the international mediators considered it to be especially important to make the Constitution a dynamic instrument and provide for their possible phasing out.'[31] The relevant provision is Article X of the BiH Constitution, which provides for amendment of the Constitution by a two-thirds majority of the Parliamentary Assembly (the lower house of the state parliament), subject to a restriction that no amendment may eliminate or diminish the rights and freedoms established in the ECHR.[32] Given that the power to amend the Constitution is vested in a domestic institution, and not the parties to the Dayton Peace Accords (BiH, Croatia and the Federal Republic of Yugoslavia) nor in the office of the High Representative (the international administrator for Bosnia and Herzegovina), the ECtHR found that Bosnia and Herzegovina could be held responsible for violations of Convention rights resulting from an application of provisions established in the Constitution through its failure to introduce the necessary amendments.[33]

In relation to membership of the House of Peoples, the ECtHR confirmed that whilst there was no obligation to introduce direct elections to legislative bodies, P1–3 would apply 'to any of a parliament's chambers to be filled through *direct* elections'.[34] The Court observed that the composition of the House of Peoples was determined through *indirect* elections – members were appointed by the legislatures of the sub-state entities of Bosnia and Herzegovina: the Federation of Bosnia and Herzegovina and the Republika Srpska. Further, the House of Peoples enjoyed 'wide powers to control the passage of legislation', in addition to certain powers in relation to the allocation of state resources and the ratification of treaties. On this basis, the ECtHR concluded that elections to the House of Peoples fell within the scope of P1–3.[35]

The focus of the judgment was the discrimination in the enjoyment of the right to stand for election to the House of Peoples on the grounds of race or ethnicity (Article 14, ECHR, taken with P1–3). Membership of the House of Peoples is limited to persons designating themselves as belonging to one of the three constituent peoples of Bosnia and Herzegovina: Bosniaks, Croats and Serbs. 'Others' are excluded, including persons belonging to the Roma and Jewish (national) minorities. According to the case law of the ECtHR, discrimination 'means treating

[31] Ibid., para.14. [32] BiH Constitution, note 20 above.

[33] *Sejdić and Finci*, note 19 above, para.30. [34] Ibid., para.40 (emphasis added).

[35] Ibid., para.41. Cf. Partly Concurring and Partly Dissenting Opinion of Judge Mijović, Joined by Judge Hajiyev, p.47.

differently, without an objective and reasonable justification, persons in similar situations'. The scope of the margin of appreciation accorded to states parties in making this judgment will vary with the circumstances, the subject matter and the background.[36] The Court affirmed that discrimination on the grounds of ethnicity is a form of racial discrimination, and 'where a difference in treatment is based on race or ethnicity, the notion of objective and reasonable justification must be interpreted as strictly as possible'.[37] The justification was provided for in the objective of concluding the constitutional settlement: the ending of violent ethnic conflict. The issue for the ECtHR was whether the regime could be justified fourteen years later. The Court observed 'significant positive developments' in the period since the adoption of the Dayton Peace Accords,[38] and concluded, by fourteen votes to three, that the automatic and complete exclusion of representatives of 'Other' communities from the possibility of election to the House of Peoples lacked an objective and reasonable justification and was a violation of Article 14 (taken in conjunction with P1–3).[39] The same approach was applied to the issue of eligibility for election to the Presidency, with the Court concluding, by sixteen votes to one, that 'the constitutional provisions which render[ed] the applicants ineligible for election to the Presidency must also be considered discriminatory and a breach of [Article 1 of (optional) Protocol No. 12 (enjoyment of any right set forth by law without discrimination)]'.[40]

The judgment was accompanied by strong dissenting judgments. Judge Mijović, joined by Judge Hajiyev, rejected the conclusion that Bosnia and Herzegovina was a 'stable and self-sustainable State', capable of withstanding constitutional reform to unravel the complex structures of power sharing between the three dominant groups.[41] The justices further questioned whether it was 'up to the European Court of Human Rights to determine when the time for change has arrived?'[42] Judge Bonello opined that the Dayton Peace Accords had 'extinguished the inferno that had been Bosnia and Herzegovina'. Whilst the constitutional settlement 'may not be perfect architecture[,] it was the only one that

[36] Ibid., para.42. [37] Ibid., para.44. [38] Ibid., para.47. [39] Ibid., para.50.

[40] Ibid., para.56. See Art. 1(1), Protocol No. 12 to the Convention for the Protection of Human Rights and Fundamental Freedoms, CETS No. 177: 'The enjoyment of *any right set forth by law* shall be secured without discrimination on any ground such as sex, race, colour, language, religion, political or other opinion, national or social origin, association with a national minority, property, birth or other status' (emphasis added).

[41] Opinion of Judge Mijović, note 35 above, p.45. [42] Ibid., p.51.

induced the contenders to substitute dialogue for dynamite'. The ECtHR '[had] told both the former belligerents and the peace-devising do-gooders that they got it all wrong. They had better start all over again . . . Back to the drawing board.'[43] Judge Bonello also questioned whether a judicial institution 'so remote from the focus of dissention' could be the best judge of the situation and the existence, or otherwise, of an objective and reasonable justification for the discriminatory measures, concluding that he 'doubt[ed] that any State should be placed under any legal or ethical obligation to sabotage the very system that saved its democratic existence'.[44]

Creating a constitutional moment

Sejdić and Finci is of interest for a number of reasons and to a number of constituencies. First, it is of direct interest to the people of Bosnia and Herzegovina, in terms of the stability of the political arrangements and basis for political negotiations around constitutional reform.[45] The judgment has been communicated to the Committee of Ministers of the Council of Europe,[46] which has stressed its significance and '[urged] the authorities of Bosnia and Herzegovina to bring the country's Constitution and laws in line with the European Convention on Human Rights as a matter of priority'.[47] The judgment creates a constitutional moment during which the people(s) of BiH are expected to engage in a process of reform to ensure the development of a constitution based on the idea of the political equality of citizens, with elements of power sharing between the main ethno-cultural groups,[48] and not the political equality of (constituent) peoples.

[43] Dissenting Opinion of Judge Bonello, p.53. [44] Ibid., p.55.

[45] See, generally. Timothy William Waters, 'Contemplating failure and creating alternatives in the Balkans: Bosnia's peoples, democracy, and the shape of self-determination' (2004) 29 *Yale Journal of International Law* 423.

[46] Art. 46, ECHR.

[47] 'Declaration on Bosnia and Herzegovina' by Micheline Calmy-Rey, outgoing Chair, and Antonio Miloshoski, incoming Chair of the Committee of Ministers, CM Document, Committee of Ministers of the Council of Europe, Document CM(2010)59 Strasbourg (11 May 2010).

[48] The majority of the Grand Chamber accepted that the time 'may still not be ripe for a political system which would be a simple reflection of majority rule[,] [although] there [was] no requirement under the Convention to abandon totally the power-sharing mechanisms peculiar to Bosnia and Herzegovina': *Sejdić and Finci*, note 19 above, para.48.

Second, *Sejdić and Finci* elaborates the content of the ECHR with its conclusions that indirect elections fall within the ambit or scope of P1–3 and that discrimination in the enjoyment of rights of political participation on grounds of race and ethnicity is capable of justification, depending on the circumstances of the case. The latter point is noteworthy as the international law norm prohibiting racial discrimination is amongst the most frequently cited candidates for the status of *jus cogens*.[49] The formal position is that any treaty that conflicts with a norm of *jus cogens* is void;[50] more generally, norms of *jus cogens* are understood to represent the established interests and values of the international legal community, distinct from those of the collective sovereign interests of states – i.e. norms of *jus cogens* reflect a concept of global justice and establish standards of legitimate behaviour in world society.

Third, *Sejdić and Finci* demonstrates the difficulties for the ECtHR in locating itself within domestic political and constitutional controversies – ten of the twenty-six justices that examined the issue at the domestic and international level reached a different conclusion to the majority of the Grand Chamber. In its judgment, the ECtHR rejected the constitutional narrative of Bosnia and Herzegovina, i.e. that ethnic power-sharing was required to avoid conflict, through its determination that the factual circumstances on the ground could no longer justify the impugned discriminatory provisions. It is, though, difficult to conclude that a supranational court is better placed than the national constitutional court (which reached the opposite conclusion)[51] to pass judgment on complex questions of fact in constitutional and political controversies.

[49] *Fragmentation of International Law: Difficulties Arising from the Diversification and Expansion of International Law*, Report of the Study Group of the International Law Commission, Finalized by Martti Koskenniemi, UN Doc. A/CN.4/L.682, 13 April 2006, para.374.

[50] Arts 53 and 64, VCLT, note 10 above.

[51] Case No. AP–2678/06, appeal of *Stranka za Bosnu i Hercegovinu* (Party for Bosnia and Herzegovina) and Mr Ilijaz Pilav. The Constitutional Court determined that the restrictions on the right to stand for election to the Presidency could be justified by reference to the 'specific nature of internal order' agreed in the form of the Dayton Peace Accords, 'whose ultimate goal was the establishment of peace and dialogue between the opposing parties' (para.21). The restrictions were 'proportional to the objectives of general community in terms of preservation of the established peace, continuation of dialogue, and consequently creation of conditions for amending the [Constitution and democratic system]' (para.22). The impugned constitutional provisions did not violate the rights guaranteed by the ECHR or its protocols, 'given the fact that there is an objective and reasonable justification for differential treatment' (para.25). Cf. Separate concurring opinion of Judge Feldman and Separate dissenting opinion of Judge Constance Grewe (joined by Judge Seada Palavrić).

Finally, the judgment highlights the complexities of the idea of legitimate political authority following the globalisation and fragmentation of governance functions. Following the Westphalian political settlement, the legitimate authority of international law norms depends on 'sovereign' consent. States parties, according to this positivist orthodoxy, accept the authority of the ECHR through their constructed identities as sovereigns subject to the international law principle *pacta sunt servanda* (promises must be kept). Bosnia and Herzegovina, as a sovereign state,[52] ratified the ECHR on 12 July 2002. The scope and content of its international law obligations under the ECHR is not, though, conditioned by the expression of sovereign will reflected in the literal terms of the Convention (which does not contain a right to stand for elective office). The ECtHR has determined that the ECHR is not a treaty 'of the classic kind'.[53] In developing a dynamic and teleological interpretation of Convention rights, the ECtHR has brought into being an autonomous legal order that is subject neither to the individual will of a state party nor the collective wills of states parties. The following sections of this chapter examine the arguments for accepting the authority of the ECtHR to determine the normative situation of states parties to the ECHR in the absence of democratic procedures for elaborating the scope and content of Convention rights or an expression of sovereign will for augmenting the obligations of states parties through signature and ratification of an agreed text.

A judicial project of political justice

The ECtHR has described the ECHR as a 'constitutional instrument of European public order' in the field of human rights.[54] Increasingly, writers refer to the regime established under the ECHR as a constitutional regime.[55] Anne Peters concludes that the ECtHR adopted a method of interpretation that is both teleological and dynamic '*because* of [the] treaty's constitutional quality'.[56] Stephen Gardbaum argues that,

[52] Cf. Opinion of Judge Mijović, note 35 above, p.44: '[BiH] does not function as an independent and sovereign State'.

[53] *Ireland* v. *UK*, note 11 above.

[54] *Bosphorus Hava Yollari Turizm Ve Ticaret Anonim Sirketi* v. *Ireland*, Reports of Judgments and Decisions 2005–VI [GC], para.156.

[55] See Steven Greer, 'Constitutionalizing adjudication under the European Convention on Human Rights', (2003) 23 OJLS 405, p.407.

[56] In Jan Klabbers, Anne Peters and Geir Ulfstein, *The Constitutionalization of International Law* (Oxford University Press, 2009), p.218 (emphasis in original).

because the ECHR has achieved de facto supremacy over domestic law through compliance with the judgments of the ECtHR, the Convention functions within the legal systems of states parties 'as an invocable and supreme law, and accordingly, can be understood as a federalized or constitutionalized regional human rights system'.[57] (The federal analogy is often relied on in relation to the ECtHR to suggest a 'vertical' separation of powers analogous to the 'horizontal' separation of powers within domestic systems, along with the taken-for-granted importance of the judicial protection of rights.) Alec Stone Sweet concludes that the ECtHR functions like a constitutional court through its construction of the law of the ECHR in a dynamic and progressive way, in light of changing circumstances and challenges to the authority of the regime; adjudication of disputes between individuals and the public interest; reliance on the constitutional principle of proportionality; and in its role in coordinating the autonomous legal domain established under the ECHR with other autonomous legal domains, including, but not restricted to, the autonomous domains of the legal systems of states parties.[58]

The judgment in *Sejdić and Finci* established a requirement for Bosnia and Herzegovina to engage in fundamental reform, notwithstanding the conclusions of the domestic court that the constitutional arrangements were, and remained, proportional to the objectives of the preservation of peace, the continuation of dialogue, and establishment of the conditions necessary for achieving a lasting political settlement.[59] The recognition that the ECtHR is a 'constitutional court' results in a situation in which the populations of states parties find themselves subject to the 'final' authority of the state 'constitutional' court dealing with human rights *and* that of the ECtHR. The lesson from legal pluralism is that autonomous legal regimes are not structured in accordance with any basic norm or principle, or constitutional settlement. It is for each legal order to structure its relationship with other regimes from a perspective that is

[57] Stephen Gardbaum, 'Human rights and international constitutionalism', in Jeffrey L. Dunoff and Joel P. Trachtman (eds.) *Ruling the World: Constitutionalism, International Law, and Global Governance* (Cambridge University Press, 2009) 233, p.247.

[58] Alec Stone Sweet, 'Constitutionalism, legal pluralism, and international regimes' (2009) 16 *Indiana Journal of Global Legal Studies* 621, pp.642–3. The idea of a 'constitution' is applied to treaty regimes which are constituted by written meta-norms or codified secondary rules and which possess judicial mechanisms that exercise compulsory jurisdiction under which 'authority to interpret and apply the regime's law is final': ibid., p.631.

[59] See note 51 above.

internal to the regime (looking outwards, as it were). There is no reason to conclude that either a state constitutional court or the ECtHR is able to claim the final, 'constitutionally decisive', word in cases of conflict between the autonomous legal systems and implicit conceptions of justice that inform the conclusions of the respective judicial organs. From the perspective of the state system, the external frame established by the ECHR does not subject the state law system to the authority of the ECtHR; it challenges the state law system to justify its normative regime and version of justice by holding up another version.

There is no doubt that the ECHR is a significant instrument in the construction of the idea of justice in the European *espace juridique* – and in the domestic constitutional systems of states parties. As a judicial project of political justice, however, the regime lacks the democratic and political legitimacy of the democratic, rule-of-law state, which rests on two principles: voluntarism in the constitution of the sovereign political community and democratic procedures for the establishment of constitutional rules about law making and political law norms, subject to the rule of law and the protection of human rights. The idea that legitimate government is constituted through the voluntary agreement of a majority of a political community is,[60] of course, contrary to our experiences of sovereign political communities being constituted by the exercise of authority: community does not constitute 'authority', community is constituted by the exercise of authority. In the case of the legal system established under the ECHR, the authority of the legal order was established by the determination of the ECtHR to develop an autonomous reading of Convention rights with regard to the object and purpose of the ECHR, as an instrument for the protection of human rights in light of present-day conditions.

A democratic conception of legitimate authority

The assertion of authority through judicial reasoning does not, by itself, accord legitimate authority to the ECtHR, i.e. the right to determine the

60 John Locke, *Two Treatises of Government*, edited with an introduction by Peter Laslett (Cambridge University Press, 1960) II § 99; also Thomas Hobbes, *Leviathan*, edited with an introduction by C. B. Macpherson (London: Penguin, 1968), p.90. The reliance on majority rule to bind dissenters is paradoxical. Cf. Andreas Kalyvas, 'Popular sovereignty, democracy, and the constituent power' (2005) 12 *Constellations* 223, p.237.

normative situation of the democratic states parties subject to the ECHR. The idea of authority (properly understood) implies some connection between the exercise of regulatory power and the interests of the subjects of the normative regime. The notable feature of institutions that assert a right to regulate others is that they invariably make a claim to legitimacy: authority is inherently related to legitimacy.[61] It might be the case that all societies regard democracy as the only basis for legitimate authority, although this seems implausible (cf. the customary laws of indigenous peoples). In democratic societies, however, it seems reasonable to conclude that individuals will not accept the exercise of authority in the absence of engagement by the governance institution with subjects through democratic procedures to determine the interests and perspectives of subjects.[62]

This chapter follows Frank Michelman in regarding democracy as a system of 'popular political self-government'.[63] A self-government conception must rely on a procedural understanding of democracy and democratic legitimacy: 'democracy is at its fullest when a country's people decide for themselves, by democratic political procedures, all of those conditions of their lives that are politically decidable.'[64] The idea applies equally to the 'constitutional' laws of law making that frame the exercise of democratic politics.[65] In the counter-factual ideal, following Jürgen Habermas, the legal system emerges by way of a consensus arrived at through dialogue in which positions are accepted as legitimate only where agreed during uncoerced rational discourses by those affected by the outcomes. In the practice of 'deliberative democracy', given that it is not possible for all persons to engage directly on all issues, citizens must be represented by others in parliamentary institutions responsible for the adoption of law norms; the function of the judiciary is limited to ensuring the procedural legitimacy of established law norms and interpreting the scope and content of laws established through political procedures.[66]

John Rawls also refers to the ideal of a 'deliberative [or well-ordered constitutional] democracy', although in a different sense to Habermas.

[61] Cf. Joseph Raz, *The Morality of Freedom* (Oxford University Press, 1986), p.53.

[62] Wojciech Sadurski, 'Law's legitimacy and "democracy-plus"' (2006) 26 OJLS 377, p.387.

[63] Frank Michelman, 'The 1996–97 Brennan Center Symposium Lecture' (1998) *Californian Law Review* 399, p.400.

[64] Ibid., p.412. [65] Ibid., p.413.

[66] Cf. Jürgen Habermas, *Between Facts and Norms: Contributions to a Discourse Theory of Law and Democracy*, trans. William Rehg (Oxford: Polity, 1996).

The definitive idea of deliberative democracy is deliberation: the exchange of views and perspectives on political questions, with arguments supported by reasons. The essential elements of deliberative democracy are the idea of public reason, a framework of democratic institutions, and the commitment of democratic citizens to the public reason.[67] Rawls concludes that the exercise of coercive political authority by a state government requires the establishment of a constitution 'the essentials of which all citizens as free and equal may reasonably be expected to endorse in the light of principles and ideas acceptable to their common human reason'.[68] The establishment of legitimate political authority requires both a narrow 'constitutional consensus' and a broader and deeper 'overlapping consensus' on the 'constitutional essentials' and elements of political justice. The constitutional consensus, reflected in the constitution, establishes certain basic political rights and liberties and establishes democratic procedures for moderating political rivalry within society.[69] The overlapping consensus is concerned with the establishment of 'deeper' political principles and ideals founded on a political conception of justice. It goes beyond political principles to establish certain substantive rights, such as freedom of conscience and thought; equality of opportunity; and certain basic requirements of the human person.[70] The transformation from a constitutional consensus to an overlapping consensus, i.e. the development of a political conception of justice, occurs through political debate, including that around constitutional reform, and through judicial review by the courts, which requires an interpretation of the meaning of constitutional provisions in accordance with a political conception of justice.[71] The function of the judiciary is to develop the 'best interpretation' of the constitution, based on the relevant body of constitutional materials and precedents, that can be justified in terms of the public conception of justice and public reason.[72] The constitution is not, however, the product of judicial

[67] John Rawls, *Political Liberalism* (New York, Chichester: Columbia University Press, 2005), p.448.

[68] Ibid., p.137. Rawls does not address the possibility of applying the analysis beyond the state. In *The Law of Peoples* (Cambridge, MA: Harvard University Press, 1999), Rawls does not identify any comprehensive international human rights norms analogous to that recognised at the domestic level. Following Rawls, Thomas Nagel argues that political justice can only be achieved in the context of the state: Thomas Nagel, 'The problem of global justice' (2005) 33 *Philosophy and Public Affairs* 113.

[69] Rawls, *Political Liberalism*, p.163.

[70] Ibid., p.164. [71] Ibid., p.165. [72] Ibid., p.236.

decision-making and judicial reasoning: 'it is what the people acting constitutionally through the other branches eventually allow the Court to say it is.'[73] One of the functions of the constitutional court is to ensure that political discussions that address constitutional questions, including the scope and content of human rights norms, are undertaken 'in line with the political values of justice and public reason.'[74]

According to Rawls, all constitutional questions and questions about justice should be settled in accordance with principles and ideals acceptable to the common reason of the subjects of the political order. Public reason is characteristic of a democratic people: 'it is the reason of its citizens'. The subject of their reason is the good of the public and the issue of political justice.[75] In a democratic society public reason is the reason of equal citizens who, as a collectivity, exercise the final political power in the enactment of law norms and the amendment of the constitution. The requirement of public reason does not apply to political law norms (although this is desirable), only the constitutional essentials and questions of basic justice, including the scope and content of human rights norms.[76] The constitutional essentials include the structures and processes of government and the basic rights and liberties that legislative majorities are required to respect, including the rights to vote and participate in elections and the rule of law. The content of public reason specifies certain basic rights, liberties and opportunities familiar to constitutional democracies; accords a certain priority to those rights in relation to the competing claims of the general good; and guarantees citizens adequate opportunities to make effective use of their rights and opportunities.[77] One of the features of the political conception of justice is that its content is expressed in terms of 'certain fundamental ideas seen as implicit in the public political culture of a democratic society'.[78]

[73] Ibid., p.237. [74] Ibid., p.239. [75] Ibid., p.213.
[76] Ibid., p.214. [77] Ibid., p.223.
[78] Ibid., p.13. In its judgments the ECtHR has observed that democracy does not simply mean that that the views of a majority must always prevail. Democracy must be based on 'dialogue and a spirit of compromise necessarily entailing various concessions on the part of individuals or groups of individuals which are justified in order to maintain and promote the ideals and values of a democratic society'. It is this 'constant search for a balance between the fundamental rights of each individual which constitutes the foundation of a "democratic society"': *Leyla Sahin* v. *Turkey*, Reports of Judgments and Decisions 2005–XI [GC], para.108.

The ECtHR and the public good

Rawls's understanding of the role of constitutional courts in developing a conception of political justice in democratic systems provides the basis for beginning to think about the role of the ECtHR in interpreting the scope and content of the ECHR. The function of the ECtHR is to develop the 'best interpretation' of the ECHR that can be justified in terms of the constitutional settlement: the Convention itself and the jurisprudence of the ECtHR,[79] and the political conception of justice implicit in the Convention. Three possibilities present themselves. First, political justice can be understood as a concept that applies only at the level of the state, with its established mechanisms for democratic will-formation and coercive institutions for the enforcement of agreed justice norms. On this understanding, the function of the ECtHR is to promote democratic decision-making procedures within states parties and the development of a plurality of political conceptions of justice. Second, if it is accepted that the ECHR is an autonomous legal system organised in accordance with its own 'constitution' (and all legal systems are organised in accordance with their own basic norm, or rule of recognition, with accepted constitutional laws about law making),[80] then it is inevitable that the regime will develop in accordance with a conception of political justice that informs the interpretation of the scope and content of Convention rights. Third, the ECtHR might understand itself as both fulfilling the function of developing a political conception of justice at the level of the ECHR and promoting the establishment of legitimate conceptions of political justice within states parties. It is this third possibility that appears, on closer inspection, most promising.

At the level of the state, a constitutional consensus on the essentials of government and fundamental rights is transformed into an overlapping consensus by way of the development of a political conception of justice through democratic debates and the judicial reasoning of constitutional courts, i.e. those concerned with the interpretation and application of constitutional provisions. The overlapping consensus includes agreement

[79] *Chapman* v. *United Kingdom*, Reports of Judgments and Decisions 2001–I [GC], para.70: 'The Court considers that, while it is not formally bound to follow any of its previous judgments, it is in the interests of legal certainty, foreseeability and equality before the law that it should not depart, without good reason, from precedents laid down in previous cases'.

[80] Cf. Hans Kelsen, *General Theory of Law and State*, trans. by Anders Wedberg (New York: Russell & Russell, 1961), p.111; H. L. A. Hart, *The Concept of Law*, 2nd ed. (Oxford: Clarendon Press, 1994), p.233.

on those human rights norms familiar to constitutional democracies; other rights emerge through political processes established under the constitution. There is an absence of political deliberation on the conception of justice in relation to the ECHR – actors can only influence the regime as participants in legal processes, as applicants, respondents, lawyers, justices etc. The 'overlapping [constitutional] consensus' emerges through judicial reasoning (only), and there is no realistic opportunity for political law-making, given the absence of any possibility of reforming the substantive provisions of the ECHR and its protocols through treaty amendment, which requires the consent of all states parties.

The question then emerges as to the nature of the legal regime established under the ECHR. First, if we accept that justice is a political value – to be determined in the context of a political community – the absence of a 'polity' in which political discourse can occur is problematic. Further, the rights in the ECHR do not apply equally to all those ultimately subject to the regime. The obligations of states parties (and by implication the 'Convention rights' of individuals) vary in accordance with the circumstances of the case and the application of the margin-of-appreciation doctrine. The difficulty could be overcome if we accepted that the ECHR has established a federal structure in which the basic norm of the (federal) legal system is reflected in the Convention, with the constituent states parties enjoying a degree of autonomy in the interpretation of Convention rights, subject to judicial review by the ECtHR. The 'federalist' argument, however, is difficult to sustain unless it is accepted that the states parties to the ECHR are no longer sovereign and that non-sovereign states can be subject to overlapping and conflicting 'federal' structures (consider, for example, how a number of states party to ECHR are subjected to the authority through membership of the legal systems established by the European Union and the United Nations); both of these arguments seem implausible.

Other-regarding conceptions of justice

The ECHR is not a 'constitutionalised' regime in the sense that it establishes a political community in which a consensus on the constitutional essentials and a political conception of justice is able to emerge through reasoned political deliberations.[81] The ECtHR is required to

[81] Cf. Neil Walker, 'Reframing EU constitutionalism', in Dunoff and Trachtman (eds.) *Ruling the World* (note 57 above), p.149.

develop a conception of justice through judicial reasoning (alone), relying on the text of the ECHR and its own jurisprudence. This limits its interpretative role to the constitutional essentials and fundamental rights, and it is not possible for the ECtHR to develop a 'deep' conception of human rights in those areas in which the rights of the individual must be balanced against the general interest, for the very reason that there is no 'general interest' reflected in the establishment of the ECHR regime. In the absence of a political community subject to the authority of the governance regime, a supranational legal system is required to develop an 'other-regarding' conception of political justice in which its judgments outline a conceptual archetype of the democratic state and democratic society in accordance with the model suggested in the ECHR. The interpretative function of the ECtHR is to determine the scope and content of fundamental rights (the identification of which may be subject to reasonable disagreement) and the procedural requirements for the development of a political conception of rights within the domestic societies of states parties.

In *Sejdić and Finci*, the ECtHR concluded that the BiH Constitution is inconsistent with the ECHR, and the impugned discriminatory provisions could not be justified. The judgment does not reflect a conflict of law norms or visions of political justice, but an attempt by the ECtHR to reconstruct the constitutional frame for democratic law-making consistent with its conception of the archetype of the democratic state. The judgment subjects the political system of Bosnia and Herzegovina to the authority of the ECHR, requiring fundamental constitutional reform. The difficulty for the ECtHR lies in establishing legitimate authority for the judgment, given its acceptance that it was *arguable* that the discriminatory provisions in the Constitution could be justified, depending on the interpretation of the factual circumstances and the constitutional narrative in the particular case.

The design of the democratic system for the establishment of political law norms is an area in which states parties are accorded a wide margin of appreciation, consistent with the aims and objectives of the ECHR: the establishment of a democratic state and democratic society and the protection of fundamental rights.[82] In developing an other-regarding conception of political justice, the function of the ECtHR is to establish

[82] See, generally, Steven Wheatley, 'Minorities, political participation and democratic governance under the European Convention on Human Rights', in Marc Weller (ed.), *Political Participation of Minorities* (Oxford University Press, 2010) p.175.

the constitutional essentials – the minimum requirements of a democratic system of political law-making at the level of domestic government and the scope and content of fundamental rights. There was no requirement for Bosnia and Herzegovina to accede to the ECHR regime (certainly not under Protocol 12), or to refrain from entering a reservation or derogation, but once BiH became subject to the ECHR, the ECtHR was required to hold to the constitutional essentials suggested in the ECHR and its own jurisprudence, which emphasise the importance of the political equality of citizens, particularly in relation to the issue of direct discrimination on grounds of race or ethnicity. Consistent with the conception of an other-regarding system of political justice, the ECtHR should have concluded that direct discrimination in the enjoyment of political rights on grounds of race or ethnicity could not be justified in any circumstances: the political equality of citizens is a 'constitutional essential' in democratic states.

Conclusion

The argument developed by David Kennedy suggests that, in order to make a contribution to a just world order, human rights activists and lawyers should embrace the possibilities (and responsibilities) of rulership. The analysis developed in this chapter proceeds from the position that in conditions of uncertainty and disagreement humanitarians cannot be certain that their policy proposals are 'welfare-enhancing' or 'just' or 'right' in the absence of legitimate authority, and that legitimate authority should be understood in terms of a modified conception of democratic legitimacy (a democratic rule of international law, if you like):[83] laws are valid where adopted through democratic procedures or developed by constitutional courts in accordance with the political conception of justice developed within the legal system (at whatever level). The exercise of authority is justified where it is consistent with the requirements for political *self*-determination, and not rulership by (well-intentioned) *others.* This is an argument to which Kennedy appears to be sympathetic when he writes about the possibilities of carrying 'the revolutionary force of the democratic promise – of individual rights, of economic self-sufficiency, of citizenship, of community empowerment, and of participation in the decisions that affect one's life – to

[83] See Steven Wheatley, 'A democratic rule of international law', 22 *European Journal of International Law* (2011) 2, 525.

the sites of global and transnational authority'.[84] The development of a just international order requires the democratisation of global, regional and domestic legal orders, not the imposition of forms of rulership by well-intentioned utopians who claim to know better.

[84] David Kennedy, 'The mystery of global governance', in Dunoff and Trachtman (eds.) *Ruling the World*, 37, p.67.

9

Universal human rights: a challenge too far

ROB DICKINSON

Introduction

The concept of human rights has expanded exponentially since the end of the Second World War and has demonstrated such vibrancy and all-embracing nature that Costas Douzinas has remarked that 'human rights have become the *raison d'être* of the state system',[1] and David Kennedy comments that 'human rights also become a practice of governance'.[2] For Eric Heinze, 'universal human rights apply to all states, irrespective of political regime',[3] and bearing in mind the word 'universal' in the expression this is arguably correct.[4] In this way human rights may be seen to challenge the long-established *jus cogens* norm of sovereignty.[5] The

My thanks are due to Elena Katselli (Newcastle University) for her advice and comments on an earlier draft and generally to members of the Human Rights Research Group at Newcastle Law School.

[1] C. Douzinas, *The End of Human Rights: Critical Legal Thought at the Turn of the Century* (Oxford: Hart Publishing, 2000), p.374.

[2] See Chapter 2 above. David Kennedy opines further that 'humanitarian voices are increasingly powerful on the international stage': ibid.

[3] See Chapter 10 below.

[4] In the context, note the Universal Declaration of Human Rights (hereafter, UDHR) – a seminal work adopted and proclaimed on 10 December 1948 by the General Assembly of the UN after a vote of 48–0, with 8 abstentions. Member states were requested to publicise the text of the Declaration but it was only with the 1966 International Covenants that legal force was given to the (originally aspirational) rights outlined in the UDHR: International Covenant on Civil and Political Rights (hereafter, ICCPR), adopted 16 December 1966, 999 UNTS 171 (entered into force 23 March 1976); also International Covenant on Economic, Social and Cultural Rights (hereafter, ICESCR), adopted 16 December 1966, 999 UNTS 3 (entered into force 3 January 1976).

[5] As William Twining puts it, 'municipal law can no longer be treated in isolation, either internally or externally... the twin doctrines of national sovereignty and non-interference in the internal affairs of independent states are being steadily challenged, most prominently, but not exclusively, by international humanitarian and human rights law': W. Twining, *Globalisation and Legal Theory* (London: Butterworths, 2000), p.51.

increasing influence of human rights may be seen in the interventionist foreign policy views of such as Tony Blair,[6] a view comprising 'a doctrine of ethical imperialism wrapped up in the language of globalisation'.[7] This has profound implications for international law, and indeed for the United Nations, since humanitarian voices are increasingly powerful on the international stage. Nevertheless, despite the increasing influence of human rights law evident in international discourse, humanitarian intervention has been criticised on the basis that it is 'deeply corrosive' of the rule of non-intervention in the internal affairs of states.[8]

In his chapter in this volume David Kennedy takes the view that, although human rights may legitimate a regime, the concept is less compelling than it once was and may be used in addition as a cover for political objectives.[9] Thus the utopian version of human rights has progressed through a chastening process. This chapter proceeds to consider, first, challenges to sovereignty, including the human rights challenge, before moving on to consider one specific aspect within the panoply of human rights, that relating to the self-determination of peoples. More specifically, the chapter analyses the evolving boundaries of the concept of external self-determination in the context of the prospective solution that has been reached in Kosovo. It also examines whether this may be perceived as a component of a retreat from the universality of human rights, perhaps a high-water mark in the challenge of human rights to the norm of sovereignty.

Human rights as a challenge to sovereignty

It would be wrong of course to view sovereignty as a static concept. A norm of customary international law may evolve, and a violation of that norm, rather than creating a new norm, may form an exception to

[6] C. Hill, 'Putting the world to rights: Tony Blair's foreign policy mission' in A. Seldon and D. Kavanagh (eds.), *The Blair Effect 2001–5* (Cambridge University Press, 2005), p.394: 'his belief in the principle of intervention to overthrow tyrannies which threatened international peace as well as their own peoples'. This then presupposes no intervention if international peace is not at stake, or indeed if intervention would conflict with such peace.

[7] R. Skidelsky, 'The reinvention of Blair' in Seldon and Kavanagh (eds.), *The Blair Effect*, p.444. From a speech made by Tony Blair in Chicago in April 1999 – hence it may be termed his Chicago Doctrine.

[8] M. Kaldor, 'American power: from "compellance" to cosmopolitanism?' in D. Held and M. Koenig-Archibugi (eds), *American Power in the Twenty-First Century* (Cambridge: Polity Press, 2004), 181, p.204, referring to H. Bull, 'Conclusion' in H. Bull (ed.), *Intervention in World Politics* (Oxford: Clarendon Press, 1984), 181, p.183.

[9] See Chapter 2 above. In the context of 'political objectives' see note 6 above.

the customary norm, thus confirming the existence of that norm.[10] As a starting point, though, '[t]he absolute power of the sovereign state has been the foundational doctrine for political theory and practice',[11] a view shared by both Thomas Hobbes[12] and Jean Bodin.[13]

Nevertheless certain factors have come about to check the powers of the sovereign state. One such has been the evolution of human rights covenants and conventions, constructs which check and control external sovereignty – the authority granted to each state by international law to exert legal control over the territory within its boundaries without deferring to any claim of legal superiority made by any organisation or third state.[14] The existence of such covenants and conventions exercises a cooling influence on the powers of a state to act without impediment within its borders. There may be criticism of the state's actions, and indeed direct interference within its territory by, for instance, human rights organisations – attached to the United Nations or otherwise.[15] Further, sectoral challenges also affect the independent function of the state – exemplified by the World Trade Organization:[16] an example of globalisation in practice.[17] Thus, then, while for such as Lawrence Farley

[10] See, for example, *Case Concerning Military and Paramilitary Activities in and against Nicaragua* (*Nicaragua* v *United States of America*) ICJ Rep 1986, 14, confirming that a violation, or conduct inconsistent with a given rule of customary international law, should not be considered as creating a new norm but as confirming the existence of an old norm: see para.186 of the Judgment dated 27 June 1986.

[11] N. MacCormick, *Questioning Sovereignty: Law, State, and Nation in the European Commonwealth* (Oxford University Press, 1999), p.124

[12] Ibid., p.123.

[13] See J. Bodin, *On Sovereignty: Four chapters from* The Six Books of the Commonwealth, ed. and trans. Julian H. Franklin (Cambridge University Press, 1992), for example at p.1: 'Sovereignty is the absolute and perpetual power of a Commonwealth' (footnote omitted).

[14] MacCormick, *Questioning Sovereignty*, note 11 above, pp.129, 134.

[15] Evidenced by, for example, Amnesty International, 'Bahraini government must end interference in human rights organization' (2010), www.amnesty.org/en/news-and-updates/bahraini-government-must-end-interference-human-rights-organization-2010–09–09 (accessed 26 February 2011): 'Amnesty International has called on the Bahraini government to reverse its decision to suspend the board of a prominent human rights organization, *after it criticized alleged violations committed by the authorities* against opposition and human rights activists within the Sh'ia community' (emphasis added).

[16] S. Tierney, 'Reframing sovereignty: sub-state national societies and contemporary challenges to the nation-state', 54 ICLQ (2005) 1, 161, p.164.

[17] Globalisation poses challenges to the independent function of the state, and presents challenges to traditional legal theory, for instance challenging '"black box theories" that treat nation states, societies, legal systems, and legal orders as closed, impervious entities that can be studied in isolation': Twining, *Globalisation and Legal Theory*, p.252.

sovereignty is 'the defining characteristic of the modern state system',[18] this has become ever less the case.

The essential purpose of the human rights regime is 'to promote and protect vital human interests',[19] a purpose made evident in the Preamble to each of the two 1966 International Covenants.[20] Even so, it has been questioned whether human rights are in fact universal, and 'the universality of both the notion of human rights and the nature of human rights has been, and remains, highly contested'.[21] Ongoing state agreement to universal human rights is of course a prerequisite to their universality but, in view of this contestation, the attribution of 'universality' to human rights can be seen to be something of a misnomer, and it has been argued that the Universal Declaration of Human Rights should be made more 'relevant for the present times and ... acceptable to all nations and peoples'.[22] In this way, principles – human rights principles – may be seen to potentially contrast with a pragmatic attitude to their implementation.[23]

The issue of 'acceptab[ility] to all nations and peoples' – of relativism, both spatially and temporally – finds expression in the 'Asian values' debate. In this, the elites

> of almost all East Asian countries insist that some of the rights included in the United Nations and other Western-inspired declarations of human rights are incompatible with their values, traditions and self-understanding, and that Western governments should be more tolerant of their attempts to define and prioritise them differently.[24]

The argument is that 'the conventional declarations of human rights explicitly or implicitly prescribe the standard Western liberal-democratic form of government and brook no departures from it'.[25]

[18] L. T. Farley, *Plebiscites and Sovereignty: The Crisis of Political Illegitimacy* (Boulder, CO: Westview Press, 1986), p.8.

[19] J. R. Bauer and D. A. Bell, 'Introduction' in J. R. Bauer and D. A. Bell (eds.), *The East Asian Challenge for Human Rights* (Cambridge University Press, 1999), 3, p.3.

[20] See note 4 above.

[21] A. Hurrell, 'Power, principles and prudence: protecting human rights in a deeply divided world' in T. Dunne and N. J. Wheeler (eds.), *Human Rights in Global Politics* (Cambridge University Press, 1999) 277, pp.291–2. Despite the view of Eric Heinze: see note 3 above and related text.

[22] Tun Daim Zainuddin, senior adviser to the Malaysian Government, quoted in Francesca Klug, *Values for a Godless Age: The Story of the UK's New Bill of Rights* (London: Penguin Books, 2000), p.210.

[23] David Kennedy (Chapter 2 above) cautions against the dangers of pragmatism.

[24] B. Parekh, 'Non-ethnocentric universalism' in Dunne and Wheeler (eds.), *Human Rights in Global Politics*, 128, p.154.

[25] Ibid., p.155. Such arguments in part explain the reluctance, for example, of the People's Republic of China to ratify the ICCPR, while it has ratified the ICESCR. In essence the

In the 1990s a backlash developed to the role played by the United Nations in setting standards applicable to human rights, 'based on a claim that alleged violations [of human rights] were being used as a pretext for a new cycle of Northern-led interventionary diplomacy', and China 'emerged as the informal leader of this movement of resistance'.[26] Thus it is argued that 'human rights norms are not persuasive in and of themselves; instead they are imposed as the values of the dominant state',[27] and essentially matters within the domestic jurisdiction.

Not the only challenge

The human rights challenge to sovereignty is buttressed by such developments as the internet, which has the potential to impinge on the sovereignty of the state.[28] The onward march of technology ensures a dissemination of information into states, which governments cannot entirely control, thus undermining the ability of governments to control their own population and, in turn, sovereignty.[29] This is evidently of particular significance in 'closed' societies: a new source of information filters into society and its members, giving new insights to the population potentially at the expense of state authority. This serves to emphasise the importance of political realism: while the state possesses considerable power it 'is a construct of social practices', therefore 'a possible object of political contestations' and open to developments in

Chinese government 'argues that human rights turn to some extent on cultural values and traditions, and that while the human rights movement emphasises the universality of rights, cultural differences cannot and should not be ignored. Human rights norms are inevitably subject to cultural mediation': R. Peerenboom, *China's Long March toward Rule of Law* (Cambridge University Press, 2002), p.536, footnotes omitted. Parekh, though, argues that the Chinese leaders' contention that their traditional values are incompatible with human rights is unconvincing, and further that the rejection of human rights is both self-serving and suspect: Parekh, 'Non-ethnocentric universalism', pp.157–8.

[26] R. A. Falk, *On Humane Governance: Toward a New Global Politics* (Cambridge: Polity Press, 1995), p.26; see also the Bangkok Governmental Declaration of 1993. The Declaration is accessible at http://law.hku.hk/lawgovtsociety/Bangkok Declaration.htm.

[27] Ming Wan, *Human Rights in Chinese Foreign Relations: Defining and Defending National Interests* (Philadelphia: University of Pennsylvania Press, 2001), p.12.

[28] As instanced by calls on websites for attack on the integrity of the state, for example by Islamists in the UK such as the British *jihad* group al Ghurabaa.

[29] See, in this context, D. S. Stern, 'State sovereignty, the politics of identity and the place of the political' in M. E. Denham and M. O. Lombardi (eds.), *Perspectives on Third-World Sovereignty: The Postmodern Paradox* (Basingstoke: Macmillan Press Ltd, 1996), 28, p.28.

the wider world, both in respect of dissemination of the views of individuals and in the dissemination of other political and legal ideas.[30]

Thus, 'ultimately a controlled press is incompatible with the socio-political dynamics of the Information Age',[31] and all states, including powerful states such as the People's Republic of China, realise the potential importance of the internet; so, for instance, at the start of 2006 a website for the Central People's Government of the PRC was launched.[32] By way of further example, the internet was seen as significant in January and February 2011 in connection with the popular unrest against the government of President Hosni Mubarak in Egypt. Accordingly, internet connections across Egypt were cut, 'as authorities geared up to a day of mass protest'.[33] The Mubarak regime fell the following month. Developments of this nature will provide one battleground for the concept of sovereignty in the early years of this century, and pragmatism again comes to the fore.

A third development impinging upon sovereignty is a combination of sub-state nationalism and supranationalism. This is particularly evident in Western liberal democracies, and is best evidenced by the continued advance of the European Union (EU) – representing an 'ever closer union' of the states of Europe.[34] Through the supranational body of the EU, states pool elements of their sovereignty, but at the same time in Europe a move towards subsidiarity pulls at the strings of sovereignty from the opposite direction. The federal principle of subsidiarity may be concisely defined as 'the principle that each social and political group should help smaller or more local ones accomplish their respective ends without, however, arrogating those tasks to itself'.[35] Thus smaller units seek greater power as against the state, at the same time as the supranational body of the EU seeks greater powers for itself. The sovereignty of the state is caught in between. Although international

[30] Ibid., p.37.

[31] R. Baum, 'Political implications of China's information revolution: the media, the minders, and their message' in Cheng Li (ed.), *China's Changing Political Landscape* (Washington, DC: Brookings Institution Press, 2008) 179.

[32] At www.gov.cn: see *People's Daily Online*, 'China effectively promotes administrative transparency' (2007), available at http://english.people.com.cn/200703/23/print20070323_360429.html (accessed 15 February 2011).

[33] BBC News, 'Egypt severs internet connection amid growing unrest' (2011), available at www.bbc.co.uk/news/technology-12306041 (accessed 15 February 2011).

[34] As in the evocative title of D. Dinan, *Ever Closer Union: An Introduction to European Integration*, 2nd edn, revised (Basingstoke: Palgrave, 1994).

[35] G. Carozza, 'Subsidiarity as a structural principle of international human rights law', 97 *American Journal of International Law* (2003) 1, 38, p.38, n.1.

law is a powerful force in defence of the power of the state, being concerned with the order of states, subsidiarity enhances human rights obligations in opposition to sovereignty, affirming diversity more than universal state values.[36]

Indeed, for Carozza, subsidiarity is seen as a structural principle of international human rights law, capable of mediating tensions between sovereignty and human rights, between the nation state and internationalism, and between various visions of human dignity and the diversity and freedom of cultures.[37] He argues that:

> despite its potential to encourage pluralism in human rights, subsidiarity does not undermine the universal and fundamental nature of human rights in theory, nor the political effectiveness of human rights norms. It respects the inherent problems of unifying law and the legal diversity in legal norms while mitigating the risk that a global rule of law will impose uniformity at the expense of the diversity of human cultures . . . Subsidiarity offers a contrast to prevailing patterns of understanding on the place of human rights in the international order, which are based largely on more limited conceptions of sovereignty.[38]

Thus in this respect, in the sphere of public international law, subsidiarity itself becomes an alternative principle to sovereignty, rather than a part of its developing concept. It is of relevance that developments at EU level are based on the consent of member states, either unanimous or through use of qualified majority voting (and it is in the EU that the main debate on subsidiarity lies), as indeed 'universality' of human rights is premised on state agreement.

Consequently it is evident that challenges are being mounted to the supremacy of the concept of sovereignty, to the nation state as the pre-eminent site of territorial integrity.[39] In turn one may perceive the declining power of the nation state, yet this may be over-emphasised.[40] Sovereignty as a construct is still of fundamental relevance. Indeed modern realists view sovereignty as a given, a fact of life,[41] and sovereignty is not something that disappears easily. The state maintains a normalising power and

[36] Ibid., especially pp.68–9; Tierney, 'Reframing Sovereignty', especially p.171.

[37] Carozza, 'Subsidiarity as a structural principle', pp.38, 68.

[38] Ibid., p.78.

[39] See Tierney, 'Reframing Sovereignty', p.164.

[40] M. O. Lombardi, 'Third-World problem-solving and the "religion" of sovereignty: trends and prospects' in Denham and Lombardi (eds.), *Perspectives on Third-World Sovereignty*, 152, p.153. See also A. James, *Sovereign Statehood: The Basis of International Society* (London: Allen & Unwin, 1986), p.275.

[41] R. B. J. Walker, 'Space/time/sovereignty' in Denham and Lombardi, ibid., 13, pp.23 and 25.

each state may be viewed as 'a continuous homogeneous project'.[42] Even in the EU, nation states act pragmatically to maintain powers and continue to seek advantage.[43]

The fact that sovereignty evolves as a concept will not necessarily diminish its importance at all, although in its development interstices may open up. This allows additional space for wider interpretation of such concepts as self-determination in an international law dominated by the rights and obligations of states toward each other; in other words in a state of affairs under the dominant system of sovereignty. With that in mind the next section proceeds to discuss self-determination within the concept of human rights as a specific challenge to sovereignty.

Self-determination

It is instructive in the current discourse on self-determination to look at the events in Kosovo, which, on 17 February 2008, issued a unilateral declaration of independence from Serbia.[44] Prior to the break-up of the former Yugoslavia in 1991, Kosovo was a self-administering province of Serbia under the 1974 Yugoslav Constitution.[45] This chapter is not the place to detail this break-up and its consequences.[46] However, so far as Kosovo is concerned, the outcome has proved to be the intervention of

[42] M. J. Shapiro, 'Moral geographies and the ethics of post-sovereignty' in Denham and Lombardi, ibid., 39, p.45.

[43] While sovereignty has been seen to erode within the EU, the concept of sovereignty does not go down without a fight. For example: 'As state sovereignty has eroded into a relative concept, a significant portion of the German juridical debate has responded by over-emphasising the sovereignty of the German state over and above its European and international commitments as part of its crusade against what is seen by many as the "withering away" of the state' (footnotes omitted) – M. Aziz, 'Sovereignty *über Alles*: (re)configuring the German legal order' in N. Walker (ed.), *Sovereignty in Transition* (Oxford: Hart Publishing, 2003), 279, p.281.

[44] To date only eighty-one countries have recognised that independence, the most recent of which was St Lucia on 19 August 2011: see, for example, Republic of Kosovo, Ministry of Foreign Affairs, 'Countries that have recognised the Republic of Kosovo' (2011), available at www.mfa-ks.net/?page=2,33 (accessed 3 October 2011).

[45] The Constitution of the Socialist Federal Republic of Yugoslavia, promulgated on 21 February 1974, and reprinted in part in S. Trifunovska, *Yugoslavia Through Documents: From its Creation to its Dissolution* (Dordrecht/Boston/London: Martinus Nijhoff Publishers, 1994), p.224. The Socialist Federal Republic of Yugoslavia was a federal state comprising five Socialist Republics and two 'Socialist Autonomous Provinces of Vojvodina and Kosovo, which are constituent parts of the Socialist Republic of Serbia': Art. 1 of the 1974 Constitution; see also Art. 2.

[46] See for example J. Summers (ed.), *A Kosovo Precedent?* (Leiden: Brill, 2011) for useful information in this regard.

the international community following a series of UN Security Council Resolutions. These culminated in Resolution 1244 (1999),[47] thereafter the Comprehensive Proposal for the Kosovo Status Settlement together with the Report on Kosovo's future status prepared by the UN Special Envoy for the future status of Kosovo, Martti Ahtisaari,[48] and more latterly the Kosovan attempts to become one of the very few entities that have achieved external self-determination through unilateral secession in the modern era. Indeed, the only other entity that has arguably achieved this is Bangladesh,[49] although even in the case of Bangladesh not all believe that the establishment of that country comes within the principle of self-determination:

> The indications are that the United Nations did not treat the emergence of Bangladesh as a case of self-determination despite good grounds for doing so, but rather as a *fait accompli* achieved as a result of foreign military assistance in special circumstances. The violence and repression engaged in by the Pakistan military made reunification unthinkable, and in effect legitimised the creation of the new State.[50]

This provides an instance of the application of pragmatism as a matter of practice.

Consequently the situation pertaining in Kosovo is of potential significance for the doctrine of self-determination as the doctrine may be said to be seeking a new role for itself.[51] This is apparent not only in the acceptance to date by eighty-one states of the declaration of independence by Kosovo,[52] but also in the fact that the UN Special Envoy was able to conclude that independence was the only viable solution for Kosovo, subject to supervision 'for an initial period by the international community'.[53] It is significant that a solution of this nature was proposed under

[47] Adopted by the Security Council at its 4011th meeting on 10 June 1999.

[48] See Letter dated 26 March 2007 from the Secretary-General addressed to the President of the Security Council, with Report of the Special Envoy of the Secretary-General on Kosovo's future status annexed, S/2007/168; and Addendum comprising the Comprehensive Proposal for the Kosovo Status Settlement, S/2007/168/Add.1.

[49] See, for instance, C. Tomuschat, 'Secession and self-determination' in M. G. Kohen (ed.), *Secession: International Law Perspectives* (Cambridge University Press, 2006), 23, p.42.

[50] J. Crawford, *The Creation of States in International Law*, 2nd edn (Oxford: Clarendon Press, 2006), pp.415–16.

[51] In the aftermath of the Second World War self-determination had found expression in its application to 'peoples under colonial self-determination': J. Crawford, 'Some Conclusions' in J. Crawford (ed.), *The Rights of Peoples* (Oxford: Clarendon Press, 1988), 159, p.161, but of course there are now few entities under colonial domination to which this could apply.

[52] See note 44 above.

[53] Report of the Special Envoy, note 48 above, para.5.

UN auspices at all, even though it was not ultimately adopted. Despite the description applied to the Kosovo situation – unique, *sui generis*[54] – the question arises whether this description in itself prevents the settlement from having the potential to form the basis for a new normative approach to external self-determination. In other words, whether the separation of an entity from the parent state such as in this instance may become a precedent, a rule of customary law emerging in validation of the self-determination and independence of Kosovo.

At this time the challenge of Kosovo to the principle of sovereignty may be seen to take two forms: first with reference to the Comprehensive Proposal for the Kosovo Status Settlement,[55] and second with regard to the unilateral declaration of independence of 17 February 2008. So far as the latter is concerned, the validity of the declaration has been referred to the International Court of Justice (ICJ) by the United Nations.[56] The Court restricted its Opinion to this narrow and specific question,[57] and therefore particular issues regarding, for example, 'the extent of the right of self-determination ... [were] beyond the scope of the question posed by the General Assembly'.[58] Thus the only question to be determined by the ICJ in their Opinion was 'whether the declaration of independence violated either general international law or the *lex specialis* created by Security Council Resolution 1244 (1999)'.[59] The Court considered that the declaration of independence violated neither international law, nor Resolution 1244 (which formed part of international law and which purported to protect the territorial integrity of all states in the region including the Federal Republic of Yugoslavia – later Serbia), nor indeed the Constitutional Framework that had been established in Kosovo.[60] The final conclusion of the ICJ, therefore, was that Kosovo's declaration of independence did not violate international law.[61]

It is noteworthy that the Court's decision that Kosovo's declaration of independence did not violate international law was a majority opinion, adopted by ten votes to four.[62] Of the four voting against, two were from the former Communist bloc (Slovakia and the Russian Federation) and two were from Africa (Sierra Leone and Morocco). All the Court judges

[54] Ibid., para.15. [55] See note 48 above.

[56] See United Nations General Assembly Resolution 63/3 of 8 October 2008, A/63/PV.22, and also Advisory Opinion of the ICJ of 22 July 2010, 'Accordance with international law of the unilateral declaration of independence in respect of Kosovo (Request for Advisory Opinion)'.

[57] Para.51 of the Advisory Opinion. [58] Para.83 of the Advisory Opinion.

[59] Ibid. [60] Paras.84, 93, 119 and 121 of the Advisory Opinion.

[61] Para.123 of the Advisory Opinion. [62] Ibid.

from Western states voted with the majority, as did a single African delegate, from Somalia, perhaps enhancing the perception of a division between the West and other states on human rights issues.

While the declaration of independence does not violate international law, that in itself does not give the entity declaring independence the right to separate from the parent state, and as indicated issues concerning 'the right to separate from a State' were beyond the scope of the question posed.[63] This then returns the argument to one revolving around the principle of external self-determination and whether the unadopted Proposal for the Kosovo Status Settlement has the potential to contribute to the expansion of that principle. The international community have been assiduous in an attempt to avoid this possibility in their use of wording such as 'unique' and '*sui generis*' to describe the Kosovo situation,[64] and it is true that Kosovo is distinguishable from states created, for example, from the other constituent parts of Yugoslavia in that it had enjoyed the status of an autonomous province, not a republic. Under the 1974 Constitution, Kosovo was a constituent part of the Socialist Republic of Serbia and was recognised as such.[65] Nevertheless, the fact that the Kosovo Status Settlement proposed that 'the only viable option for Kosovo is independence, to be supervised for an initial period by the international community',[66] is demonstrative of the evolving boundaries of the concept of self-determination, speaking of a dynamic to the legal right of peoples to self-determination that is continuing, an extension of the conditions in which the right may be justified and a considerable attack on the supposed illegality of unilateral secession. It reflects the purported potential creation of a state in international law – state building from the outside.

The continuation of this dynamic to the right to external self-determination, a right to secede, is evident too in respect of events in Georgia in August 2008, when, following armed conflict, the independence of South Ossetia and Abkhazia was recognised by Russia, Moscow drawing on Kosovo as a direct parallel.[67] This then demonstrates the potential of the proposed Kosovo Status Settlement as a trend (albeit the Settlement itself

63 Para.83 of the Advisory Opinion.

64 See, for example, note 54 above and related text. In similar fashion, it may be argued that Bangladesh did not fall within the principle of self-determination: see note 50 above and related text.

65 See note 45 above. 66 Report, note 48 above, para.5.

67 President Medvedev of Russia remarked that Moscow felt obliged to recognise South Ossetia and Abkhazia 'as other countries had done with Kosovo': BBC News, 'Russia recognises Georgian rebels' (2008), http://news.bbc.co.uk/2/hi/in_depth/7582181.stm (accessed 16 February 2011).

may be seen as an unsuccessful diplomatic initiative) and the start prospectively of a new normative approach to external self-determination.

However, if independence for Kosovo, fully recognised by the international community, is the ultimate result of the Kosovo Status Settlement and the declaration of independence of Kosovo, with Kosovo becoming a member of the key international institutions, this will not necessarily bring about a new norm permitting secession, or an extension of the existing norm of self-determination. It may take the form of an exception to norms of sovereignty and territorial integrity.[68] It is arguable that any extension to the concept of self-determination may find its limits here in the instance of Kosovo and it is worth recalling that secession is not in itself a right under international law, nor, more specifically, of self-determination.[69] It is noteworthy that Kosovo has been able to make progress – if not yet definitive progress – in its goal of achieving independence from Serbia, whereas other entities have not been able to make similar progress. One such entity is Tibet, which has failed to harness the support of the international community in its dealings with the People's Republic of China.

A pragmatic approach

What may be termed the Tibet Question is one resonating particularly since 1950, when the People's Liberation Army of China entered Tibet in numbers and what may be termed a Tibetan polity and Tibetan de facto independence ceased,[70] since Tibet then fell under political control of China.[71] Thus, the Tibet Question is one that centres on territory and control and it is a question at the heart of which is independence.

[68] See in this regard, note 10 above and related text. In another context, the case of the 2003 invasion of Iraq in probability constitutes an exception to and violation of the customary rule against the use of armed force rather than the creation of a new norm: see David Kennedy, Chapter 2 above.

[69] G. Nolte, 'Secession and external intervention' in Kohen (ed.), *Secession*, 65, p.84.

[70] See M. C. van Walt van Praag, *The Status of Tibet: History, Rights, and Prospects in International Law* (London: Wisdom Publications, 1987), p.140: 'On 7 October 1950, troops of the People's Liberation Army crossed into Tibet'; see also M. C. Goldstein, *A History of Modern Tibet, 1913–1950: The Demise of the Lamaist State* (Berkeley and Los Angeles: University of California Press, 1989), p.813: 'In the next few months, several thousand troops of the People's Liberation Army arrived in Lhasa; although the old system continued to exist in some form for another eight years, October 1951 marks the end of the de facto independent Lamaist State'.

[71] See, for example, The Agreement of the Central People's Government and the Local Government of Tibet on Measures for the Peaceful Liberation of Tibet, 23 May 1951, translated in van Walt van Praag, *The Status of Tibet*, pp.337–40.

It will be recalled that Kosovo had the status of an autonomous province – a constituent part of Serbia.[72] Similarly, Tibet – in the guise of the Tibet Autonomous Region – is an autonomous region within the People's Republic of China.[73] Equally, in both autonomous regions there has been an ongoing pattern of human rights abuse.[74] Yet, in the one, Kosovo, the creation of a new state appears to have been legitimised; in the other, Tibet, the dominance of the Chinese state holds sway. The Chinese focus on the interpretation of self-determination is one factor of pertinence here. China regards Tibet as an integral part of the Chinese state and consequently not open to foreign interference; the right of the state to its own self-determination is seen as a defence to interference in the state.[75] Following on from the argument that human rights norms are imposed as the values of the dominant state,[76] that human rights are essentially matters within the domestic jurisdiction of the country, is the fact that by virtue of Article 2(7) of the UN Charter, the UN are not entitled to intervene in matters that are essentially within a domestic jurisdiction.

So, assuming that there are equivalences between Kosovo and Tibet, as to the status of each entity and patterns of human rights abuse, why has one new state (Kosovo) potentially been legitimised while another (Tibet) is as far as ever from the Tibetan goal of independent statehood? In other words, why is it that it may be said that the effects of the legitimisation of statehood for Kosovo – the potential new normative approach to external self-determination[77] – find their limits, for example, in Tibet within the People's Republic of China?

It would seem that self-determination has been treated pragmatically rather than as an indivisible interest even though self-determination is said to be indivisible.[78] If so, this has implications for international norms

[72] See note 45 above.

[73] See, for example, van Walt van Praag, *The Status of Tibet*, p.156.

[74] See, for example, R. A. Dickinson, 'Twenty-first century self-determination: implications of the Kosovo Status Settlement for Tibet', 26 *Arizona Journal of International and Comparative Law* (2009) 3, 547, pp.553–6, 562–3 and 573.

[75] R. Emerson, 'Self-determination', 65 *American Journal of International Law* (1971) 3, 459, p.466.

[76] See note 27 above and related text. [77] See 'Self-determination' above.

[78] G. Seidel, 'A new dimension of the right of self-determination in Kosovo?' in Christian Tomuschat (ed), *Kosovo and the International Community: A Legal Assessment* (The Hague: Kluwer Law International, 2002), 203, p.213. It may also be noted that violence has played its part both in Kosovo and in the case of Bangladesh. The lack of violence in Tibet is predicated on the fact that violence is antithetical to Buddhism. If violent disorder is perceived to be a prerequisite for successful external self-determination

of sovereignty and territorial integrity, and since self-determination of peoples is a group human right the issue of the universality of human rights comes into focus. If the divisibility of self-determination is demonstrable then the question of the universality of human rights is directly brought into question.

Kosovo as a step too far for universal human rights

The legitimisation of a new state of Kosovo – even in embryonic form – is a step too far in the human rights movement and is a challenge too far for the universality of human rights. Perhaps, indeed, it is more properly seen as a retreat from the notion of the universality of human rights. It calls into question the whole concept of universality, and it seems that some entities, some states, are more equal than others: power and *Realpolitik*, therefore, become the crux of the matter and in appearance the political may extract the legal from the idea of self-determination and therefore the universality of human rights. If Kosovo is successful in obtaining full recognition of its independence, has it succeeded in seceding because it can, rather than because it is entitled to do so on principle?

The indivisibility of self-determination becomes questionable.[79] It is one thing for an entity such as Kosovo to be able to break away from a state such as Serbia; it is an entirely different thing for an entity such as Tibet to break away from a state such as the People's Republic of China. In this respect Blair's Chicago Doctrine falls perfectly into place; there will be no intervention by the international community against a state if intervention would conflict with international peace.[80] This has a consequence so far as sovereignty is concerned. Although human rights may challenge the *jus cogens* norm of sovereignty,[81] it becomes clear that some states are indeed more equal than others: the sovereignty of a strong state, such as the People's Republic of China, is protected, whereas the sovereignty of a less strong state, such as Serbia, is not.

Therefore lack of indivisibility in self-determination calls into question the very universality of human rights – and hence may be perceived as an element of a retreat from a high point in the interpretation of human rights. At the same time, however, all states are nevertheless

through secession from a parent state this in itself raises disturbing questions about the indivisibility of self-determination and the universality of human rights.

[79] Cf. Seidel, ibid. [80] See notes 6 and 7 above. [81] See note 5 above and related text.

affected directly by the concept of human rights. This is evidenced by the fact that China issues annual White Papers delineating progress in its human rights cause – thus demonstrating to the outside world an appearance of bowing to the human rights regime; it is also evidenced by Serbia's loss of sovereignty over Kosovo.

All this gives us pause for thought when considering human rights as 'the *raison d'être* of the state system'.[82] It leads to the question whether Kosovan independence is a bridge too far for human rights, a challenge to sovereignty too far for universal human rights, and may lead to an acceleration of the retreat from human rights, for it is certain that Kosovo can be perceived as a component of a retreat from the universality of human rights. There is a selective implementation of the human rights regime, which brings to the forefront the political and the concept of power at the expense of the law. Principle loses out to pragmatism; power brokers acting only when they want to – when they perceive that it is in their interests so to do. China invokes the Western principle of self-determination to buttress its own power and its power is sufficient to ensure that it is able to protect its own interests against any possibility of humanitarian intervention. Thus the issue becomes one of whose self-determination? whose rights are in issue? and a problem that once one people has self-determination that people may deny self-determination to entities within its boundaries.

Self-determination can serve the interests of elites rather than peoples. And once humanitarian intervention occurs – as in the case of Kosovo – where might that lead, and, ultimately, who might it benefit? In the case of Kosovo, in December 2010 the Council of Europe reported that Kosovo's prime minister was 'the leader of a "mafia-like" criminal organisation with links to organ and drug smuggling'.[83] In a wider context, as Andrew Hurrell remarks, 'writers such as Berlin and Elster have underlined the extent to which formal political democracy can entrench murderous majorities of all kinds – but most dangerously, perhaps, murderous ethnic majorities'.[84] Thus external self-determination is not necessarily a solution

[82] See note 1 above and related text.

[83] P. Lewis, 'Kosovo's prime minister denies "mafia" claims: Council of Europe report accuses Hashim Thaci of leading criminal organisation linked to organ trafficking', *The Guardian*, 17 December 2010, available at www.guardian.co.uk/world/2010/dec/17/kosovo-pm-denies-mafia-claims (last accessed 16 February 2010).

[84] Hurrell, 'Power, principles and prudence', p.280 – see in this regard I. Berlin, 'Two concepts of liberty' in *Four Essays on Liberty* (Oxford University Press, 1969), especially pp.165–9; J. Elster, 'Majority rule and individual rights' in S. Shute and S. Hurley (eds.), *On Human Rights: The Oxford Amnesty Lectures* (New York: Basic Books, 1993), p.111.

for ‘the people’. There is no guarantee that the elites who achieve power as a result of self-determination – as a result of independence – will hold that power for the benefit of the people. With this in mind the assertion that Kosovan independence is a bridge too far for human rights which might lead to an acceleration of the retreat from human rights may prove something not to be regretted. It becomes clear that human rights may be seen as a cover for objectives, both political and (indeed) economic, of those in the wider international community and of those within a seceding unit as well as those already in power in an extant territory.

PART IV

Theoretical perspectives on human rights

10

The reality and hyper-reality of human rights: public consciousness and the mass media

ERIC HEINZE

Introduction

Scholarship on international human rights generally adopts two approaches. The normative approach focuses on treaties or other authoritative sources. The institutional approach emphasises governments, organisations or other actors charged with the norms' implementation. Much writing inevitably involves both approaches. Any critical stance is then often limited either to examining obstacles within the norms or their interpretation, or to pointing out the shortcomings of actors responsible for implementation.

The authors of human rights scholarship are often activists, lawyers, diplomats or judges, and may include scholars with professional affinities to those circles. They largely confine their critical scope to those normative or institutional levels. Some theoretical writings go further, proposing broader frameworks, such as liberal, legal-realist, post-Marxist, post-colonial, feminist, communitarian or deconstructionist. Those analyses too, however, frequently focus either on prevailing norms (individually or as a system) or on the performance of the relevant actors.

In this chapter, I shall examine a third layer of activity, the mass media. I shall treat the media as being on a par with, or more powerful than, the dominant systems of norms, insofar as the media determine the situations with which those norms are associated in the public mind; and as being at least on a par with organisations and governments,

This chapter benefited from discussions within the Newcastle Law School's 'Retreat from Human Rights' series, session of 27 November 2009, chaired by Colin Murray. Equally helpful was the conference 'Law and Politics: Democracy, Human Rights and Power', University of Westminster, 10 June 2010, chaired by Daniela Nadj. Many thanks also to Rob Dickinson, and to William Linton for his research assistance.

insofar as the media determine which situations are most visibly and urgently acted upon. The neglect of this decisive strand underscores the ongoing formalism of legal practice: norms and institutions receive the most attention, since they assume the official status proper to the promulgation, interpretation and implementation of rights. In most scholarship on international law and human rights, the role of the media, lacking any such formalised status, is cited, if at all, only tangentially.

Some international bodies, like the treaty-based Committees of the United Nations, or the Sub-Commission on Human Rights, do exhibit some independence from media trends.[1] Their roles, however, have remained minor. Even leading politicians scarcely know about them. In the world of real power politics, they do not need to know about such agencies. The Committees or the Sub-Commission may influence cooperative states in a symbolic hope that other states will someday follow suit; but they have wielded no real influence over the most heinous situations and regimes, either because responsible actors are not states parties to the respective treaties,[2] or because they disregard the various agencies' findings or recommendations, which lack any enforcement mechanism. Meanwhile, bodies like the former UN Human Rights Commission, or its successor, the Human Rights Council, grimly display the irrelevance of any genuine and balanced picture of global human rights to countless UN member states.[3] Even high-profile NGOs, like Amnesty International, attract only sporadic attention, and usually only in the elite media.

To be sure, a good deal has been written on the portrayal of human rights in the media. As of this writing, however, little of that work appears in publications on international law or on international human rights. It is conducted mostly by political and social scientists, and is published in journals far from the mainstay of international lawyers. The

[1] For periodically updated archives, see Office of the United Nations High Commissioner for Human Rights, 'Human Rights Bodies', at www.ohchr.org/EN/HRBodies/Pages/HumanRightsBodies.aspx (accessed 15 December 2010); University of Minnesota Human Rights Library, 'United Nations Documents', at www1.umn.edu/humanrts/un-orgs.htm (accessed 15 December 2010).

[2] For ratification information, see United Nations Organisation (UNO), 'United Nations Treaty Collection, Chapter IV: Human Rights', at http://treaties.un.org/pages/Treaties.aspx?id=4&subid=A&lang=Den (accessed 15 December 2010).

[3] See, e.g., Rosa Freedman, 'Improvement on the Commission?: The UN Human Rights Council's inaction on Darfur', *University of California-Davis Journal of International Law & Policy* 16 (2010), 81.

human rights community focuses upon formally empowered instruments, organisations or governments, with little appreciation for the mass consciousness of human rights that overwhelmingly decides the issues that attract or deflect power brokers' attention in the first instance; which mass consciousness is a media creation. If the media lacks any formal role, it more than compensates in its functional influence.

It is worth briefly noting two caveats. First, although I shall not speculate further on this point, even if we were to substitute rights discourse for a law or ethics that is less individualist or litigious in its origins or effects, the role of the global media, unless it were organised vastly differently than it is today, would still remain decisive. The problem of media dominance is not a problem for human rights *per se*. It would be a problem for anything conceivable, in today's sense, as a globally applied ethics. Accordingly, I am less interested in whether a rights discourse is better or worse than any alternatives, and more interested in the role the media assumes with arguable indifference to our legal or ethical paradigms. Secondly, in discussing the role of the media in international human rights, I shall consider them only as actors in generating a public consciousness of human rights. This analysis will not cover the media as, collectively, an object of legal or professional regulation, subject to their own positive norms, such as freedom of speech, defamation or other standards of press conduct. We must bear in mind, however, that the two sets of questions do remain linked. The link becomes evident in times of media blockades, or under totalitarian regimes, since the media's creation of a mass human rights consciousness crucially depends on what the media can report.

Human rights in hyper-reality

In his chapter in this volume, David Kennedy warns that to frame certain issues as raising distinct concerns about human rights can divert our attention from other problems: 'a well-implemented ban on the death penalty, for example, can easily leave the general conditions of incarceration unremarked'. In that case, singling out capital punishment as a distinct human rights issue 'can make life-without-parole more legitimate, more difficult to challenge'.[4]

The example of the death penalty is probative, since the two other problems Kennedy cites, prison conditions and excessive sentences, are

[4] See p.24 in Chapter 2 above.

themselves subject to human rights norms. The problem Kennedy evokes is *not* that some important issues enjoy, while others lack, the protections of higher-law norms. We would be hard-pressed nowadays to find an issue of any seriousness that does not in some way involve human rights. Rather, and particularly in our world of bloated and ever-expanding norms and instruments, the problem is that adequate attention cannot possibly be paid to all of them. What is decisive in our world is not which norms do and do not count as human rights, but rather which concrete situations attract attention.

Taking a converse scenario, if the media were suddenly to direct massive and concerted attention to prison conditions or excessive sentences, and to ignore the problem of criminal punishment, it is the death-row inmates who would then suffer. It would not be the sheer existence of formal norms, but rather the media that would have created the shift. The media drive human rights because there are already norms for virtually any situation that the media may report or overlook, and because organisations, institutions and governments overwhelmingly respond to the public pressures generated by the media.

Among the broader public, and among ruling elites, dominant understandings of what international human rights 'are' have little to do with the realities of actual abuses, and most to do with media choices. For example, following the USA-led invasions of Afghanistan in 2001 and then of Iraq in 2003, just under 800 'enemy combatants' were imprisoned at the detention centre in Guantánamo Bay, Cuba.[5] Meanwhile, throughout that period, armed conflict in the Democratic Republic of Congo (DRC) was counting its victims of death, torture, rape, mutilation, orphaning and displacement in the millions.[6] While coverage of Guantánamo during George W. Bush's second presidential

[5] See, e.g., Gordon Cucullu, *Inside Gitmo: The True Story Behind the Myths of Guantánamo Bay* (New York: Harper, 2009); Joseph Margulies, *Guantánamo and the Abuse of Presidential Power* (New York: Simon & Schuster, 2007).

[6] Gerard Prunier, *Africa's World War: Congo, the Rwandan Genocide, and the Making of a Continental Catastrophe* (London: Oxford University Press, 2010); Phoebe Okawa. 'Congo's war: the legal dimension of a protracted conflict', 77 *British Yearbook of International Law* (2006) 203. See also, e.g., 'Congo death toll up to 3.8m', *Guardian Unlimited*, 10 December 2004, available at www.guardian.co.uk/congo/story/0,12292,1370528,00.html (accessed 15 December 2010); Lydia Polgreen, 'War's chaos steals Congo's young by the millions', *New York Times*, 30 July 2006, available at www.nytimes.com/2006/07/30/world/africa/30congo.html?ex=1311912000&en=b51825fef1e20057&ei=5088&partner=rssnyt&emc=rss (accessed 15 December 2010).

term became more-or-less daily, not just in the American media, but throughout much of the world,[7] DRC went almost entirely unreported.

That kind of comparison, seemingly compassionate when the spotlight shifts to DRC's real victims, nevertheless breeds intractable dilemmas. We cannot escape the embarrassment that the question 'why should Guantánamo receive so much attention, and Congo so little?' is a mere variation on the positive assertion, 'Guantánamo should receive less attention!' But who would ever voice that demand? Once an event raises undeniably urgent questions of politics, ethics or rights, it becomes disconcerting, and evokes a spectre of authoritarianism, to call for less discussion of it. However noble one's intentions might be in encouraging coverage of other global situations, that desire would seem to stray too close to downright complicity in the camps. After all, the Bush administration would have relished a call for less coverage, particularly if replaced by a focus on human rights abuses by other governments. Any attempt to redress 'too much' reporting on Guantánamo would appear to undermine the democratic value of maximum discussion on issues of state action or public interest. Such a shift would also invite a grisly number-crunching game, wherein we weigh a few hundred victims of the camps against a few million in Congo or elsewhere. Such a calculus would degrade human rights to utilitarian, cost–benefit analyses in order to decide who 'deserves' how much coverage. Comparisons are odious.

The dilemma allows no easy resolution. We cannot approve of the extent of the Guantánamo coverage, so completely does it eclipse millions of other violations around the world. Yet nor can we condemn it, since the loudest possible noise against Guantánamo is crucial to the self-critical dialogue without which a democracy's essential elements of legitimacy and accountability are destroyed.

A common attitude towards the media might be called 'loosely pluralist'. We know that not every problem can be reported. Every day, the world is cluttered with millions of problems. The sheer notion that a given situation does or does not constitute a human rights 'problem' already presupposes some normative criterion that, in many cases, can be disputed. We instead hope for some balanced mix over the long run. Any given day's reporting will emphasise some problems over others. So we accept that the media are doing their job if, over time, we feel that an

[7] Cf. Eric Heinze and Rosa Freedman, 'Public awareness of human rights: distortions in the mass media', 14 *International Journal of Human Rights* (2010) 491, pp.507–8.

overall picture has emerged, at least of the world's gravest abuses. The problem, of course, as 'Guantánamo *versus* Congo' suggests, is that a 'reasonably complete and balanced picture' does *not* inevitably emerge 'over time'.

Nor does the problem reduce to one of elite *versus* popular media, or of left-wing *versus* right-wing media, or of privately *versus* publicly owned media. Although the elite outlets may provide better pictures than the popular press, they too privilege concerns with only tangential bearing upon human rights. The elite *New York Times*, or the centre-left *Guardian*, showed only marginally more interest in DRC than their more colourful counterparts.[8] The public BBC showed little more interest than the privately operated Murdoch outlets.

Only through the media can we glean what might be called a 'functional ontology' of human rights violations: not merely a study of norms on paper, nor even of violations that actually 'exist' in the world, but rather one (a) of those of which the existence matters, because the world's attention is sufficiently drawn to them; and (b) of those of which the existence does not matter, those which do not exist in any functional way, because the media bypass them. In theory, the falling tree makes a sound even if no one hears it: a violation exists even if it is never discovered or publicised. In practice, the decisive mode by which human rights exist, the only mode of existence which makes human rights in any way known to the public at large and to those in power, lies not in the real, but in the so-called 'hyper-real' world. In hyper-reality, the falling tree makes a sound only when someone hears it – and indeed not just a single sound, but through steady repetition. Jean Baudrillard sees hyper-reality, in opposition to reality, where our encounter is fundamentally driven not by lived experience of the object in question (for example a personal encounter with a human rights violation) but rather through media representations.[9] A pre-modern European might have understood a report, or story, about a famine in some faraway place by having experienced hunger at home. Today's Western Europeans will know hunger, or genocidal murders, rapes or limb-hackings, only through televised images of faraway places; not as mirrors of their own lived experiences, but through representations ('simulacra') of societies experienced as alien or 'Other'. The result is that even an existential experience as basic, as primary to the human condition as simple bodily

[8] See ibid.

[9] See, e.g., Jean Baudrillard, *Simulacres et simulation* (Paris: Éditions Galilée, 1981).

hunger will, for most in the West, be a sheer media contrivance. For most audiences in the West, in the context of our post-industrial states, human rights abuses are a hyper-real media invention. Even those of us with direct experience of our own, or others', violations will know, through direct experience, only a tiny fragment of any genuinely global human rights picture.

Human rights: absolute *versus* zero-sum

A commitment to human rights is a commitment to an ethical code. If we believe in human rights as a matter of principle, then, on human rights' own terms, we cannot rate any other interest as being above them, able to trump them. Even God's will cannot stand above human rights in that sense, but can only be, at best, coextensive with them. Admittedly, some details of human rights (for example, the precise maximum number of hours for holding detainees in pre-trial detention, or the precise amount of money that government, or private enterprise, must spend to accommodate the physically handicapped) may allow considerable variation without violating express religious precepts. By contrast, if we believe in core human rights, but only with qualification (for example, only insofar as we think God allows – if we believe, for example, that God requires or permits killing people for the crime of homosexual conduct) then, however much we might accommodate certain positive elements of the prevailing human rights codes, our highest ethical code is, ultimately, something other than human rights. In that case, our ethics might maintain some degree of overlap with human rights, but human rights as such could not be said to be the ultimate ethical value.

If, after all, we do believe in international human rights more or less in their dominant form, then they must represent not only a highest value, but a universal one. There can be no principle admitting the enjoyment of human rights in solely conditional ways (barring conditions legitimated by human rights law itself, such as exceptions clauses or derogations clauses). In other words, human rights, in principle, preclude any zero-sum calculus. Contrary to a classical utilitarian ethics,[10] and contrary to

[10] See generally, John Rawls, *A Theory of Justice*, 2nd edn (Oxford University Press, 1999). Rawls's analysis amounts neither to an unqualified attack on utilitarianism, nor to the suggestion that utilitarian calculations are altogether incompatible with liberal rights regimes. He argues, rather, that utilitarianism in itself cannot provide an adequate foundation for a just political order. Utilitarian considerations are feasible, then, within

more ordinary legislative procedures beyond the core issues of human rights (such as routine deliberations on such issues as tax rates, or financial regulation, or zoning rules), there is no principle of fundamental human rights that can be construed as granting only some rights, on condition that others be withheld: neither can one individual be expected to secure some human rights solely on the condition of forgoing others; nor can any group of people be denied human rights on condition that others may enjoy them.[11]

In other words, even-handedness is not simply an aspiration of human rights, but a conceptual presupposition, without which they make no sense at all. By 'even-handedness', I mean not merely the obvious element of equal enjoyment of rights by all rights holders (as has always been expressly stated in the relevant instruments),[12] but also, and of the same stature, condemnation of all perpetrators in general proportion to their respective levels of abuse.[13] (Levels of abuse, in turn, must be determined by taking account, for example, under legitimate states of emergency, of states' available means;[14] or, in the case of social and economic rights, of states' available resources.[15])

Under that principle of even-handedness, a state like Israel would certainly have been subject to criticism and legitimate media attention,[16] from the time of her creation at least into the twenty-first century, but no more than any number of her non-democratic neighbours during that same period, who, before the 2011 uprisings, attracted a media spotlight mostly on their international acts, with very little attention – certainly in comparison to that on Israel – to their internal repression.

rights regimes, but can never override rights. Utilitarianism thus becomes not altogether destroyed by, but simply subordinated to, liberalism.

[11] See generally, e.g., Ronald Dworkin, *Taking Rights Seriously* (Cambridge, MA: Harvard University Press, 1977).

[12] See, e.g., Universal Declaration of Human Rights, Arts. 1 and 2, GA Res. 217A (III), at 71, UN Doc. A/810 (1948).

[13] See generally, Eric Heinze, 'Even-handedness and the politics of human rights', 21 *Harvard Human Rights Journal* (2008) 7.

[14] See, e.g., UN Human Rights Committee, 'General comment 29: states of emergency (Article 4)', UN Doc. CCPR/C/21/Rev.1/Add.11 (2001).

[15] International Covenant on Economic, Social and Cultural Rights (ICESCR), GA Res. 2200A (XXI), 21 UN GAOR Supp. (No. 16) at 49, UN Doc. A/6316 (1966), 993 UNTS 3, entered into force 3 January 1976, Art. 2(1).

[16] See, e.g. UN Human Rights Committee, 'Concluding observations of the Human Rights Committee: Israel', report of 29 July 2010, UN Doc. CCPR/C/ISR/CO/3 (2010); UN Committee on Economic, Social and Cultural Rights, 'Conclusions and recommendations of the Committee on Economic, Social and Cultural Rights: Israel', UN Doc. E/C.12/1/Add.90 (2003).

Once again, the ability of the media to construct such a situation is striking. A media-disseminated phrase like 'Occupied Territories', directly drawn from international law, too readily serves to distinguish Israel from her self-declared adversaries. An 'occupied territory' raises problems because an entity legitimately claiming self-determination is denied it. Surely, however, we cannot call the people of Tunisia, Egypt, Bahrain, Libya, Syria or Saudi Arabia (as opposed to their small ruling elites) in any sense more self-determining than the Palestinians at any time throughout the late twentieth or early twenty-first centuries.

As with Guantánamo, a common claim is that the brighter media spotlight is justified, since self-proclaimed democracies must be held to higher ethical standards. The problem is that such a criterion, far from applying international law, flatly contradicts it. Universal human rights apply to all states, irrespective of political regime. Nothing in the Universal Declaration of Human Rights or its progeny suggests (and it would be legally and conceptually absurd for them to suggest) that internationally responsible actors acquire a privilege of lower-level scrutiny by formally institutionalising regimes that are repressive either of democracy,[17] or of other human rights principles. Arguably, insofar as non-democratic states by definition contradict some of the most fundamental rights (notably, the right to political participation, not to mention free speech and fair trials),[18] lack of democracy must not lighten, but rather should intensify, the scrutiny a state receives. (In fact, the more one contemplates such a criterion, the more bizarre it appears: presumably, any historian explaining the Second World War would then have to take a hard line on The Netherlands, in view of its democratic traditions, while mentioning Nazi Germany only in passing – 'after all, the Nazis never claimed to be democratic!')

Palestinians have certainly lived in unacceptable conditions. Nevertheless, even conditions in other democracies, such as India or Brazil, with far more millions of people living with comparable deprivation,[19] have scarcely received any such censure, despite the aggravation of such

[17] UDHR Art. 21(1) states '[e]veryone has the right to take part in the government of his country, directly or through freely chosen representatives.'

[18] See UN Human Rights Committee, 'General comment 25 (57)' (on rights of political participation) UN Doc. CCPR/C/21/Rev.1/Add.7 (1996).

[19] See, e.g., UN Committee on Economic, Social and Cultural Rights, 'Concluding observations of the Committee on Economic, Social and Cultural Rights: Brazil', report of 22 May 2009, UN Doc. E/C.12/BRA/CO/2 (2009); UN Committee on Economic, Social and Cultural Rights, 'Concluding observations of the Committee on Economic, Social and Cultural Rights: India', report of 16 May 2008, UN Doc. E/C.12/IND/CO/5 (2008).

conditions through official corruption[20] and gross disparities of wealth.[21] As there is nothing like the complexity of a military occupation linked to the poverty in India or Brazil, they presumably have less of an excuse, and, in any case, no better one.[22] Yet not only do they suffer nothing like pariah status, but have counted among the most highly regarded candidates for permanent membership of a reformed UN Security Council. By analogy, examining the daily newspaper *The Australian* over an extended period, Virgil Hawkins – criticising the limited number of narratives that qualify a story for press coverage – approximated that 100 times more attention had been devoted to Israel than to DRC, despite the Congo conflict claiming 1,000 times more victims.[23] Although it is sometimes suggested that the media only spotlight stories with a 'good guy' and a 'bad guy', that view is probably too simplistic. Hawkins's analysis does suggest, however, that journalists prefer a narrative of the stronger and the weaker, and either fail to report, or misleadingly report, situations in which the power relations, and ethical dilemmas, are more complex.

Perhaps we should not read too much into such disparate media focus? Perhaps everyone somehow knows, deep down, that Israel is not much worse than countless other states? The facts suggest otherwise.

[20] In Transparency International's 2009 rankings for corruption, Brazil takes 75th place and India takes 84th place. Transparency International, 'Corruption Perceptions Index 2009', at www.transparency.org/policy_research/surveys_indices/cpi/2009 (accessed 26 February 2011).

[21] Under ICESCR Art. 2(1), a state party is bound only to 'achieving progressively the full realization' of economic and social rights, and only 'to the maximum of its available resources'. Respect for that progressive principle becomes questionable, however, when massive and entrenched poverty is tolerated alongside a privileged class entitled to great accumulation of private wealth.

[22] According to the UN Committee on Economic, Social and Cultural Rights, 'while the full realization of the relevant rights may be achieved progressively, steps towards that goal must be taken within a reasonably short time after the Covenant's entry into force for the States concerned. Such steps should be deliberate, concrete and targeted as clearly as possible towards meeting the obligations recognized in the Covenant.' Committee on Economic, Social and Cultural Rights, 'General comment 3: the nature of states parties' obligations', para.2 (Fifth session, 1990), UN Doc. E/1991/23, annex III at 86 (1991), reprinted in *Compilation of General Comments and General Recommendations Adopted by Human Rights Treaty Bodies*, UN Doc. HRI/GEN/1/Rev.6 at 14 (2003).

[23] Virgil Hawkins, 'National interest or business interest: coverage of conflict in the Democratic Republic of Congo' in *The Australian* newspaper, 2:1 *Media, War & Conflict*, April 2009, 67–84, 71–2. See also, generally, Virgil Hawkins, *Stealth Conflicts: How the world's worst violence is ignored* (Aldershot, UK: Ashgate, 2008); Philip Knightley, *The First Casualty: The War Correspondent as Hero, Propagandist and Myth-maker from the Crimea to Iraq* (London: Andre Deutsch, 2003).

A broad-based 2008 poll, commissioned by the BBC, surveying more than 17,000 people in 34 countries, revealed that even North Korea was perceived throughout the world as more benign, a better international actor, than Israel.[24] Without our having to deny serious abuses committed by Israel, then, such a perception nevertheless reflects not the reality of the two countries' comparative levels of violations, so much as the hyper-reality of both quantitative and qualitative media coverage devoted to the everyday lives of people living under them.[25]

We need not go so far as to claim that the disproportion accrues 'to Israel's detriment', at least not in an unqualified sense, since, as the spotlight on Guantánamo suggests, attention to human rights abuses can never be called a detriment. Rather, we should say, 'to the detriment of over 20 million North Koreans', who also have individual lives and stories, yet whose suffering attracts only fleeting and superficial attention. Well into the twenty-first century, North Korea may have fallen under the occasional spotlight due to its militarism or nuclear technologies; however, if only because North Korean totalitarianism is so perfect as to preclude press coverage, it draws remarkably little of the humanised, day-to-day interest that global media have devoted to Israeli injustices.

It is a platitude to think that the way for a state to avoid scrutiny is by improving its human rights. But platitudes can be false. States with good human rights records, like Sweden[26] or Norway,[27] have democratic cultures and a free press. Ironically, their media keep their populations awash with constant domestic human rights reporting, hence incessant internal scrutiny. The worst tactic, if a state wishes to avoid scrutiny,

[24] 'World views US "more positively"', report of 2 April 2008, *BBC News*, available at http://news.bbc.co.uk/1/hi/world/americas/7324337.stm (accessed 26 February 2011). The title of the article refers to a boost, albeit modest, in the otherwise poor image of the USA during the final years of the George W. Bush administration.

[25] See also Dov Shinar, 'Can peace journalism make progress?: the coverage of the 2006 Lebanon War in Canadian and Israeli media', 71:6 *International Communication Gazette* October 2009, pp.451–71.

[26] See, e.g., UN Human Rights Committee, 'Concluding observations of the Human Rights Committee: Sweden', UN Doc. CCPR/CO/74/SWE/Add.1 (2003); UN Committee on Economic, Social and Cultural Rights, 'Conclusions and recommendations of the Committee on Economic, Social and Cultural Rights: Sweden', UN Doc. E/C.12/1/Add.70 (2001).

[27] See, e.g. UN Human Rights Committee, 'Concluding observations of the Human Rights Committee: Norway', UN Doc. CCPR/C/NOR/CO/5 (2006); UN Committee on Economic, Social and Cultural Rights, 'Conclusions and recommendations of the Committee on Economic, Social and Cultural Rights: Norway', UN Doc. E/C.12/1/Add.109 (2005).

is not to abuse rights brutally, but to abuse them carelessly. In the world not of human rights reality, but of media-generated hyper-reality, the best way for a state to avoid scrutiny is not to improve its conditions, but to create a regime so perfectly and pervasively abusive that no real reporting, by either a domestic or a foreign press, can take place at all, and all political dissent is swatted like a fly at the first signs of life.

So it is that North Korea, Libya, Burma, Syria, and, to large extent still, China have often avoided the exhaustive, painstaking, deeply humanised scrutiny that their conditions would require. Israel–Palestine, then, ends up in the same dilemma as Guantánamo. We cannot accept less reporting, insofar as there can never be too much critical dialogue within and among democracies and their democratic allies; yet nor can we accept the massive reporting focused on Israel–Palestine, insofar as it eclipses coverage of far more abusive states, within the region and beyond, including some of Israel's harshest, and often – either individually or as a bloc – most powerful, critics.[28]

In practice, human rights may often boil down to the sheer horse-trading of the zero-sum mindset. Certainly in its early years, the practices of the UN Human Rights Council have glaringly illustrated that reality, as very large blocs of Israel's adversaries, and their allies, push their own states off the agenda while keeping Israel on it.[29] However, even if such outright trade-offs are what states or institutions often do, it is never (again, unlike utilitarians or legislators) what they officially *say* they do. They never formally embrace sheer deal-making as any part of the international human rights movement's declared principles or procedures, at least not insofar as they wish to be seen as promoting rights. We can certainly acknowledge that the ideal of even-handed application of norms and procedures currently remains far from view. At the same time, we must recall that it remains an ideal conceptually presupposed by human rights.

The norms and institutions of human rights law, then, may shun any zero-sum calculus in principle. No true believer in human rights would ever accept that one population should be given fewer human rights so that another may enjoy more. Nevertheless, the mass media expressly

[28] On the role of the Organisation of the Islamic Conference in sabotaging the work of the Human Rights Council, particularly by directing criticism at Israel in order to deflect attention from its members and friends, see, e.g., Rosa Freedman, 'The United Nations Human Rights Council: a critique and early assessment' (Ph.D. thesis, University of London, 2011), ch.5.

[29] See generally ibid.; and Freedman, 'Improvement on the Commission?'.

and necessarily play that zero-sum game. And it is an inscrutable one. In a steadily globalising era, public interest in international affairs remains limited.[30] Much of the media scarcely venture beyond a brief selection of headlines. They cannot feasibly stray anywhere near a comprehensive picture of global human rights. Any choice to report one situation is perforce a choice to overlook countless others. Believers in human rights may place them as a highest ethical value, and may shun the *principle* of human rights as zero-sum; however, most of what we know about human rights comes through sources that expressly decline to place human rights as a highest value (regardless of the individual views of particular editors or reporters, many of whom might well, and with utmost sincerity, profess personal allegiance to that code), instead subordinating human rights to the specific, overriding concerns of journalistic interest, and thereby structuring human rights around a rigidly zero-sum calculus.[31]

In the media, instead of representing the highest, unconditional value – as that would require no other concomitant ethical or political value to justify exhaustive coverage – human rights (even in cases of their most egregious abuses) are routinely subordinated to other values, such as high-profile wars (which generally entail Western involvement),[32] terrorism, or political corruption, all of which certainly involve important human rights issues, but are not primarily reported for the sake of comprehensive human rights coverage. Throughout much of the late twentieth and early twenty-first centuries, a journalist covering Libyan-sponsored terrorism, or a North Korean missile testing, might, as an incidental matter, have dropped in some mention of those states' mechanisms of internal repression. But those have rarely been the focus of detailed and sustained coverage for its own sake. During that same period, states like Belarus or Tunisia have merely had to refrain from high-profile provocations altogether in order to avoid virtually all

[30] See, e.g., Knightley, *The First Casualty*, pp.106–9, 118–19.

[31] Even the largest news agencies do not have unlimited resources, nor do their audiences have unlimited time or interest. Moreover, compared to a generation or two ago, political problems today, and certainly human rights issues, are far more intricately tied to detailed national and international legal frameworks. Yet most of us know what we know about human rights from agencies the editors and reporters for which may hold degrees in politics or even international relations, but have little if any specialised training in the theory or practice of international human rights law. (A comparison could be drawn with science or business reporters, who are generally expected to have, or to develop, a level of background or training commensurate with the precision required.)

[32] See, e.g., Heinze & Freedman, 'Public awareness of human rights', p.504.

scrutiny. Even sporting events can become a kind of pretext for such scrutiny, which supersedes and subordinates, rather than being superseded by and subordinated to, human rights violations. Reporting on Tibet may have swept in with the 2008 Olympics, but swept out just as rapidly once the Games were a humdrum memory.

Any demand that the attention paid to problems be strictly tailored to their relative gravity would be an illusion, not least because human rights abuses entail heavy symbolism, beyond the purely personal interests of actual and discretely identifiable victims; and the gravity of a deeply laden symbol resists easy quantification. In 2010, for example, a global campaign was launched to protest the Iranian sentencing of Sakineh Mohammadi Ashtiani to death by stoning for adultery.[33] On a too-literal proportionality test, it would scarcely seem that the intensity of media scrutiny was justified for just one victim. Crucial to such a campaign, however, is that Ashtiani is not a lone victim. The protest arguably has multiple targets. It rages not solely against her punishment, but also against such penalties imposed on any woman, or on any person, in Iran and arguably in other non-democratic or weakly democratic states. It can also be said to protest women's subordination, or harsh sexual moralities, in general, throughout the world. Moreover, such campaigns can have preventative effects, the best result of all for human rights, by warning Iran or other regimes that they are being watched, possibly discouraging future repression.

On the other hand, there must be a limit to the extent to which some victims stand as symbols for others. It would be questionable to justify the media's neglect of victims in China or Libya by arguing that Guantánamo or Palestine stand as global symbols for victims everywhere. Moreover, we must wonder why, for example, some situations generate no such symbols. Has the DRC, for example, been so bereft of them? According to one 2008 report, 'in the last ten years in Congo, hundreds of thousands of women have been raped, most of them gang raped'. That ten-year time span is itself significant, raising questions about where the media have been. Dr Denis Mukwege, director of a local hospital, notes that 'the youngest was three years old', while 'the oldest was seventy-five'. He adds: 'You know, they're in deep pain. But it's not just physical pain. It's psychological pain that you can see. Here at the hospital, we've seen women who've stopped living.' Mukwege describes how soldiers, armed

[33] See, e.g., Jon Leyne, 'Iran's dilemma over stoning', report of 12 August 2010, at www.bbc.co.uk/news/world-middle-east-10956520 (accessed 26 February 2011).

with machetes, attacked one woman. Despite her being pregnant, the soldiers 'just cut her at many places', including her genitals.[34]

I am not suggesting that there is any easy template for the media to follow. The relative significance and symbolism of human rights abuses will always involve judgement calls. And yet, by the late twentieth century, it became clear that it is the media's neglect of the world's most egregious situations, from Congo, to Libya, to Belarus, to North Korea, in comparison to those stories that attract exhaustive coverage, which has generated a hyper-reality of human rights pervasively at odds with their reality.

The number of people who systematically study professional human rights reports, such as the published opinions of the UN treaty-based committees, or reports by Amnesty International, Human Rights Watch, Article 19 and other leading non-governmental organisations (NGOs), as well as leading scholarly journals, is presumably slight, perhaps a few thousand in the entire world. We can assume that they comprise only a small minority even among those individuals who, either as politicians or as experts, are involved in international affairs. Not even full-time human rights professionals can easily keep pace with the sheer volume of materials, outside their own areas of specialisation, in a way that would constantly furnish them with a current, comprehensive overview of global human rights. Beyond that small circle of human rights professionals, the numbers of politicians and diplomats both willing and able to keep abreast of the specialised literature surely hovers around nought, although it is they who hold the greatest power to make change. What they know about human rights will draw largely from the media sources that everyone else receives.

Human rights in Hollywood

Returning to an earlier example, international norms now strongly condemn capital punishment and advocate its progressive elimination.[35] At the same time, as has been suggested, we must compare the enormous

[34] 'War against women: the use of rape as a weapon in Congo's civil war', report of 17 August 2008, *CBS News*, available at www.cbsnews.com/stories/2008/01/11/60minutes/main3701249.shtml (accessed 26 February 2011).

[35] See, e.g., Second Optional Protocol to the International Covenant on Civil and Political Rights (ICCPR), aiming at the abolition of the death penalty, GA Res. 44/128, annex, 44 UN GAOR Supp. (No. 49) at 207, UN Doc. A/44/49 (1989), entered into force 11 July 1991, preamble, paras.4, 5 and 6.

scale, and the concomitant time, effort, and costs, of the campaigns against it, with the paucity of attention paid to countless global abuses, exacting an exponentially greater number of victims. Once again, merely to introduce that comparison raises suspicions that we may be lurching towards positive indifference about the death penalty, or devaluing the kinds of debate about criminal punishments that ought to occur in a democratic society.

Kennedy's example of the death penalty is also important insofar as, among Western states, it now stands out as a distinctly American kind of violation,[36] in comparison to European states which have generally abolished it.[37] (Even in European states with voices favouring reinstatement, few appear to feel strongly enough to make this a major issue.) In 2009, Amnesty International reported on the excessive suffering of death-row inmates in Japan. Inmates enjoy no meaningful contact with others, are left uninformed of the date of their execution, and develop alarming levels of mental illness:

> The government has a policy of not allowing access to prisoners on death row and denied Amnesty International's request for access . . . Each day could be their last. The arrival of a prison officer with a death warrant would signal their execution within hours. Some live like this year after year, sometimes for decades . . . Apart from visits to the toilet, prisoners are not allowed to move around the cell and must remain seated.[38]

For most people in the West and beyond, however, the face of the death penalty in a prosperous society is more likely to be a film like *Dead Man Walking*, or simply the routine diet of reports, documentaries and television drama shows about capital punishment in the USA, than anything from Japan. Rightly, Europeans in particular condemn the

[36] Although only some US states currently impose the death penalty under general criminal law, certain federal offences also provide for it. See UN Human Rights Committee, 'Concluding observations of the Human Rights Committee: United States of America', UN Doc. A/50/40, paras.266–304 (1995), para.281.

[37] See, e.g., Protocol No. 13 to the Convention for the Protection of Human Rights and Fundamental Freedoms, concerning the abolition of the death penalty in all circumstances (ETS No. 187), Vilnius, 3 May 2002. For global ratification information on the ICCPR Second Optional Protocol, see UNO, 'United Nations Treaty collection, Chapter IV' (note 2 above).

[38] Amnesty International, 'Japan continues to execute mentally ill prisoners', report of 10 September 2009, at www.amnesty.org/en/news-and-updates/report/japan-continues-execute-mentally-ill-prisoners-20090910 (accessed 26 February 2011). See also, e.g. on forced confessions, Norimitsu Onishi, 'Pressed by police, even innocent confess in Japan', *New York Times*, report of 11 May 2007, at www.nytimes.com/2007/05/11/world/asia/11japan.html (accessed 15 December 2010).

persistence of the death penalty in the USA, particularly in view of ongoing concerns about racism, poverty and adequate legal representation.[39] However, recalling Kennedy's reference to competing concerns, throughout the late twentieth century and early twenty-first century prison conditions in France have continued so poor as to prompt hundreds of suicides.[40] The numbers are not altogether disproportionate to those of executed Americans, in view of the countries' respective populations. Yet there has been no pan-European, let alone global, discussion of those French conditions.

If we care about differences between formal norms and actual conditions, we might ask whether that French *de facto* condemnation to death is much better than the American *de jure* one (or indeed whether it is not worse, providing a more diffuse target than the formally sanctioned norms or practices of capital punishment). While US criminal justice has long been scrutinised for problems of racism, the traditional French government policy of declining to compile statistics on citizens' race, religion or ethnicity has inevitably diminished the attention paid to those issues within the prison context.[41] The distinctly American image of the death penalty presumably arises from its iconic status in Hollywood, together with Hollywood's global reach, in contrast to the lack of any comparable mediatisation of European or other global situations.

Small wonder that the USA has traditionally been so widely seen as racist, certainly before President Obama's electoral victory: not because its racism or other abuses are so very different from those in other complex, industrialised, multi-ethnic societies, but because it has been far more mediatised. A colleague whose course covers racism in Britain told me recently that he wanted to assign his students something other than a British source, and was thinking about a novel by Alice Walker or Toni Morrison. I told him both were good choices, but also very usual ones, both within the USA and beyond. Why not choose a novel from some country other than the USA? His face went blank.

Admittedly, the occasional news feature will focus outside the USA at times of special flare-up, as in Rwanda, Bosnia or Tibet. Films like *Hotel*

[39] See, e.g., Andre Kaspi, *La peine de mort aux Etats-Unis* (Paris, FR: Plon, 2003).

[40] See, e.g., Gérald Andrieu, 'L'administration pénitentiaire "camoufle"-t-elle des suicides?' *Marianne*, 18 August 2009, at www.marianne2.fr/L-administration-penitentiaire-camoufle-t-elle-des-suicides_a181826.html (accessed 26 February 2011).

[41] See, e.g., Molly Moore, 'In France, prisons filled with Muslims', *Washington Post*, 29 April 2008, p.A–01, at www.washingtonpost.com/wp-dyn/content/story/2008/04/28/ST2008042802857.html (accessed 26 February 2011).

Rwanda or *The Last King of Scotland* are perhaps stirring greater mass awareness than we had seen in the past. Curiously, even those films emphasise individuals at one remove from the carnage, without inviting us into a *Color Purple* type of intimacy with victims, their families, or their communities. More importantly, such coverage, still intermittent, cannot compare to the rich palette of highly personalised, often intimate, racially informed programming, from 'Bill Cosby' and 'Oprah', to numerous and detailed documentaries on American slavery, to major Hollywood films, which cross the globe, constantly evoking issues of race in the American past and present. American introspection about racism becomes global. French or Dutch introspection about racism remain, for the most part, French or Dutch. As to Russian, Indian, Chinese, or Japanese introspection, it is questionable how much had gone on at all through their own mass media by the beginning of the new century, let alone through any global distribution.

That strongly US-centred human rights consciousness may well change, as European films like *Made in Britain, La Haine* or *Gegen die Wand*, within a broader world-cinematic context, attract greater interest. But such films are still consigned to art-house status as soon as they leave home, and can scarcely boast global or even large European audiences. One might expect that the US media would be admired for its pioneering role in dealing with race. To some degree, it probably is. Ironically, however, it has also created a constant mental association of the USA with racism and other forms of social injustice – an association not so spontaneously drawn to other states, even those with worse records, that lack such media presence. I have no reservation about that US image *per se*, grounded as it is in an undeniable past and present. My objection, rather, is that countless other racisms, countless other histories, countless other abuses throughout the world go mostly unfilmed, and so are largely ignored.[42]

I have no illusion that in a state like Belgium human rights would or should receive the attention lavished on the far larger and more powerful USA. Nevertheless the EU increasingly functions, and wishes to be seen, as a composite cultural entity. Given its fervently proclaimed human rights aspirations, we should ask about how the history of racism, including its colonial element, is communicated, not only with respect

[42] Cf. generally Eric Heinze, 'Truth and myth in critical race theory and LatCrit: human rights and the ethnocentrism of anti-ethnocentrism', 20 *National Black Law Journal* (2006–7) 107.

to any given European's own country, but with respect to other European countries, and how its media presence compares to that of US racial history.

It would be dishonest for the EU to represent its cultural unity only in reference to da Vinci and Proust, while presenting its darker elements, past or present, merely as the unfortunate deviations of individual states. It would be remarkable to argue that Mozart was a European but Hitler an Austrian. However, that seems to be the dominant message. Any assumption, for example, that Leopold II created only a Belgian history, distinct from a European one, reflects not Leopold's irrelevance to Europe's past and present, so much as Europeans' own amnesia about their fellow nations. Belgium, the EU's primary host country, retains (in Brussels, the EU 'capital' city) publicly displayed statues of Leopold II, a monarch who implemented systematic murders of millions of Congolese, along with routine chaining and amputations of both children and adults, and the enslavement of virtually that entire population, within just forty years (circa 1880–1920), for the sake of rubber and other raw materials.[43] To this day, that African history is taught and discussed only minimally, if at all, among a European population which, curiously, has often taken a keener interest in US racism than in that of its own European neighbours (to be clear, then, I make that observation not in reference to Europeans' awareness of racism in their own home countries, but in reference to their awareness of racism within EU member states *other* than their own). It is remarkable that today Europeans often pay far more attention to the history of the West African slave trade, which turns into a fundamentally *American* story, than to that Central African history, which does not let Europe so easily off the hook.

The ongoing, murderous consequences for Central Africa, recently tolling over three million dead, and countless others maimed, raped or internally displaced, continue to this day.[44] Both that history, and its ongoing consequences, are scarcely discussed by modern Europeans (or anyone else), who certainly do not commemorate it, and are indeed mostly ignorant of it. A 2004 documentary, one of the very few of its kind, still needed to recite the most basic facts, effectively introducing them as a novelty.[45] The BBC journalist Mark Dummett used that occasion to comment:

43 See, e.g., Adam Hochschild, *King Leopold's Ghost* (New York: Mariner, 1998).

44 See, e.g., Okawa. 'Congo's war', p.203. See also, e.g., 'Congo death toll up to 3.8m', *Guardian Unlimited*; Polgreen, 'War's chaos steals Congo's young by the millions'.

45 'Congo: white king, red rubber, black death', London, UK: BBC, 2004 (dir. Peter Bate).

> Of the Europeans who scrambled for control of Africa at the end of the nineteenth century, Belgium's King Leopold II left arguably the largest and most horrid legacy of all . . . He claimed he was doing it to protect the 'natives' from Arab slavers, and to open the heart of Africa to Christian missionaries, and Western capitalists. Instead . . . the king unleashed new horrors on the African continent.
>
> He turned his 'Congo Free State' into a massive labour camp, made a fortune for himself from the harvest of its wild rubber, and contributed in a large way to the death of perhaps 10 million innocent people. What is now called the Democratic Republic of Congo has clearly never recovered.
>
> 'Legalised robbery enforced by violence', as Leopold's reign was described at the time, has remained, more or less, the template by which Congo's rulers have governed ever since. Meanwhile Congo's soldiers have never moved away from the role allocated to them by Leopold – as a force to coerce, torment and rape an unarmed civilian population.
>
> As the BBC's reporter in DR Congo, I covered stories that were loud echoes of what was happening 100 years earlier, [which included] children and adults whose right hands had been hacked off by [Leopold's] agents. They needed these to prove to their superiors that they had not been 'wasting' their bullets on animals. This rule was seldom observed as soldiers kept shooting monkeys and then later chopping off human hands to provide their alibis.[46]

As a superpower, the USA has inevitably attracted greater attention than any given EU member state. That is not entirely a bad thing. We should indeed take a particular interest in the conduct of the most powerful states. It is difficult, however, to justify that disproportionately greater attention strictly from the standpoint of human rights. The EU counts as a composite entity, boasting a shared culture, with a combined wealth and population greater than those of the USA.[47] It is implausible to imagine that either the history or the ongoing realities of racism in Europe merit so much less European or global interest.

Only European Nazism, increasingly associated more with a concluded past than an ongoing present, receives both the quantity and the dramatic quality of attention that is otherwise directed towards US racism, in Europe, in the USA and throughout the world. The

[46] Mark Dummett, 'King Leopold's legacy of DR Congo violence', *BBC News*, 24 February 2004, at http://news.bbc.co.uk/1/hi/world/africa/3516965.stm (accessed 15 August 2011).

[47] For regular updates, see, e.g., European Commission, *Eurostat*, at http://epp.eurostat.ec.europa.eu/portal/page/portal/eurostat/home (accessed 26 February 2011); US Census Bureau, at www.census.gov/compendia/statab/ (accessed 26 February 2011).

extermination of Jews was so thorough that the tiny numbers who survived in Europe, which represented a far smaller proportion of the population after the Second World War than African Americans in the USA, meant that European governments could make amends with comparatively little complication or resistance. More importantly, any Euro-American parity in the respective levels of media attention is attained only because European Nazism and US racism were deeply internal affairs. Europe's Nazi atrocities, like America's racist ones, were committed largely on domestic minority populations. European 'black/white' or 'brown/white' racism, by contrast, differs markedly from that of the USA, having, until the later twentieth century, played out largely on non-European soil. Before the Second World War, Europe's racism was of a wholly different order to American racism, its atrocities committed outside European frontiers and not experienced in any direct sense by ordinary Europeans.

It is no surprise, then, that the internal racial tensions have not festered, as they have in the USA over many years, making it far easier for Europeans to 'forget' a past that they could so easily walk away from, leaving the 'natives' to themselves. A Hollywood-style panorama of Leopold's Congo extending to the ongoing consequences, might spur not only Americans, but also Europeans, to view *Roots* or *In the Heat of the Night* within a far more nuanced global context than the strongly US-centred media has ever provided. If a group of Germans or Austrians were to raise a statue of Hitler in a public place, it would become a European, arguably a global, media event, with hefty condemnation at home and abroad, and likely legal sanctions. Within an hour, the statue would be removed by law or by force. By contrast, in the very 'capital' of the European Union, at the heart of one of Europe's most materially prosperous democracies, statues of Leopold II welcome officials from all EU member states, without a word of European protest. Far from condemnation, proud public commemoration of Leopold still takes place. As recently as 2007, the Belgian Royal Mint issued commemorative coins featuring his effigy. Astoundingly, in its handsomely presented sales brochure, the Mint brushed aside the monarch's atrocities in a question-begging subordinate clause: 'The second Belgian king is certainly, in view of his Congo policy, the most reviled *(de meest verguisde)* of our heads of state . . .' Given the brochure's money-making aim, that caveat serves more to add an edgy *frisson* than to evoke anything like a memory of the monarch's atrocities. The Mint's aim is to honour the king, not to shame him, praising his government's period of 'economic *and cultural* expansion'.[48] The European press and populace scarcely notice such chilling gestures. As of this writing, even the European Commission against Racism and Intolerance, which should be most vigilant about Europe's historical memory, has taken no official stand against these public honours commemorating the king.[49] I have emphasised this Belgian example not least because of Belgium's special status within the EU, but others might be cited.[50]

The frequent attention of US film or television to issues of race probably does have some progressive effect, promoting a more critical awareness of those issues. The consciousness it promotes must surely prompt some viewers to think about racism 'generally'. Above all, however, it creates an immediate, and constantly reinforced, awareness of racism *in the USA*. Other societies either actively prohibit any such portrayals of themselves (for example, Western consciousness of the Soviet Union and its allies generally focused on political repression, or militarism, and not specifically on racism), or willingly accept such works, but with nothing like the global distribution enjoyed by their US counterparts. Racism in Western Europe, and around the world, may well receive media attention, but rarely at the scale of *The Color Purple* or *Do the Right Thing*.

A crucial insight of the US civil rights movement was to awaken us to the dominant media's inherent racism. Racism takes forms far beyond the crudest insult and invective. More insidious, more effective, are the media's sheer absences and silences. In the twentieth century, popular US sitcoms from *I Love Lucy* through to *The Brady Bunch* presented an all-white America, on the heels of a long Hollywood tradition of either excluding ethnic minorities, or featuring them in caricatured and

[48] Koninklijke Munt van België, *MuntInfo*, No. 45, October 2007, p.8, available at http://treasury.fgov.be/intermunt/En/Muntinfo/MI45nl.pdf (accessed 26 February 2011) (emphasis added).

[49] Albeit formally attached, not to the European Union, but to the Council of Europe, there can be no suggestion that the ECRI's mandate would have no bearing upon European states' attitudes towards such gross historical incidents. For regularly updated policy statements, see Council of Europe, European Commission against Racism and Intolerance, www.coe.int/t/dghl/monitoring/ecri/default_en.asp (accessed 26 February 2011).

[50] Note also that most continental Europeans now learn English as their second language, often from a very young age. Teachers seek materials that will spur students' interest and provoke thought, finding a treasure trove in both fictional and non-fictional accounts of American cultural history, with its inevitable attention to race. For the most part, the languages of former colonial powers, such as Spanish, Portuguese, Italian, Dutch and even French, along with many non-European languages, are increasingly neglected in the race for English, attracting that same depth of interest only at more specialised levels.

subservient, if not altogether demeaning, roles.[51] That first wave of silencing witnessed changes towards the end of the twentieth century, as the mass media made more room for non-white faces. A reactionary, right-wing view could be associated with nostalgia for the earlier images and hostility towards alternative ones, as the left rightly pushed for diversity.

Since that time, we have been living through a second wave of silencing. If the US popular media have changed since the 1950s, one thing has remained the same: overwhelmingly, coverage is *about the USA*. That's no shock. Popular media always include a strong local component. Mass German audiences watch German serials, or chat or variety shows; mass French audiences watch French serials, or chat or variety shows; and so on. In recent years, Western European popular media have paid increasing attention to issues of race and ethnicity at home.

But a question arises about what the audiences view beyond their local fare. What are popular (as opposed to elite) British, French, German or Italian audiences watching when they are not watching home-grown films or television shows? Are they watching *each other's*, motivated by a political and cultural interest in their own European neighbours? European elites may do so to a limited degree. Overwhelmingly, however, the second media source for mass European and indeed global audiences is American. The average German viewer will have seen more about racism in the USA than about racism in fellow EU-member states France or Italy; the average French viewer will have seen more about racism in the USA than about racism in fellow EU-member states Italy or Germany; and so on. Yes, German viewers will have seen the rioting in British cities or French suburbs, in the form of routine news reports. They will not, however, have fed upon the steady diet of more intimate, personalised, fictionalised, or fly-on-the-wall exposure – the storytelling[52] – which they will have experienced about racism both in their own country *and in the USA*. Meanwhile, the average US viewer (again, as distinguished from small elites) will have seen little if anything about contemporary social conflict either in Western Europe, or indeed in Russia, India, Japan, Brazil or other places.

[51] See generally, e.g., Clint C. Wilson *et al.*, *Racism, Sexism, and the Media: The Rise of Class Communication in Multicultural America*, 3rd edn (New York: Sage Publications, 2003); John D. H. Downing and Charles Husband, *Representing Race: Racisms, Ethnicity and the Media* (New York: Sage Publications, 2005).

[52] Cf. Heinze, 'Truth and myth in critical race theory and LatCrit', pp.115–16 and 120–3.

Solutions?

At several levels, including not just hard-news reporting but also, perhaps more importantly, popular entertainment, the mass media generate a hyper-reality pervasively at odds with the realities of global human rights. It is the most repressive regimes who benefit most, and their victims who lose most. That media-generated consciousness of human rights becomes a far more powerful factor in actual discussions and actions on human rights than most of what is done within the formally legal confines of norms and institutions. Or, more precisely, it is the media that too often determine the situations towards which, and away from which, those norms and institutions are directed.

That failure to grasp the media's role underscores lawyers' ongoing entrapment in legal formalisms. Human rights professionals and scholars focus almost entirely on norms and institutions, paying too little attention to the overwhelming force of the mass media in determining the use and abuse of those official channels. Remedies are available, but only to a limited extent. Much of the mass media could certainly redress some of the grosser imbalances, by injecting greater diversity and even-handedness into their hard-news reporting. In contrast, the degree to which one might expect the entertainment industry to diversify its topics, or the public to enjoy a greater range, is far from clear.

As we have seen, the problem is not specific to the nature of human rights norms. Any ethics that resists a zero-sum calculus, shunning the idea that ethics towards some individuals or groups can only come at the expense of ethics towards others, must inevitably be sacrificed on the altar of the media's own fiercely zero-sum game. That game remains fundamentally damaging to the ethos of universal human rights, where the sum is not zero. Yet the media will not shed that zero-sum approach for as long as they retain anything like their familiar forms. Even the internet age, which can overcome some of the shackles of traditional editorial practices, scarcely offers a superior alternative, since information turns into a scarcely filtered wasteland through which few can navigate effectively.

At the very least, diplomats, activists and scholars must openly acknowledge the limitations and distortions underlying even our well-informed notions about global violations. Nevertheless, from states conspicuously benefiting from those defects, few such acknowledgements can be expected.

11

Human rights and the struggle for change: a study in self-critical legal thought

CHRISTINE BELL

Part I: Introduction: revisiting anger

Anger

It is rare that an academic piece makes me angry. But when I first read David Kennedy's 'The Problem with the International Human Rights Movement' I remember feeling quite angry to the point that it made me reflect on why.[1] I read lots of academic analysis, I disagree with much of it and it frequently challenges matters which I hold dear. But I am an academic and, worse than that, a lawyer and so I tend to enjoy reading these pieces and arguing with them in my head. So why the anger?

There were a few concrete matters. I felt that despite the caveats, which suggested a mere rehearsal of 'hypothetical' arguments about the downside of human rights aimed at encouraging 'practical thinking' and 'pragmatic evaluation' of interventions, this was a frontal attack on both the practice and the discourse of human rights which was duplicitously being presented as a much lower-scale scuffle. Where Kennedy said that many good things had been achieved by the human rights movement, and that costs might be outweighed by benefits, I could not see anything other than a quick nod to cover a rejection of the enterprise of human rights activism in totality.

A part of my anger was born of having been a human rights activist in Northern Ireland in a situation that was somewhat dangerous and stressful, and where there were easier ways to live one's life. My own

I would like to thank Maggie Beirne, Ita Connolly, Rob Dickinson, Christopher McCrudden and Catherine Turner for comments on an earlier draft, and in addition thank Ita Connolly for valuable research assistance.

[1] D. Kennedy, 'The international human rights movement: part of the problem?' 15 *Harvard Human Rights Journal* (2002) 101 (the article was originally published in another journal in 2001).

difficulties, I felt, were a fraction of those of human rights activists in virtually any other conflict situation. I did not identify with Kennedy's 'international human rights movement'; it was not the international human rights movement I felt I knew. It seemed to refer to the professionals, the big international NGOs, operatives in bureaucratic, intergovernmental, human rights machinery or even professionals within governments. The international human rights movement of which I felt a part was a movement of local activists operating locally across the world, with whom I interacted and felt myself to be in solidarity: ordinary people, often marginalised in terms of their politics and their identity, ethnicity or gender, who lived with much more risk and took much braver decisions at greater cost than I. We did not particularly view ourselves as linked to those higher up the human rights food chain; in fact, in ways we felt that they were useful to us only so far as we could 'use them' to access international fora. They were someone else to be lobbied in the hope that they might in turn lobby on our behalf.

Moreover, Kennedy's actual criticisms – his 'costs' – left me with a sense of 'so what'. Many of the charges which Kennedy made appeared to me to accuse human rights activists of ignoring dilemmas which in my experience we engaged with daily. The capacity of human rights to monopolise emancipatory vocabulary, to view both problem and solution too narrowly, to be too general in some instances and too particular in others, to institutionalise liberalism and so on, were matters we agonised about continually and could not avoid agonising over because these are charges which had a local version and against which we constantly had to defend. We were often accused by one side or another of being reformist and therefore pro-state (and so, really British Unionists), or statist and therefore ignoring the activities of 'terrorists' (and so, really Irish Nationalists or Republicans). Even without the charges, most people saw human rights as irrelevant to the host of other political problems. For those who thought beyond the 'constitutional problem' there were problems of poverty, equality, reconciliation and 'community relations' between Catholic and Protestant communities to consider. Human rights did not figure very highly on anyone's agenda, and far from pushing it as the only or even the predominant paradigm, our mantra was that just as 'human rights abuses were part of the problem, so they had to be part of the solution'. That word 'part' was important to us, because it claimed a place for human rights on the agenda while acknowledging the breadth of that agenda (and indeed any claim to have been the whole thing would have been immediately rejected as ridiculous because for most people the conflict was self-evidently about other things).

From this experience, I felt that Kennedy's rehearsal of costs added little to our analysis or effectiveness and everything to those who most oppose radical change, and support violence, continued oppression, denial of state complicity in the conflict and denial of equality. It was fine for Kennedy, I felt, sitting in Harvard applying critical thought to concepts in a cool and rational way, as part of a project which it seemed to me amounted to little else than showing that he could conduct critical analysis of things that he was supposed to like, as well as of things he could be assumed to dislike. But was it really a good use of his time to hurt political projects to which he claimed to be sympathetic, for analysis that he claimed amounted to little more than 'let us look at some of the bad things and not just think it is all easy and good'? Was this not a little self-indulgent?

Linked to these objections, my anger was definitely rooted in an 'et tu, Brute?' sense that now we not only had to defend against our enemies but also against our friends. This new friendly fire was an unwelcome distraction from what could literally be life-and-death battles. Why should our enemies be handed their arguments on a plate? I was particularly annoyed at what I saw as an attempt to foreclose objections on this front, in the argument that 'human rights was now a mature enough discourse' to withstand critical engagement so we just had to endure it. To express any anger would now place me in the category of those who could not tolerate criticism or engage intellectually. This was a pre-emptive defence that operated to protect less against academic rejoinder (because academics will find ways to reply), than against the righteous anger of those on the barricades justifying its righteousness. I felt I could easily accept the need for critical engagement with human rights, the need for questioning, the need to be challenged. It was just that this broadside polemic, with its sneaky caveats and rehearsal of our opponents' arguments, had no real 'take home' for how we might do things differently. If the article was not rejecting the usefulness of all human rights activism (and remember, I suspected that it was), then what was it advocating? The most concrete suggestion was greater attention to the costs of human rights interventions, but beyond what we already did there did not seem to be any coherent way to measure and weigh the benefits and costs of interventions, just a range of further 'what ifs'. The pragmatic rationale given for the critique seemed to boil down to little more than an injunction: human rights activists should agonise even harder over the difficulties of human rights activism than we already did. Could Kennedy really justify this attack in terms of the need to encourage us all to indulge in ever-bigger mind-warps? Did the benefits of his own article outweigh the costs?

Revisited reflection

It was the memory of this article and the anger it prompted, that led me to accept the invitation to be involved in a ten-year evaluation of David Kennedy's piece, with David Kennedy himself participating in the debate. I had always felt that I should revisit my rejection of the piece, and in particular consider where my initial anger had come from and whether it had any justification beyond my own sensitivities. On a quick reread I could hardly even conjure up my past emotions. So what had changed? Was it the context in which human rights language was now used and a new-found ambivalence? Or ambivalence rooted in the new expanded reach of human rights in which human rights had become everything and therefore nothing? Was it my own relationship to human rights activism and discourse that had changed? Or was it just a change in my 'reading' of what Kennedy was saying? Or perhaps it was all of these things.

In the intervening period I had read much more of David Kennedy's work and found it very useful.[2] In part, reading his work cumulatively had made me more sympathetic to what I now understand to be a broader project of criticising regimes and the dynamics of 'professionalisation' and regime protection which characterise the new post-Westphalia international legal system.[3] His critique of the human rights movement is part of a critique of regime experts and the mutual process by which experts and regimes reshape each other, but also wield a power of stealth decision-making by controlling how key political choices are framed, understood and responded to. In place of the anti-human rights diatribe to which I had reacted so strongly I now saw in the original piece

[2] See in particular comparative law work: D. Kennedy, 'The methods and politics of comparative law' in M. Bussani and U. Mattei (eds.), *The Common Core of European Private Law* (The Hague, London: Kluwer Law International, 2003), p.131.

[3] The pieces on which I draw further include *Of Law and War* (Princeton University Press, 2006), *The Rights of Spring: A Memoir of Innocence Abroad* (Princeton University Press, 2009); 'The mystery of global governance' in J. L. Dunoff and J. P. Trachtman (eds.), *Ruling the World? Constitutionalism, International Law, and Global Governance* (Cambridge University Press, 2009), p.37.

the beginnings of a broader project linked to a broader context: how to respond to the collapse of Westphalia and a state-centric way of understanding international law, which regimes and regime experts have come to replace.

Secondly, the position of human rights had indeed changed in Northern Ireland and beyond, and with it my own relation to human rights. The 'dark side of virtue' had come to the fore for many activists internationally, most notably with international intervention in Kosovo and then Iraq, both of which were justified *inter alia* in terms of the need to respond to human rights violations. But for me personally, in my local context, I now realised that from the 1998 Agreement onwards I had increasingly come to look much more like the international human rights professional that Kennedy had lambasted in 2001. In Northern Ireland – against the odds – human rights issues had been placed centrally in a peace agreement which had started life as a rather un-normative attempt to split power between Protestant Unionists and Catholic Nationalists (two different types of nationalism) with a nod to the sovereign aspirations of Catholics for a united Ireland.[4] The peace agreement included a section on human rights, and had created a range of human rights institutions.[5] As human rights had moved from 'margin to mainstream' so had we. I and erstwhile activist friends now sat on a range of local human rights institutions as part and parcel of a complicated new system of governance. The state's opponents – who had been sceptical of the reformist agenda of human rights – were now at the heart of a power-sharing government, in a complex new constitutional order with confederal dimensions.[6] Pro-state actors who had opposed the discourse now found themselves in a redefined state that they struggled to accept and implement, except in so far as they could articulate it to be part and parcel of a broader UK constitutional reform package of devolution and 'modernisation' with no sovereign implications.[7] Human rights appeared

[4] See, C. McCrudden, 'Mainstreaming equality in the governance of Northern Ireland', 22 *Fordham International Law Journal* (1998) 1696, and P. Mageean and O'Brien, M. 'From the margins to the mainstream: human rights and the Good Friday Agreement', 22 *Fordham International Law Journal* (1998) 1499.

[5] *The Belfast Agreement: An Agreement Reached at the multi-party talks on Northern Ireland* (Cm. 3883, April 1998), Strand One, 'Democratic institutions in Northern Ireland', para.5.

[6] B. O'Leary, 'The nature of the Agreement', 22 *Fordham International Law Journal* (1998) 1628 (describing the Agreement's constitutional arrangements as 'consociationalism plus', the plus part being its cross-border, bi-national dimension).

[7] C. Bell, C. Campbell and F. Ní Aoláin, 'Justice discourses in transition', 13 *Social and Legal Studies* (2004) 306, p.319.

to the state's opponents to hold out the possibility of radical change to the nature of the state in the absence of an immediate change of sovereignty. To the state's friends human rights offered a possibility of conservative change and a tolerable concession in place of an intolerable change of sovereignty. Debates over the reach and implementation of the Agreement's human rights measures therefore lay at the heart of struggles to 'own' the direction of transition. As one of the appointees to the first human rights commission established under the terms of the agreement, I had found myself at the heart of the new order and experienced first-hand, and somewhat painfully, a very clear move from activist to joint partner in a complex and contested project of 'governance'.[8] In short, some of Kennedy's charges seemed better placed ten years on in terms of how they spoke to my own position, and in particular the implicit injunction to 'own your own power' seemed to have a new and important relevance. Had he just been more prescient than the rest of us?

Thirdly, however, it seemed to me that not only had I become more critical, but that in recent years, with the attack (as part of the 'war on terror') on rights and international law, the critics had mellowed (although I am sure they would reject all that the word implies and that this analysis would not win me friends). Indeed, on rereading Kennedy's contribution to this collection I find myself asking, more than ever, have I changed or is Kennedy's restatement a much more tempered document than the original? With no difficulty I now read the honouring of human rights achievements as genuine, and the reflective engagement with the difficulties of humanitarian enterprises as deeply constructive. Perhaps also delusionally, I have perceived similar changes in the work of other critics: Martti Koskenniemi and his 'culture of formalism',[9] or Conor Gearty's struggles to accept that judges sometimes do seem to have a role in protecting rights that supplements rather than depleting broader

[8] I was a member of the Northern Ireland Human Rights Commission from 1999–2003, when I resigned, publicly disagreeing with Human Rights Commission positions and its way of doing business. For a more objective account of the difficulties of the Commission, see S. Livingstone, R. Murray and A. Smith, 'Evaluating the effectiveness of national human rights institutions: the Northern Ireland Human Rights Commission with comparisons from South Africa' (Nuffield Foundation, 2005), and Joint Committee on Human Rights, 'Work of the Northern Ireland Human Rights Commission', Fourteenth Report of the Session 2002–3, HL Paper 132; HL 142.

[9] M. Koskenniemi, *The Gentle Civilizer of Nations: The Rise and Fall of International Law 1870–1960* (Cambridge University Press, 2001) (Koskenniemi has now retracted the support for the 'culture of formalism' that he asserted in this book (conversation with author)).

democratic participation.[10] So, strangely, at the point at where I – in part persuaded by the critics – was now prepared to be more critical of human rights discourse, the critics seemed, on occasion at least, to be less critical. This too drew me back to Kennedy's article and appeared worth exploring.

Finally, I had met David Kennedy and had a brief but interesting conversation about the personal motivations and drive for his focus on criticising the discipline of law and international law in particular. This conversation fed into a type of 'mid-life crisis' I was undergoing at the time as I reflected on how academics do and should link or not link with the practical politics of progressive social transformation. What was the point of being an academic lawyer? What was the 'meaning of life' for legal academics – from where do we find our purpose and motivation and how do we decide to place our energies? How should we understand our role and our responsibilities with relation to projects of social change where political imagination is everything, and commentary itself therefore has a political impact? Should we mix practical engagement with law with scholarly contribution and the construction or deconstruction of 'fields' of analysis; and if so, how? This too seemed to prompt a revisiting of the piece and my reaction to it.

A self-critical evaluation

So, with the ghosts of past anger exorcised and my self-critical legal glasses on, what follows is a more sober attempt to respond to Kennedy's critique of human rights drawing on my own experiences. This evaluation includes that of the original essay, as bolstered by the Newcastle conference discussion that underlies this collection, by his subsequent work, including his own self-critical analysis of an experience of human rights activism, and by the critiques of others.[11] I engage in three ways. In part II of this chapter I partially accept Kennedy's account of possible costs of human rights and partially rebut them by re-arguing that benefits attach to human rights advocacy, in particular in deeply divided societies, which traditional legal analysis tends to undervalue. In part III, I consider the deeper and more comprehensive underlying attack on human rights as stultifying political responsibility. In the final part IV, I use the discussion to reflect further on how legal academics engage with

[10] C. Gearty, *Can Human Rights Survive?* (Cambridge University Press, 2006).
[11] See note 3 above.

movements which aim for progressive social change, and what the responsibilities and costs of such engagement might be.

Part II: Recalculating the costs and benefits of human rights

Kennedy's list of possible costs of human rights interventions is long, including: that human rights focus on the state to the exclusion of issues such as economics; that human rights hold out limited possibilities for knowledge and justice; that they do more to produce and cause violations than to prevent and remedy them, because they treat symptoms and not causes; that human rights bureaucracy is itself part of the problem, often strengthening bad governance; and that human rights produce bad politics in certain contexts.[12] Most crucially, perhaps, these criticisms are linked in the deeper charge that human rights discourse is a limited one which depoliticises and neutralises broader political battles at the local and international level. It does this, because the bureaucracy and professional practice of human rights obscures the contradictions and uncertainties in the discourse.[13] Human rights interventions, it is charged, articulate legal certainties and right and wrong answers in the place of contested concepts and political struggle.

I do not seek to reject outright Kennedy's account of these costs. Rather, I accept them but argue that, when translated into a local context, there is a need to question not just the politics of human rights activism, but the politics of the alternatives. In Northern Ireland Kennedy's costs capture well a range of tensions that human rights activists experienced. To speak in generalisations, local nationalist or Republican (Catholic) communities engaged in a broader political struggle around a change in statehood and, while wanting some accountability and change with regard to specific human rights violations, they often did not want what they understood as a broader national struggle to be depoliticised by human rights activists, and did not have faith in the project of state reform that they felt human rights held out. To use Kennedy's words, they did not view human rights (seen as a stand-alone concept) as a field of emancipatory possibility. Local unionist (Protestant) communities felt that human rights discourse was one that cast them as perpetrators of discrimination and domination when they experienced life as victims

[12] See in particular Kennedy, 'The international human rights movement'.

[13] Somewhat implicit in his original article, the argument is more explicit in the essay in this collection and elsewhere in Kennedy's writings.

of a brutal IRA campaign. A focus on the state seemed to leave untouched (and therefore fail to sanction) the violence of non-state actors or 'terrorists', and was charged to be anti-state and subversive. Human rights was therefore the enemy's language and agenda in another guise, its legalism at best a blind spot and at worst cover for immoral commitment. They viewed many of the state's instruments of human rights abuse – the police, emergency legislation, and forms of coercive detention and interrogation – as protecting them. The state resisted the discourse of rights and attempted to present the conflict as entirely a problem of bad intercommunal relationships: human rights activists were at best naïve and at worst evil, and were stultifying the possibility of intercommunal dialogue by suggesting that structural change on communally 'divisive' issues such as policing, emergency legislation and discrimination were important to communal relationships and a less violent future. Better not to mention the war; human relationships could be better built by funding Protestant and Catholic schoolkids to go plant trees together (an activity I myself had taken part in with little consequence for the trajectory of the conflict or deforestation but with great opportunities for meeting boyfriends parents might disapprove of).

The case of Northern Ireland illustrates the deep divisions of politics, the centrality of rights issues to these divisions, and the need for political space in which to address divisions. This space, I argue, was enabled and facilitated by human rights discourse. The costs of human rights therefore deserve to be critiqued in terms of a fuller articulation of the possible benefits on the other side of the balance sheet. While it is often assumed that the key benefit of human rights activism is 'accountability' and some form of remedy for human rights violations, there are often further instrumental benefits to human rights interventions, particularly in deeply divided societies, which are little commented on or factored into legal analysis. In practice, paradoxically, some of the very limitations and apparent inadequacies of rights as a discourse can enable political dialogue where there is little possibility of it; can produce new ways of knowing across social divisions; can constitute good politics when presented with violent agendas; and can be one of the only available ways to talk about state accountability in a world where, despite much talk of its demise, the state still continues to intrude violently in people's lives.

Maybe because Kennedy's charges of the excessive legalism of human rights discourse have a truth, these strategic arguments for human rights are less often made than a simpler articulation of human rights as 'the right thing to do' and requiring remedial action (such as release of the prisoner of conscience). Yet a strategic and even political concept of human rights lies at the heart of most legal articulations of rights. The Universal Declaration's preamble states that 'it is essential if man is not to be compelled to have recourse, as a last resort, to rebellion against tyranny and oppression, that human rights should be protected by the rule of law'.[14] The domestic incorporation of rights in many Western liberal constitutions talks of rights as having a pragmatic as much as a principled end.[15] The experience of human rights activism in Northern Ireland points to some of these pragmatic roles for human rights discourse – roles which for many activists were much more crucial factors in becoming involved in human rights struggles than an abstract principled commitment to rights.

Human rights activism and political dialogue

While political dialogue can be stifled, it can also be enabled, by human rights law. As local activists in Northern Ireland we worked very hard to 'carve out' some sphere of operation in the name of human rights around which both Catholics and Protestants could find some common conversation where there was none. These were articulated in the three core principles (or consensus) for the organisation I worked for – the Committee on the Administration of Justice (hereafter CAJ, a sister group to the Scottish Council for Civil Liberties, Liberty and the Irish Council for Civil Liberties).[16] Interestingly these principles spoke much

[14] Preamble, United Nations Universal Declaration of Human Rights, 1945. Cf. also '[r]eaffirming their profound belief in those fundamental freedoms which are the foundation of justice and peace in the world and are best maintained on the one hand by an effective political democracy and on the other by a common understanding and observance of the human rights upon which they depend', Convention for the Protection of Human Rights and Fundamental Freedoms, 1950; 'the upheavals of European history have shown that the protection of national minorities is essential to stability, democratic security and peace in this continent', Council of Europe, Framework Convention on National Minorities 1995.

[15] See, for example, the Swedish Constitution, contained in four documents, The Instrument of Government, SFS 1974: 152; The Act of Succession SFS 1810: 0926; The Freedom of the Press Act SFS 1949: 105; The Fundamental Law on Freedom of Expression, SFS 1991: 1469, all available in English at www.riksdagen.se/templates/R_Page____6357.aspx (accessed 16 August 2011).

[16] For background on this organisation see L. Wheelan, 'The challenge of lobbying for civil rights in Northern Ireland: the Committee on the Administration of Justice', 14 *Human Rights Quarterly* (1992) 149; for an account of CAJ and others' role in the peace process see McCrudden, 'Mainstreaming equality', Mageean and O'Brien, 'From the margins to the mainstream' and B. Campbell, *Agreement: The State, Conflict and Change in Northern Ireland* (London: Lawrence and Wishart, 2008).

more to the attempt to create a space of engagement – a mini-democratic space if you will – among ourselves and our quite different views of the conflict and the connections with human rights abuses. First, we took no position on the 'constitutional' status for Northern Ireland – we claimed that whether Ireland or Britain were sovereign human rights should be protected; second, as a group we disavowed the use of political violence as a tool for political ends; and third, we sought to root our interventions in international human rights standards.

In some ways our three self-imposed constraints prove Kennedy's points in being at once too legalistic and not legalistic enough. In avoiding the constitutional position we artificially avoided what the rest of the political spectrum viewed as the central issue. One needs only to examine Palestinian human rights groups, whose number one human right is the right to self-determination, to see the contingency of our position. From one point of view this avoidance eschewed a legalistic approach to the right to self-determination, constituting perhaps an implicit acceptance that self-determination as a human right did not inform the situation helpfully. More importantly, however, avoidance of the constitutional question constituted a pragmatic attempt to take a portion of the political space beyond the politics of 'what was the legitimate state', to question the nature of the state whether a British or Irish state ultimately resulted. Neutrality on the constitutional issue was also a deeply practical attempt to ensure that both Catholic/Nationalists and Protestant/Unionists, who had very competing notions of what self-determination would involve, could engage with human rights standards and in essence a moral notion of 'fairness'.

By basing our activism in legal human rights standards, as per Kennedy's charge, we looked very legalistic. A faithfulness to the technical remit of international standards made our choices over what violence to monitor look partisan with respect to a mess of violence, placing us in constant controversy over where we would and would not intervene. But again, the commitment to international standards was driven more by the need for a political placing of human rights attuned to local context, than a naïve belief in these standards *per se*. The turn to process was not an attempt to use law to smooth over the issues of political division that we faced. Rather, it was an attempt to try to find some common ground from which to address issues which were at the heart of that division – a project to create political space. From a very practical point of view, the state had committed publicly in international law to these standards and so it was hard for it to argue that these standards were particular to one side in the conflict or had no relevance to state actions. Moreover, in the many, many charges as to whose political agenda we were serving, international human rights law gave us a touchstone with which to comment on developments such as new forms of emergency legislation and abuse in custody or in prisons. But importantly, rooting analysis in international standards also enabled intercommunal discussion. Negotiation experts advise that a useful way to move people from hard positional bargaining is to test claims against objective standards: such as standards external to the parties to the conflict.[17] Human rights standards, for all their vagueness and difficulties of application, are external to particular conflicts and can play a role in moving people towards a conversation about common values *versus* particularistic clientelism. In Northern Ireland, the legal formulation of human rights as international law binding the state also assisted the involvement of the Protestant community on issues that were seen as 'for Nationalists', by appealing to a broader set of values that had acceptance beyond our shores and were indeed ultimately statist and conservative.

Finally, the commitment not to support political violence again was a deliberate choice, not directly constrained by human rights standards, but flowing from the idea that those who promote rights should not deny rights, and that the advocacy of human rights is itself part of a wider commitment to human dignity. This commitment signalled that our activism would be rooted in the politics of non-violence and would have an independence from projects and political positions which viewed such violence as necessary, even as we worked to represent those who supported such violence. But here too choices were implicitly made as regards the applicability of human rights law, and the non-application of humanitarian law which might have justified forms of state and non-state violence.[18]

In all three governing commitments we can stand charged with being simultaneously too legalistic and not legalistic enough. We were too legalistic in using human rights standards as our means of intervention; and yet unable to come up with satisfactory legal justification for non-intervention on the question of sovereignty or commitments to non-violence. However, to assert that the legalism of our work may have

[17] R. Fisher and W. Ury, *Getting to Yes: Negotiating Agreement Without Giving In* (New York: Penguin Books, 1983).

[18] For the complicated relationship of the Northern Ireland conflict see F. Ní Aoláin, *The Politics of Force: Conflict Management and State Violence in Northern Ireland* (Belfast: Blackstaff Press, 2000), p.218.

displaced broader political responsibility for addressing the conflict misunderstands the connections between the failure of law and the failure of politics. The difficulty we faced in Northern Ireland, common to other societies with protracted social conflict, did not result just from the failure of the rule of law but also from the failure of politics. The only central political issue that mattered and on which people voted was the zero-sum game of united Ireland *versus* continuing the union with Britain. In practice, the failure of politics, and the partisan nature of the state as 'a Protestant State for a Protestant people',[19] had resulted in direct rule by Britain and a democratic deficit whereby Northern Irish votes signified a border referendum and no other policy. The very limitations of the political space made issues that should have been central to any political discussion (such as the need to end the violence, ensure equality and social inclusion, and reduce poverty) secondary to the issue of who constituted the state. At a more informal political level, strong social taboos existed over the discussion of divisive issues.

In such a context it is difficult to find any conceptual or literal meeting ground for political discussion. For me, and others I suspect, human rights activism was one of the few places in which one could be politically active without joining an organisation that had some sort of sectarian dimension (including rationales focused only on ending sectarianism), or required pre-commitment to a particular sovereign outcome. If one wanted to try to make a contribution to the crisis in which we lived that was not rooted in projects of violence, of particularising the nation state, or sectarianism, or belief in mass personal transformation (and non-contributions felt like a contribution to the status quo), then human rights activism was one of the few places in which to do it. While not engaging in elaborate theoretical angst, I think none of us would have denied that we were 'doing politics' in the sense of constructing and finding a space for political engagement, but we would have strongly denied that we were doing 'party politics' or could automatically be aligned as a group with particular constitutional or sectarian positions.

Our politics was one of questioning how a broader political space could be constructed, rooted in debating the transcendent values through which we might seek community and constitutional reform which might be necessary. These were values which at one level we

[19] 'All I boast of is that we are a Protestant Parliament and a Protestant State', Sir James Craig, Prime Minister of Northern Ireland, 24 April 1934, Northern Ireland House of Commons Official Report, Vol. 34, col. 1095, available at http://stormontpapers.ahds.ac.uk/stormontpapers/pageview.html?volumeno=16&pageno=1095 (accessed 16 August 2011).

believed were 'non-negotiable' rather than contingent to security situations, and so our commitment to human rights standards was more than purely strategic. Simultaneously, however, we viewed ourselves as being in constant negotiation over the acceptance and implementation of rights as part of a broader battle to win some kind of conception of common humanity and peaceful coexistence out of the anarchy of competing particularistic claims to own the state. Joining a group such as CAJ was a way of practising the politics of democracy not just within the constitution and organisation of a group, but also by trying to reframe and promote a new politics of democracy in practice by promoting consideration of what values should underlie constitutional claims.[20] From the vantage point of divided societies such as Northern Ireland criticism of law as stultifying political discourse therefore seems particularly badly placed and to invest in the very law/politics distinction that the critique calls critical attention to. In fact our activism self-consciously sought to work in the dialectic between law and politics in a project to create political space.[21]

Human rights and the state

Human rights, Kennedy argues, can occupy the space of emancipation while being unable to offer emancipation. However, emancipation will never emanate from a single form of intervention in any case and, despite all the problems which Kennedy identifies, the language of human rights has an enduringly radical quality as one of the only languages through which to hold the state to account. In Northern Ireland, arguing that human rights were *part* of the problem ran into a deeper difficulty than that people were focused on other problems. That difficulty was that of the state's opposition to the relevance of human rights in the Northern Irish context. Some of the violent dimensions of our conflict lay not in wrong relationships between Catholics and Protestants, but in the relationship between the state and its nationalist/republican dissenters. Throughout the conflict the state remained adamant politically and legally that no conflict existed (as most states with

[20] See e.g. N. Fraser, *Justice* Interruptus: *Critical Reflections on the 'Postsocialist' Condition* (London: Routledge, 1997), p.81 (noting how civil society groups can create 'subaltern counterpublics' where they generate alternative meaning).

[21] Cf. C. Campbell and I. Connolly, 'Making wars on terror: global lessons on Northern Ireland', 69 MLR (2006) 6, 935, who provide an in-depth analysis of the ways in which law can be a tool of political opportunity and a resource for social movements, as well as a state tool of repression.

internal conflicts do)[22] – rather, there was a massive, almost inexplicable crime wave. The government maintained throughout that humanitarian law protocols dealing with internal conflict did not apply (although they refused to ratify them just in case);[23] it attempted to not derogate from human rights law (although eventually derogation was forced by losing cases before the European Court of Human Rights),[24] and it asserted that there were no political prisoners (just prisoners who self-organised with military chains of command, in segregated units, wearing their own clothes and associating freely).[25]

The government did, however, have policies with which to respond to the conflict. The main 'progressive' agenda promoted by the state as a value-driven response to the conflict was a discourse of 'community relations' which had its roots in a model of pacification rather than reconciliation.[26] Where the IRA presented the conflict as a war over sovereignty between Irish people and the British state, the state presented the problem as one of warring ethnic (Catholic and Protestant) communities in Northern Ireland to which they were a neutral, external arbitrator. From this perspective, the very worthy enterprise of

[22] O. Gross and F. Ní Aoláin, *Law in Times of Crisis: Emergency Powers in Theory and Practice* (Cambridge University Press, 2006).

[23] The UK signed Protocol I and II to the Geneva Conventions but noted in Parliament at the time (1977) that

> [n]either in Northern Ireland nor in any part of the United Kingdom is there a situation which meets the criteria laid down for the application of either Protocol. Nor is there any terrorist organization operating within the United Kingdom that fulfils the requirements which a national liberation movement must meet in order to be entitled to claim rights under Protocol I. There is therefore, no question of any of the provisions of either Protocol benefiting the IRA or any others who may carry out terrorist activities in peacetime.

Hansard, HC Debates, Vol. 941, col. 237 (written answer) (14 December 1977). Cf. also Ní Aoláin, *The Politics of Force*, pp.234–8, and K. McEvoy, 'Human rights, humanitarian activities and paramilitary activities in Northern Ireland' in C Harvey (ed.) *Human Rights, Equality and Democratic Participation in Northern Ireland* (Oxford: Hart, 2001), pp.215–49.

[24] The case after which the derogation was implemented was *Brogan* v. *United Kingdom* (1989) 11 EHRR 117. The derogation was unsuccessfully challenged in *Brannigan and McBride* v. *United Kingdom* (1993) 17 EHRR 539. (A previous derogation enabling 'internment' (administrative detention) had been considered valid in *United Kingdom* v. *Ireland* (1978) but had been withdrawn on 22 August 1984.)

[25] See K. McEvoy, *Paramilitary Imprisonment in Northern Ireland: Resistance, Management and Release* (Oxford University Press, 2001) for a full account of the dynamic of imprisonment in the conflict and how the concept of 'political prisoners' was treated.

[26] See R. McVeigh 'Between reconciliation and pacification: the British state and community relations in the North of Ireland', 37 *Community Development Journal* (2002) 1, 47.

promoting good community relations became entwined with a state agenda of denying its own involvement as protagonist in the conflict. In insisting that issues such as equality of access to jobs, public goods and services, neutral policing (representative and serving the entire community), and an end to emergency legislation were prerequisites – or at least requisites – of good community relations, human rights activists stood at odds with a state approach that preferred that people 'look to the sectarianism within themselves'. The attempt to get us all to look for the sectarianism within ourselves was central to years of huge commercial campaigns, complete with its own set of glossy mini-drama ads on the TV that played out to Cat Stevens, and the dedication of untold state resources which communities tried to subvert to community development ends. 'Community relations' was much easier for the state to do than addressing how it had structured, legislated for, and wittingly and unwittingly, directly and indirectly, aided violent conflict. But community relations policy was more than a displacement activity – it was an attempt by the government to win the meta-conflict – the conflict about what the conflict was about.[27] Because if the real problem was hatred between Catholics and Protestants, then there was one set of solutions, and if the problem was a lack of democratic values and inclusiveness at the heart of the state, then a whole other set of solutions would come into play.

While not setting themselves in opposition to community relations discourse, human rights standards pushed at the state's underlying internal and external logic. A record of cases lost before the European Court of Human Rights that is on a par with Turkey's carried some shame for the British government, as well as a foreign policy cost in the loss of reputation as 'one of the good guys' and the promoters of human rights.[28] Internationally, the human rights record kept the problem from being seen as a problem of 'terrorism' alone, but placed an enduring question mark over the state's tactics and legitimacy.

In divided societies with protracted social conflict, some language through which to press the accountability of the state for its violence is vital to addressing violent conflict across the board. A monopoly on the legitimate use of force is central to the definition of statehood and

[27] On meta-conflict see J. McGarry and B. O'Leary, *Explaining Northern Ireland: Broken Images* (Oxford: Blackwell, 1995), p.1; on the relationship to human rights and peace processes see C. Bell, *Peace Agreements and Human Rights* (Oxford University Press, 2000).

[28] For a full account of the European Convention on Human Rights and the conflict see B. Dickson, *The European Convention on Human Rights and the Conflict in Northern Ireland* (Oxford University Press, 2010).

so a state using violence within its borders tends to control to a disproportionate extent the capacity to present that violence as legitimate. The state uses legal restraints on its violence, such as democratic accountability and human rights standards, as one of the factors that legitimates its use of violence. Challenges to the legitimacy of state violence made through the language of law and rights therefore have a particular purchase. Campbell and Ní Aoláin have pointed out how in formally democratic states the state's sense of its own legitimacy often obscures from itself its role as a human rights abuser: a dynamic that 'if we do it, it's OK, and not the same as when "they" do it'.[29] Human rights claims challenge this dynamic. Moreover, Campbell's work on combatants illustrates how even a very attenuated state commitment to the rule of law can provide a 'dampening effect on conflict' more generally,[30] while McEvoy describes in practical terms how state-focused human rights activism constrained non-state actors.[31] Northern Ireland indicates how human rights discourse often remains one of the few tools with which to cut through the state's arguments over its own legitimacy and call it to account for its actions, and also has a broader impact on violence. Clearly there is a cost to this focus on the state; however, the price is not a given. How one calibrates the cost depends on the severity of the state's human rights violations in its public sphere of operation, the broader 'dampening' effect of the discourse, and the extent of one's commitment to other forms of accountability for non-state actions.

Human rights and political imagination

Kennedy justifies his articulation of the cost of human rights in terms of the need to encourage activists to factor costs as well as benefits into decision making. Again, it is difficult to argue that any action purporting to be a beneficial action should not undergo regular cost–benefit analysis. And perhaps the sureties of the professional engagement of human rights have indeed meant that increasingly such analysis is not seen as valued or undertaken with any genuine commitment. The injunction to reintroduce some of the circumspection present in the initial days of human rights activism is therefore useful.

[29] F. Ní Aoláin and C. Campbell, 'The paradox of transition in conflicted democracies', 27 *Human Rights Quarterly* (2005) 172, p.187.

[30] Campbell and Connolly, 'Making wars on terror', p.945.

[31] McEvoy, 'Human rights, humanitarian activities and paramilitary activities in Northern Ireland'.

However, once we move beyond a basic command to stop and think a little, it is very difficult to see exactly how to conduct a cost–benefit analysis in any more scientific sense. Counting social change is not like counting money, or even a counting of deaths in conflict, or proportionality of military response. Often the benefits and disadvantages of attempts to bring about progressive social change, such as improved respect for rights, are difficult to calibrate as a practical matter. If a human rights intervention is likely to lead to more repression, at least in the short term, should one move forward or not? Even in hindsight the calculations are difficult to make, as a few Northern Irish examples illustrate.

On 30 January 1972 ('Bloody Sunday'), thirteen marchers were shot dead by British troops in a civil rights demonstration. A government-established inquiry chaired by Lord Widgery found, on quite flawed evidence, that 'there is a strong suspicion that some [of the deceased and wounded] had been firing weapons or handling bombs in the course of the afternoon and that yet others had been closely supporting them . . . .'[32] The event and the injustice of Widgery's victim-blaming judgment were very significant in reducing belief in reform of the state as an option and fuelling recruitment for the IRA, escalating and solidifying the conflict into what would become a thirty-year trajectory.

A campaign by families eventually led to a second inquiry being established, as part of a 'confidence building measure' by the British government during the peace negotiations.[33] This second inquiry resulted in the converse finding that:

> [t]he firing by soldiers of 1 PARA on Bloody Sunday caused the deaths of 13 people and injury to a similar number, none of whom was posing a threat of causing death or serious injury. What happened on Bloody Sunday strengthened the Provisional IRA, increased nationalist resentment and hostility towards the Army and exacerbated the violent conflict of the years that followed. Bloody Sunday was a tragedy for the bereaved and the wounded, and a catastrophe for the people of Northern Ireland.[34]

This second Tribunal constituted the first time in British legal history that a second inquiry had been established into an incident that had already been investigated. The inquiry took twelve years, involved

[32] J. P. W. Widgery, *Report of the tribunal appointed to inquire into the events on Sunday, 30 January 1972, which led to loss of life in connection with the procession in Londonderry on that day* (London: HMSO, 1972).

[33] See Bloody Sunday Inquiry website at www.bloody-sunday-inquiry.org/index.html.

[34] *The Report of the Bloody Sunday Inquiry* (Saville Report) (HC 29-I–X, Volumes 1–10) (15 June 2010) (London: Stationery Office, 2010), Volume 1, Chapter 5.5.

lengthy court battles between the Ministry of Defence, the Tribunal and the families, and cost £195 million.[35] The ultimate report (published in ten volumes) vindicated the victims, finding that none of them were involved in criminal activities which contributed to their deaths, but was rather weak on institutional accountability for the day – concentrating blame on the wayward actions of key soldiers as 'unjustifiable' and 'unjustified'.[36]

How would one calibrate costs and benefits in this chain of repression, activism and response? Repression rather than reform was a clear possible outcome of the initial civil rights marches. Indeed, the civil rights marches at that time were part of a more global trend in which marches were at times targeted most where they would be likely to elicit and therefore reveal a brutal response. Despite past similar behaviour, however, it was not foreseeable that soldiers would open fire with live ammunition and shoot dead so many civilians – most of them teenagers – in broad daylight. Had march organisers thought this was going to happen it is clear that they would not have organised the march, and in fact they took steps to ensure no IRA presence or guns at the march so as to protect the civilian marchers from the possibility of the army's violent reprisal.

With a measure of due process, fairness and impartiality, the first inquiry (itself a process designed to deliver accountability) could have led to a measured conclusion but failed to. In its failure it carried a huge cost – the double-wronging of the families in labelling them perpetrators rather than victims, with much pain and ultimately a great cost in the wider effect on the conflict. In fact here the scales tip so far in the cost direction that they fall over. The second inquiry, although largely putting the matter to rest for the families and the state, also came at a huge personal and financial cost. However, there was also a wider cost for all those who would seek accountability from the state in the future. Reaction to the cost and scale of the inquiry led to the passing of a new Inquiries Act 2005 which reformed the tribunals process to give government ministers new powers to control, curtail and even stop inquiries.[37]

[35] The Inquiry cost had reached £190.3 million to the end of February 2010. See www.bloody-sunday-inquiry.org/questions-and-answers/index.html. On the release of the Report Prime Minister Cameron stated in his speech to the Commons that the cost had reached £195 million.

[36] See e.g., Volume 1, Chapter 4, *Report of the Bloody Sunday Inquiry.*

[37] Inquiries Act 2005 (c.12).

So, knowing the actual costs and benefits, how would we now 'weigh them'? Should the marchers not have marched for their civil rights, on the chance that this would trigger disproportionate violence? Should accountability not have been pursued because injustice and further violence was a likely result? Should a second inquiry not have been sought, because it could have led to more injustice, or because it might be effective and lead to the inquiry mechanism itself being curtailed? And what numbers do we use to price the matter? Do we count up the fourteen Bloody Sunday dead (one died later) and their families, and then anticipate the numbers of those across the UK who might be killed by state agents, in custody, car chases or counter-insurgency operations and who might want an inquiry in the future, and guess how the sum might work out? Or should we dismiss this line of reasoning altogether because, if using the mechanism leads to losing it then it may as well be used once, while if its loss was down to the length and cost of the Bloody Sunday Inquiry then this could not have been anticipated? Or should we measure the cost of the inquiry and compare it with other things – related to social justice – that we could have 'bought', such as new hospitals or schools? Or what if the Bloody Sunday Inquiry in fact proved to be the confidence-building exercise that made the sliver of difference in ending the conflict, and against the £195 million we must hang in the balance the cost in lives and money of continuing conflict? Then it might seem cheap at the price.

Or take the peace process and removal of emergency legislation. During the peace process human rights groups pushed very hard to win the argument that emergency legislation, responsible for human rights abuses, should be repealed as unnecessary following the end of conflict. Looking ahead, a clear cost to repeal was predictable and predicted: that the government would use the repeal of emergency legislation to move many of its key features into 'ordinary' legislation. But what were human rights groups to do about this? All we could do was anticipate the move and make arguments that emergency powers should not be made permanent and 'ordinary'. While I have no illusion that these arguments would have won the day, in fact what did happen was unpredictable. A large bomb planted by anti-agreement 'dissidents', a few months after the peace agreement was signed in 1998, killed thirty civilians in the greatest loss of life in a single incident during the entire Troubles. In response both the United Kingdom government and the Irish government passed new legislation extending the remit of emergency legislation well beyond what would have been politically acceptable during the

Troubles.[38] With the state's opponents, its supporters and third-party 'friends' of the process now all working together to 'promote' the agreement and address the destabilising capacities of violent 'outbidders' there was no political impetus to curb the state,[39] even though this move contrasted starkly with the human rights dimension of the new peace agreement.[40] Later, in 2000, 'normalisation' of what had been emergency powers was further buttressed after the attacks of 11 September 2001.[41]

As regards the 'normalisation' of emergency law post-conflict, while the broad impetus of the government not to let go of power was predictable, the political moments that enabled it to reconfigure and extend emergency powers were not. The reconfiguration might well have occurred without any human rights intervention, of course. What therefore is the lesson for intervening against emergency legislation? How would we now do things differently, and could we have factored in these 'lessons learned' at a pre-intervention stage to change how we intervened? Should we not have intervened to dismantle an emergency law application in Northern Ireland because change could lead to a normalised national framework? Could we have predicted violent acts on the scale of Omagh and 9/11? What would we have said and done about emergency legislation if we could have? Should we have put all our energies into campaigning against 'terrorism' (and how)? Or into something different altogether?

In fact, the lesson which I take is that if political support for the protection of human rights depends on one's political stance *vis-à-vis* the legitimacy of a state, then rights protections are very vulnerable to the state's projects for political inclusion and self-rehabilitation, and the new political dispensation will create new 'outsider' groups whose

38 Criminal Justice (Terrorism and Conspiracy) Act 1998 (c. 40) and the Offences Against the State (Amendment) Act 1998.

39 Outbidders are groups who try to 'outbid' rivals within a peace process by adopting more radical positions that reject the process and its fruits, so as to attract the former supporters of their closest political rivals.

40 Through the investigations of the Police Ombudsman another story later emerged to complicate the question of accountability for the bomb. These investigations revealed a police failure to act on informer evidence and perhaps prevent the bomb. See Police Ombudsman's Press Statement of 12 December 2001 on her Investigation into Matters Concerning the Omagh Bombing on August 15, 1998, available at www.policeombudsman.org/publicationsuploads/Omagh-press-statement.pdf (accessed 16 August 2011).

41 The Terrorism Act 2000 became a permanent piece of legislation and consolidated previous 'temporary' legislation. After 9/11 the Anti-Terrorism, Crime and Security Act 2001 was passed, followed by the Prevention of Terrorism Act 2005; then the Counter-Terrorism Act 2008.

rights can be abridged precisely because they are outside the political consensus. Paradoxically, at this point only arguments about principle and about the counter-productive dimension of abridging rights – human rights argued in their least particular form – can claim any traction politically or legally.[42] This reinforces human rights activism rooted in universal legal articulations of rights, rather than becoming over-dependent on the particularities of any instance of conflict.

In short, it seems quite impossible to undertake a cost–benefit analysis in any sensible way. It is impossible because the costs and benefits are impossible to predict, and difficult to calibrate even if we could predict them. However, the problem goes much deeper than these practical difficulties. A cost–benefit analysis is impossible because any intervention has a number of related short-term and long-term goals, and in fact disagreement exists regarding what precisely the long-term goals of any intervention are. In the longest term the goal of any intervention is inevitably a political goal for progressive change on which activists themselves will have no consensus – in our case a fairer, more just society the broad values of which we addressed but the constitutional parameters of which we left open to ongoing political negotiation.

Kennedy charges that the inability to link intervention with goal undermines the movement, and evidences a lack of clear thinking. To use his analogy: one would not begin to build a road without undertaking some appraisal of whether it could in fact be finished and where it is going. But in fact the construction of impossible-to-build roads to possible destinations that we might raise from the waste ground in front of us is in some ways a wonderful metaphor for the project of democracy as essentially contested concept. Where Kennedy rejects the 'magical thinking' of unthought-out roads, I love the phrase and want to run down those roads. In the very grey and unmagical world in which I grew up, it often seemed that it was only magical thinking that could save us. The never-ending need to chart in advance the inevitable trajectory and failure of all the possible roads out of our conflict was one of its most depressing features, and in my view just as responsible for a silly conflict's prolongation as the existence of guns and sectarian intent. If one is not to battle conflict and repression with further conflict and

[42] Cf. L. Roniger and M. Sznajder, *The Legacy of Human Rights Violations in the Southern Cone: Argentina, Chile and Uruguay* (Oxford University Press, 1999), arguing that the link between human rights and the struggle for democratisation led to failure to struggle for human rights within the democratised state which in turn undermined the quality of the democracy.

repression, it must be battled with political imagination and projects which stimulate the body politic into new ways of being, and here human rights have a role.[43]

In Northern Ireland, some human rights activists engaged because they saw practices around them that they thought were wrong and should be stopped; some engaged because they thought the logic of human rights would push the state to reveal itself as unreformable and produce a radical change in the nature of the state; and some engaged believing that the state could be reformed and that this would undermine violent opposition and contribute to conflict resolution. But in some sense we all embarked on a journey not knowing which broader political outcomes would result from the journey undertaken together. Had any particular destination been predestined or entirely predictable, the road could not have been built, nor the journey undertaken. Whether we all ended up where we wanted, or thought we should, is another story. Clearly, we could not all end up at our preferred destination, but more interestingly, the destination that we have arrived at is still contested and a little up for grabs and we continue to negotiate it.

Human rights and good government

Kennedy accuses human rights activism of producing bad government as well as good by causing bad governments to become more acceptable. Better 'bad government' can attend any attempt to reform the practice of government – a partial and limited reform always carries the risk of legitimising more bad practice than it changes. However, Kennedy's charge also applies in a new context in which 'governance' is now a more complicated practice than 'government', involving diverse permutations of state and non-state partnership, of which my own experience in the Human Rights Commission was a small part. Here the charge is not merely that bad government may be produced, but that human rights actors/professionals will become part-and-parcel of bad government and even directly produce bad practices of administration themselves.[44]

On the good government side of the ledger, however, it is also possible for the practice of human rights to open up new avenues of democratic

[43] Cf. J. P. Lederach, *The Moral Imagination: The Art and Soul of Building Peace* (Oxford University Press, 2005).

[44] See also M. Koskenniemi, 'Human rights mainstreaming as project of power' 5 February 2006, unpublished paper, Michigan School of Law. Available at: www.iilj.org/courses/documents/Koskenniemi.pdf (accessed 16 August 2011).

participation and underwrite new conceptions of 'good government'. In Northern Ireland, for example, the Belfast Agreement responded to the inequalities which had generated the conflict by providing for a new equality duty to reach beyond concepts of direct and indirect discrimination to affect the structural legacy of discrimination.[45] This duty essentially requires all policies and practices to be 'equality proofed' in terms of a range of categories such as gender, race, religion and sexual orientation. Where a policy will have a negative impact on equality, those promulgating it have to consider other options which will reduce this impact and to consult widely with the affected groups. The equality duty moves the concept of rights from one of 'trumps' to 'a language that creates the basis for deliberation'.[46] Indeed, one of the most significant 'side effects' of the equality duty has been the way in which it requires policy making to be opened up to consultation so as to give groups who would have been excluded from the legislative and policy process a line of legally required access. The duty, while not trouble-free in implementation,[47] enables ongoing monitoring of the structural equality implications of a whole gamut of decision making that would have otherwise remained closed and un-negotiable. It provides a basis for groups and individuals to challenge decision making before it happens – not by handing them the tool of immediate judicial review, but rather by providing for processes of political dialogue, consultation and negotiation.

Paradoxically, however, the move of human rights from 'margins to mainstream' and from trump cards to process frameworks, can make the concept more problematic for critics, rather than less.[48] For critics, mainstreaming 'downgrades' human rights from trump cards to 'just another part of the policy decision-making process' and has two difficulties. First, 'rights as deliberative process' fail to address the problem of the ever-expanding reach of human rights claims: if everything is human rights, human rights appraisal of policies becomes meaningless.[49] Second, and worse, human rights mainstreaming is charged with enabling a project involving even more straightforward hegemonic co-option

[45] The Northern Ireland Act 1998, s.75.

[46] C. McCrudden, *Buying Social Justice* (Oxford University Press, 2007), p.617, quoting M. Ignatieff, 'Human rights as idolatry' in M. Ignatieff (A. Gutman ed.), *Human Rights as Politics and Idolatry* (Princeton University Press, 2003), pp.53 and 95.

[47] For an assessment see E. McLaughlin and N. Faris (eds.), *Section 75 Equality Duty: An Operational Review* (2004), available at www.nio.gov.uk/section_75_equality_duty_an_operational_review_volume_1.pdf (accessed 16 August 2011).

[48] See Koskenniemi, 'Human rights mainstreaming as project of power'.

[49] See ibid.

of the human rights movement into bad government because the (meaningless) project of mainstreaming pushes the movement into administrative roles for which it is not competent and simultaneously undermines its more achievable ambition to be the 'revolutionary' voice of opposition.[50]

In response, it could be argued that an 'equality' duty is much more focused than a general duty to proof for 'human rights' implications, which insulate it from the expand-and-burst dynamic of human rights claims. It can further be argued that the criticism does not connect fully enough with particular processes of mainstreaming, where a move from no consultation to some consultation with affected groups may itself deliver a primary benefit in terms of democratic deliberation. For McCrudden, for example, the difficulties of attempting reflexive regulation of equality are answered not by throwing out mainstreaming, but by placing conditions on its procedures.[51] With respect to the attempt to promote 'reflexive regulation' of equality he suggests three conditions: that public sector organisations assess their equality practices on the basis of evidence that is objective and comparable across sectors (such as workforce monitoring); that they need to consider seriously those alternative approaches available that might shift entrenched patterns of inequality, and to be monitored in this; and that there must be a mechanism that requires consultation with stakeholders.

However, further answer to the criticism requires us to turn to the idea that there is an underlying tension between the 'revolutionary' dimension of human rights as trumps and a human rights practice that is able to view itself as part and parcel of democratic deliberation and new governance.

Part III: Human rights, revolutionary politics and a new world order

Running through Kennedy's 'costs' and 'problems' is a much more fundamental critique of human rights than a set of doubtful musings (noted subconsciously by my anger ten years ago). This critique, made even clearer in later work including the chapter in this collection,[52] is the

[50] Ibid.

[51] C. McCrudden, 'Equality regulation and reflexive regulation: a response to the Discrimination Law Review's Consultative Paper', 36 *Industrial Law Journal* (2007) 255.

[52] See Chapter 2 above, note 3 above, and compare also C. Gearty, 'Is the idea of human rights now doing more harm than good?', Inaugural Lecture, LSE, 12 October 2004,

critique that human rights as a discourse and a practice has a cost for the body politic. By placing contentious political matters into a legal world focused on certainty and answers, we lose something of our capacity for political engagement, and perhaps lose it unwittingly. This loss arises at the local level or the level of a particular human rights intervention, where a direct cost to political debate and projects of common humanity may be exacted.

However, at its deepest level, the charge that human rights is stultifying the political sphere is made in terms of our increasingly globalised world order and our capacity to find a new revolutionary politics with which to search for justice. Kennedy worries that human rights may be a 'delay and a diversion' on the road to this new politics: '[a] status quo project of legitimation and an establishment career option for those who might otherwise have contributed to a new global politics'.[53] Human rights as legal standards of state restraint; the inevitable bursting of the human rights bubble as it expands to inform everything and bursts into 'nothing special'; the co-option of human rights professionals as part of new systems of governance: all appear to demonstrate how human rights have become part of the problem of globalisation rather than something which can stand above it and inform progressive change. At its heart the critique questions whether the revolutionary voice of human rights, with its state-centric perspective, has any relevance to the attempt to find a revolutionary voice with respect to the globalised power of this new world.

How then to respond to this much broader, deeper criticism? First of all, whether human rights activism is a diversion from the project of a new political discourse of power relations depends to some extent on what is one's view of the role of the state in the new era. While I accept criticisms of the state-centredness of human rights as codified in law, I am reluctant to jettison wholesale the power of human rights to provide some basis for requiring state accountability, either because it does not do the whole job, or because we have decided that state accountability is *passé*. Even though we still lack 'workable maps of global power' at the global level, it is far from certain that the state will not figure.[54] If we turn to the 'hollowed-out' state at the domestic level, increasingly the gap in the middle can be viewed as a space for dialectical competition where state power and control remain in subtle ways

available at www2.lse.ac.uk/humanRights/articlesAndTranscripts/121004_CG.pdf (accessed 16 August 2011) and C. Douzinas, *The End of Human Rights: Critical Legal Thought at the Turn of the Century* (Oxford: Hart, 2000).

[53] See Chapter 2 above. [54] Kennedy, 'The mystery of global governance', p.65.

through their regulation of the hollow, rather than a space from which the state is permanently absent.[55] The state remains a key part of institutional configuration at the international level. In focusing on the state, human rights force us to question not just what to do when the state is absent, but when and where the state continues to be present. In days when we search for a new, radical, post-nation state politics, is it so impossible that a tapestry of human rights engagement with the complex, hollowed-out state and its post-state dimensions might serve to clarify the political choices at stake in our move from the nation state, rather than obscure them? For example, if the state does not provide security, who does and what are the consequences for accountability?[56] If someone other than the state provides security, what language and mechanisms do we use to talk of concepts such as democratic legitimacy and accountability?

As will become evident, I share many of Kennedy's concerns that the professionalisation of human rights and the involvement of human rights professionals in projects of governance and international intervention have negated the radical dimensions of human rights. However, I would also assert that the radical potential of human rights can never be completely defeated. In places Kennedy seems to advocate recapturing a more uncertain, politically contingent practice of human rights.[57] In other places he seems to view its moment as having come and gone irretrievably.[58] But there is an important difference between the two arguments and in the decision whether it is bathwater or baby that cannot and should not be saved.

Part IV: Life projects, social change and legal academics

For me Kennedy's 2001/2 essay raised questions about where academics, including myself, choose to put their energies, and why. Clearly Kennedy

[55] See e.g. G. Ellison and M. O'Rawe, 'Security governance in transition: the compartmentalizing, crowding out and corralling of policing and security in Northern Ireland', 14 *Theoretical Criminology* (2010) 31 (arguing in essence that the state has taken back control of dimensions of policing discourse that had been put beyond it, but indirectly rather than directly).

[56] See e.g, I. Loader and N. Walker, *Civilizing Security* (Cambridge University Press, 2007), p.7, arguing that the state is 'indispensable to the task of fostering and sustaining liveable political communities in the contemporary world', while providing a nuanced reading of the state's actual role in contemporary Western societies.

[57] Kennedy, *The Rights of Spring*, pp.98–104.

[58] See Chapter 2 above, and in particular p.34.

had an academic freedom to write the article and clearly human rights lawyers have to be prepared to answer criticism. However, I questioned whether (in a short life during which none of us will be able to write all we want to, and in which human rights is one of the only vocabularies available to those who want to argue for state accountability) this was the best use of his time and powers of analysis. At heart I questioned the politics of his own intervention.

Critical legal scholarship aimed at critiquing both law and modes of legal analysis has always been aware that it must self-critique at the point of production. These concerns manifest variously as concerns about 'standpoint', in worries about how to connect critical analysis with constructive projects of reform, indeed about whether strands of critique themselves suffer from the same professionalisation–failure-to-own-power dynamic that they identify in others. As an activist who began increasingly to marry activist intervention with interests pursued in academia – initially as a project to give me more time for activism, but over time growing into an intellectual project in its own right – I continually battle internally with the ways in which my dual commitment to activism and to the honesty of intellectual critique can sit together.

What does it mean to choose to be 'critical of one's discipline' or a particular 'field'? Is it to criticise the whole enterprise of constructing a discipline or field? Well then, fine: I do not feel that I have much at stake in preserving and maintaining disciplinary or field boundaries for their own sake – they are to some extent themselves constructs for analytical purposes.[59] But neither, therefore, can I get too excited about deconstructing them, particularly when there is a social cost.

Or is it to be critical of the political dynamics of the field, as is Kennedy's work on humanitarian enterprises? This I can be concerned with (and of course this links to how the field is constructed).[60] However, critical discourse is also itself a part of that field rather than something that stands apart from it. In fact, to some extent, such is the post-modern, post-structuralist world we live in, that the construction and deconstruction of any field now form 'nested oppositions' which evidence the field's coming of age in academic terms. All too often, one has the uneasy sense that intellectual pursuits can themselves constitute a game (and conferences

[59] Cf. J. Conaghan 'Reassessing the feminist project in law', 27 *Journal of Law and Society* (2000) 3, 351.

[60] See Kennedy 'The methods and politics of comparative law'; cf. my own criticisms of field construction in C. Bell, 'Transitional justice, interdisciplinarity and the state of the field or non-field' 3 *International Journal of Transitional Justice* (2009) 5.

often bring this feeling on). Just as Kennedy sees a loss in the legalisation and 'expertisation' of humanitarian enterprises, so I feel a loss that I think is related to his, revolving around the 'academicisation' of the activism of movements. I wonder whether we can stop our critique of the deadening hand of legal analysis of human rights at the movement or whether we need to include academic voices and even critical discourse as a part of the overall tapestry. In movements in which I have been loosely involved – feminism, human rights, equality, through both practical lobbying for change and as a teacher and researcher in academia – I can see a similar trajectory: from social movement outside academia, to praxis involving academics, to accepted status as new (multi-disciplinary) field, to new established field to be critiqued. En route through this trajectory, at the same time as academic legitimacy is gained, something is also lost. What is this something? Is it the assumed common commitment to a project of social change as academics scent the latest 'new thing' and the uncommitted join in? Or the wearying and time-consuming business of constructing, deconstructing, analysing, re-analysing? Or the academic crushing of law's possibilities for good as doomed to inevitable co-option in the quicksand of legalisation? Is it possible that the business of the academy is itself part of the problem?

A part of the cost of entry to the legal academy is the idea that, because we can twist the arguments every which way, none of it really has any consequence. We are in the ultimate performative world where law's power and the power of legal analysis reside in the strength and persuasiveness of the performance. It is inevitable that in this world we also end up asking whether the subversion is indeed subversive or whether it merely reinforces one status quo or another?[61] Concern about the implications of criticism for the status quo can perhaps be understood as having produced a critical self-wrestling with the ways in which, on occasion, law and formalist argumentation can appear to be one of the last bulwarks against oppressive actions.[62] When the chips are down and the stakes are high, often law, with its association with the right and the good, is one of the only ways in which to appeal rhetorically against the injustices of unbridled political power, and litigation is a partner of political intervention. To criticisms of judicial

[61] For an interesting discussion relating to feminism see 'Is subversion subversive?' 13 *Texas Journal of Women and the Law* (2003–4) 159.

[62] See Koskenniemi, *The Gentle Civilizer of Nations*, and Gearty, *Can Human Rights Survive?* as examples.

responses as 'flabby subjective response dressed up in the guise of objectivity' let us respond with Sachs: 'while one should always be sceptical about the law's pretentions, one should never be cynical about the law's possibilities'.[63]

The law's possibilities are often sought out by those in struggle as one of the few resources available. How, then, can the academic who takes academic contribution seriously enough to consider it an intervention best respond? I imagine it here as a range of imaginary answers that the human rights academic might give the local activist.

Stay on the barricades if you wish, you are fighting a good fight; I support wholeheartedly but we all have our place in the struggle, and fortunately mine is at my desk formulating the legal brief – I was never good at barricades. Wait there a minute: soon I will give you a piece of definitive analysis which will help with your struggle. Wait, I am coming with you, even though we may both end up pissing in the wind. Whether you stay up there or come down is not really my business; yes, I am a human rights academic but that never implied any commitment to the practice and in fact I resist anyone implying that it does – to do so would be to undermine the place human rights has won in the academy. Nothing: we have nothing to do with each other and there is no special reason why I should talk to you.

Come down off the barricades, and consider how you may be doing more harm than good. Come down and we can explore the possibly better alternative roads to emancipation. Come down off the barricades because you are engaged in a diversion which may delay us all in finding a new, more radical politics from which to address the wider project of global power. Come down, because you are very embarrassing and drawing me, the stranger, into a colonial encounter in your pleas for help, from which I cannot escape looking good.

Come and talk to me a minute to see if together we can find a way to create the political space and change we both search for.

[63] A. Sachs, *The Strange Alchemy of Life and Law* (Oxford University Press, 2009).

12

Lawfare and the international human rights movement

RICHARD MULLENDER

Introduction

[P]articipation in war is not only physically but morally perilous.[1]

The United States Army Air Force swept over and bombed an industrial facility dedicated to the production of components for nuclear weapons.[2] The bombers failed to destroy their target. They did, however, bring death to the local community.[3] As a consequence, the US administration found itself fielding sharply worded complaints from a disgruntled government.[4] This is not an outline of effects that might flow from an American raid on Iran in the years ahead. Rather, it concerns the USAAF's attack on the Norsk Hydro Works in occupied Norway in 1943. We do not need to take the providential view of history propounded by Hegel to find the outlines of the future in the USAAF's fleet of Flying Fortresses.[5] For the raid took place at the beginning of what Henry Luce (the proprietor of *Time* and *Life* magazines) had (before America's entry

Newcastle Law School. I owe thanks to Francesco de Cecco, Colin Murray, Patrick O'Callaghan and Ole Pedersen for their comments on earlier drafts. I am also grateful to those who offered comments on a related seminar paper I gave in Newcastle Law School, and to David Campbell and Keith Ewing for their assistance with particular points.

[1] J. McMahan, 'Laws of war', ch.24 in S. Besson and J. Tasioulas, *The Philosophy of International Law* (Oxford University Press, 2010), p.508.

[2] M. Burleigh, *Moral Combat: A History of World War II* (London: Harper Press, 2010), p.301.

[3] Ibid. (noting that twenty-two civilians died in the raid).

[4] Ibid. (noting the complaints of the Norwegian government-in-exile).

[5] G. W. F. Hegel, *The Philosophy of History*, J. Sibtree, trans. (New York, Amherst, MA: Prometheus Books, 1991), pp.1–100. See also R. Plant, *Hegel: On Religion and Philosophy* (London: Orion Publishing, 1997), p.54 (on the metaphysic of rational progression that features in Hegel's account of the historical process).

into the Second World War) called the 'American Century'.[6] On Luce's account, this would be a century in which the USA exerted power in ways that demonstrated that it was 'the powerhouse of the ideals of Freedom and Justice'.[7] Moreover, it would be an epoch in which the USA would seek to advance the cause of human rights. President Roosevelt had made this plain before taking his country to war. The USA and its allies fought the war on precisely this basis – with the protection of human rights as a war aim.[8] This war aim provided part of the justification for the raid on Norsk Hydro. But so too did a developing commitment to what we would now call the proportionality principle. For earlier attempts to destroy (or, at least, disable) the plant by the British had made it clear that a raid such as that mounted by the USAAF would be necessary in order to advance the Allied cause.[9]

While we may now be better able to talk the language of human rights and proportionality than was the case in the 1940s, the world of the Norsk Hydro raid remains, in many respects, our world. As they were during the Second World War, human rights are a tantalising ideal. In the decades since the defeat of the Axis powers, critics of human rights have regularly pursued the theme that they give expression to a distinctly Western practical agenda and serve Western interests.[10] This is a criticism on which David Kennedy has dwelt, and to which he lends some support, in 'The international human rights movement: part of the problem?'.[11] Moreover, in some of his more recent writings, he has examined a practice in which an association between American (or, more broadly, Western) power and human rights is plain to see. This practice features prominently in what Kennedy has called the 'new law of force' and involves the use of military power for the purpose of advancing a humanitarian agenda

[6] N. Ferguson, *Colossus: The Rise and Fall of the American Empire* (London: Penguin Books, 2005), pp.65–6.

[7] Ibid.

[8] M. Gilbert, *Second World War* (London: Weidenfeld and Nicolson, 1989), p.222, G. Robertson, *Crimes Against Humanity: The Struggle for Global Justice*, 3rd edn (London: Penguin Books, 2006), p.28, and P. Sands, *Lawless World: Making and Breaking Global Rules* (London: Penguin Books, 2006), pp.8–9.

[9] Burleigh, *Moral Combat*, pp.299–301.

[10] See, for example, A. J. Langlois, *The Politics of Justice and Human Rights: South East Asia and Universalist Theory* (Cambridge University Press, 2001).

[11] D. Kennedy, 'The international human rights movement: part of the problem?' 15 *Harvard Human Rights Law Review* (2001) 101, pp.114–16.

(e.g. to secure human rights).[12] More recently, Kennedy has used the term 'lawfare' when referring to this practice.[13]

On Kennedy's account, the practice of lawfare has gained currency and become more refined in the decades since the collapse of the Axis powers.[14] However, we can (as the Norsk Hydro raid shows) trace it back to the Second World War. But this (as we will see) is only the beginning of a much longer story. For lawfare is a practice that has deep roots in the American (or, more broadly, Anglo-American or Western) political tradition. This being so, we might make the leap from the fact that lawfare is a local (American, Anglo-American or Western) enthusiasm to the conclusion that it serves sectional rather than universal interests. However, we will also explore the possibility that, while rooted in a particular tradition, lawfare (when suitably refined) is an appropriate means by which to pursue a universal agenda. While examining this matter, we will also consider Kennedy's ambivalent relationship with the movement on which he has concentrated critical fire. As we will see, his analysis exhibits moral urgency of a sort that bears family resemblances to that on display in the practice of lawfare (and the international human rights movement with which he associates this practice).[15] But before turning to these matters we must examine the practice of lawfare and relevant politico-legal history.

[12] On the 'new law of force', see D. Kennedy, *The Dark Sides of Virtue: Reassessing International Humanitarianism* (Princeton, NJ: Princeton University Press, 2004), ch.8. See especially pp.262ff.

[13] See Chapter 2 above, p.30–1 (where Kennedy notes that the US military has been employing the term 'lawfare' – with no great commitment to precision – for some time). Kennedy's decision to embrace the term 'lawfare' is regrettable since it bears (as he notes) a range of meanings. For example, some commentators employ 'lawfare' to refer to the use made of law by, *inter alios*, terrorists (e.g. instruments that secure human rights) to raise the profile of the causes that they seek to advance. (See D. B. Rivkin and L. A. Casey, 'Lawfare', *Wall Street Journal*, 23 February 2007, p.11(A).) In the remainder of this chapter, we will refer to 'lawfare' exclusively in the sense specified in the text. Used in this way, it provides a label by means of which we can conveniently capture a central feature of the 'new law of force' (as described by Kennedy).

[14] The history of lawfare lends support to the point made by Michael Oakeshott that practices begin naïvely and typically become more refined over time as a result of the pursuit of intimations within them. See M. Oakeshott, *The Vocabulary of a Modern European State*, L. O'Sullivan ed. (Exeter: Imprint-Academic, 2008), p.108.

[15] L. Wittgenstein, *Philosophical Investigations*, G. E. M. Anscombe, trans. (New York: Macmillan, 1968), para.67 (where Wittgenstein uses the phrase 'family resemblances' to capture partially overlapping similarities that overlap and crisscross in the same way as 'the various resemblances between members of a family'). See also H. Fenichel Pitkin, *Wittgenstein and Justice: On the Significance of Ludwig Wittgenstein for Social and Political Thought*, revised edn (Berkeley, CA: University of California Press, 1972), p.64.

Lawfare: an analysis of the practice

Kennedy's writings on humanitarianism and the development of the new law of force enable us to pick out at least some of the more prominent features of lawfare. He tells us that humanitarians are troubled by the 'extreme gap between the peaceful . . . aspirations associated with international law and the political freedom – and violence – associated with war'.[16] This, he adds, is because 'international humanitarians abjure war'.[17] However, some among them have embraced lawfare because they see it as an element in the project of 'mak[ing] the world more just'.[18] More particularly, Kennedy identifies lawfare as a component of the 'new legal order' inaugurated by the UN Charter system.[19] This, on his account, is an order within which sovereigns are part of an 'international community'.[20]

As well as identifying lawfare as a component in a larger humanitarian project (concerned with the pursuit of justice), Kennedy also describes it as 'an integrated way of thinking about warfare'.[21] This is because it is a practice that 'combines elements of the human rights tradition, as well as the traditions of humanitarian law and collective security'.[22] But integration has to do with more than a commingling of traditions in the service of the same goal. We can see in the practice of lawfare both consequentialist and deontological moral impulses. Consequentialism is the body of moral philosophy according to which we should assess our conduct by reference to its (actual or anticipated) effects.[23] Deontology, by contrast, enjoins us to act in ways that are properly attentive to sources of intrinsic value.[24] Pinning down the consequentialist impulses at work in lawfare is a straightforward task. At the most general level, they find expression in the pursuit of a world that is 'more just'.[25] More concretely, we find them in efforts to prosecute war in ways that take adequate account of human rights.

Kennedy brings into view the deontological impulses within the practice of lawfare when he states that 'international humanitarians abjure war'.[26] War is an assault on a state of affairs (peace) and a set of interests (those of the human rights bearers who live in the midst of conflict) to which international humanitarians appear to ascribe

[16] Kennedy, *The Dark Sides of Virtue*, p.236. [17] Ibid., p.235. [18] Ibid., p.236.
[19] Ibid., p.254. [20] Ibid. [21] Ibid., p.237. [22] Ibid. See also pp.253–4.
[23] S. Blackburn *The Oxford Dictionary of Philosophy* (Oxford University Press, 1994), pp.77–8.
[24] Ibid., pp.100 and 205–7. [25] See note 18 above, and associated text.
[26] See note 17 above, and associated text.

intrinsic value. For this reason, they seek to specify tight restrictions on the use of military force. Thus it comes as no surprise to find that the proportionality principle occupies a place of prominence in the practice of lawfare. Moreover, if we contrast the proportionality principle's place in lawfare with proportionality-talk in the (general) law of war, it becomes possible to gain greater analytic purchase on the practical impulses we are considering. Typically, proportionality-talk within the law of war proceeds on the basis of an analogy with the defence of self-defence in municipal criminal law.[27] In criminal law, a defendant can successfully run this defence by establishing that they used no more force than was necessary to secure their interest in physical security.[28] Many commentators on the law of war talk, *mutatis mutandis*, in this way when specifying the requirements of proportionality in their field.[29] But this approach does not seem to capture the full complexity of lawfare as a practice. For 'proportionality' in this context seems to refer to a more richly elaborated principle. This principle specifies that those pursuing an outcome that serves the interests of all relevant people should only override or compromise interests that they may adversely affect where it is strictly necessary to do so.[30] Since this principle simply assumes the value of the interests under threat, we can detect a deontological impulse within it (notwithstanding the fact that it attaches priority to the pursuit of outcomes).

To the extent that the proportionality principle is a component of lawfare, it brings into view another of the practice's features. This is the assumption that peace and war occupy space in the same legal universe (shaped by the bodies of law and practice we noted earlier). In this, the thinking of those who have elaborated this practice differs from nineteenth century commentators. Kennedy tells us that, by the end of the

[27] See T. Hurka, 'Proportionality in the morality of war' 33 *Philosophy and Public Affairs* (2005) 34, p.38, McMahan, 'Laws of war', pp.497–8, and M. Walzer, *Just and Unjust Wars: A Moral Argument with Historical Illustrations*, 4th edn (New York: Basic Books, 2006), pp.58–9. David Kennedy's position on proportionality as a feature of lawfare exhibits some similarities to that of Hurka, McMahan and Walzer but is hard to pin down with any degree of precision. See D. Kennedy, *Of Law and War* (Princeton, NJ: Princeton University Press, 2006), pp.120 and 143–4.

[28] A. Ashworth, *Principles of Criminal Law*, 6th edn (Oxford University Press, 2009), pp.118–19.

[29] Hurka, 'Proportionality in the morality of war', p.42.

[30] For detailed examination of the proportionality principle, see R. Mullender, 'Theorizing the Third Way: qualified consequentialism, the proportionality principle, and the new social democracy' 27 *Journal of Law and Society* (2000) 493, pp.503–6. As to when military intervention to protect human rights is 'strictly necessary', see R. Dworkin, *Justice for Hedgehogs* (Cambridge, Mass.: Harvard University Press, 2011), p.344 (arguing that 'military sanctions are justified only to stop truly barbaric acts').

nineteenth century, 'leading treatise writers' identified war and peace as situated in 'two different legal universes'.[31] Lawfare departs from this view by, *inter alia*, identifying war and peace as states of affairs to which the same legal norms have relevance. The proportionality principle (as it features in the practice of lawfare) is one such norm. Those who seek to act in accordance with this norm take into account the interests of those who will (or may) benefit from the use of military force. Likewise, they seek to accommodate the interests of those who will or may suffer adverse consequences. This readiness to take account of these (opposing) sets of interests reveals the practice we are examining to be (as we would expect in the sphere of human rights) egalitarian.

The readiness to use force in this egalitarian, human rights-focused way has, on Kennedy's account, become a practical possibility in the years since 1945 and the collapse of the Axis powers.[32] However, he recognises that long before the end of the Second World War states were adopting practices of the sort that are a feature of lawfare. For example, he notes that during the American Civil War 'the US government published a manual of instruction for Union troops' on the acceptable use of force.[33] This manual – the work of Francis Lieber, a professor at Columbia University – became a 'model' from which various European states derived inspiration when working up codes of their own.[34] Given that Lieber presented his manual to troops who were seeking to advance an egalitarian war aim (freeing African Americans from slavery), we can see the outlines of lawfare in this approach to the use of force. If this is correct, it yields a basis on which to suggest that we can best understand lawfare as the upshot of an incremental process of development.

The manual Lieber provided for Union troops during the American Civil War is relevant to this discussion for a further reason. Kennedy states that lawfare is a practice that 'has had its share of blind spots and biases'.[35] One such blind spot may be a failure to recognise the extent to which it has emerged from and continues to be rooted in a distinct politico-legal tradition rather than being (in some sense) universal. Kennedy's reference to Lieber's manual and a range of points we will explore shortly suggest that we should treat lawfare as a local enthusiasm (rooted in an 'American', or 'Anglo-American', or 'Western' tradition). Alongside this possible blind spot we should set a potential bias in the practice that we can explore by returning to the proportionality principle. The proponents of lawfare appear to assume that it is possible

[31] Kennedy, *The Dark Sides of Virtue*, p.241. [32] Ibid., p.237. [33] Ibid., pp.238–9.
[34] Ibid., p.239. [35] Ibid., p.235.

to calibrate the use of military force finely so as to minimise its negative effects. Proportionality has relevance here because it appears to be (for reasons we will examine later) the witness and external deposit of this belief. To the extent that this belief has shaped lawfare, we might see it as a practice afflicted by misplaced optimism (or even a species of utopianism).[36]

Optimism of the sort we have just been considering is relevant to lawfare for a further reason: for it gives expression to the assumption that we can and should fashion a legal framework that effectively bridles military operations. To take this view is to give priority to law and to identify the use of force as a process that must conform to its requirements. But Kennedy, in his contribution to this collection, discusses conceptions of lawfare that challenge the optimistic assumption we are exploring. For he notes that some proponents of lawfare see law as 'a strategic asset' within a process that is primarily military – rather than legal – in orientation.[37] When we juxtapose this latter view with the optimistic one, there are reasons for thinking that an ineliminable tension exists within lawfare. This is certainly the case if we view its two elements – law and force – as standing in a relationship of binary opposition. For each of the two has claims to priority over the other ('respect for human rights and law more generally' *versus* 'effectiveness arising from the deployment of military assets untrammelled by law'). Hence, an understanding of lawfare in which law enjoys priority (relative to force) is vulnerable to a reversal of the sort described by deconstructionists.[38]

Assuming that there is a tension within lawfare of the sort to which deconstruction directs attention, we will adopt the optimistic view outlined earlier and assume that law (and not force) enjoys priority within the practice. For this view affords a basis on which to present

[36] We could expect uncharitable critics of lawfare to offer harsher analyses. They might see it, for example, as just one more example of the 'well-meaning guff' that features in the mainstream of the international human rights movement. (See D. Sandbrook, 'Friends in high places', *The Sunday Times*, 13 March 2011, p.36 ('Culture' section).) Alternatively, they might describe it as a practice informed by 'unscrupulous optimism'. On this form of optimism, see R. Scruton, *The Use of Pessimism and the Danger of False Hope* (London: Atlantic Books, 2010), pp.22–3 (describing unscrupulous optimism as 'typified by . . . the "best case" fallacy': the assumption that we will (notwithstanding lack of supporting evidence) achieve 'the best outcome').

[37] See Chapter 2 above, p.30 (where Kennedy also notes that some commentators describe lawfare as a 'tactical ally' of the military).

[38] J. M. Balkin, 'Deconstructive practice and legal theory' 96 *Yale Law Journal* (1987) 743, pp.746–51.

lawfare in what we might call (following Ronald Dworkin) its best light.[39] Moreover, there are reasons for thinking that this more positive view is more faithful to the relevant politico-legal history – to which we now turn.

Lawfare and the American political tradition

In 1815, John Adams (in a letter to Thomas Jefferson) looked back on the War of Independence. He stated that the War had been 'an Effect and Consequence' of a revolution that had taken place before blood flowed at Lexington.[40] He added that the revolution had taken place in 'the minds of the People' between 1760 and 1775.[41] These terse observations are, for the purposes of the present discussion, highly important. For they point to an association between a particular set of ideas and the use of military force that we might regard as – at least – approximating 'lawfare' (as Kennedy uses that term). Moreover, this combination of ideas and force is (as we will see) also apparent in the prosecution of the American Civil War by the Union and in the USA's war aims in the two World Wars.

But before turning to these later conflicts, we must look in some detail at the reasons for the War of Independence. In the mid-eighteenth century, Britain adopted a more interventionist stance towards the regulation of her colonies on what is now the eastern seaboard of the USA.[42] In 1650, an Act of Parliament identified these colonies as subject to the sovereign imperial legislature in London.[43] Moreover, Britain's victory over France in the Seven Years War encouraged this more assertive approach to her colonies.[44] This approach found expression in the Sugar Act 1764 and the Stamp Act 1765. These Acts imposed tax burdens on the colonies with the aim of funding the activities of the

[39] R. Dworkin, *Law's Empire* (London: Fontana Press, 1986), p.53 (arguing that 'all interpretation strives to make an object the best it can be').

[40] K. Burk, *Old World, New World: The Story of Britain and America* (London: Little, Brown, 2007), p.109.

[41] Ibid. John Searle's account of 'the construction of social reality' provides a basis on which to develop Adams's point concerning 'the minds of the People' (between 1760 and 1775). For Searle identifies collective intentionality as a necessary condition for the emergence of social institutions (including frameworks of law). See J. Searle, *Making the Social World: The Structure of Human Civilization* (Oxford University Press, 2010) and J. Searle, *The Construction of Social Reality* (London: Penguin Books, 1996).

[42] Burk, *Old World, New World*, pp.110–11.

[43] Ibid. [44] Ibid.

British military in North America.[45] The Sugar Act also established that those breaching its requirements would face trial in vice-Admiralty Courts.[46] Colonial critics of these Acts were able to attack them on grounds that they (with good cause) regarded as principled. In the Virginia House of Burgesses, Patrick Henry placed emphasis on the fact that the colony's royal charters stipulated that only those elected by Virginians could tax them.[47] In this feature of Virginia's relationship with the Crown he found support for the conclusion: 'no taxation without representation'.[48]

Alongside these developments, we must set the fact that Britain began to use troops with the aim of ensuring that the colonies acted in accordance with the will of Parliament. As a result, Britain's authority (already under strain) began to 'bleed away'.[49] By 1774 increasing numbers of colonists were ready to embrace the idea that the British were seeking to 'enslave America'.[50] Likewise, more and more colonists were ready to accept that citizens need not obey unjust laws.[51] In the light of these and the other developments we have noted, we can see that a rich body of thought that had to do with the pursuit of justice motivated the colonists. And in 1775, they made it clear to the British (at Concord and Lexington) that they were ready to use force in pursuit of their agenda.[52]

Thus we can trace a timeline that lends force to Adams's claim that the revolution took place in the minds of a significant number of people before they resorted to force. Moreover, we might see the events that we have been examining as establishing a politico-legal grammar that finds

45 Ibid., pp.118–19, and I Judge, '"No tax without representation": a British perspective on Constitutional arrangements' (lecture delivered at Broadmore, Colorado Springs, 28 August 2010), pp.4–5 (copy held on file in Newcastle Law School). (The Stamp Act was 'the first "direct" tax' imposed by the Westminster Parliament on the colonies. See D. Reynolds, *America, Empire of Liberty: A New History* (London: Penguin Books, 2010), p.58.)

46 Burk, *Old World, New World*, p.118. 47 Ibid., p.119.

48 Ibid. While the phrase 'no taxation without representation' gained great currency during the struggle between the American colonists and the British Crown, we can trace the (legitimacy-related) issue it raises back to seventeenth-century England. For extra-Parliamentary taxation by the Stuart monarchs was a practice that those who rebelled against them identified as a factor that led them to employ military force. See S. Schama, *A History of Britain*, Volume II, *The British Wars 1603–1776* (London: BBC, 2003), pp.40 and 54. See also P. Kellner, *Democracy: 1,000 Years in Pursuit of British Liberty* (Edinburgh: Mainstream Publishing, 2009), pp.94–6 (on The Petition of Right 1628).

49 Burk, *Old World, New World*, p.138. 50 Ibid., p.143. 51 Ibid.

52 Ibid., pp.151–3.

expression in the Declaration of Independence.[53] Those who led the revolution against the Crown regarded force as a means necessary to the pursuit of an egalitarian end. And in revolting only when these conditions could be met, they established a basis on which others might 'go on' in (or incrementally develop) the same practice.[54] Moreover, on the evidence of the American Civil War and the two World Wars, we have (as we will see) grounds for supposing that those who dwelt on the politico-legal grammar worked up by the American revolutionaries were attentive students.

While the American Civil War was not solely about slavery, the abrogation of this institution provided the Union with one of its central war aims. Lincoln made this clear in his Emancipation Proclamation.[55] The Proclamation 'exalted the war to the level of a moral crusade'.[56] Moreover, Lincoln saw the preservation of the Union as itself being an urgent moral matter.[57] For he identified the United States and its commitment to egalitarianism as 'the last best hope of the earth'.[58] This statement repays close attention. It indicates that Lincoln regarded the use of force in pursuit of an egalitarian practical agenda (and a form of life in which it found expression) as something more than a local (American) concern. The 'hope' to which he refers seems to betoken a world in which all people enjoy equal standing underwritten by law.[59]

[53] On the (Wittgensteinian) notion of 'grammar', see Fenichel Pitkin, *Wittgenstein and Justice*, pp.116–39 (describing it as associated with learning from cases and as yielding criteria that are reliant on connections that we have already made between word and world). See also Wittgenstein, *Philosophical Investigations*, para.90 (describing 'grammar' as governing 'the *possibilities* of phenomena' by regulating 'the *kind of statement* that we make about phenomena'). Wittgenstein's account of grammar intersects with the account, in his later writings, of the 'work' of philosophers. For he described this work as 'consist[ing] in assembling reminders for a particular purpose'. We might see a grammar as a set of such reminders. Wittgenstein, ibid., para.127.

[54] Wittgenstein uses the phrase 'going on' to capture the process by which the participants in a practice elaborate it. To indicate what he means by 'going on', he describes someone who extends a series of numbers by 'adding 2' thus: '2, 4, 6, 8 . . .', etc. See Wittgenstein, ibid., paras.185–7. While we might see the incremental elaboration of the practice we are considering as broadly similar, it is more complex. For it proceeds by reference to a range of considerations (or grammar-generating criteria) (including the necessity and proportionality of force in pursuit of an egalitarian goal).

[55] T. Keneally, *Lincoln* (London: Phoenix, 2005), pp.135–6.

[56] Ibid., p.176. [57] Ibid., p.103. [58] Ibid., p.139.

[59] 'Hope' of the sort described in the text plainly informed the thinking of Thomas Jefferson. In 1802 (and while US President), Jefferson stated that '[i]t is impossible not to be sensible that *we are acting for all mankind*'. He also observed that '[favourable] circumstances . . . have imposed on us the duty of proving what is the degree of self-government in which a society may venture to leave its individual members'. See L. Hunt,

The egalitarian impulses that found expression in the War of Independence and the American Civil War are also apparent in the USA's decision to enter the First World War in 1917. This becomes apparent when we examine the war aims of President Woodrow Wilson. He sought to create a system of self-determining, democratic, nation states.[60] To this end, he also aimed to establish a League of Nations embodying the egalitarian principle that its members were legally equal.[61] In Wilson's view and that of his close adviser, Colonel Edward House, the USA's war aims promised nothing less than a new world order.[62] In their account, the relationship between the League of Nations and states would be analogous to that between states and citizens.[63] They also made the further (and hopelessly naïve) assumption that their plan would more adequately secure the interests of those who lived within the order they hoped to establish.[64]

When historians seek to sum up this toweringly ambitious plan, they typically make reference to the Fourteen Points that Wilson proposed at the Versailles Peace Conference in 1919. But if we examine the relevant history more closely, we find that the Fourteen Points provide no more than a chapter in a longer story. Moreover, it is a story in which House figures at least as prominently as Wilson. The story begins in 1912 with the publication in New York of the novel, *Philip Dru*.[65] The novel became a talking point for a variety of reasons. It contemplated a world federation in which the principle of popular sovereignty and the ideal of the rule of law would limit the power of states.[66] Here we see something very much like the vision that Wilson sought to make a reality in 1919. And this is no accident. For, while he did not identify himself as such,

Inventing Human Rights: A History (New York: W. W. Norton & Company, 2008), p.68 (drawing on *The Writings of Thomas Jefferson*, A. A. Liscombe and A. E. Bergh, eds (Washington, DC: Thomas Jefferson Memorial Association of the United States, 1903–4) Vol. 10, 324 (emphasis added)).

60 P. Bobbitt, *The Shield of Achilles: War, Peace and the Course of History* (Harmondsworth, Middx: Penguin Books, 2003), p.394.

61 Ibid., p.395. 62 Ibid., p.407. 63 Ibid., p.379.

64 The naïvetë exhibited by Wilson and House derives from the fact that they were arguing for the creation of states within which '[r]ank majorities' (to use Grattan's phrase) would give nations bodies of law that might be spectacularly insensitive to the interests of minorities. On rank majorities, see L. O'Sullivan, ed., *Michael Oakeshott: The Concept of a Philosophical Jurisprudence: Essays and Reviews 1926–1951* (Exeter: Imprint-Academic, 2007), p.204. See also Bobbitt, *The Shield of Achilles*, p.405 (noting John Maynard Keynes' description of Wilson as a 'blind and deaf Don Quixote'), and N. Ferguson, *The War of the World: History's Age of Hatred* (London: Allen Lane, 2006), pp.160–63.

65 Bobbitt, ibid., p.375. 66 Ibid., p.401.

House was the author of *Philip Dru*. House's vision (as became apparent in the inter-war years) was deeply flawed.[67] For minorities were victims of abuse in the crudely majoritarian nation states that came into existence in Central Europe after the First World War.[68] Nonetheless, the vision is important for our purposes. For it reveals a strong form of egalitarianism (concerned with democratic governance) as having motivated the USA's resort to arms in 1917.

While Wilson and House saw the self-determining and democratic nation state as an institution in which they could repose their hopes, Franklin Roosevelt (before and during the Second World War) placed emphasis on the individual. For he was a proponent of human rights at a time when they were gaining currency as a matter of urgent practical concern. But this does not mean that this agenda was a creation of the years immediately preceding the USA's entry into the Second World War. At first in a rather muted form, this agenda had begun to win adherents during and after the First World War.[69] And during the second half of the 1930s and in the early 1940s, a number of prominent commentators, including H. G. Wells, boosted the cause of human rights. As well as writing an influential pamphlet on this topic, Wells argued that those waging war on the Axis should identify human rights as a war aim. Roosevelt and Churchill acted on this proposal when they met in 1941 and signed the Atlantic Charter. Among other things, the Charter indicated that the struggle against the Nazis and their allies had to do with fashioning institutions that guarantee freedom to all people.[70] Following US entry into the war, Roosevelt returned to the subject of human rights. In conjunction with twenty other nations fighting against the Axis, he made it plain that the United Nations were committed to the protection

[67] We might sum up the flaw in the agenda that Wilson and House sought to advance in a term much used by comparative lawyers: 'transplantation'. For Wilson and House assumed that it would be possible to introduce into other countries a politico-legal framework that had its life in the USA. They thus exhibited a staggering insensitivity to historical and cultural particularity. On transplantation, see O. Kahn-Freund, 'On Uses and Misuses of Comparative Law' 37 MLR (1974) 1, p.6.

[68] Ferguson, *The War of the World*, pp.185–6 (on 'the new states created by the peacemakers' as 'the graves of nations' (quoting Alfred Döblin)).

[69] See for example, *Minority Schools in Albania* (1935) PCIJ, Ser. A/B, No. 64. See also Robertson, *Crimes Against Humanity*, pp.22–3.

[70] D. Dimbleby and D. Reynolds, *An Ocean Apart: The Relationship Between Britain and America in the Twentieth Century* (London: Hodder & Stoughton, 1988), p.136 (identifying the Atlantic Charter as 'embody[ing] America's distinctive vision of the post-war world').

of fundamental human rights. To underscore the point, 'the Allies . . . signalled their intention to bring German war criminals to book'.[71]

As in the earlier conflicts we have surveyed, we find the USA identifying the use of military force with the pursuit of an egalitarian practical agenda. At various points in the struggle against the Axis powers, those playing prominent roles in the US war effort echoed Lincoln by pointing out that their cause served the interests of humankind as a whole. This was true of the Supreme Allied Commander Dwight D. Eisenhower. On the eve of the D-Day landings he declared that the eyes of the world would fasten, in eager anticipation, on the invasion force.[72] By this time, the USA had assumed the position of a 'colossus' or hegemonic power – thus lending support to Luce's talk of 'the American century'.[73]

With a greater weight of expectation on the USA than at any previous point in its history, the tension between the ideals animating its war effort and the need for military effectiveness comes sharply into view. The position adopted by, for example, the Secretary for War, Henry Stimson, makes this tension vivid. A teetotal Presbyterian, Stimson had, in the inter-war years, been 'a great believer in disarmament, international law and a World Court'.[74] This led some to characterise him as 'a New England conscience on legs'.[75] There was certainly something in this. Stimson had described the Allies' decision to bomb Dresden as 'terrible and probably unnecessary'.[76] He was implacably opposed to the use of an atomic bomb on Kyoto.[77] More generally, he feared that use of

[71] Burleigh, *Moral Combat*, p.543.

[72] S. Ambrose, *Band of Brothers: E Company, 506th Regiment; 101st Airborne from Normandy to Hitler's Eagle's Nest* (London: Simon & Schuster, 2001), p.66 (emphasis added) (Eisenhower declared: 'You are about to embark upon *the Great Crusade* . . . The eyes of the world are upon you . . . And let us all beseech the blessing of Almighty God upon this great and noble undertaking.')

[73] Ferguson, *Colossus*, ch.2. (Just as Luce directs our attention to what we might call the dawning of American hegemony, the novelist Philip Roth directs our attention to some of its earliest effects. Through the medium of one of his characters (Nathan Zuckerman), he says: '[l]et's remember the energy. Americans were governing not only themselves but some two hundred million people in Italy, Austria, Germany, and Japan. *The war-crimes trials were cleansing the earth of the devils once and for all.*' See P. Roth, *American Pastoral* (London: Vintage Books, 1998), p.40 (emphasis added). See also J. Didion, *Sentimental Journeys* (London: Flamingo, 1994), p.45 (on the USA as a 'liberating force'), Reynolds, *America, Empire of Liberty*, p.574 (noting that (in 2004) President George W. Bush rejected the view that the USA is an 'imperial power' and described it as 'a liberating power'), and G. Vidal, *The Last Empire: Essays 1992–2001* (London: Abacus, 2002), p.173 (on the Truman Doctrine (1947), which (according to Vidal) 'made the entire world the specific business of the United States').

[74] Burleigh, *Moral Combat*, p.522. [75] Ibid. [76] Ibid., p.525. [77] Ibid., p.523.

this new technology on Japan would erode the legitimacy of the American war effort. Nonetheless, he ultimately concluded that the USA would be justified in dropping atomic bombs on Japanese cities. This has led Michael Burleigh to describe Stimson as 'capable of [making] ruthless decisions dextrously veiled in ... preachy moralism'.[78] But it would surely be nearer the mark to identify Stimson as one who found himself wrestling with tensions that are internal to the practice that Kennedy calls lawfare.[79] For he was seeking (like the Founding Fathers, Lincoln, Wilson and House) to advance an egalitarian cause by military means.[80] He was also seeking to do so in ways that, while effective, would not undercut the USA's legitimacy as the bearer of an egalitarian tradition that, by 1945, had embraced the cause of human rights as we now understand them.

Situating lawfare

Local enthusiasm?

While the USA has, on occasion, departed from the sort of practices that suggest a commitment to lawfare, we have grounds for arguing that this approach to the use of force is a local enthusiasm. Our examples enable us to trace the practice we are examining back to the War of Independence and to argue that it has (since its naïve beginnings) developed over the last two centuries. In the War of Independence, the nascent state used force to advance an egalitarian cause. Lincoln prosecuted the Civil War not merely with the aim of preserving the Union but so as to advance the cause of egalitarianism by emancipating those in slavery. He thus took a step that made good a source of imperfection in the Founding Fathers' expressions of commitment to egalitarianism.[81] In the World Wars, Presidents Wilson and Roosevelt placed emphasis on dimensions of this

[78] Ibid., p.522.

[79] On the tensions within lawfare, see note 38 above and associated text.

[80] As well as treating military force as a means by which to advance its agenda, the USA made full use of General Douglas MacArthur's plenipotentiary status in postwar Japan to the same end. Among other things, the Americans abolished Shinto (which identifies the Japanese as superior to other races) as a state religion. They also mounted an assault on Japanese patriarchy by conferring rights to divorce, property and inheritance on women. See Burleigh, *Moral Combat*, p.555.

[81] See R. Rorty, *Truth and Progress: Philosophical Papers* (Cambridge University Press, 1998), ch.9.

egalitarian project (self-determination and human rights) that they regarded as having relevance not just to Americans but to people everywhere.[82]

The influence exerted by Edward House on Wilson certainly lends plausibility to the argument that the USA used force in the First World War so as to give expression to a local enthusiasm. For House saw in this conflict and its aftermath an opportunity to apply the US constitutional blueprint globally and, thereby, do egalitarian work. When we turn to the Second World War, Roosevelt's advocacy of individual human rights is, among other things, a response to shortcomings in Wilson's favoured vehicle for egalitarian reform: the democratic nation state. For these rights afford a means by which to counter the danger that minorities will be abused by a majority in a position to exercise power in discriminatory ways. Moreover, Roosevelt was able to identify his own country's Bill of Rights as an eligible model when human rights became a matter of pressing concern among those fighting against the Axis.

While we can work up an account of lawfare as a distinctively American practice, we might also situate it in a broader and more long-lived form of life, that of Anglo-America.[83] We can find support for this suggestion in the writings of an English political philosopher, John Locke. Locke's thinking exerted a significant influence on the Founding Fathers of the Union. This was, among other things, because he argued that, where rulers conduct themselves tyrannically, those over whom they wield power may legitimately rebel.[84] Moreover, we can find in English political history an example of just the sort of rebellious response to tyranny (later) described by Locke. Those who took up arms

[82] Cf. G. Greene, *The Quiet American* (London: Vintage, 2002 [first published in 1955]) in which Greene offers a sustained assault on the claims made by one of his American characters, Pyle, to be advancing a universal-egalitarian agenda of a sort that bears obvious resemblances to those of Wilson and Roosevelt. See, for example p.10 where Greene (who is clearly repelled by Pyle's hubris) says of his character: 'he was absorbed ... in the dilemmas of Democracy and the responsibilities of the West; he was determined to do good, not to any individual person but to a country, a continent, a world ... [H]e was in his element now with the whole universe to improve.' See also viii–ix, where Zadie Smith (in her Foreword) is critical of 'big, featureless, impersonal ideas like Pyle's' and calls attention to his 'ossifying rhetoric'.

[83] On 'Anglo-America' as a distinct social formation, see A. Gamble, *Between Europe and America: The Future of British Politics* (New York: Palgrave Macmillan, 2003), ch.5.

[84] J. Waldron, 'John Locke', in D. Miller, ed., *The Blackwell Encyclopaedia of Political Thought* (London: Blackwell, 1987), p.295. See also D. Boucher, *Political Theories of International Relations* (Oxford University Press, 1998), p.259 (noting that 'Locke established the right to resistance by grounding it in just war theory').

against Charles I during the English Civil War did so with the aim of countering tyranny.[85] Moreover, they used force with the aim of establishing a politico-legal framework that paid adequate regard to the rule of law and an existing (if rather limited) democratic principle. This rebellion was a source of inspiration to the American colonists before and during their struggle with the Crown.[86] However, they regarded themselves as seeking to establish a more attractive form of government than that contemplated by their English predecessors.

These are not the only reasons for regarding lawfare as a practice with an Anglo-American provenance. Britain has, on occasion, used military force to secure fundamental interests of the sort now embraced by the human rights movement. This is, for example, true of the deployment of the Royal Navy in the nineteenth century to stop other nations from participating in the slave trade (following the passage of the Slave Trade Act 1807).[87] We can also find support for the claim that lawfare is an Anglo-American practice in the British approach to its bombing campaign against Germany in the Second World War. In 1938, the British Prime Minister, Neville Chamberlain, told the House of Commons that the use of bombers to target civilians would be contrary to international law.[88] When war came a year later, British unease about the use of bombers against its Nazi adversary found expression in the decision to attach priority to precision bombing.[89] However, there was 'a slippage towards bombing urban areas' that became increasingly 'promiscuous'.[90] An Air Directive of February 1942 underwrote this development by reversing the priority given to precision bombing over area attacks.[91] But while the Royal Air Force (RAF) adopted this morally troubling approach, it was in receipt of informal legal advice from J. M. Spaight.[92] We see in this rather rough-and-ready practice a commitment to the use of force on a model that approximates the practice of lawfare.[93]

[85] R. Mullender, ch.13 (on militant democracy in the United Kingdom), in M. Thiel, ed., *The 'Militant Democracy' Principle in Modern Democracies* (Burlington, VT: Ashgate, 2009), pp.321–3, and Robertson, *Crimes Against Humanity*, pp.4–8.

[86] See note 48 above, and associated text.

[87] The Slave Trade Act 1807 placed a ban on the slave trade. Thereafter, Britain treated slaving as equivalent to piracy and, as such, punishable by death.

[88] Burleigh, *Moral Combat*, p.486. [89] Ibid., p.490. [90] Ibid., pp.484 and 488.

[91] Ibid., p.490. [92] Ibid., p.486.

[93] J. M. Spaight, however, was clear on the point that the use of the RAF to bomb Germany was far from being (and could not be) a finely calibrated use of military power. See J. M. Spaight, *Bombing Vindicated* (London: Geoffrey Bles, 1944), p.60 (stating that 'it was impossible for anyone, however credulous, to accept the repeated and solemn assertion of His Majesty's Ministers in Parliament that the bombing of Germany was

Moreover, the RAF's concerns intersected with those of President Roosevelt. For (prior to American entry into the war) he sought assurances from Britain, France and Germany that they would not indiscriminately bomb civilians.[94]

Much more recently, Tony Blair (when Prime Minister) advocated a far-reaching commitment to the use of military force in the service of human rights. In 1999, he argued in a speech in Chicago that the 'international community' could use force to secure the human rights of people facing abuse from their own government.[95] While speaking of the 'international community' as the intervening agency, it was plain that Blair regarded the USA (aided by Britain) as playing a prominent role in the type of operations he had in mind. NATO's 'humanitarian war' against the Federal Republic of Yugoslavia provides an example of (or, at least, approximates) the sort of intervention Blair contemplated.[96] However, this intervention raises awkward questions about the relationship between the practice of lawfare and the general law of war (as a component of public international law). On the analysis of John Gray, NATO's 'humanitarian war' provides an example of '[a] new international order . . . under construction with America in the lead'.[97]

This is a point that has obvious relevance to the response, in both Britain and the USA, to events in Libya in early 2011. When faced with a revolt, Muammar Qaddafi used force as a means by which to cling to power in his country. This prompted the British Prime Minister, David Cameron, to table (in conjunction with France and Lebanon) a United Nations Security Council resolution calling for a 'no-fly zone' on

being carried out with strict regard to the dictates of humanity in accordance with the rules of civilised warfare'). See also W. G. Sebald, *On the Natural History of Destruction*, A. Bell, trans. (New York: The Modern Library, 2004), p.3ff. (on the 'devastation' and 'horrors' resulting from Allied bombing raids).

94 Burleigh, *Moral Combat*, p.486.

95 J. Gray, *Black Mass: Apocalyptic Religion and the Death of Utopia* (London: Allen Lane, 2007), pp.97–8, and H. Young, *Supping with the Devils: Political Writing From Thatcher to Blair* (London: Atlantic Books, 2004), p.187.

96 D. Zolo, 'Humanitarian militarism', ch.27 in Besson and Tasioulas, *The Philosophy of International War*, p.554ff.

97 Gray, *Black Mass*, p.97. (While we cannot tackle the point in detail in this chapter, Blair (while British Prime Minister) made at least one statement concerning the use of military force that suggests that he was less committed to its finely calibrated deployment than are the proponents of lawfare. While visiting British troops in Basra, Iraq, in 2007, he said 'so we kill more of them than they kill us . . . It's brilliant actually.' See M. Amis, *The Second Plane: September 11: 2001–2007* (London: Jonathan Cape, 2008), p.185.)

humanitarian grounds.[98] While the Security Council responded affirmatively to the resolution, the British Foreign Secretary, William Hague, had stated earlier that (in the absence of such support) Britain could engage in military action.[99] We must, however, set these responses to the Libyan crisis alongside those made by the US administration. For, when juxtaposed, the two sets of responses are relevant to Gray's critique of 'humanitarian war'. On Gray's account, this approach to the use of military force is the harbinger of a new international order. But we find in the responses that we are considering evidence of a more equivocal position. Like Cameron, President Barack Obama contemplated resort to military force. However, his Secretary of State, Hilary Clinton, was at pains to point out that (to meet the requirements of public international law) any such intervention would need the authorisation of the United Nations. In this respect, her position clearly differs from that of Hague. However, Clinton and Hague have much in common. The tests of necessity and proportionality (central to the practice of lawfare) inform their respective responses. And while Hague's position is less procedure-bound than that of Clinton, he stated that the use of force requires a basis in international law.[100] Both Hague and Clinton thus exhibit fidelity to a body of law shaped by the (grammar-generating) efforts of Wilson (during and after the First World War) and of Roosevelt (before and during the Second World War).[101] For this reason (and *contra* Gray), it would be wrong to see them as proponents of distinct practices. We would be nearer the mark if we viewed their statements

[98] R. Watson, G. Whittell and W. Pavia, 'Cameron rift with Obama over Libya', *The Times*, 17 March 2011. See also D. Aaronovitch, 'Go for a no-fly zone over Libya or regret it', *The Times*, 24 February 2011, p.23.

[99] R. Crilly, A. Porter, N. Ramdani and R. Spencer, 'We will crush the rebellion in 48 hours, warns Gaddafi', *The Daily Telegraph*, 17 March 2011, p.17, and 'Libya: President Obama gives Gaddafi ultimatum', available at www.bbc.co.uk/news/world-africa-12791910 (accessed 18 March 2011).

[100] 'Libya revolt: Hague urges "legal basis" for no-fly-zone', available at www.bbc.co.uk/news/uk-politics-12697639 (accessed 17 March 2011). For discussion of more recent developments in Libya (culminating in the collapse of the Qadaffi regime), see D. Owen, 'We have proved in Libya that intervention can still work', *Daily Telegraph*, 24 August 2011, p.18 (arguing that 'a West chastened by its experiences in Iraq and Afghanistan' and 'enfeebled by debt' has, nonetheless, demonstrated the viability of 'the doctrine of humanitarian intervention').

[101] See notes 53, 54 and 67–70 above, and associated text. See also P. Kennedy, *The Parliament of Man: The United Nations and the Quest for World Government* (London: Penguin Books, 2006), p.30ff.

as having to do with the grammatical requirements of a (long-lived but developing) practice to which they are each committed.

To the two accounts of lawfare (American and Anglo-American) we have so far considered, we can add a third that (as with the other two) presents it as a local enthusiasm. For we can identify it as a contribution to a Western tradition with a very long history. The tradition in question is composed of the writing and practice concerned with the prosecution of a just war. The roots of this practice (and reflection on it) are Hebraic, Greek and Roman.[102] And since its emergence, a diverse group of thinkers (including Augustine, Suarez and Grotius) has sought to elaborate it.[103] More recently, debate on the topic of a just war has unfolded in the field of public international law.[104] However, the main outlines of just war doctrine were discernible by the Middle Ages: the proportionate use of force in pursuit of a just cause.[105] Moreover, these components of just war doctrine yield a basis on which to argue that lawfare is a more refined variation on the same theme. For it picks out highly specific considerations (the protection of human rights or, at least, humanitarian concerns) as grounds for the (proportionate) use of force.

While it is possible to identify lawfare as the embodiment of local enthusiasms (American, Anglo-American or Western), there are reasons for viewing it as universal in orientation. The elements of American history over which we have raked certainly lend support to this view. For the War of Independence, the Civil War, and the World Wars involve the use of force as a means by which to secure interests shared by all people. Moreover, we can see in the process of development we have traced a strong commitment to establishing a form of life with universal appeal and the capacity to endure. Thus we find Lincoln, in the midst of the Civil War, declaring that, '[i]n giving freedom to the *slave* we *assure* freedom to the *free*'.[106] These are features of the developing

[102] J. Turner Johnson, 'Just war', in Miller, ed., *The Blackwell Encyclopaedia of Political Thought*, p.258.

[103] Ibid., pp.258–9. [104] Ibid., pp.257–8.

[105] Those who have contributed to debate on just war doctrine have taken widely divergent views on the considerations embraced by the notion of a suitable ground for the use of force. Grotius, for example, argued that, in order to be just, war must aim at peace (and should, under no circumstances, be a matter of mere expediency). By contrast, Vitoria took the view that the justifiable facilitation of free exchange is a just cause. See Boucher, *Political Theories of International Relations*, pp.214–15 (on Grotius) and 218 (on Vitoria). See also L. W. Sumner, *The Hateful and the Obscene: Studies in the Limits of Free Expression* (Toronto: University of Toronto Press, 2004), pp.212, n.9 and 214, n.31 (noting that the principle of proportionality features in just war doctrine).

[106] Keneally, *Lincoln*, p.139.

practice on which we have dwelt that provide grounds for arguing that the impulses that inform it bear similarities to those in Hegel's political philosophy.

Lawfare, Hegel, and the spectre of metaphysics

Hegel seems apt as a source of support for the claim that universal impulses are at work in the practice of lawfare. This is because his political philosophy (as we will see) provides a bridge between local enthusiasms and a universal practical agenda. However we should note, before proceeding any further, that he is something of a mixed blessing for those minded to argue that lawfare is universalist in character. This is because metaphysical assumptions that have little contemporary appeal inform his political philosophy.[107] These assumptions are apparent in Hegel's reworking of an idea that features prominently in Kant's political philosophy. This is Kant's idea of a universal history. By 'universal history', Kant means a protracted but progressive process that ultimately issues in practical arrangements that accommodate the interests of all people defensibly.[108]

While embracing Kant's idea of a universal history, Hegel presents it in terms quite different from those used by his compatriot. According to Hegel, throughout history humans have sought adequate (by which he means reciprocal) recognition from others.[109] To this end, they have been prepared to use force to ensure that they receive the recognition they seek. Hegel develops this point in two ways. In his story of a primitive 'first man' (who lives at the beginning of history), he describes a 'life-and-death struggle' between two people each of whom is motivated by the desire for more adequate recognition.[110] The battle yields an

[107] See note 5 above, and associated text. See also F. Beiser, *Hegel* (New York: Routledge, 2005), p.1 (on '"the taste for the absolute", which was the inspiration for Hegel's metaphysics'). See also T. Pogge, *John Rawls: His Life and Theory of Justice*, M. Kosch, trans. (New York: Oxford University Press), p.14 (noting Rawls's rejection of Abraham Lincoln's claim that the victory of the Union in the Civil War yielded evidence of 'God . . . acting justly').

[108] H. Reiss, ed, *Kant: Political Writings* (Cambridge University Press, 1991), pp.41–53 ('The idea of a universal history from a cosmopolitan point of view'). See also F. Fukuyama, *The End of History and the Last Man* (London: Penguin Books, 1992), pp.55 and 349, n.11.

[109] Fukuyama, ibid., chs 18 and 19, and R. R. Williams, *Hegel's Ethics of Recognition* (Berkeley: University of California Press, 1997).

[110] G. W. F. Hegel, *The Phenomenology of Spirit*, A. V. Miller, trans. (Oxford University Press, 1977), p.114.

unsatisfactory outcome, for one of the two subjugates the other. As a result, neither of the two enjoys reciprocal recognition: for the victor receives recognition not from an equal but from a person in servitude. This story throws light on a second narrative in which Hegel seeks to outline the way in which universal history, on his account, has unfolded. Hegel begins this narrative in 'the Oriental world' and describes a state of affairs much like that in the story of the first man. For only one is free while all others in this context occupy inferior positions.[111] Hegel next turns to Ancient Greece and Rome and describes an improved set of circumstances. For now some are free.[112] But, as in the Oriental world, others languish in servitude. This narrative draws to a close in the West of Hegel's day – of which the USA (described by him as 'the Land of the Future') is a part.[113] In the West he finds a state of affairs in which all enjoy (or, at least, have a realistic prospect of enjoying) freedom and the reciprocal recognition that comes with it.

Given the part played by the West in the *dénouement* of Hegel's historical narrative, we might see it as the expression of a local enthusiasm (liberal-democratic egalitarianism) rather than a practical agenda that is universal. But this is not Hegel's view. On his account, if we look closely enough, we can see that humankind has moved haltingly over the slaughterbench of history towards a set of practical arrangements that accommodate the interests of all people adequately.[114] Moreover, he explains that local enthusiasms carry within them universal impulses that find full realisation in Western politico-legal institutions and practices. But he does not leave matters there. He argues that metaphysics is a feature of and not external to the forms of practical life he scrutinises. For he finds in the process of development he traces intimations of a spirit (*Geist*) that (in some mysterious way) propels humankind in the direction of just practical arrangements.[115] He adds that this spirit finds expression in the activities of 'world-historical' societies (e.g. Greece, Rome and the USA). Likewise, he identifies spirit or *Geist* as present in the activities of individuals who bear the burden of world history: for example, Napoleon ('history [or *Geist*] on horseback').[116] In light of

[111] Beiser, *Hegel*, p.266. [112] Ibid.

[113] Hegel, *The Philosophy of History*, p.86 (where Hegel also states that, in America, 'the burden of the World's History shall reveal itself').

[114] Ibid., ch.11, and Fukuyama, *The End of History*, ch.19.

[115] Hegel, *The Philosophy of History*, p.72 (describing 'History' as 'the development of Spirit in *time*').

[116] R. M. Burns and H. Rayment-Pickard, eds, *Philosophies of History: From Enlightenment to Postmodernity* (Oxford: Blackwell, 2000), pp.84–9, J. McCarney, *Hegel on History*

these points, we could argue that the history of the USA and the practices in which its politico-legal form of life find expression are the embodiment (or external deposit) of a universal agenda.[117]

As we noted earlier, Hegel is a mixed blessing for those who want to identify practices such as lawfare as universal in orientation. We can use his political philosophy to present them in this light. But by doing so, we embrace a body of thought in which metaphysics features prominently.[118] We might seek to sidestep this difficulty by identifying Hegel's practical concerns as intersecting with, for example, the avowedly non-metaphysical (or 'political') 'liberalism of freedom' propounded by John Rawls.[119] But even if we conclude that such a move insulates the proponents of lawfare from the charge of metaphysics, they still have to face a further and more immediate difficulty. This is the possibility that lawfare is a practice that exhibits a degree of ruthlessness that is quite at odds with a commitment to human rights.

Lawfare and ruthlessness

As we noted in our analysis of lawfare, it is a practice that attaches priority to the pursuit of egalitarian outcomes (states of affairs in which victims of human rights-related abuses enjoy more adequate protection). This emphasis on the pursuit of outcomes means that lawfare stands in a tense relationship with the human rights movement of which it is a part. For the moral impulses central to human rights are deontological. The discourse of human rights makes this immediately apparent. For example, to talk of the 'violation' of a human right is to give expression to the assumption that the violator has trampled on a good that is intrinsically valuable.

(London: Routledge, 2000), pp.1–2, and A. W. Wood, *Hegel's Ethical Thought* (Cambridge University Press, 1990), pp.226–7.

117 In his response to the crisis in Libya in early 2011, Tony Blair lends some support to the Hegelian claim that the USA and the West more generally are the bearers of a universal agenda. For he argues that 'there is no doubt that the best, most secure, most stable future for the Middle East lies in the spread of democracy, the rule of law and human rights'. To this he adds the further claim that these goods 'are not "Western"'. Rather they are 'universal values of the human spirit'. A. Blair, 'We can't just be spectators in this revolution', *The Times*, 19 March 2011, p.27. See also A. Davutoğlu, 'We have been insulted and humiliated. But finally history is bringing us dignity', *The Guardian*, 16 March 2011, p.33.

118 Cf. those commentators who seek to bleach the metaphysics out of Hegel: e.g. A Patten, *Hegel's Idea of Freedom* (Oxford University Press, 1999).

119 J. Rawls, *Lectures on the History of Moral Philosophy* (Cambridge, MA: Harvard University Press, 2000), p.349.

Tension arises since it is impossible for a practice simultaneously to prioritise two types of moral impulse – deontological in the case of human rights and consequentialist in that of lawfare.

Proponents of lawfare might respond to this line of argument by noting that the proportionality principle is sensitive to and seeks to secure sources of intrinsic value. While this is true, proportionality does not eliminate the source of tension we are considering. For proportionality (in common with the practice of lawfare more generally) is informed by a type of composite moral philosophy to which we can give the name qualified consequentialism. This form of moral philosophy prioritises outcomes. However, deontological considerations place limits on the range of ways in which those pursuing a particular outcome may seek to do so. The proportionality principle provides a way of operationalising this moral philosophy. For it specifies that those pursuing an outcome can only override or compromise a source of intrinsic value where they can satisfy a test of necessity.[120] This test merits close attention. Where the proponents of lawfare can satisfy it, consequentialist impulses will override deontological ones – thus bringing the uneasy relationship between the practice they have embraced and the wider human rights movement into sharp relief.[121]

We can press this analysis further by drawing on the account of ruthlessness offered by the philosopher Thomas Nagel. In 'Ruthlessness in public life', Nagel draws a number of distinctions between 'private' (or 'individual') morality and 'public morality'.[122] He identifies private morality as having to do with close interaction between individuals.[123] In contrast, he associates public morality with 'institutions that are designed to serve purposes larger than those of particular individuals or families'.[124] In light of these points, Nagel states that public morality exhibits a 'discontinuity' from individual morality.[125] He develops this point by arguing that those who work within public institutions demonstrate 'a heightened concern for results'.[126] He adds that they typically focus impartially on the means by which to achieve 'the best overall results' rather than on individuals who might be adversely affected by

[120] The sources of intrinsic value to which the proportionality principle is sensitive yield defeasible, exclusionary reasons for action. See J. Raz, *Practical Reason and Norms* (Princeton, NJ: Princeton University Press, 1990), pp.35–48 and 182–6.

[121] Mullender, 'Theorizing the Third Way', pp.493 and 513.

[122] T. Nagel, *Mortal Questions* (Cambridge University Press, 1979), ch.6. (While Nagel draws the distinctions referred to in the text, he nonetheless states that 'public and private morality may share a common basis without one being derived from the other').

[123] Ibid., pp.78 and 83. [124] Ibid., pp.83–4. [125] Ibid., p.78. [126] Ibid., p.82.

their decisions.[127] This leads him to identify public morality as strongly consequentialist in orientation.[128] This feature of public morality has a corollary that is highly relevant to this discussion. When compared with private morality, public morality exhibits reduced concern with 'action-oriented constraints', i.e. constraints that limit the means that public institutions may employ to pursue their ends.[129] Insofar as public bodies and public officials enjoy some measure of 'insulation' from these constraints, Nagel concludes that public morality 'licenses ruthlessness'.[130]

Nagel's account of ruthlessness enables us to grasp more fully the significance of the fact that, within the practice of lawfare, consequentialist impulses can override deontological ones. In attaching priority to the pursuit (by means of violence) of benign outcomes, lawfare exhibits 'a heightened concern for results'. Moreover, where the pursuit of these results collides with countervailing deontological considerations, those who propose to use force may do so if they can satisfy the necessity test specified by the proportionality principle. Here we see a readiness to weaken action-oriented (or deontological) constraints. To these points proponents of lawfare might respond by arguing that the outcomes to which priority attaches are themselves intrinsically valuable (human rights and a peaceful environment within which individuals can exercise them). But even if we accept this point, the fact remains that the practice we are scrutinising is one to which Nagel's account of ruthlessness has obvious application.

Just as we can throw the brickbat of ruthlessness at the proponents of lawfare, so too we can charge them with unjustified optimism. And as with our ruthlessness-related analysis, this is a line of criticism to which

[127] Ibid., p.83. The impartiality that Nagel identifies as a feature of public morality provides a basis on which to distinguish his use of 'ruthlessness' from another sense (associated with the political philosophy of Machiavelli) in which the term is employed. 'Ruthlessness' (in the Machiavellian sense) is partial. This is because it has to do with employing whatever means are necessary in order to secure one's own interests: see N. Machiavelli, *The Prince*, Q. Skinner and R. Price, eds (Cambridge University Press, 1988), pp.62 and 104. Likewise, we should distinguish Nagel's account of 'ruthlessness' from that of the Nazis. Within National Socialist ideology '*Vernichtung*' (ruthlessness) has to do with the 'liquidation' (extirpation) of political opponents and racial inferiors: see M. Mazower, *Hitler's Empire: Nazi Rule in Occupied Europe* (London: Allen Lane, 2008), pp.64–6 and 176–7.

[128] Nagel, *Mortal Questions*, p.83.

[129] Ibid., pp.84–5. (See also M. Oakeshott, *On History and Other Essays* (Oxford: Basil Blackwell, 1983), p.181, identifying 'the sovereignty of the *utilitas publica*' as a feature of practical life where 'the prosperity of all' overrides private interests.)

[130] Nagel, *Mortal Questions*, pp.82 and 76.

the proportionality principle is relevant. This principle seems to hold out the promise that we can make finely calibrated judgements concerning the pursuit of desirable ends and the circumstances in which we may have to override countervailing sources of value in order to secure them. But it is by no means obvious that this is the case in some contexts of the sort we are contemplating. While the proponents of lawfare may present us with the prospect of a better future in which human rights enjoy more adequate protection, the use of force is fraught with risks that resist precise assessment. Thus we might describe those who ignore this rather obvious point as falling victim to unjustified optimism.[131] For they assume that they are in a position to make precise assessments of ends and means in circumstances where this is unlikely to be the case.[132] Assuming that unjustified optimism is a feature of lawfare, this may go some way towards explaining why its proponents are ready to act ruthlessly. For they may harbour in their minds the confident assumption that the end justifies the (attainable) means.[133] If this is the case, their thinking is very different from that of Kennedy, to which we now turn.

Ambivalence definitely; aporia maybe

We can gain purchase on Kennedy's thinking on human rights by situating him in the tradition we have been examining. But before doing this, we must return to the politico-legal grammar that we identified as guiding the founders of the USA as they inched towards and then prosecuted the War of Independence. As we noted, this grammar established conditions for the use of force in pursuit of egalitarian objectives.[134] On the analysis offered earlier, it was a source of guidance not just to the Founders but also to Lincoln in the American Civil War and

[131] See also note 36 above, on unscrupulous optimism.

[132] See R. Smith, *The Utility of Force: The Art of War in the Modern World* (London: Penguin Books, 2006), p.6 (arguing that 'to apply force with utility implies an understanding of the context in which one is acting, a clear definition of the result to be achieved, an identification of the point or target to which the force is being applied – and – as important as all the others, an understanding of the nature of the force being applied'). See also C. von Clausewitz, *On War* (Oxford University Press, 2007) bk.II, ch.2, para.24 (pp.88–89) (noting that, in war, 'all action takes place ... in a kind of twilight, which like fog or moonlight, often tends to make things seem grotesque and larger than they really are'). Cf. D'Ancona, 'Libya Won't make Cameron's Name, but it's certainly a Start', *Sunday Telegraph*, 28 August 2011, p.22 (noting the pleasant surprise of British Ministers at accurate artillery targeting).

[133] See T. Pynchon, *Gravity's Rainbow* (London: Picador, 1975), p.30 (on 'the illusion of control'). See also p.96 (on 'the absolute rule of chance' as a feature of war).

[134] See notes 53 and 54 above, and associated text.

to Wilson and Roosevelt in the World Wars. Moreover, it has (in the various conflicts we have examined) undergone development. In the Civil War, Lincoln identified its egalitarian component as sufficiently strong to require not just the preservation of an existing but imperfect egalitarian order:[135] rather, he identified it as requiring an end to slavery. In the First World War, Wilson likewise intensified its informing egalitarianism by identifying self-determination as a principle with global reach. Roosevelt further intensified its egalitarianism when he identified individual human rights as placing restrictions on national self-determination. In this way, he sought to counter the crude (and all too often persecutory) approach to majoritarian rule that was a feature of life in many of the states that came into existence after the First World War.[136]

As Lincoln, Wilson, Roosevelt and others have gone on in the practice we are considering, tensions within it have become more apparent to those who participate in it. We see one such tension in the collision between the principle of self-determination and concern for the interests of individuals. Another such source of tension is that between the consequentialist and the deontological impulses that feature in it. These tensions are apparent when we consider, for example, Henry Stimson's attitude towards bombing in World War Two. As a 'New England conscience on legs', Stimson was highly sensitive to the sources of intrinsic value that have come to feature in human rights law. But at the same time, he was committed to the successful prosecution of the war so as to establish conditions in which these individual protections could become a prominent feature of the global scene.

These points bring us to the context in which Kennedy has worked up his analysis of human rights. This is a context within which deontological impulses feature prominently. They manifest themselves in commitment to, among other things, human rights and peace. But we also find in this context a commitment to making the world a better place. Thus we have to set this consequentialist strand of thought alongside the deontological one typically associated with human rights. Moreover, we have to keep in mind the fact that the two types of practical impulse we are considering stand in an uneasy relationship. This uneasiness is on display in Kennedy's thought. For he is a bearer of the same tradition as Stimson. Like Stimson, he is a deontologist who quails at the prospect

[135] See Rorty, *Truth and Progress*, Vol III, p.167ff. (on Thomas Jefferson's blindness to the injustice of slaveholding).

[136] See note 68, above, and associated text.

of adopting inappropriate means. However, the note of urgency that rings out in 'The international human rights movement: part of the problem?' suggests hunger for action – the delivery of justice on an alternative (but unspecified) model. These features of Kennedy's thinking provide support for the conclusion that ambivalence is a feature of his thinking. But we might also draw from them the conclusion that there is in his thinking an element of aporia – a hesitancy or overpowering sense of doubt in the face of alternative courses of action.[137] If this is the case, it is far from surprising. We might explain this feature of his thinking by reference to the uneasy relationship between consequentialist and deontological impulses in the body of thought we have surveyed. For we find in this relationship clear signs of competitive pluralism.[138] This is because each of these two sets of impulses provides widely applicable reasons for action. As a result, those who take them seriously find themselves contemplating fields of activity to which both deontological and consequentialist reasons for action are relevant and, hence, stand in a competitive relationship.[139] Little wonder then that those who think hard about both sets of impulses – as Kennedy does – exhibit some hesitancy when seeking to derive guidance from them.[140]

[137] 'Aporia' refers to 'those irresolvable doubts and hesitations which are thrown up by . . . [a] text [or other object of interpretation]'. See J. Hawthorn, *A Concise Glossary of Contemporary Literary Theory*, 2nd edn (New York: Edward Arnold, 1994), p.7.

[138] J. Raz, *The Morality of Freedom* (Oxford: Clarendon Press, 1986), pp.404–7 (on competitive pluralism)

[139] Alongside competition between values, we should also place the competing claims of eligible models of human association. This is because the pursuit of a world that is 'more just' (to use Kennedy's phrase) might, for example, be pursued on the model of civil association or on that of enterprise association. On these two models, see R. Mullender, 'Human rights, responsibilities and the pursuit of a realistic utopia' 61 *Northern Ireland Legal Quarterly* (2010) 33, p.44 (drawing on the political philosophy of Michael Oakeshott). Civil association takes the form of a modest, rule-governed framework within which the individual is free to pursue his or her plans free from interference by governmental bodies with large plans for social improvement. By contrast, enterprise association is highly instrumental. Those who wield governmental power in an enterprise association seek to pursue a desired goal or end-state. This may be, for example, a set of social relations that is distributively just. While the pursuit of such an end-state may lend an enterprise association moral appeal, it constitutes a standing threat to the individual (who finds him- or herself co-opted (more or less intrusively) into the projects that invest the relevant context with a strong sense of social purpose).

[140] While we cannot pursue the matter in detail here, there are also reasons for thinking that Kennedy's thinking exhibits the admixture of 'world-weariness and cleverness' that, on one analysis, is a feature of postmodern thought; see B. McHale, *Constructing Postmodernism* (New York: Routledge, 1992), p.39.

Conclusions

If the analysis of lawfare offered in this chapter is broadly correct, it is a practice that we can interpret in at least two ways. We can see it as giving expression to practical impulses within a particular politico-legal tradition. This tradition is itself open to a range of interpretations. We can characterise it as American, as Anglo-American and as Western. Of these three views, the first – the American reading – is the one on which we have placed emphasis. This seems apt since we can trace a timeline along which we can identify key moments in the development of the politico-legal tradition we have been scrutinising. This process of development has found dramatic expression in the American Civil War, the First World War and the Second World War, and on each occasion it has proceeded in accordance with the (developing) politico-legal grammar that guided the American Founding.[141] For on each occasion the USA has used force to advance an egalitarian agenda that, at this late point in its development, involves efforts to secure human rights across the globe. But alongside this reading of this tradition, we must set the universalist, Hegelian alternative we examined earlier. For we might argue that the local enthusiasms on which we have focused our attention make apparent the means humankind must adopt in order to secure the interests of individuals.

As well as offering these readings of lawfare, we also found two sources of tension within this practice. The first of the two has to do with the relative positions within lawfare of law and force. While we have, in this chapter, assumed that priority attaches to law rather than to the use of military force, there are reasons for thinking that the relationship between the two is inherently unstable. Perhaps this is not simply on account of the fact that they constitute (on our earlier analysis) the poles in a binary opposition. In order to explain why this may be so, we must turn briefly to the political philosophy of David Hume. Hume tells us that 'cool' and 'violent' passions are at 'war' within each person.[142]

[141] Since Wittgenstein associates 'grammar' (in his sense) with distinct forms of life (or cultures), it should not surprise us to discover that Matt Groening's cartoon character, Bart Simpson, is able to identify the American Revolutionary War and World War Two as 'good' wars. See R. Richmond and A. Coffmann, eds, *The Simpsons: A Complete Guide to Our Favourite Family* (London: HarperCollins, 1997), p.21 (discussing 'Bart the General'). See also Fenichel Pitkin, *Wittgenstein and Justice*, p.132ff., and Wittgenstein, *Philosophical Investigations*, para.23.

[142] D. Hume, *A Treatise of Human Nature*, L. A. Selby-Bigge, ed. (Oxford: Clarendon Press, 1978), p.438.

Moreover, he identifies law as an institution in which the cool passions find expression and place a (much needed) bridle on the violent ones.[143] By contrast, war is a context in which the violent passions are likely to find their most intense expression. Thus we have reason to regard lawfare as a practice in which the violent passions threaten to overwhelm the cool ones. The practice of the US military in the Second World War is again instructive. For we can set the ('cool') scrupulousness with which the USAAF planned and conducted the Norsk Hydro raid alongside General George Patton's ('violent') order to 'kill devastatingly'.[144]

The second of the two sources of tension we identified became apparent when we examined the proportionality principle – which embraces the consequentialist and deontological impulses within lawfare. Proportionality gives sequential priority to the pursuit of benign outcomes. But the proponents of human rights typically identify deontological considerations as their primary concern. As a result, a problem of uncombinability arises for those who see in lawfare a means to advance the cause of human rights. For they cannot prioritise outcomes in accordance with proportionality and simultaneously with the deontological considerations that feature most prominently within the (wider) human rights movement.[145] If, as we have assumed in this essay, the proponents of lawfare prioritise consequentialist impulses, they are open to the charge of ruthlessness in Nagel's sense. This remains the case notwithstanding the fact that the proportionality principle is a prominent feature of lawfare, for proportionality does not eliminate the source of tension that we are considering. Rather, it enables those who apply it to mediate between consequentialist and deontological impulses. Moreover, those who engage in this process may convey the impression that they are going about their business in a finely calibrated way. To the

143 G. J. Postema, *Bentham and the Common Law Tradition* (Oxford: Clarendon Press, 1986), p.105.

144 Burleigh, *Moral Combat*, p.380. Patton issued this order while his troops were participating in the operation to capture Sicily. In their efforts to act in accordance with it, a unit of American troops shot Italian prisoners (whom they suspected of being snipers). Subsequently, a US Army chaplain complained about these killings to General Omar Bradley. As a result, Bradley went to see Patton (who took the view that the killings were 'thoroughly justified'). Bradley disagreed and forced Patton to court-martial an officer and a sergeant. Patton's response was to issue the order: 'Try the bastards'. The officer secured an acquittal at his court-martial (having cited Patton's order), while the sergeant returned to active service as a private one year after receiving a sentence of life imprisonment.

145 On uncombinability, see J. Gray, *Post-Liberalism: Studies in Political Thought* (London: Routledge, 1993), p.301.

extent that they act in this way, there is reason to suppose that they are claiming rather too much and may, indeed, be the victims of unjustified optimism. For precision seems unlikely to be a feature of the judgements they have to make (most obviously about anticipated outcomes) in circumstances where the fog of war descends.

As well as throwing light on lawfare, our examination of relevant history provides a basis on which to embed Kennedy within the tradition out of which the movement he critiques has grown. On the analysis offered earlier, he is a bearer of the tradition within which the international human rights movement and the practice of lawfare have grown up. As such he is the heir to over two centuries of reflection and practical activity that have yielded a richly elaborated body of thought. Within this body of thought consequentialist and deontological impulses stand in a relationship that we can theorise by reference to Joesph Raz's idea of competitive pluralism. For each set of impulses seeks to occupy space to which the other makes intelligible claims.[146] This is, as we have noted, a state of affairs that can induce ambivalence and quite possibly aporia. Moreover, we can find in Kennedy's response to the international human rights movement evidence that both of these conditions have shaped his thinking.

Before closing, some words seem appropriate on the method adopted in this chapter (which has been in large part historical). Rather than taking the international human rights movement on its own terms (a universalist project rooted in and serving a global community) our focus has been on local enthusiasms in the American, or Anglo-American, or Western contexts. In dwelling on these enthusiasms we have (to use Michael Oakeshott's phrase) pursued intimations within a particular tradition.[147] In the course of doing so, we have not only picked out grand events on the timeline mentioned earlier. We have also devoted attention to the fine-grained detail of relevant history. This includes Francis Lieber's manual of instruction to Union troops in the American

[146] See note 138 above, and associated text.

[147] See P. Franco, *Michael Oakeshott: An Introduction* (New Haven, CN: Yale University Press, 2004), ch.3. (While our focus has been, for the most part, on the USA, the pursuit of intimations within the British context reveals, among other things, that the proportionality principle informed the thinking of those in government long before they began to invoke it in terms. Jenifer Hart's account of Home Office practice in the 1930s reveals this to be the case. For she speaks of 'the Home Office *tradition* that civil liberties should be restricted as little as possible and only then as a result of urgent administrative necessity'. See S. Dorril, *Blackshirt: Sir Oswald Mosley & British Fascism* (Harmondsworth, Middx: Penguin Books, 2007), p.481 (emphasis added).)

Civil War. Likewise, it includes the USAAF's raid on the Norsk Hydro plant in 1943. Interpretative activity of this sort can encourage a rather romantic outlook – as those who engage in it grasp the richness of the tradition under scrutiny. We see just this sort of thing happening when, for example, Don DeLillo scrutinises the first half of the American century and declares:

> You have a history . . . that you are responsible to . . . You're answerable. You're required to make sense of it. You owe it your complete attention.[148]

Delillo, intoxicated by the attractions of US culture, overstates his case. We are not required to make sense of any tradition. Doing so is only worthwhile if it is or promises to be a source of attractive reasons for action. Where this is the case, we do owe it 'our complete attention'. For only in this way can we hope to pursue intimations within it.

148 D. DeLillo, *Underworld* (London: Macmillan, 1998), p.512.

INDEX